Hymns On Various Passages of Scripture

Thomas Kelly

HYMNS

ON

VARIOUS PASSAGES OF SCRIPTURE.

BY

THOMAS KELLY.

SEVENTH EDITION,
WITH MANY ADDITIONAL HYMNS.

DUBLIN
PRINTED FOR MARCUS MOSES,
Publisher of the Rev. T. Kelly's Hymns set to Music by the Author,
PIANO-FORTE, HARP, AND MUSIC WAREHOUSE,
4, AND 5, WESTMORELAND-STREET,
AND 40, AND 41, FLEET-STREET.
SOLD BY JOHN ROBERTSON, 8, GRAFTON-STREET, DUBLIN;
SIMPKIN, MARSHALL AND CO., LONDON;
JOHNSTONE AND HUNTER, EDINBURGH.

MDCCCLIII.

or three Hymns which ought to have had a place under one of the defined classes. This, however, is not a matter of much consequence.

It will be perceived by those who may read these Hymns, that though there is an interval between the first and the last, of near sixty years, both speak of the same great truths, and in the same way. In the course of that long period, the Author has seen much, and heard much; but nothing that he has seen or heard, has made the least change in his mind, that he is conscious of, as to the grand truths of the Gospel. What pacified the conscience then, does so now. What gave hope then, does so now. "Other foundation can no man lay, than that is laid, which is Jesus Christ." Brethren, pray for the Author; you can confer no greater favour upon him.

INDEX.

INDEX TO NEW HYMNS.

INDEX TO NEW HYMNS.

INDEX TO NEW HYMNS.

INDEX TO SUBJECTS.

ERRATUM.

Hymn 23, verse 4, line 3, omit "on."

HYMNS.

Nativity.

HYMN I.

"*Ye shall find the babe . . . in a manger.*"—LUKE ii. 12.

1 CHRIST is born, go tell the story,
Tell the nations of his birth:
Tell them that the "Lord of glory"
Comes from heav'n to dwell on earth:
Let the tidings
Fill the world with sacred mirth.

2 See he lies in yonder manger;
"Prince of Life" his title is:
Midst his own, and yet a stranger,
All things seen and unseen his;
Yet neglected:
Wonder, O ye heav'ns, at this.

3 See fulfill'd prophetic vision,
"Unto us a child is born;"
Though an object of derision,
Though the theme of human scorn:
Yet his people
Hail his birth, and cease to mourn.

4 Hail Emmanuel, child of promise,
"Lord of all," in humble guise;
Long detain'd, and absent from us,
Come at length to bless our eyes:
Hail Emmanuel!
God the Saviour, only wise!

HYMN II.

"*There shall come a star out of Jacob.*"—NUMBERS xxiv. 17.

1 JACOB'S star is ris'n at last,
Brighter than the brightest sun:
Darkness is for ever past,
And the joyful day begun.

2 Sing aloud, the cause is great;
Sing, ye heav'ns, and sing, thou earth:
Still the joyful theme repeat;
Joyful theme, Emmanuel's birth.

3 This is Jacob's promis'd star,
Giving light to all around;
Shining clear, and seen afar,
Seen to earth's remotest bounds.

4 Sing the Infant, virgin-born,
He a King, a King by birth;
Though the mark of human scorn,
Heir of all in heav'n and earth.

5 Now, ye saints, dry up your tears;
See the day is come at last:
Jacob's promis'd star appears,
Darkness is for ever past.

HYMN III.

"*A multitude of the heavenly host praising God.*"
LUKE ii. 13.

1 WHENCE those sounds symphonious,
Solemn, sweet, and rare,
Music, how harmonious!
Filling all the air?
Hark! 'tis angels singing,
Singing here on earth:
Joyful tidings bringing
Of the Saviour's birth.

2 In that region yonder,
Where the angels sing,
Bursts of joy and wonder
Make the air to ring;
"Praise and adoration
"Be to God above:
"And to man, salvation,
"Object of his love."

3 Now, ye heavens, sing ye;
Earth, break forth and cry;
O ye mountains, ring ye
With the sound of joy;
For the Lord has done it:
His the victory.
His own arm has won it:
Israel shall be free.

HYMN IV.

"*And all that heard it wondered.*"—Luke ii. 18.

1 FLY abroad, and tell the story
Of the mighty Saviour's birth;
Say ye, that the Lord of glory
Leaves his throne and comes to earth.
He, before whom angels bow,
Takes the form of man below.

2 Hither come, and view the stranger,
View the infant lately born;
See he lies in yonder manger,
By the world cast out in scorn.
Mark him well, for this is he,
Born to set his people free.

3 Wonder not that thus you see him
Lying in this humble place;
Nor indulge a wish to free him
From a state so low and base.
Worldly pomp the Saviour scorns,
Him no outward state adorns.

4 Sing, ye saints, the Saviour's praises:
'Twas for you he suffer'd shame;
Yes, he stooped, that he might raise us
To the place from whence he came.
Though he now appears so low,
Crowns shall soon adorn his brow.

5 Learn, from his obscure condition,
How to think of all below:
Scorn he meets, and opposition:
Jesus finds in man his foe.
Such our Master was, and we
Must expect like him to be.

HYMN V.

"*For unto us a Child is born, unto us a Son is given.*"
ISAIAH ix. 6.

1 WE'LL sing in spite of scorn;
Our theme is come from heav'n;
"To us a child is born,
"To us a son is giv'n."
The sweetest news that ever came,
We'll sing, tho' all the world should blame.

2 The long-expected morn
Has dawned upon the earth;
The Saviour Christ is born,
And angels sing his birth:
We'll join with heav'n's seraphic throng,
We'll share their joys, and swell their song.

3 O 'tis a lofty theme,
Supplied by angels' tongues!
All other objects seem
Unworthy of our songs.
This sacred theme has boundless charms,
It fills, it captivates, it warms.

4 Now sing of peace divine,
Of grace to guilty man;
No wisdom, Lord, but thine,
Could form the wondrous plan:
Where peace and righteousness embrace,
And justice goes along with grace.

5 Give praise to God on high,
With angels round his throne;
Give praise to God with joy;
Give praise to God alone;
'Tis meet his saints their songs should raise,
And give the Saviour endless praise.

HYMN VI.

"*We have seen his star in the east, and are come to worship him.*"—MATT. ii. 2.

1 HARK! what sounds salute our ears,
"CHRIST THE LORD at length appears:"
"Unto us a son is giv'n:"
Angels bring the news from heav'n.

2 Come, ye saints, arise and sing,
Glory be to God our King!
"Unto us a child is born,"
Zion is no more forlorn.

3 Who are these that come from far,
Led by Jacob's rising star?
Lo! they gather like a cloud,
Or as doves their windows crowd.

4 Strangers these, to Zion come,
There to seek a peaceful home.
Zion wonders at the sight;
Zion feels a strange delight.

5 Zion now no more shall sigh;
God will raise her glory high:
He will send a large increase;
He will give her people peace.

6 Sons of Zion, sing aloud;
See her sky without a cloud:
God will make her joy complete:
Zion's sun shall never set.

HYMN VII.

"Behold, I bring you glad tidings of great joy, which shall be to all people."—Luke ii. 10.

1 ANGELIC messenger, repeat
Those joyful sounds once more;
For sure no accents half so sweet,
E'er reach'd my ears before.

2 "Glad tidings from heaven I bring,
"Glad tidings to all upon earth:
"This day is Christ born to be King,
"And Bethl'hem's the place of his birth."

3 Sounds seraphic fill the air,
Angel bands assemble there:
Heav'n itself, come down to earth,
Celebrates the Saviour's birth.

CHORUS.

"Glory to God on high be giv'n;
"And on earth peace, good will from heav'n."

HYMN VIII.

"Glory to God in the highest, and on earth peace, good will toward men."—Luke ii. 14.

1 "UNTO us a Son is giv'n;"
'Tis the promis'd Christ is meant,
Bands of angels come from heaven
To announce the tidings sent,
Fill'd with rapture,
Celebrate the great event.

2 "Glory in the highest! glory
"Be to God, and peace on earth."
Now proclaim the joyful story
Of the mighty Saviour's birth;
Let the tidings
Fill the world with sacred mirth.

3 This is "the desire of nations"
Promis'd to the church so long;
Object of its expectations;
Burden of prophetic song;
Sing, ye people,
Join with heav'n's angelic throng.

4 Lo! he comes, the Lord from heaven;
Lo! the mighty God appears.
"Unto us a Son is given:"
This is music in our ears;
Nothing sweeter,
Mortal or immortal hears.

HYMN IX.

"*Thy holy child, Jesus.*"—ACTS iv. 30.

1 BORN in a stable he,
And cradled in a stall,
In whom his people see
The very "Lord of all."
No wonder carnal men
The claims of one should scorn,
So weak, to human ken,
And so ignobly born.

2 Yet all the pow'r in earth,
And all in heav'n is his;
Entitled by his birth,
He "Heir of all things is."
"The First" he is, "and Last,"
Who does not, cannot change;
The Future, as the Past,
Is his. 'Tis passing strange.

3 To those who judge by sense,
The stable and the cross
Are folly and offence,
But theirs the shame and loss.
While Faith a glory sees,
A majesty above,
Whatever outward is;
The majesty of love.

4 All hail "The Holy Child,"
"The first-begotten" Thou;
By men on earth revil'd,
Before whom angels bow.
The kingdom is thine own,
The glory and the pow'r;
The praise be thine alone,
Both now and evermore.

HYMN X.

"*For mine eyes have seen thy salvation.*"—LUKE ii. 30.

1 CHILD of promise, look'd for long!
Child of promise, come at length!
Thou, our Hope, our Joy, our Song;
Thou, our "Righteousness and Strength;"
Hallow'd be thy name for ever,
Thine a kingdom ending never.

2 Arms of flesh uphold thee now,
Though thine arm upholds us all;
Royal crowns adorn thy brow,
Though thy chamber be a stall,
And thy bed an humble manger,
Strange it is, there's nothing stranger.

3 While the great and wise, with scorn,
Look upon a sight like this,
They who from above are born,
Know that nothing is amiss,
All is right, and as it should be,
Nothing greater, wiser could be.

4 'Tis the case of one who rich,
Poor became, and lowly was;
Riches his, compared to which
Other wealth no value has,
He bestows his wealth on others,
This is love beyond a brother's.

5 Holy Child! those lips of thine,
Mute though now they seem, and are,
Soon will utter words divine,
Words that will be heard afar,
To the distant nations reaching,
Till "the end of all things" teaching.

6 And that feeble arm of thine
Destin'd is to do a deed,
Other deeds that will outshine,
And their measure far exceed;
One of love, of grace abounding,
One, all human thought confounding.

7 Hail! mysterious Infant, hail!
Thee we honour and adore;
Thine a throne that will not fail,
Thine a name all names before,
Thine a pow'r, all pow'r transcending,
Thine a glory never ending.

HYMN XI.

"*Emmanuel, which, being interpreted, is, God with us.*"—
MATT. i. 23.

1 SEED of the woman, look'd for long,
He comes at the appointed time.
With joy we hear the angels' song,
'Tis sweet, 'tis solemn, 'tis sublime.

2 "To God on high let glory be,
"To man, good will and peace on earth;"
We give the praise, O Lord, to thee,
And hail with joy the Saviour's birth.

3 Mysterious Child! to thee we bow;
To thee a willing homage yield;
To thee, of all things heir, though now
A babe, by mortal arms upheld.

4 A mystery confounding thought!
And yet a fact to childhood plain!
A fact with blessings richly fraught,
What angels love, what men disdain.

5 But those there are throughout the earth
Who know what others do not know;
They own the royal infant's birth,
And meekly in his presence bow.

6 A glorious day will come, they know,
When he, who now appears so weak,
Will, "conqu'ring, and to conquer," go,
And all the other sceptres break.

7 But he has much to suffer ere
That glorious day arrive. For pain
And shame, and death, await him here;
Till this is pass'd, he cannot reign.

6 I leave the world for this;
Let others share its toys:
I envy not their fancied bliss,
The cross yields purer joys.

HYMN XIV.

"*Smitten of God, and afflicted.*"—ISA. liii. 4.

1 "STRICKEN, smitten, and afflicted,"
See him dying on the tree!
'Tis the Christ by man rejected!
Yes, my soul, 'tis he! 'tis he!
'Tis the long-expected prophet,
David's son, yet David's Lord;
Proofs I see sufficient of it:
'Tis a true and faithful word.

2 Tell me, ye who hear him groaning,
Was there ever grief like his?
Friends thro' fear his cause disowning,
Foes insulting his distress.
Many hands were raised to wound him,
None would interpose to save;
But the awful stroke that found him,
Was the stroke that justice gave.

3 Ye who think of sin but lightly,
Nor suppose the evil great,
Here may view its nature rightly,
Here its guilt may estimate.
Mark the sacrifice appointed!
See *who* bears the awful load!
'Tis the WORD, the LORD'S ANOINTED,
Son of man, and Son of God.

4 Here we have a firm foundation;
Here's the refuge of the lost:
Christ's the rock of our salvation;
His the name of which we boast.
Lamb of God, for sinners wounded!
Sacrifice to cancel guilt!
None shall ever be confounded,
Who on him their hope have built.

HYMN XV.

"*O my Father, if it be possible, let this cup pass from me.*"—
MATT. xxvi. 39.

1 JESUS drains the cup of sorrows;
See he lies beneath our load;
Gives his life a ransom for us,
And redeems us by his blood.
Was there ever love like this?
Was there ever grief like his?

2 Jesus is "a man of sorrows,"
Here he claims pre-eminence;
See him pierc'd by heav'n's own arrows;
See him die for our offence.
We, like sheep, had gone astray;
Jesus takes our sin away.

3 Jesus suffers—wondrous victim!
'Tis the Son of God that dies!
Heav'n, and earth, and hell afflict him:
Justice claims the sacrifice.
Darkness now exerts its power;
Darkness reigns this fearful hour.

4 Come, ye saints, look here and wonder;
Come behold what love could do:
Gaze upon the victim yonder:
Jesus suffer'd thus for you.
Bid adieu to low desire;
Here let earthly love expire.

HYMN XVI.

"*He was wounded for our transgressions.*"—Isa. liii. 5.

1 JESUS is the victim offer'd;
On him fell vindictive fire:
When he died, the victim suffer'd
All that justice could require.
This is welcome news from far,
Why should any now despair?

2 Now let others boast of doing,
We have no such plea as this:
Grace alone prevents our going
Down to hell's profound abyss.
Jesus came to save the lost;
In his name alone we boast.

3 Resting on this "faithful saying,"
We are safe from force and guile;
On the Lord our spirits staying,
We may look around and smile:
Leaning on his powerful arm,
Who or what can do us harm?

4 Fair our lot—in pleasant places
God has cast the lines for us;
Well may we shew forth his praises,
Who has loved his people thus.
Of his love we'll gladly talk,
By its pow'r constrain'd we'll walk.

HYMN XVII.

"*He is brought as a lamb to the slaughter.*"—Isa. liii. 7.

1 AS a lamb led forth to slaughter,
Jesus on his way proceeds:
See his foes are filled with laughter,
While the patient victim bleeds.
Jesus dies, by man abhorr'd;
Jesus, chosen of the Lord.

2 Jesus dies in love to others;
Greater love hath none than this:
Love of kindred, love of mothers,
Feeble is, compared to his.
Who can tell its breadth and length?
Who its depth, its height, its strength?

3 Come, my soul, look here and wonder,
Here's a sight to cause surprise:
Well the rocks might cleave asunder;
Well might darkness veil the skies:
'Twas the voice of nature then;
Nature's voice reproving men.

4 Nature's voice, again reproving,
Would be heard should I not speak:
None has greater cause for loving
Him who came the lost to seek:
Yet my love, how cold it is!
O how different mine from his!

5 Ah, my Lord, thou know'st thy servant,
Weak, unfaithful, apt to slide;
Make his love more pure and fervent,
Let him at thy feet abide.
Thine the tribute of his praise,
Thine the remnant of his days.

2 In his suff'rings no complaint is,
Smitten though he be to death.
Yes, the Lord of glory faint is,
And he yields his latest breath;
But his dying words, what were they?
"It is finish'd!" Wondrous words!
But the world around, how hear they?
Truth to them no joy affords.

3 Little know they what's impending,
When the Lord shall come again;
Come with clouds, from heav'n descending.
Every eye shall see him then,
They who seiz'd and who condemn'd him,
They who pierc'd his hands and feet,
They who slighted and contemn'd him;
All before his throne shall meet.

HYMN XXI.

"*The Lord God shall give unto him the throne of his father David.*"—LUKE i. 32.

1 DAVID'S royal son behold,
Long expected, long foretold;
Him of whom the prophets show'd
Coming as they taught he would.
Hosanna to the Son of David.

2 Rightful heir of David's throne,
His the title, his alone.
But ere this admitted is,
Toil and strife and pain are his.
Hosanna, &c.

3 Sore the conflict is, and strange;
But his purpose knows no change;
And in this eventful hour,
Darkness fails, and all its power.
Hosanna, &c.

4 David's royal son prevails,
His a pow'r that never fails;
His the sceptre and the crown,
His the spoil and the renown.
Hosanna, &c.

5 'Tis to him the praise belongs,
Raise, ye saints, triumphal songs,
His the suff'ring, ours the gain,
Reign, O Lord, for ever reign.
Hosanna, &c.

HYMN XXII.

"For it is the blood that maketh an atonement for the soul."—
LEV. xvii. 11.

1 WITHOUT blood is no remission,
Life for life the sentence is;
Pardon comes on this condition,
Tremble we when hearing this:
Where's the victim?—make him known;
Say ye, is his life his own?

2 Can he deal with it as one who
No superior owns, or has?
This belongs to him alone, who
Fills the throne that ever was,
And for ever will remain,
His an everlasting reign.

3 But will he whose voice is thunder,
And whose bolt the lightning is,
Whom the angels view with wonder,
Majesty and glory his;
Will he do what he alone
Equal is to, else undone?

4 Seest thou one, who, more than others,
Seems to know what sorrow is?
Love is his beyond a brother's;
Grace, and power, and truth are his,
Yet he comes, and dwells with men,
Dies, and takes his life again.

5 He could do it, but no other;
None whose life was not his own.
How could one redeem his brother?
Could he for his sin atone?
Were his life a gift bestow'd,
Had he ought but what he ow'd?

6 But the Lord who comes from heaven,
Is the Holy One of God;
Life is his—his own—not given,
Hence the value of his blood,
Hence he could atone for sin,
Hence impart new life within.

7 Sing we then, it well befits us,
'Tis a sweet, a blessed theme;
Wonder upon wonder meets us,
Tracing God's myterious scheme;
Sing of him who came to save,
Who his life for sinners gave.

HYMN XXIII.

"*God forbid that I should glory, save in the cross.*"—Gal. vi. 14.

1 TO the cross, away, away!
'Tis the place for you and me;
'Tis the place, again I say,
Where a sinner ought to be.

2 There it is, and only there;
What the sinner wants is found;
There he breathes a purer air,
All is tainted, all around.

3 Light is there, and there alone;
All is dark but one bright spot:
That on which the Lord has shone,
Light is there, but elsewhere not.

4 To the cross away, away,
While forbearance still endures;
Haste ye on, "while 'tis call'd to-day,"
For to-morrow is not yours.

5 Ere another dawn begins,
Who can tell what change may be?
He that dieth in his sins
Life in heav'n will never see.

6 Happy they who life have found
In the cross, of life the spring.
Joy is theirs, and shall abound
When in heav'n they see their king.

HYMN XXIV.

"*Father, if thou be willing, remove this cup from me.*"—
LUKE xxii. 42.

1 'TWAS a dark and fearful hour,
'Twas beyond example so,
When, as one bereft of pow'r,
Or as one oppress'd with woe,
Jesus to his Father pray'd,
That the cup might pass away:
What a load on him was laid,
When the Saviour thus could pray!

2 But it was the Father's will,
Not his own, he came to do,
All his pleasure to fulfil,
And for this all else forego.
Hence the cup his Father gave,
Drank he, bitter as it was.
This, and nothing else could save;
Nothing, nothing but the Cross.

3 Through this channel, this alone,
Mercy flows, all others barr'd;
He who mediates, must atone
For the guilt, nor can be spar'd;
Though his Son the victim is,
God will magnify his law;
Ponder this, O ponder this.
Let our minds be fill'd with awe.

Resurrection.

HYMN XXV.

"*He is not here, but is risen.*"—LUKE xxiv. 6.

1 THE Lord, who late was dead,
Now lives; then haste away,
And through the world the tidings spread,
THE LORD IS RIS'N TO-DAY.

2 While foes are fill'd with fear,
His joyful friends may say,
What glorious news is this we hear?
THE LORD IS RIS'N TO-DAY.

3 His triumph is complete,
Let all his people say;
And let ten thousand tongues repeat,
THE LORD IS RIS'N TO-DAY.

4 Let all his people sing,
For well his people may;
The theme is sweet, of hope the spring,
THE LORD IS RIS'N TO-DAY.

5 On him our souls rely,
Desponding thoughts away;
We know 'tis true, and sing with joy,
THE LORD IS RIS'N TO-DAY.

HYMN XXVI.

"*If Christ be not raised, your faith is vain.*"—1 COR. XV. 17.

1 IF Jesus rose not from the grave,
The faith of all his saints is vain:
That he can have no power to save,
If death detains him still, is plain.

2 If Jesus rose not from the grave,
We're guilty still, our sins remain:
The hope is vain his people have;
If Jesus rose not, hope is vain.

3 If Jesus rose not from the grave,
His foes were right in all they said;
For he to all assurance gave,
That he would rise and leave the dead.

4 If Jesus rose not from the grave,
Then all he said was empty boast:
His claims no good foundation have,
And they who sleep in him are lost.

5 If Jesus rose not from the grave,
The thief, that perish'd by his side,
As just a claim as he would have
To be the sinner's hope and guide.

6 But now is Jesus ris'n indeed;
The first-fruits he of those who sleep:
Rejoice, ye saints, the pris'ner's freed,
For who could such a pris'ner keep?

7 He fought with Death, the saints' last foe,
And though he seem'd to lose the day,
'Twas Death sustain'd the overthrow,
Subdu'd by him who seem'd his prey.

8 Doubt then no more, ye saints, nor grieve,
The Lord is ris'n, is ris'n indeed;
Because he lives, his saints shall live,
Shall live with him, their glorious Head.

9 He sits at God's right hand above,
The dread of foes, the joy of friends;
Supreme in pow'r, in truth, in love;
His kingdom, one that never ends.

10 The glorious day is drawing near,
When he who lay in yonder tomb,
With crowds of angels shall appear,
And take his waiting people home.

HYMN XXVII.

"*Death is swallowed up in victory.*"—1 Cor. xv. 54.

1 HARK! ten thousand voices cry,
Vict'ry, vict'ry, through the sky!
Swiftly flies the welcome sound,
Spreading rapt'rous joy around.

2 Jesus comes, his conflict over;
Comes to claim his great reward:
Angels round the victim hover,
Crowding to behold their Lord.

3 O what honours now await him!
Friends and foes shall hear his voice:
Tremble, tremble, ye that hate him;
Ye who love his name, rejoice.

4 Yonder throne, for him erected,
Now becomes the victor's seat;
Lo, the man on earth rejected!
Angels worship at his feet.

5 Day and night they cry before him,
"Holy, holy, holy Lord!"
All the pow'rs of heav'n adore him,
All obey his sov'reign word.

CHORUS.

Then haste, ye saints, your tribute bring,
And crown him everlasting King.

HYMN XXVIII.

"*So they went, and made the sepulchre sure, sealing the stone, and setting a watch.*"—MATT. xxvii. 66.

1 GO, and seal the sepulchre,
Make it sure, for much depends;
Jesus living did aver,
He would rise and meet his friends.

2 Hell its utmost aid will give;
Go and hold the pris'ner fast:
Satan knows that should he live,
Long his kingdom cannot last.

3 O, ye vain and foolish men,
What though earth and hell combine,
Jesus will revive again,
Death his pris'ner must resign.

4 Lo! th' appointed hour is come!
All suspense for ever ends;
Jesus lives, and leaves the tomb;
See, he stands among his friends!

5 When he meets their wond'ring eyes,
Whom he call'd, and made his own,
Many doubts at first arise,
But the Lord dispels them soon.

6 Happy they who have not seen,
Yet believe the record true;
They shall see the Saviour reign,
They shall share his glory too.

7 'Tis a sweet, reviving hope,
Saviour, let thy kingdom come;
Haste, and take thy people up
To their bright, eternal home.

HYMN XXIX.

"*The Lord is risen indeed.*"—LUKE xxiv. 34.

1 "THE Lord is ris'n indeed,"
And are the tidings true?
Yes, they beheld the Saviour bleed,
And saw him living too.

2 "The Lord is ris'n indeed,"
Then Justice asks no more;
Mercy and Truth are now agreed,
Who stood oppos'd before.

3 "The Lord is ris'n indeed,"
Then is his work perform'd;
The captive surety now is freed,
And death, our foe, disarm'd.

4 "The Lord is ris'n indeed,"
Then hell has lost his prey;
With him is ris'n the ransom'd seed,
To reign in endless day.

5 "The Lord is ris'n indeed,"
He lives to die no more;
He lives, the sinner's cause to plead,
Whose curse and shame he bore.

6 "The Lord is ris'n indeed,"
This yields my soul a plea;
He bore the punishment decreed,
And satisfied for me.

7 "The Lord is ris'n indeed,"
Attending angels hear.
Up to the courts of heav'n, with speed,
The joyful tidings bear.

8 Then take your golden lyres,
And strike each cheerful chord,
Join all the bright celestial choirs,
To sing our risen Lord.

HYMN XXX.

"*And your joy no man taketh from you.*"—JOHN xvi. 22.

1 REJOICE, the Lord is ris'n;
Let all his friends rejoice;
This day the Lord has left his pris'n;
The grave has heard his voice.

2 The grave has felt his pow'r,
And yielded up his prey;
For darkness had its fearful hour;
But now again 'tis day.

3 The Lord is ris'n indeed;
And he will die no more.
He lives again, and lives to plead,
The mercy-seat before.

4 We see him not, 'tis true;
But still we may be glad.
The work is done he came to do;
Then why should we be sad?

5 The Lord who risen is,
Whose place is now in heav'n,
Will come again: rejoice in this,
All pow'r to him is giv'n.

6 And when the Lord appears,
His people then are blest.
A place in heav'n is theirs; and theirs
An everlasting rest.

HYMN XXXI.

"*Then he said unto them, O fools, and slow of heart to believe all that the prophets have spoken!*"—LUKE xxiv. 25.

1 O FOOLS, and backward to receive
What God by all his prophets said,
That Christ a suff'ring life should live,
And then be number'd with the dead.

2 Why are ye pensive thus, and sad?
Why, like to men astonish'd, flee?
Why now resign the hopes ye had,
That Jesus should the Saviour be?

3 Go, search the prophets and the law,
And find the true Messiah there;
Then meditate on all ye saw,
So shall the joyful truth appear.

4 But see, he comes! the very same
Who lately hung on yonder tree:
Ye can no more resist his claim;
Behold his wounds! 'tis he! 'tis he!

5 Till the appointed hour arriv'd,
He lay a pris'ner in the grave;
(Death could no more), he then reviv'd,
And now he lives, and lives to save.

6 All hail! victorious Lord, all hail!
Thy people's life! thy people's joy!
Thy love to them shall never fail;
Thy praise shall all their pow'rs employ.

HYMN XXXII.

"*He is not here: for he is risen, as he said.*"—MATT. xxviii. 6.

1 HE'S gone! see where his body lay,
A pris'ner till th' appointed day,
Releas'd from prison then:
"Why seek the living with the dead?"
Remember what the Saviour said,
That he should rise again.

2 O joyful sound! O glorious hour!
When Jesus, by almighty pow'r,
Reviv'd, and left the grave.
In all his works behold him great!
Before, almighty to create!
Almighty now to save.

3 "The first begotten from the dead,"
Behold him ris'n, his people's head!
To make their life secure.
They too, like him, shall yield their breath,
Like him, shall burst the bands of death:
Their resurrection sure.

4 Why should his people now be sad?
None have such reason to be glad,
As reconcil'd to God.
Jesus, the mighty Saviour, lives;
To them eternal life he gives,
The purchase of his blood.

5 Why should his people fear the grave?
Since Jesus will their spirits save,
And raise their bodies too.
What though this earthly house shall fail?
Almighty pow'r will yet prevail,
And build it up anew.

6 Ye ransom'd, let your praise resound,
And in your Master's work abound,
With strong and patient faith:
Be sure your labour 's not in vain;
Your bodies shall be rais'd again,
No more to suffer death.

HYMN XXXIII.

"*Why seek ye the living among the dead?*"—Luke xxiv. 5.

1 YES, the Lord no more is found
In the grave, the dead among;
Seek him not beneath the ground;
They who seek him there, do wrong.

2 First among the living he,
First in pow'r and first in place;
"Lord of all," ordain'd to be:
"Full of truth, and full of grace."

3 Hail the Lord return'd to life;
Living, and to die no more;
Past the suff'ring and the strife;
His the name all names before.

4 Hail the blessed name he bears;
He who came from heav'n to die.
This is he who "sows in tears;"
This is he who "reaps in joy."

5 Yes, the day not distant is
When he shall collect his own.
O what joy will then be his!
His the glory, his alone.

HYMN XXXIV.

"*I am he that liveth and was dead.*"—Rev. i. 18.

1 CROWNS of glory, ever bright,
Rest upon the victor's head:
Crowns of glory are his right,
His "who liveth and was dead."

2 Jesus fought and won the day;
Such a day was never fought;
Well his people now may say,
See what God, our God, has wrought.

3 He subdu'd the pow'rs of hell;
In the fight he stood alone;
All his foes before him fell,
By his single arm o'erthrown.

4 They have fall'n to rise no more:
Final is the foe's defeat:
Jesus triumph'd by his pow'r,
And his triumph is complete.

5 His the fight, the arduous toil;
His the honours of the day;
His the glory and the spoil;
Jesus bears them all away!

6 Now proclaim his deeds afar;
Fill the world with his renown:
His alone the victor's car;
His the everlasting crown.

HYMN XXXV.

"*A little while, and ye shall not see me, and again, a little while, and ye shall see me.*"—John xvi. 16.

1 THO' foes should triumph in his death,
And friends should mourn and fear,
Yet Jesus will resume his breath,
And in the world appear.
His friends shall then confess his claim,
And all his foes be fill'd with shame.

2 The name of Jesus shall be borne
To lands involv'd in night;
And like the rising of the morn,
Shall bring the welcome light.
Though now a pris'ner with the dead,
His name throughout the world shall spread.

3 Hail, mighty Lord, a conqu'ror thou!
With this peculiar boast,
That then thine honours brightest grow,
When men despise them most;
And Death, that boasts his myriads slain,
Appears a captive in thy train.

HYMN XXXVI.

"*Behold the place where they laid him.*"—Mark xvi. 6.

1 COME, ye saints, look here and wonder,
See the place where Jesus lay;
He has burst his bands asunder;
He has borne our sins away;
Joyful tidings!
Yes, the Lord is ris'n to-day.

2 Jesus triumphs! sing ye praises:
By his death he overcame:
Thus the Lord his glory raises;
Thus he fills his foes with shame:
Sing ye praises!
Praises to the victor's name.

3 Jesus triumphs! countless legions
Come from heav'n to meet their King:
Soon in yonder blessed regions
They shall join his praise to sing.
Songs eternal
Shall through heav'n's high arches ring.

HYMN XXXVII.

"*Then were the disciples glad when they saw the Lord.*"—
JOHN XX. 20.

1 GLAD they were, how should they not?
Glad to see the Lord again;
When he breath'd his last, they thought
All was lost; they sorrow'd then;
But the world rejoic'd to be
Rid of him they loath'd to see.

2 But his people's grief is now
Turn'd to joy, as he had said;
While his hands, his feet, his brow,
Proof afford that he was dead;
Dead, indeed; but now he lives,
And to others life he gives.

3 All the pow'r above, below,
All is his, by compact his,
Fruit of strife, and toil, and woe.
But his conflict over is;
Him in glory now we see,
"Lord and Christ" ordain'd to be.

4 His we are, we love his name,
And would serve him as we ought,
But, we own it to our shame,
What we would, we do it not.
Thine it is to pardon, Lord,
Pardon us, and strength afford.

Exaltation of Christ.

HYMN XXXVIII.

"In the midst of the throne . . . a Lamb as it had been slain."—
REV. v. 6.

1 BEHOLD the Lamb, with glory crown'd!
To him all pow'r is giv'n;
No place too high for him is found,
No place too high in heav'n.

2 He fills the throne, the throne above;
He fills it without wrong;
The object he of angels' love,
The theme of angels' song.

3 With faces veil'd yon seraphs bright
Upon his glory gaze;
Not seraphs could endure the light,
The full resplendent blaze.

4 Though high, yet he accepts the praise
His people offer here:
The faintest, feeblest cry they raise,
Will reach the Saviour's ear.

5 Well may his people then be found
Transported with the sight;
To see the Lamb with glory crown'd,
Must yield them sweet delight.

6 This song be ours, and this alone,
That celebrates the name
Of him that sits upon the throne,
And that exalts the Lamb.

7 To him whom men despise and slight,
To him be glory giv'n:
The crown is his, and his by right,
The highest place in heav'n.

HYMN XXXIX.

"*And on his head were many crowns.*"—REV. xix. 12.

1 LET crowns of glory wreathe the head
Of him who bore the cross:
He liveth now; he once was dead;
He died and rose for us.

2 For us the Saviour died and rose,
For us whom he has sav'd;
For us, who once appear'd his foes;
Whom sin had once enslav'd.

3 How rich the grace, how free the love,
That saves a people thus!
The theme is high, our thoughts above,
'Tis far too high for us.

4 Nor can the brightest seraph there,
In yonder world above,
The subject fathom, and declare
The mystery of love.

5 Its breadth and length, its depth and height,
Are such, that he alone
Can measure its extent aright,
To whom all things are known.

6 But this we know, that God is love;
A truth by heav'n confess'd:
And those below, and those above,
Who know his name are bless'd.

7 And when to yonder place we go,
Where soon we hope to be;
We then shall know what angels know,
And see what angels see.

HYMN XL.

"*Endured the cross, despising the shame, and is set down at the right hand of the throne of God.*"—HEB. xii. 2.

1 FOR whom is yonder crown prepar'd,
Of workmanship divine?
For Jesus is the bright reward;
For him its glories shine.

2 Beneath the earth awhile he lies,
A pris'ner with the dead;
A victor soon the Lord will rise,
And glory wreathe his head.

3 He saw the cross, despis'd its shame,
And bow'd beneath its weight;
For this he bears the greatest name,
And gains the highest seat.

4 To him shall ev'ry knee be bow'd;
His claim shall angels own;
Around the rising victor crowd,
And bear him to his throne.

5 Behold, ye saints, behold your King,
By hosts angelic crown'd:
They shout, and heav'n's high arches ring
With the triumphant sound.

6 Let saints on earth their tribute bring,
And echo back the sound;
For he who saves them is the King,
By hosts angelic crown'd.

HYMN XLI.

"*Worthy is the Lamb.*"—Rev. v. 12.

1 HARK the notes of angels singing—
"Glory, glory to the Lamb!"
All in heav'n their tribute bringing,
Raising high the Saviour's name.

2 Ye for whom his life was given,
Sacred themes to you belong:
Come assist the choir of heav'n;
Join the everlasting song.

3 Saints and angels thus united,
Songs imperfect still must raise;
Though despised on earth, and slighted,
Jesus is above all praise.

4 See th' angelic hosts have crown'd him,
Jesus fills the throne on high:
Countless myriads, hov'ring round him,
With his praises rend the sky.

5 Fill'd with holy emulation,
Let us vie with those above:
Sweet the theme—a free salvation!
Fruit of everlasting love.

6 Endless life in him possessing,
Let us praise his precious name:
Glory, honour, power and blessing,
Be for ever to the Lamb.

HYMN XLII.

"*Let all the angels of God worship him.*"—Heb. 1. 6.

1 HARK, ten thousand harps and voices
  Sound the note of praise above!
Jesus reigns, and heav'n rejoices:
  Jesus reigns, the God of love:
See he sits on yonder throne;
Jesus rules the world alone.

2 Well may angels bright and glorious,
  Sing the praises of the Lamb;
While on earth, he prov'd victorious;
  Now, he bears a matchless name:
Well may angels sing of him,
Heav'n supplies no richer theme.

3 Come, ye saints, unite your praises
  With the angels round his throne;
Soon we hope our Lord will raise us
  To the place where he is gone.
Meet it is that we should sing,
Glory, glory to our King.

4 Sing how Jesus came from heaven,
  How he bore the cross below;
How all pow'r to him is given;
  How he reigns in glory now:
'Tis a great and endless theme:
O 'tis sweet to sing of him!

5 Jesus hail, whose glory brightens
  All above, and gives it worth.
Lord of life, thy smile enlightens
  Cheers and charms thy saints on earth:
When we think of love like thine,
Lord, we own it love divine.

6 King of glory, reign for ever,
Thine an everlasting crown:
Nothing from thy love shall sever
Those whom thou hast made thine own;
Happy objects of thy grace,
Destin'd to behold thy face.

7 Saviour, hasten thine appearing;
Bring, O bring the glorious day,
When the awful summons hearing,
Heav'n and earth shall pass away:
Then, with golden harps, we'll sing—
"Glory, glory to our King."

HYMN XLIII.

"*King of kings, and Lord of lords.*"—Rev. xix. 16.

1 "KING of kings, and Lord of lords!"
These are great and awful words;
'Tis to Jesus they belong:
Let his people raise their song.

2 Hark, how angels sound his praise!
Fill'd with transport while they gaze:
Glory, honour, praise and power,
These are thine for evermore.

3 Crown him, then, whom angels sing;
Crown him everlasting king!
Jesus fills the throne above,
Jesus is the God of love.

4 Holy, holy, holy Lord!
Heav'n and earth thy name record;
Pow'r and praise to thee belong;
Lord, accept our feeble song.

5 Rich in glory, thou didst stoop:
This is now thy people's hope:
Thou wast poor, that they might be
Rich in glory, Lord, with thee.

6 When we think of love like this,
Joy and shame our hearts possess:
Joy, that thou couldst pity thus;
Shame, for such returns from us.

7 Yet we hope the day to see,
When we shall from earth be free;
Borne aloft, to heav'n be brought,
There to praise thee as we ought.

8 While we still continue here,
Let this hope our spirits cheer.
Till in heav'n thy face we see,
Teach us, Lord, to live to thee.

HYMN XLIV.

"*Sing praises unto our King, sing praises!*"—PSALM xlvii. 6.

1 GLORY, glory to our King!
Crowns unfading wreathe his head!
Jesus is the name we sing;
Jesus risen from the dead;
Jesus conqu'ror o'er the grave;
Jesus mighty now to save.

2 Jesus is gone up on high,
Angels come to meet their King;
Shouts triumphant rend the sky,
While the victor's praise they sing:
"Open now, ye heav'nly gates!
"'Tis the King of glory waits."

3 Now behold him high enthron'd!
Glory beaming from his face!
By adoring angels own'd,
God of holiness and grace!
O for hearts and tongues to sing
"Glory, glory to our King."

4 Jesus, on thy people shine!
Warm our hearts, and tune our tongues!
That with angels we may join,
Share their bliss, and swell their songs.
Glory, honour, praise and pow'r,
Lord, be thine for evermore!

HYMN XLV.

"*That at the name of Jesus every knee should bow.*"—
PHIL. ii. 10.

1 EV'RY knee shall bow to Jesus,
'Tis decreed, and must be done;
God ordains it, whom it pleases
Thus to glorify his Son:
Honour is to Jesus giv'n,
All the pow'r in earth and heav'n.

2 He who without usurpation,
Claims equality with God,
Comes from his exalted station,
And with men has his abode:
Though we see him humbled now,
Ev'ry knee to him shall bow.

3 See the Lord, "A man in fashion,
"Of no reputation made."
See, he dies without compassion!
In the tomb behold him laid!
Though he seems deserted now,
Ev'ry knee to him shall bow.

4 See the Saviour ris'n victorious,
Late a pris'ner with the dead:
Look, ye saints, the sight is glorious!
Jesus ris'n his people's head;
Crowns adorn the victor's brow;
Ev'ry knee to him shall bow.

5 See him now to glory raised,
Bearing an unrivall'd name:
Angels, at the sight amazed,
Worship, and confess his claim;
All in heav'n adore him now:
Ev'ry knee to him shall bow.

6 Hark! the trumpet loudly sounding,
Now proclaims the Judge is near:
Jesus comes, his foes confounding,
Jesus, to his people dear:
Lo! he comes on yonder cloud;
Ev'ry knee to him is bow'd.

HYMN XLVI.

"*Who coverest thyself with light.*"—PSALM civ. 2.

1 SEE where the Lord his glory spreads,
Thro' yonder mansion fill'd with light;
His least perfection far exceeds
The reach of fancy's boldest flight.

2 Around his everlasting throne
Ten thousand times ten thousand sing:
They worship him as God alone,
And crown him everlasting King.

3 Approach, ye saints, this God is yours;
'Tis Jesus fills the throne above;
Ye cannot fail while God endures;
Ye cannot want while God is love.

4 Come then, and swell the note of praise,
In Jesu's name rejoice and sing:
While angels on his glory gaze,
The saints may cry, "Behold our King."

5 Jesus, thou everlasting King,
To thee the praise of heav'n belongs;
Yet smile on us, who fain would bring
The tribute of our humbler songs.

6 Though sin defile our worship here,
We hope, ere long, thy face to view;
In heav'n with angels to appear,
And praise thy name as angels do.

HYMN XLVII.

"*God our Saviour.*"—Titus iii. 4.

1 LO! the infant Saviour lies;
Angels call him "only wise;"
To his name they join the words—
"King of kings, and Lord of lords."

2 See! he stands at Pilate's bar;
Most despis'd of all by far;
Still to him belong the words—
"King of kings, and Lord of lords."

3 He who wears the crown of thorns,
He whom man reviles and scorns,
Claims exclusively the words—
"King of kings, and Lord of lords."

4 On the cross 'tis still the same;
Never does he yield his claim:
Clear his title to the words—
"King of kings, and Lord of lords."

5 Past the conflict of his love;
See! he takes his place above:
On his vesture shine the words—
"King of kings, and Lord of lords."

6 O ye bright seraphic choirs,
Strike anew your golden lyres:
While ye gaze, proclaim the words—
"King of kings, and Lord of lords."

7 Join, ye saints, with heav'n agree,
Let the name of Jesus be
Still united to the words,
"King of kings, and Lord of lords.

HYMN XLVIII.

"*And he hath on his vesture, and on his thigh, a name written, King of kings, and Lord of lords.*"—REV. xix. 16.

1 WHENCE those unusual bursts of joy,
Whose sound through heaven rings?
They welcome Jesus to the sky,
And crown him "King of kings."

2 At sight of him, yon seraphs bright
Exulting clap their wings;
They hail their Lord with new delight,
And crown him "King of kings."

3 The brightest angel glory boasts,
To him his tribute brings,
And joins high heav'n's assembled hosts,
To crown him "King of kings."

4 Look up, ye saints, and while ye gaze,
Forget all earthly things:
Unite to sing the Saviour's praise,
And crown him "King of kings."

5 While heav'n, in honour of his name,
With exultation sings,
His saints on earth will own his claim,
And crown him "King of kings."

6 When here, he bore our sin and shame;
And thence our comfort springs:
'Tis meet we should exalt his name,
And crown him "King of kings."

7 We hope, ere long, beyond those clouds,
To tune celestial strings;
And join with heav'n's exulting crowds,
To crown him "King of kings."

HYMN XLIX.

"*And he shall reign for ever and ever.*"—Rev. xi. 15.

1 LOOK, ye saints, the sight is glorious,
See "the Man of Sorrows" now;
From the fight return'd victorious,
Ev'ry knee to him shall bow:
Crown him, crown him;
Crowns become the victor's brow.

2 Crown the Saviour, angels crown him:
Rich the trophies Jesus brings:
In the seat of pow'r enthrone him,
While the vault of heaven rings:
Crown him, crown him;
Crown the Saviour "King of kings."

3 Sinners in derision crown'd him,
Mocking thus the Saviour's claim;
Saints and angels crowd around him,
Own his title, praise his name:
Crown him, crown him;
Spread abroad the victor's fame.

4 Hark! those bursts of acclamation!
Hark! those loud triumphant chords!
Jesus takes the highest station:
O what joy the sight affords!
Crown him, crown him;
"King of kings, and Lord of lords."

HYMN L.

"*Who is this King of Glory?*"—Psalm xxiv. 8.

1 YE who dwell in heav'n, declare
Who "the King of Glory" is;
Who is first and highest there?
His the pow'r, the kingdom his?

2 'Tis the Lamb, the Lamb alone,
Claims the title justly his;
He it is that fills the throne;
He "the King of Glory" is.

3 Blessed news! the Lamb is King:
Glorious truth! he reigns alone:
Come, ye saints, your tribute bring,
Bow before the Saviour's throne.

4 Let the world deride his claim;
Let the world refuse to bow:
Angels triumph in his name;
All in heav'n adore him now.

5 Jesus hail! whom angels sing;
Lamb of God, for sinners slain;
Reign for ever, glorious King;
Thou art worthy, Lord, to reign.

HYMN LI.

"*Who is this that cometh from Edom?*"—ISAIAH lxiii. 1.

1 "WHO is this that comes from Edom?"
All his raiment stain'd with blood,
To the slave proclaiming freedom,
Bringing and bestowing good;
Glorious in the garb he wears,
Glorious in the spoils he bears.

2 'Tis the Saviour, now victorious,
Trav'lling onward in his might;
'Tis the Saviour, O how glorious
To his people is the sight!
Jesus now is strong to save,
Mighty to redeem the slave.

3 Why that blood his raiment staining?
'Tis the blood of many slain;
Of his foes there's none remaining,
None the contest to maintain;
Fall'n they are, no more to rise,
All their glory prostrate lies.

4 This the Saviour has effected,
By his mighty arm alone;
See the throne for him erected,
'Tis an everlasting throne;
'Tis the great reward he gains,
Glorious fruit of all his pains.

5 Mighty Victor, reign for ever,
Wear the crown so dearly won;
Never shall thy people, never
Cease to sing what thou hast done:
Thou hast fought thy people's foes;
Thou wilt heal thy people's woes.

HYMN LII.

"*He hath triumphed gloriously.*"—Exod. xv. 1.

1 SONS of Zion, raise your songs,
Praise to Zion's King belongs;
His the victor's crown and fame,
Glory to the Saviour's name!

2 Sore the strife, but rich the prize,
Precious in the victor's eyes;
Glorious is the work achiev'd,
Satan vanquished, man reliev'd.

3 Sing we then the victor's praise.
Go ye forth and strew the ways;
Bid him welcome to his throne,
He is worthy, he alone.

4 Place the crown upon his brow;
Ev'ry knee to him shall bow;
Him the brightest seraph sings,
Heav'n proclaims him "King of kings."

HYMN LIII.

"*Perfect through sufferings.*"—Heb. ii. 10.

1 THE head that once was crown'd with thorns,
Is crown'd with glory now;
A royal diadem adorns
The mighty victor's brow.

2 The highest place that heav'n affords
Is his, is his by right,
"The King of kings, and Lord of lords,"
And heaven's eternal light.

3 The joy of all who dwell above,
The joy of all below
To whom he manifests his love,
And grants his name to know.

4 To them, the cross, with all its shame,
With all its grace, is given;
Their name an everlasting name,
Their joy the joy of heav'n.

5 They suffer with their Lord below,
They reign with him above;
Their profit and their joy to know
The myst'ry of his love.

6 The cross he bore is life and health,
Though shame and death to him;
His people's hope, his people's wealth,
Their everlasting theme.

HYMN LIV.

"*His right hand, and his holy arm, hath gotten him the victory.*"
PSALM xcviii. 1.

1 SEE! he comes, his work is done,
See the victor coming!
See! he comes, the day is won;
Fresh his honours blooming:
This is he whom many foes
Threaten'd and assaulted;
But above them all he rose,
Now the more exalted.

2 JESUS is the victor's name,
JESUS, Lord of glory;
Fly, ye heralds, spread his fame,
Tell the joyful story:
Make the Saviour's triumph known,
Let the nations hear it;
He alone deserves the crown,
He alone shall wear it.

3 Jesus comes, he won the day,
Go ye forth to meet him;
Bring the palm, and strew the way,
And with singing greet him:
Well his people now may sing,
Sing with exultation,
Since the victor is their king,
And he brings salvation.

The Day of Christ.

LV.

"*The earth and the heaven fled away.*"—Rev. xx. 11.

1 O WHAT a sound was there!
'Tis nature's final groan:
And Jesus bids the world appear
Before his awful throne.

2 The day at length is come,
As threaten'd, like a snare;
A source of endless joy to some;
To others, of despair.

3 The Saviour is at hand;
Behold he comes with clouds;
And angels, at their Lord's command,
Appear in joyful crowds.

4 But who may stand this day,
Destroying far and wide?
When heav'n and earth shall flee away,
Who can the storm abide?

5 The saints alone shall stand,
The people of his love;
He sets them at his own right hand,
And gives them joys above.

6 Into his presence brought,
They see him face to face:
No other grace his people sought;
And now he grants this grace.

HYMN LVI.

"And what I say unto you, I say unto all—watch."
MARK xiii. 37.

1 AWAKE, ye saints, awake and watch,
The bridegroom may be near;
How awful, should the summons catch
His people slumb'ring here!

2 They who are ready to attend
The Lord when he appears,
With him to glory shall ascend;
Eternal life is theirs.

3 With him they shall sit down, and feast
On heav'n's unbounded store;
Enjoy an everlasting rest,
And never hunger more.

4 When once the chamber door shall close,
Be sure beyond a doubt,
No further hope remains for those
Who then are found without.

5 Awake, and be ye like to those
Who wait their Lord's return;
Awake, nor yield to that repose,
Whose end it is to mourn.

HYMN LVII.

"*To wait for his Son from heaven.*"—1 Thess. i. 10.

1 SAVIOUR, come! thy friends are waiting,
Waiting for the final day;
Thence the promis'd glory dating:
Come and bear thy saints away.
Come, Lord Jesus,
Thus thy waiting people pray.

2 Base the wish, and vain th' endeavour,
While on earth to find our rest;
Till we see thy face, we never
Shall or can be fully blest.
In thy presence
Nothing shall our peace molest.

3 Lord, we wait for thine appearing;
Tarry not, thy people say;
Bright the prospect is, and cheering,
Of beholding thee that day;
When our sorrows
Shall for ever pass away.

4 Till it comes, O keep us steady,
Keep us walking in thy ways;
At thy call may we be ready,
And our heads with triumph raise.
Then with angels
Sing thine everlasting praise.

HYMN LVIII.

"*Behold! He cometh with clouds.*"—Rev. i. 7.

1 JESUS comes, the Judge of all:
Heav'n's bright hosts adore him:
All the people, great and small,
Now must stand before him.

Crowns of glory wreathe his head:
Christ, the Lord's anointed;
Judge of living and of dead;
Judge of old appointed.

2 Heav'n and earth, that stood so long
Shewing forth his glory,
Now are, though they seem'd so strong,
Like a finish'd story.
Caus'd to cease by him whose pow'r
Gave them first a being;
Lo! they perish from this hour;
'Tis the Lord's decreeing.

3 Saviour, in that awful day
Keep our hearts from sinking:
For ev'n now we feel dismay,
Of the season thinking.
May we lift our heads that day—
Day of God's salvation;
May we joyful hear him say,
"Yours a glorious station."

HYMN LIX.

"*For the Lord himself shall descend from heaven with a shout.*"—1 Thess. iv. 16.

1 HARK! that shout of rapt'rous joy,
Bursting forth from yonder cloud;
Jesus comes, and, through the sky,
Angels tell their joy aloud.

2 Now the world's duration ends;
Now the Lord will meet his foes;
These shall perish, but his friends
Shall in heav'n obtain repose.

3 Hark! the trumpet's awful voice
Sounds abroad through sea and land;
Let his people now rejoice,
Their redemption is at hand.

4 See! the Lord appears in view;
Heav'n and earth before him fly;
Rise, ye saints, he comes for you;
Rise to meet him in the sky.

5 Go, and dwell with him above,
Where no foe can e'er molest;
Happy in the Saviour's love!
Blessing, and for ever blest.

HYMN LX.

"*To wait for his Son from heaven.*"—1 Thess. i. 10.

1 TO wait for that important day,
When Jesus will his pow'r display,
Be this my one great care;
To do his will, my bus'ness here;
No toil to shun, no danger fear,
Resolv'd his cross to share.

2 Should men pronounce me fool, and say,
I never need expect the day,
And all are fools who do;
Their word I never can receive,
For well I know whom I believe;
I know his word is true.

3 Though he should still prolong his stay,
And sinners mock at the delay,
His people need not fear:
The man who wore the crown of thorns,
Whose claim the world rejects and scorns,
In glory will appear.

4 Bright angels shall attend their King,
And heav'n with acclamations ring,
When Jesus comes with clouds:
Methinks I see the dazzling train;
It seems to fill yon azure plain
With heav'n's exulting crowds.

5 Transported with the glorious sight,
My soul prepares her wings for flight,
Resigning all below.
But, ah! the charm is quickly past,
She feels a chain that holds her fast,
Nor suffers her to go.

6 Be patient, then, my soul, and rest,
Be sure the Saviour's time is best,
And cannot be too late:
Rejoice in hope, the day will come
When Jesus will convey thee home;
Till then in patience wait.

HYMN LXI.

"*The night is far spent, the day is at hand.*"—ROM. xiii. 12.

1 THE night is now far spent,
And day comes on apace;
The veil will soon be rent,
That hides the Saviour's face;
The clouds that now obstruct our sight
Will all be quickly put to flight.

2 Ye saints, lift up your heads,
Salvation draweth nigh;
See where the morning spreads
Its radiance through the sky;
Oh, let the sight your spirits cheer;
The Lord himself will soon appear.

3 Though men your hope deride,
Nor will themselves believe;
Yet in his word confide,
Who never can deceive;
When heav'n and earth shall pass away,
The saints shall see a glorious day.

4 For you the Lord intends
A bright abode on high;
The place where sorrow ends,
And nought is known but joy:
With such a hope, ye saints, rejoice;
We soon shall hear th' archangel's voice.

HYMN LXII.

"*But he shall appear to your joy, and they shall be ashamed.*"—
ISAIAH lxvi. 6.

1 FROM far I see the glorious day,
When he who bore our sins away,
Will all his majesty display.

2 "A man of sorrows" once he was;
No friend was found to plead his cause,
For all preferr'd the world's applause.

3 He groan'd beneath sin's awful load;
For in the sinner's place he stood,
And died to bring him back to God.

4 But now he reigns with glory crown'd,
While angel-hosts his throne surround,
And still his lofty praises sound.

5 To few on earth his name is dear;
And they who in his cause appear,
The world's reproach and scorn must bear.

6 But yet there is a day to come,
When he will seal the sinner's doom,
And take his mourning people home.

7 Jesus, thy name is all my boast;
And though by waves of trouble tost,
Thou wilt not let my soul be lost.

8 Come then, come quickly from above,
My soul, impatient, longs to prove
The depths of everlasting love.

HYMN LXIII.

"*The trumpet shall sound.*"—1 Cor. xv. 52.

1 THE trumpet shall sound,
And fill the world round;
From shore it shall echo to shore;
The angel shall stand
With uplifted hand,
Proclaiming that time is no more.

2 And now shall the tomb
Discharge from its womb
The load it no more can contain;
The earth and the sea
The call shall obey,
And give up their myriads of slain.

3 The Saviour with crowds
Shall come in the clouds;
His glory to all shall appear:
All power is giv'n,
In earth and in heav'n,
To him who was crucified here.

4 Then joy to the saints;
Whatever complaints
Attend on their state here below,
They all in that day
Shall vanish away;
No more shall their tears ever flow.

5 Their Lord they shall see;
With him they shall be;
With him in his kingdom above;
For ever to gaze:
For ever to praise;
For ever to sing of his love.

HYMN LXIV.

"*But who may abide the day of his coming?*"—MAL. iii. 12.

1 THE day of God at length appears,
But who its terrors may abide?
It far exceeds the sinner's fears;
It humbles all the sons of pride.

2 Hark! 'tis the trumpet's awful sound;
It shakes the pillars of the earth;
Its mighty voice is heard around:
O where is now the worldling's mirth!

3 The Judge appears; around his seat
Ten thousand times ten thousand shine;
The dead are quicken'd, small and great;
The living chang'd by pow'r divine.

4 But mark the issue of the day!
Some are receiv'd with joy to heav'n;
While others, turn'd with shame away,
From God and happiness are driv'n.

5 How blest are they who welcome now,
In him who fills the judgment-seat,
The Saviour whom they lov'd below,
And long'd with great desire to meet.

6 Their cup is full, their joys abound,
No wish unsatisfied have they;
In seeing him their heav'n is found,
And ev'ry sorrow flies away.

HYMN LXV.

"*Even so, come, Lord Jesus.*"—REV. xxii. 20.

1 FLY, ye seasons, fly still faster;
Let the glorious day come on,
When we shall behold our Master
Seated on his heav'nly throne;
When the Saviour
Shall descend to claim his own.

2 What is earth, with all its treasures,
To the joy the Gospel brings?
Well may we resign its pleasures,
Jesus gives us better things.
All his people
Draw from heav'n's eternal springs.

3 But if here we taste of pleasure,
What will heav'n itself afford?
There our joy will know no measure;
There we shall behold our Lord;
There his people
Shall obtain their bright reward.

4 Fly, ye seasons, fly still faster;
Swiftly bring the glorious day;
Jesus come, our Lord, our Master!
Come from heav'n without delay;
Take thy people,
Take, O take them hence away!

HYMN LXVI.

" *For the trumpet shall sound.*"—1 Cor. xv. 52.

1 HARK! 'tis the trumpet's sound;
It closes earthly things;
It echoes all around,
And great the news it brings:—
It tells that Jesus is at hand,
And bids the world before him stand.

2 The sound is heard afar,
It goes through sea and land;
And now, before his bar,
Th' assembled nations stand:
His friends are mingled with his foes,
But who are his, the Saviour knows.

3 And now he calls his own
To dwell with him above;
To sit upon his throne,
And share his endless love:
With joy they meet him in the clouds,
And mix with heav'n's exulting crowds.

4 But oh! what storms await
The trembling crowds below!
Their pleas are now too late;
This is the time of woe:
The Judge decrees their final doom;
Their portion is " the wrath to come."

5 O that, in that great day,
We may with those appear,
To whom the Lord will say,
"Ye blessed, now come near;
"To you eternal life is giv'n;
"The glory and the joy of heav'n."

HYMN LXVII.

"*For he cometh to judge the earth.*"—PSALM xcviii. 9.

1 JESUS comes, by crowds attended,
Heav'n the dazzling train supplies:
Call the dead; the night is ended;
Bid the sleeping dust arise:
Let the ransom'd
Join the Saviour in the skies.

2 'Tis the day so long expected;
Shout, ye saints, and triumph now;
See your Lord, by man rejected;
Many crowns adorn his brow;
'Tis his triumph:
Ev'ry knee to him shall bow.

3 While dismay on others seizes,
Go and share your Master's joy;
Sound the sacred name of Jesus;
Let his praise your tongues employ:
Praise him, praise him!
Pleasures yours that never cloy.

4 Yonder mansion, fill'd with glory,
Is the place where Jesus reigns;
Go, repeat the joyful story
Of his love, in rapt'rous strains;
For his people
An eternal rest remains.

5 There around his throne assembling,
All his people see his face;
Here their joy was mix'd with trembling,
But in heav'n no fear has place:
Happy people!
Happy made by sov'reign grace.

HYMN LXVIII.

"And said to the mountains and rocks, fall on us."—
Rev. vi. 16.

1 "FALL, ye rocks, and fall, ye mountains,
"Hide, O hide us by your fall!
"Wrath is pour'd from all its fountains;
"God is come, the Judge of all:"
Thus will sinners
On the rocks and mountains call.

2 But can rocks or mountains hide them,
When the mighty God appears?
Refuge will be then denied them,
'Spite of wishes, sighs, and tears.
Then the sinner
Goes where hope no creature cheers.

3 They who witness'd Sinai's thunders,
Fled with terror and dismay;
Who then can abide the wonders
Of that great and awful day?
When the Saviour
Comes, his glory to display.

4 God will then for ever banish
All the wicked from his sight;
Then delusive hope will vanish;
Dreams of joy be put to flight;
And the sinner
Sink into eternal night.

5 Sinners hear, for O there's reason!
When shall wisdom guide you, when?
Think of the approaching season,
When the Lord will plead with men:
Hear, O hear him!
So shall ye be blessed then.

HYMN LXIX.

"*And the angel which I saw . . . lifted up his hand to heaven, and sware by him that liveth for ever and ever . . . that there should be time no longer.*"—Rev. x. 5, 6.

1 LOUD thunders shake the earth and sky,
And lightnings flash from pole to pole:
Methinks I hear the angel cry,
(How awful to the guilty soul!)
"The mystery of God is o'er,
"'Tis done! there shall be time no more."

2 The Lord appears! before his face
An all-consuming fire destroys;
The worldling's glory sinks apace,
With all that pleases or employs;
But man survives the gen'ral doom,
Man destin'd to a life to come.

3 Ah! sinner, living without God,
What shame will fill thee in that day!
How canst thou bear the iron rod?
How stand—when nature flees away?
Creation now an awful void!
Thy hopes, thy prospects all destroy'd!

4 O may we all be found that day,
With those whom Jesus will confess!
When heav'n and earth shall flee away,
The Lord will yield us happiness:
New heav'ns and earth he then will make,
And bless them for his people's sake.

5 Sweet prospect of unfading joys!
My soul anticipates the day;
And leaving to the world its toys,
To Christ, my Lord, would haste away;
With him for ever to remain,
And share the glories of his reign.

HYMN LXXII.

"*Behold, the Lord cometh.*"—JUDE 14.

1 WHAT were Sinai's awful wonders,
To the wonders of that day,
When a voice, like many thunders,
Shall be heard from heav'n to say,
Come to judgment!
Lo! the Judge is on his way.

2 Lo! he comes, the Lord from heaven,
He who bore the cross below;
All the pow'r to him is giv'n,
He appears in glory now;
Great his glory!
Ev'ry knee to him shall bow.

3 See! the nations all assembling,
Stand before the Saviour's throne;
Thousands at his presence trembling;
Hope extinguish'd, pleasures gone;
Calling, seeking
For relief, and finding none.

4 But his people, they who knew him,
And on earth his name confess'd,
These the Saviour welcomes to him,
These he makes supremely blest:
Sweet their portion!
Theirs an everlasting rest.

HYMN LXXIII.

"*The day is at hand.*"—ROM. xiii. 12.

1 YES, the day is at hand; rejoice, then, ye saints;
The Saviour is coming, away with complaints.
With pleasure we hail the approach of the day;
Come quickly, Lord Jesus, come quickly, we say.

2 But often, alas! too like others we are;
We think as they think, and their feelings we share.
Forgetting our lot, and our heavenly birth,
We cleave to the dust, as if born for the earth.

3 Ah! Lord, how perverse, how unworthy are we!
How little we are what thy servants should be!
We are not consumed, because thou changest not,
Our Lord is unchanging, how blessed the thought!

4 The favour, O Lord, that we ask thee is this,
To know the amount of our debt what it is;
Then to live as they should do who owe thee so much:
Thou art glorified then, when thy people are such.

5 Thy love in our hearts, and in prospect the day,
When sorrow and sighing shall vanish away;
When all the redeem'd shall be gathered in one,
Themselves without sin, and their dwelling thy throne.

HYMN LXXIV.

"*Unto him that loved us, and washed us from our sins in his own blood . . . be glory.*"—REV. i. 5.

1 IN the region of light and of glory,
The people whom Jesus has sav'd
Will be telling the wonderful story,
Of how they had once been enslaved;
And how the Redeemer had bought them
With blood, with his own precious blood;
And from bondage the vilest had brought them;
How pleasant their work, and how good!

[illegible]

HYMN [illegible]

"Surely I come quickly."—Rev. xxii. 20.

1 What a grand and awful sight!
Jesus comes with all his saints;
Nothing eye has seen so bright;
Nothing equal fancy paints:
Jesus comes from heav'n to judge the nations;
Object of his people's expectations.

2 Great the change from what was here;
They who were despis'd on earth,
Now the sons of God appear:
Sons of God by heav'nly birth:
Yes, the Lord his people now confesses,
And how blest are they whom Jesus blesses!

3 Rich their portion, high their place,
Full their cup of blessing is;
Now they see the Saviour's face;
All is theirs since they are his;
In his favour ev'ry good possessing;
All enjoying in the Saviour's blessing.

4 Henceforth they shall never be
Separate from him they love;
All his glory they shall see,
All his goodness they shall prove;
Theirs a treasure, never, never wasting,
Life is theirs, and glory everlasting.

HYMN LXXVI.

"*Not to me only, but to all them also that love his appearing.*"—
2 TIM. iv. 8.

1 WELCOME sight! the Lord descending!
Jesus in the clouds appears;
Lo! the Saviour comes, intending
Now to dry his people's tears.
Lo! the Saviour comes to reign:
Welcome to his waiting train.

2 Long they mourn'd their absent Master;
Long they felt like men forlorn;
Bid the seasons fly still faster,
While they sigh'd for his return:
Lo! the period comes at last;
All their sorrows now are past.

3 Now from home no longer banish'd,
They are going to their rest;
Though the heav'ns and earth have vanish'd,
With their Lord they shall be blest:
Blest with him his saints shall be;
Blest throughout eternity!

4 Happy people! grace unbounded,
Grace alone exalts you thus;
Be asham'd, and be confounded;
Sing for ever—"Not to us,
"Not to us be glory giv'n—
"Glory to the God of heav'n!"

HYMN LXXVII.

"*The upright shall have dominion over them in the morning.*"—
PSALM xlix. 14.

1 THE saints shall have joy in the morning,
Their triumph will not be till then;
Their Master has given them warning
To look for the hatred of men.
But what is contempt or aversion?
Our Lord felt them both in his day:
Shall we think of retreat or desertion?
Ah! Lord, put the thought far away!

2 'Tis honour enough that we should be
As he whom we imitate was;
We ought not to wish, if it could be,
To shun the reproach of the cross.
Ah! Lord, let us count it our blessing,
To be in the world as thou wast;
Enough in thy favour possessing,
Though every thing else should be lost.

3 The morning is dawning, we greet it;
We hail the approach of the day:
Our spirits go forward to meet it,
Come quickly, come quickly, we say.
The wheels of his chariot, why move they
So slowly? and why this delay?
His people, while waiting, why love they
The things that are passing away?

4 Forgive us, our Master, forgive us,
To thee it belongs to forgive;
From all this corruption relieve us,
Thy people to glory receive.
'Tis then we shall be where we would be,
Enjoying thy presence above;
'Tis then we shall be what we should be,
Made perfect for ever in love.

5 Then welcome the dawn of the morning!
'Tis thus that thy people should say;
And, earth with its vanities scorning,
Should hasten the wonderful day.
When thou, by thine angels surrounded,
Shalt come to relieve the opprest,
Thy foes will all then be confounded,
Thy people be perfectly blest.

HYMN LXXVIII.

"*For the Lord himself shall descend from heaven with a shout.*"—
1 Thess. iv. 16.

1 THE Lord is coming in the clouds,
Is coming with angelic crowds;
An universal shout will rend
The air, and Jesus will descend.

2 How grand the pomp of his descent!
What glory waits on the event!
The glory that to heav'n belongs
Is his, and his angelic songs.

3 Upon his awful word depends
The joy or woe that never ends;
From his award is no appeal—
Th' alternative is heaven or hell.

4 If blessedness, without alloy,
Is theirs who share the Saviour's joy,
What holiness becoming is,
The men who look for things like these!

5 Unlike to those who nothing see
Beyond the world, the men should be,
Who look for Jesus in the air,
And know that they shall meet him there.

6 Their girded loins, and lamps on fire,
Should tell what is their soul's desire,
To see the object of their love,
And dwell with him in heaven above.

HYMN LXXIX.

"*And to wait for his Son from heaven.*"—1 Thess. i. 10.

GLAD when the trumpet sounds;
But when the Lord appears,
Our joy will know no bounds:
He wipes away our tears.
Then let the trumpet sound aloud,
Let Jesus come on yonder cloud.
Why tarries our Master?
Why comes he not faster?
The wheels of his chariot seem slowly to move,
Yet shall we presume the delay to reprove?
Ah! Lord, let us feel as we should do, we pray,
Impatient to go, and yet willing to stay.
Contented, with reason,
To wait for the season
Appointed by wisdom that never can err,
Our wish is, thy will to our own to prefer.
Submissive then make us,
And never forsake us,
Till, kept by thy power, thy glory we see;
And dwell, O our Saviour, for ever with thee.

HYMN LXXX.

"*For the trumpet shall sound.*"—1 Cor. xv. 52.

1 'TIS the last trumpet's voice,
Now let the saints rejoice,
Jesus appears.
'Tis the day look'd for long,
Theme of prophetic song;
Angels around him throng,
Our King and theirs.

2 Jesus, the Lord confess'd,
Jesus, for ever bless'd,
High is his place.
His name all names above,
Symbol of truth and love,
What man knows nothing of,
Man without grace.

3 What a place now is his!
Glorious the Saviour is,
High is his throne.
All eyes behold him now,
All knees before him bow,
Crowns many grace his brow,
All is his own.

4 They who are heirs of grace
Now fill their destin'd place,
Near to their King.
Now that their Lord appears,
He will dry up their tears:
Triumph and joy are theirs;
Henceforth they sing.

5 Numbers unnumbered they;
"Worthy the Lamb," they say,
He that was slain.
Fountain of truth and grace,
Saving a ruin'd race,
Worthy the highest place,
Worthy to reign.

6 Reign then for ever thou,
Lord, at thy feet we bow;
Thou art our King.
Thy name we now adore,
Thy name all names before,
Thy name for evermore,
Thine will we sing.

HYMN LXXXI.

"*It is done.*"—Rev. xvi. 17.

1 THE trumpet is sounding, the Lord is appearing;
The earth and the heavens are passing away;
Here end, and for ever, our doubting and fearing;
It all disappears in this wonderful day.

2 How awful, how glorious, how dazzling the sight is!
The Saviour descending to gather his own;
'Tis the day that we look'd for, and vanish'd the night is;
'Tis the day with a sun that will never go down.

3 Then joy to his people, their griefs are all over,
No evil can ever approach them again;
The Lord will to them all his glory discover;
What joy must be theirs, and what blessedness then.

4 No tongue could describe it, no thought could conceive it,
What eye had not seen, and what ear had not heard;
A promise so great, it was hard to believe it,
Though written in God's own infallible word.

5 A promise no longer, but now a possession;
His people are blest with their Master above;
They feel as they ought, and they give full expression
To feelings of wonder, of joy, and of love.

6 They sing of the Saviour, who loved and who bought them,
Who died for their sin, and who made them his own;
Who raised them from death, and who graciously brought them
To dwell with himself, and to sit on his throne.

HYMN LXXXII.

"*The night is far spent.*"—ROM. xiii. 12.

1 THE night is far spent, the day is at hand;
Already the dawn may be seen in the sky;
Rejoice then, ye saints, 'tis your Lord's own command;
Rejoice, for the coming of Jesus draws nigh.

2 What a day will that be, when the Saviour appears!
How welcome to those who have shared in his cross!
A crown incorruptible then will be theirs,
A rich compensation for suff'ring and loss.

3 What is loss in this world, when compared to that day,
To the glory that then will from heaven be reveal'd?
The Saviour is coming, his people may say;
The Lord whom we look for, our sun and our shield.

4 O pardon us, Lord, that our love to thy name
Is so faint, with so much our affections to move!
Our deadness should fill us with grief and with shame,
So much to be loved, and so little to love!

5 O kindle within us a holy desire,
Like that which was found in thy people of old,
Who felt all thy love, and whose hearts were on fire,
While they waited impatient thy face to behold.

HYMN LXXXIII.

"*For the trumpet shall sound.*"—1 Cor. xv. 52.

1 THE trumpet shall sound at the Saviour's appearing;
Be ready, ye saints, for the day;
His people no cause have for doubting or fearing,
'Tis his foes he will strike with dismay.

2 They do not believe that the Lord is preparing
To meet both his friends and his foes;
And while he delays, they are only more daring
His cause and his friends to oppose.

3 The promise they say, of his coming, where is it?
The world, as it was, so it is.
The time when our Master the earth will revisit,
We know not. This knowledge is his.

4 "The Lord is not slack, concerning his promise,
As some men count slackness," we know:
The hope of his coming they cannot take from us;
And the world, for this hope, we forego.

5 As a thief in the night, is the Saviour's appearing;
Unlooked for, and sudden, the sight:
When men are secure, and no enemy fearing,
The Saviour will come in his might.

6 Then judge ye, "what manner of persons they should be,"
Who look for this wonderful day;
Like him, they should walk, in whose presence they would be,
Till he takes them for ever away.

7 Then make us, oh! make us, Lord, what thou wouldst have us;
No power nor goodness have we:
From evil within and without do thou save us;
We cast ourselves wholly on thee.

HYMN LXXXIV.

"*Seeing then that all these things shall be dissolved.*"—
2 Pet. iii. 11.

1 FAST the years are flying,
Few remain in store;
Time itself is dying,
Soon to be no more.
All that measures time is
Soon to pass away;
That which so sublime is
Has its final day.

2 All we see will soon be
In oblivion lost;
Where will sun and moon be,
And the starry host?
Sunk, to lie for ever,
In the vast abyss.
He who changes never
Has appointed this.

3 Grieve we not that this is
By the Lord decreed;
The believer his is,
Blessed news, indeed;
News to gladden those who
For his coming long.
Why then fear the foes who
Would repress their song.

4 Glad they are when thinking
Of the final day;
When the world is sinking,
Sing his people may;
In that fearful season,
Those he owns as his,
May rejoice with reason,
Life their portion is.

5 Life with him in heaven,
Him to whom they owe
All that here is given,
All hereafter too.
Gladness ending never,
This their portion is,
Glory, and for ever;
Think, O think of this.

HYMN LXXXV.

"*The end of all things is at hand.*"—1 Pet. iv. 7.

1 WHAT words are these? Awake, my soul,
"The end of all things is at hand."
One common doom awaits the whole,
The fluid sea, the solid land,
The moon and stars that rule the night,
The sun, its substance, with its light.

2 "The end of all things is at hand,"
How fearful and how strange is this,
The very earth on which we stand,
Will perish in the great abyss;
And those who have no other lot,
Will lose their all—a fearful thought!

3 "The end of all things is at hand,"
Then why my soul thus full of care,
As though the earth, its sea, and land,
Both solid and enduring were?
Arise, my soul, shake off the dust,
In that which is not, cease to trust.

4 "The end of all things is at hand,"
Be glad all ye that love the Lord;
Before him shall his people stand,
Himself his people's great reward.
Redeemed by blood, and saved by grace,
They then shall see the Saviour's face.

5 "The end of all things is at hand,"
The world which is; but we shall see
A new one rise at his command,
Who makes what is not come, to be
The place where saints for ever dwell,
In blessedness no tongue can tell.

5 But, lo! he maketh all things new;
Things go and come at his command.
New heavens, new earth appear in view,
And have their being from his hand.

6 'Tis here his people have their home,
The place of rest from toil and strife.
'Tis conflict all, this side the tomb;
Beyond it is eternal life.

HYMN LXXXVIII.

"*Love his appearing.*"—2 TIM. iv. 8.

1 I LOVE to think of that bright day,
When Jesus shall with clouds appear;
When heav'n and earth shall pass away,
It serves the drooping heart to cheer.

2 The bed of death, the grave, the shroud,
The sight of friends in grief and tears;
From this I shrink, and fain I would
Escape from what so sad appears.

3 To hear "the trump of God" resound
O'er sea and land, thro' earth and sky,
To see the Lord with glory crown'd,
The hope of this is full of joy.

4 But tho' the thought of death is sad,
And things that unto death belong;
The pardon'd sinner may be glad,
And ev'n in death may raise his song.

5 Then be it mine no choice to have,
But on the Lord my care to cast;
Content to know that he will save,
And bring me to himself at last.

HYMN LXXXIX.

"*All that are in the graves shall hear his voice.*"—John v. 28.

1 HARK, a voice! it comes from heaven,
'Tis the final trumpet's sound;
Graves are open'd, tombs are riven,
All who sleep beneath the ground
Are awaking;
Jesus comes with glory crown'd.

2 Yes, the Saviour comes in glory,
Not as once when here below;
But the poorer then, the more he
Dazzles by his greatness now.
'Tis his triumph,
Every knee to him shall bow.

3 This is he who made the heaven
And the earth, with all their host;
He, whom none would own, not even
They whom he had favour'd most.
None would know him,
Yet he came to save the lost.

4 See him now, all eyes upon him,
Who so glorious now as he?
They who when on earth would shun him,
Now amazed his glory see,
And, despairing,
Learn with him they cannot be.

5 But his people, they who knew him,
Lov'd and serv'd him here below;
These are all now gather'd to him,
And with him to heav'n they go,
There to praise him,
And as they are known to know.

HYMN XC.

"*What manner of persons ought ye to be?*"—2 Pet. iii. 11.

1 "WHAT manner of persons" should they be,
Who wait for the Saviour from heav'n?
The day may be distant—or may be
At hand—this to know is not giv'n.
But come when it may, 'tis his pleasure
His people should look for the day,
When a joy will be theirs without measure,
A joy that will never decay.

2 Our Saviour has said what we should be,
Like servants expecting their Lord;
And this is, we trust, what we would be,
Conform'd to his will and his word.
With loins girt about, and lamps burning,
Awaiting the signal from heav'n,
That tells us our Lord is returning,
The pledge to redeem he has giv'n.

3 All ye who expect him, be ready,
The day is advancing apace;
"Hold fast that ye have," and be steady,
Take heed, lest ye fail of his grace.
A little more patient endurance,
And Jesus from heav'n will descend;
Hold fast, then, the blessed assurance,
"Assurance of hope to the end."

HYMN XCI.

"*Time no longer.*"—Rev. x. 6.

1 THE trumpet sounds, the angel cries,
That time is past and gone;
The Judge appears, the dead arise,
And stand before his throne.

2 The day is come, the awful day,
By prophets long foretold;
And heav'n and earth now pass away,
'Twas so ordain'd of old.

3 But who his coming may abide,
Or who his presence bear?
And where are now the sons of pride?
The foe, the scorner, where?

4 And where are they who would not hear
The word of truth and grace?
The sinner, where will he appear?
Where find a hiding-place?

5 But they whom God has sav'd by grace,
Whom he has made his own,
Shall dwell with him, shall see his face,
And "know as they are known."

HYMN XCII.

"*The day of Jesus Christ.*"—PHIL. i. 6.

1 BRIGHT the prospect is and cheering,
Of that day, the last and best;
When the Lord, from heav'n appearing,
Will bring in the promis'd rest.
And his people
Thenceforth be for ever blest.

2 Much and oft his people should be
Thinking of the glorious day;
Doing so, his people would be
Cheer'd, and often would they say,
Come, Lord Jesus!
Why, O why this long delay!

3 But how much the things around us
Draw us from the Lord away;
'Tis a thought may well confound us,
Pardon, Lord, our sin we pray:
Freely pardon,
We have nothing, Lord, to pay.

4 Further, Lord, we pray, renew us,
"In the spirit of our mind;"
Show thy grace and mercy to us,
To thyself our spirits bind.
Nor forsake us,
Till in heav'n our rest we find.

HYMN XCIII.

"*Surely I come quickly.*"—Rev. xxii. 20.

1 JESUS soon will come to bless us;
Thenceforth nothing will distress us;
We shall then the Saviour meet:
Let us hail the coming season,
Let us sing, for we have reason:
Hope is ours, and hope is sweet.

2 Yes, the blessed hope of seeing
Him we love, and ever being
With the Lord, is sweet indeed:
Saviour, let our love be greater,
And our hope will then be sweeter,
This is what thy people need.

3 While on earth remaining, let us,
Tho' ten thousand ills beset us,
Put our steadfast trust in thee:
Let the thought of thine appearing,
Ever sweet, and ever cheering,
To our souls a blessing be.

4 What we should be, Saviour, make us;
Never leave us, nor forsake us,
Till thy face in heav'n we see.
'Tis thy grace alone can save us:
Grace, the very grace that gave us
Hope, when first we turn'd to thee.

HYMN XCIV.

"*Enter thou into the joy of thy Lord.*"—MATT. xxv. 21.

1 WHAT pleasure there is in expecting the season,
When Jesus will come, and his glory be seen;
His people are looking, and not without reason,
For joys they must patiently wait for till then.

2 'Tis "the joy of the Lord," 'tis a joy without measure,
Too holy, too blessed, too much for us here;
'Tis having a rich inexhaustible treasure,
With nothing to wish for, and nothing to fear.

3 'Tis to be with the Saviour for ever and ever,
Before him to stand without blemish or blame;
With hearts and with voices to praise him, and never
Be weary of hearing the sound of his name.

4 'Tis this, and far more, but no language can show it,
What the eye does not see, and the ear does not hear;
In the day of the Lord, it is then we shall know it,
For till then what his people are, does not appear.

5 With a prospect like this, O how much it behoves us
To walk as they should, who are born from on high;
Our Saviour is coming, our Saviour who loves us,
To him let us live, and to him let us die.

HYMN XCV.

"*Can ye not discern the signs of.*"—MATT. xvi. 3.

1 A DAWNING of light in the east,
Gives notice that day is at hand;
The saints will be speedily blest,
But others do not understand.
A sound will be heard before long,
Both sudden and loud it will be;
'Twill scatter the proud and the strong,
And in that day the valiant will flee.

2 'Tis "the great and the terrible day,"
Predicted by prophets of old;
When the earth and the heavens pass away
Like a dream, or a tale that is told.
There it is—'tis the terrible sound,
The earth is dissolving with heat;
There's a cry of despair all around,
And for sinners no place of retreat.

3 But joy to the saints! they behold
Their master appearing from heav'n;
Their joy is too great to be told,
Such joy to his people is giv'n.
'Tis joyful to see him they love,
To see him in glory appear;
'Tis joyful to praise him above,
In a way they could never do here.

HYMN XCVI.

"*New heavens and a new earth.*"—2 PET. iii. 13.

1 A LOUD, a dreadful sound is heard,
'Tis nature's dying groan;
What late to men so fair appear'd,
Is gone, for ever gone.

2 No wreck remains, no trace appears,
Of what so goodly was;
'Tis like a tale of by-gone years,
It now no being has.

3 But see, the Lord comes forth to bless,
Ye happy saints, draw near;
The dwelling-place of righteousness,
New heav'ns and earth appear.

4 For you the Lord is doing this,
The objects of his grace;
For you this new creation is,
This holy dwelling-place.

5 The Lord will there make known to you
What cannot here be told;
His love, with interest ever new,
The Lord will there unfold.

6 To him who wash'd us in his blood,
The Lord of earth and heav'n,
Who made us kings and priests to God,
Eternal praise be giv'n.

HYMN XCVII.

"*For the great day of his wrath is come.*"—Rev. vi. 17.

1 THE trumpet sounds loudly,
Who now will deal proudly?
The heart of the valiant no longer is brave:
His courage forsakes him,
To flight he betakes him,
And calls on the rocks and the mountains to save.

2 This the day of the Lord is,
For faithful his word is;
'Tis come, tho' so many said, when will it be?
A snare it resembles—
And now the earth trembles—
And wonder on wonder around us we see.

3 The day, O how cheering—
The Saviour's appearing,
To those who were waiting, midst many, the few:
Their conflicts are over,
And now they discover,
The glory once hid, but now open'd to view.

4 No language is equal
To tell of the sequel,
When saints to the promis'd possession are brought;
The blessedness given,
The glory of heaven,
'Tis something beyond either language or thought.

HYMN XCVIII.

"*For the trumpet shall sound.*"—1 Cor. xv. 52.

1 SOON the trumpet sounding loudly,
Will proclaim the Judge at hand;
Then will those who here deal proudly,
Feel the pow'r they now withstand.
Awful summons!
'Twill be heard thro' sea and land.

2 'Tis a sound, that will awaken
All who sleep beneath the ground.
Heav'n and earth will then be shaken,
And their place no more be found.
But the ransom'd,
How their joy will then abound!

3 Pure and full, and never wasting,
Is the joy for them in store.
Theirs is glory everlasting,
They shall never hunger more:
All they hop'd for,
Then is theirs, but not before.

4 Would they wish it sooner should be,
Than the time the Lord sees best?
Were it right, it sooner would be,
They who wait his time are blest.
At his coming,
They shall gain their promis'd rest.

HYMN XCIX.

"*And the seventh angel sounded.*"—Rev. xi. 15.

1 HARK! the trumpet last of seven,
Sends its voice thro' earth and heaven:
Louder than the thunder peals.
All who sleep are now awaking,
Earth is to its centre shaking,
Universal nature reels.

2 'Tis the day so long expected:
When the man on earth rejected,
Comes in majesty and pow'r.
Fly ye moments, fly still faster,
Jesus comes, "our Lord and Master!"
Hail, ye saints, the joyful hour.

3 Rest is yours, the strife is over,
And the Lord will now discover
All his glory to your view.
Yours to dwell with him for ever,
Yours a glory ending never;
Yours enjoyment ever new.

HYMN C.

"*At midnight there was a cry made.*"—MATT. XXV. 6.

1 HARK! hark a midnight cry!
 'Tis loud and terrible;
It echoes through the sky,
 The world's departing knell.
The peal of thunder nothing is,
'Tis nothing when compar'd to this.

2 It finds the world asleep;
 But who can slumber now?
The time is come to weep,
 For where escape or how?
The sinner, whither can he fly?
To hide from God's all-seeing eye?

3 The Lord appears in view,
 "Rejected once of men."
The word he spoke is true,
 For, lo! he comes again.
He comes the second time from heav'n,
To him the judgment-seat is giv'n.

4 His foes, where are they now?
 How feel they in this hour,
When ev'ry knee must bow,
 To Jesus in his pow'r?
How bear they such a sight as this?
To them his coming dreadful is.

5 But, oh! how glorious is
 The coming of the Lord,
To those he owns as his,
 Himself their great reward!
Henceforward all their troubles cease,
They dwell with him in endless peace.

HYMN CI.

"*To meet the Lord in the air.*"—1 THESS. iv. 17.

1 SHOUTS of joy shall fill the air,
When the Saviour comes again;
All his friends shall meet him there;
Great will be their triumph then.
Happy they he owns as his—
They shall see him as he is.

2 Hark the trumpet! hark it sounds,
And its voice is heard abroad,
To the earth's remotest bounds;
Through the wide domain of God.
What a fearful crash was there!
Some rejoice, and some despair.

3 'Tis the end of all below;
Wreck of worlds no more to be;
Who can bear to see it? Who?
Who the ruin bear to see?
He whom Jesus deigns to own,
He can bear it, he alone.

4 Midst the ruin he can say,
Jesus comes, my hope, my crown;
Hail the day, the joyful day;
His it is—'tis all his own.
Who is he that does not bow
At the name of Jesus now?

HYMN CII.

"*The end of all things is at hand.*"—1 PET. iv. 7.

1 "THE end of all things is at hand"
The world we live in soon will be
No world; dissolved by his command
Who made it—'tis his stern decree.

2 And yet, how solid does it seem!
As if it could not but endure;
How hard to think, that as a dream
It ends—yet so it is, be sure.

3 The earth we stand upon is doom'd.
The sun, the moon, the stars of light,
In one great gulph will be entomb'd;
A fearful, an amazing sight!

4 New heav'ns, new earth will then arise;
The saints' abode—their place of rest;
Where all is pure, where nothing dies,
Where all are safe, and all are blest.

5 Then let this earth we stand upon,
And all around us cease to be;
When all that now we see is gone,
Then what we see not, we shall see.

6 If we are his who reigns above,
Whom all his people then shall see,
The God of grace, the God of love,
How blessed will our portion be!

HYMN CIII.

"*Then look up . . . for your redemption draweth nigh.*"—
LUKE xxi. 28.

1 SING we loudly, sing we gladly;
There is reason why we should.
While the world around us madly
Presses on in thoughtless mood,
Be it ours to watch and pray,
Waiting for the final day.

2 When the trumpet sounds, what terror,
What amazement will there be!
They who in the path of error
Wander now, with dread will see
Him, whose word they slighted here;
Him they did not, would not fear.

3 What a day for them that day is!
Where is now the sinner's boast?
To escape his doom, no way is;
All is lost, for ever lost:
His "the worm that dieth not;"
'Tis a sad, a fearful thought.

4 But how blest the lot of those is,
Who shall be with him they love!
Who shall sing "the song of Moses
And the Lamb," in heav'n above:
Dwelling there, where all is bright;
God their everlasting light.

5 Welcome, then, the glorious season,
When the Lord from heav'n appears.
Let us sing, for we have reason;
He will wipe away all tears.
Jesus gives his people rest;
He it is that makes them blest.

HYMN CIV.

"*As a thief in the night.*"—1 THESS. v. 2.

1 'TIS midnight and dark;
'Tis silence—but hark!
Whence this sudden alarm thro' the sky?
This shaking of all,
As if to its fall;
Whence is it?—"What means it?"—we cry.

2 The Saviour it is;
The trumpet is his,
Proclaiming the terrible day.
His coming is felt;
The elements melt;
Things present are passing away.

3 How blessed it is,
For those who are his!
How blessed the Saviour to see!
The man crown'd with thorns;
Whom all the world scorns;
How mighty, how glorious is he!

4 Rejected he was;
He hung on a cross;
No sorrow was equal to his.
But look at him now;
A crown on his brow;
The fruit of his suffering it is.

5 Dominion and pow'r,
Are his in this hour;
His foes are all under his feet.
His people are blest;
They enter their rest;
With glad salutations they meet.

6 In triumph they sing,
The praise of their King,
Who brought them, and rais'd them to heav'n.
No name is like his,
No theme is like this,
For sinners redeem'd and forgiv'n.

HYMN CV.

"*The heavens shall pass away with a great noise.*"—2 PET. iii. 10

1 HARK! what sound is that!
Sudden, loud, and strange;
And this motion, what!
Whence this sudden change!
Think upon us, Lord, O think!
Now sustain us, or we sink.

2 Who can now be strong?
Or what heart endure?
Falling worlds among,
Who can be secure?
Saviour, in this fearful hour,
O sustain us by thy power!

3 Earth, with its contents,
Fails beneath our feet;
And the elements
Melt with fervent heat.
But behold, the Lord appears;
And his presence calms our fears.

4 Welcome, welcome, Lord,
'Tis the glorious day,
Promis'd in thy word,
Welcome, then, we say;
Welcome to thy waiting train;
Long they waited, not in vain.

5 Past their grief and care;
Past their toil and strife;
Sav'd and blest they are;
Theirs eternal life.
Theirs to dwell in heav'n above;
Theirs to be with him they love.

HYMN CVI.

"And sware . . . that there should be time no longer."—
Rev. x. 6.

1 YES, the stern decree has pass'd;
Henceforth "time shall be no more;"
And the end is come at last,
Seen by prophets long before.
Heaven and earth have pass'd away;
'Tis the great, the final day.

2 Great it is, and final too;
All that is ordain'd this day,
Will remain for ever so;
Change there will not be, nor may.
Some to endless life will go;
Some to shame, and endless woe.

3 Sun and moon, where are they now?
And the stars of heaven, where?
Gone, for ever gone, and how?
By his hand who placed them there.
Gone their light, their substance gone;
Not a trace remaining—none.

4 But the Lord, who made them all,
Still the same, makes all things new;
Pow'r is his, and at his call,
Other heav'ns appear in view,
And another earth is seen;
Mourn we not for what has been.

5 Here it is where saints repose,
After toil, and after strife;
Here their labours reach a close;
Theirs is joy and endless life.
Nothing henceforth to molest;
Nothing to disturb their rest.

HYMN CVII.

"*We shall see him as he is.*"—1 John iii. 2.

1 WHAT love, what pleasure, what surprise
Shall fill th' enraptur'd heirs of heav'n,
The day the Saviour meets their eyes,
The day the promis'd rest is giv'n!

2 Their love is kindled here below,
The author of their hope they love;
A purer, brighter flame will glow
In yonder glorious world above.

3 Of pleasure too they taste below,
But pleasure not unmix'd with pain;
In yonder world 'twill not be so,
For there no sorrow will remain.

4 And if obscure and transient views
Of heav'nly things yield such surprise,
What wonder must the sight produce
When God appears before their eyes!

5 O joyful sight! O glorious day!
When God the Saviour shall be seen,
When earthly things shall pass away,
And heav'n's unchanging state begin!

HYMN CVIII.

"*That unto me every knee shall bow.*"—Isaiah xlv. 23.

1 THUS the mighty God has spoken,
"Ev'ry knee shall bow to me;"
Shall the word of God be broken?
No, this will not, cannot be;
Heav'n and earth shall be destroy'd,
But his word shall not be void.

2 Yes, the proudest shall be humbled,
In the day when God appears;
They who at his message stumbled,
And against it clos'd their ears,
Then must see and own his pow'r,
Then they must, if not before.

3 While his friends, with exultation,
See and own the Saviour's right,
All his foes, with consternation,
Shall behold the glorious sight;
And in that triumphant hour,
They must own the Saviour's pow'r.

4 Ye who live at awful distance
From the God who gave you breath,
Who can then afford assistance?
Who can save you then from death?
Kiss the Son, O kiss him now,
To his golden sceptre bow.

State of Blessedness.

HYMN CIX.

"I shall be satisfied, when I awake, with thy likeness."—
Psalm xvii. 15.

1 WHAT tongue can tell, what fancy paint
The joys that fill th' enraptur'd saint,
When mix'd with heav'n's triumphant throng,
He shares their bliss, and swells their song?

2 He feels no pain, he fears no want;
His portion all that God can grant;
To see the Saviour as he is,
And dwell in heav'n with him and his.

3 No darkness now obscures his mind:
The darkness all is left behind:
And objects lately half conceal'd,
In full resplendence stand reveal'd.

4 His love, so cold, so mix'd before,
In heav'n is cold and mix'd no more;
It gains the region whence it came,
And lives a pure eternal flame.

5 He dwells exempt from all alarm:
No world is there to fright or charm;
No foes to plot against his peace;
No sin to give their schemes success.

6 O may I reach that blest abode,
Where saints obtain their rest in God!
For this, let ev'ry conflict here
As nothing in my sight appear.

HYMN CX.

"*And God shall wipe away all tears from their eyes.*"—
REV. vii. 17.

1 SEE the saints in heav'n appearing;
Heav'n that yields them sweet repose:
Nothing wanting, nothing fearing,
Safe from ev'ry storm that blows;
Free from sorrow, sin, and fear,
Having all they hop'd for here.

2 All their conflicts now are over;
All their dangers are no more;
And with joy they now discover
All that lay concealed before.
Fill'd with wonder they survey
All the perils of the way.

3 Perils past and gone for ever;
O how cheering is the thought!
Once we pass through yonder river,
Then we rest and labour not.
Nothing is to those oppress'd
Grateful as the thought of rest.

4 Rest from toil, and rest from terror;
Rest from all assaults of foes;
Rest from those who, loving error,
Hate the Saviour, and oppose;
Rest from all that causes grief,
Sweet the hope of such relief.

5 Hope of this our toils can lighten;
Hope has pow'r to cheer the faint;
Hope of this our gloom will brighten;
Hope sustains the trembling saint;
Hope is ours, then farewell fear;
Hope the darkest hour can cheer.

HYMN CXI.

"*Eye hath not seen, nor ear heard.*"—1 Cor. ii. 9.

1 IT has not fully yet appeared
What blessedness to saints is giv'n:
No eye has seen, no ear has heard,
Nor heart conceiv'd the joys of heav'n.

2 In heav'n itself, and there alone,
The joys of heav'n are understood;
Where saints shall know, as they are known,
And shall behold the face of God.

3 The face of him, who, here below,
Appear'd and died, to save his own:
The same who reigns in glory now,
And fills yon bright eternal throne.

4 A sight of him his people fills
With transport never known before:
They feel no want, they fear no ills;
And sin and sorrow are no more.

5 They view the Lord, whom angels view,
(He there without a cloud appears;)
And praise the Lord, as angels do,
With joy, perhaps, exceeding theirs.

6 How blest our lot, if we are his!
We too shall dwell with him above;
Yea, we shall see him as he is,
In yonder world of light and love.

HYMN CXII.

"*A land that floweth with milk and honey.*"—DEUT. xxvi. 9.

1 CANAAN flows with milk and honey,
Round the world no spot's so fair;
Fruits, whose price is more than money,
Are the fruits that flourish there;
Happy Isra'l,
Destined all its sweets to share.

2 There eternal summer glowing,
Never yields to winter's force;
Streams of living water flowing,
All enliven in their course;
Streams that issue
From a never-failing source.

3 Trees of life, spontaneous growing,
There on every side are found:
Softest breezes ever blowing,
Rich with fragrance, breathe around:
Purest pleasure
There in all its forms abound.

4 Canaan's sun abides for ever,
Hers is day without a night;
Darkness there approaches never,
All is pure and all is bright;
Great her glory!
Canaan shines with endless light.

5 When on Canaan's beauties musing,
Nothing seems to me so fair;
Ev'ry other lot refusing,
I would dwell for ever there:
Earthly treasures
Fading all and worthless are.

6 But when on the dangers thinking
That await me in the way,
Then I feel my spirit sinking,
Sadness comes and deep dismay:
"Come not hither,"
Foes unnumbered seem to say.

7 O! my soul why thus despairing?
Look to God and cease to sigh;
In his promis'd succour sharing,
Thou may'st smile at danger nigh;
At his presence,
All thy foes shall trembling fly.

8 O! my God, tho' faint and trembling,
Yet my soul shall trust in thee,
When I see my foes assembling,
To thy pow'r for help I'll flee;
And thy promise
Shall my hope and refuge be.

HYMN CXIII.

"*These are they which came out of great tribulation.*"—
REV. vii. 14.

1 SEE how many thousands yonder
On the Saviour's glory gaze,
Fill'd with love, and joy, and wonder,
While they celebrate his praise;
Jesus is their glorious theme,
Ev'ry eye is fixed on him.

2 Those are they, whose foul offences
Have been wash'd away with blood,
Blood that by its virtue cleanses,
Flowing from the Lamb of God;
Therefore do they now appear,
Praising and rejoicing there.

3 They were brought thro' tribulation,
In their way to yonder place;
Now with joy and exultation,
They behold the Saviour's face;
They are sav'd from foes and fears,
Jesus wipes away their tears.

4 'Tis the Lamb himself that feeds them,
Theirs is heav'n's eternal store;
He to living fountains leads them,
They shall thirst again no more;
Dwelling in the Saviour's light,
They shall serve him day and night.

5 Where they dwell with full enjoyment,
There we hope ere long to be;
Praise his people's sweet employment,
Through a bright eternity;
While we still remain on earth,
Let us prove our heav'nly birth.

HYMN CXIV.

"*They shall behold the land that is very far off.*"—Is. xxxiii. 17.

1 THE world with all its pageantry,
Is nothing in the pilgrim's eyes;
He aims at immortality;
He seeks a home beyond the skies:

2 A land of pure and hallow'd joy,
Where all is peace, and all is love;
Where sweets are found that never cloy,
A land the world knows nothing of.

3 Compar'd to this, the blessed isles
By poets feigned, possess no charms;
Though there eternal verdure smiles,
Though nought offends, and nought alarms.

4 A blessedness surpassing thought
Is theirs, in measure and in kind,
Who, by the sacred Spirit taught,
This holy land of promise find:

5 This land, where all the saints shall meet,
Shall see the Saviour face to face,
Shall cast their crowns before his feet,
And sing for ever of his grace.

6 If we are his, our hearts are there;
In prospect we enjoy our home;
And, while on earth, an earnest share
Of joys above, of joys to come.

7 If all the joys that earth supplies
Were offer'd in exchange for this,
'Twould seem as nothing in our eyes,
For all is ours, if we are his.

HYMN CXV.

"*And I said, O that I had wings like a dove!*"—Psa. lv. 6.

1 O HAD I the wings of a dove,
I'd make my escape and begone;
I'd mix with the spirits above,
Who encompass yon heavenly throne:
I'd fly from all labour and toil,
To the place where the weary have rest;
I'd haste from contention and broil,
To the peaceful abode of the blest.

2 How happy are they who no more
Have to fear the assaults of the foe!
Arriv'd on the heavenly shore,
They have left all their conflicts below:
They are far from all danger and fear,
While remembrance enhances their joys,
As the storm, when escap'd, will endear
The retreat that the haven supplies.

3 Around that magnificent throne,
Where the Lamb all his glory displays,
United for ever in one,
His people are singing his praise:
How holy, how happy are they,
No tongue can express their delight!
My soul, now unwilling to stay,
Prepares for her heavenly flight.

4 But why do I wish to be gone?
Do I want from the danger to flee?
And shall I do nothing for one
Who was once such a suff'rer for me?
Ah, Lord, let me think of the day,
When thou wast "rejected of men,"
And put the base wish far away,
And never be fearful again.

5 Nor less my perverseness forgive,
That when ease and prosperity come,
Thy servant is willing to live,
And his exile prefers to his home:
Ah, Lord, what a creature am I!
Sure nothing can heighten my guilt;
Forgive me, forgive me, I cry,
And make me whatever thou wilt.

HYMN CXVI.

"*Now they do it to obtain a corruptible crown, but we an incorruptible.*"—1 Cor. ix. 25.

1 LET others labour to possess
A temporary fame,
We cannot be content with less
Than an immortal name.

2 Not such as poets can bestow
On those whom they extol;
The brightest honours here below
For us are far too small.

3 The honour we desire to have,
From God alone descends;
The honour that survives the grave,
That never, never ends.

4 A real immortality,
Substantial blessedness,
'Tis this we seek, nor can we be,
Though poor, content with less.

5 For ever be his name ador'd,
Who bids us hope for this!
Eternal honour to the Lord,
Who sav'd and made us his.

6 Yes, 'tis our hope, that thro' his love,
We shall at last arise,
And from the springs of life above,
Drink everlasting joys.

HYMN CXVII.

"*Blessed is he whose transgression is forgiven.*"—Psa. xxxii. 1.

1 HOW blest is he, whom God forgives,
The man who by his favour lives,
And hopes to see his face;
The child of God by heav'nly birth,
He scorns the highest place on earth,
For yonder higher place.

2 The God he serves, is God alone,
He fills yon bright, eternal throne,
The pow'r and kingdom his;
He rules, he reigns with sov'reign sway,
And they who will not, must obey:
His arm almighty is.

3 When he forgives, then peace is known,
The peace that comes from him alone:
The sacred peace of God;
And hope, that lifts the soul on high,
That points to yonder world of joy,
And lightens ev'ry load.

4 How blest is he whom God forgives;
The man who by his favour lives,
In hope already blest;
But O what joys await him there,
Where sav'd from sin, from toil, from fear,
He gains his heav'nly rest!

HYMN CXVIII.

"*How great is thy goodness which thou hast laid up for them that fear thee.*"—PSALM xxxi. 19.

1 LORD, 'tis good to know thy grace,
Better still to taste thy love;
Best of all to see thy face,
In the realms of light above.

2 There it is thy people rest;
Rest from toil, and rest from strife;
And of blessedness possess'd,
There they live an endless life.

3 O what good thou hast prepar'd,
For thy people in that day;
When, thyself their "great reward,"
Thou wilt wipe their tears away.

4 Something seen but darkly here,
Tasted only, not enjoy'd;
There possess'd, and without fear,
Pleasure, full and unalloy'd.

5 Such the prospect is for those,
Who on earth confess thy name;
Who in presence of thy foes,
Bear the cross, nor shun the shame.

6 Welcome, Lord, reproach for thee;
Thou hast borne our guilt and shame;
Everlasting honour be,
To thy great, thy glorious name.

State of Wrath.

HYMN CXIX.

"*Where their worm dieth not.*"—MARK ix. 44.

1 WHENCE come those loud and mournful cries,
That speak a mind bereft of joy?
They come from him who yonder lies,
Where flames devour, but don't destroy.

2 I wonder not that he should fill
The world with loud incessant cries;
He feels no joy, nor ever will:
His foe the worm that never dies.

3 One drop of water! one! he cries:
Unhappy wretch! what woe is thine!
While Justice with a frown replies,
"It cannot be—the pris'ner's mine."

4 Beholding such a sight as this,
Let things eternal be my care;
And never may my case be his,
Whom God abandons to despair.

5 I'll keep in view the sinner's friend,
Whose arms I see extended wide:
At sight of him my terrors end;
His merit all my guilt will hide.

HYMN CXX.

"*I said unto thee, when thou wast in thy blood, Live.*"—EZEK. xvi. 6.

1 WHEN we lay in sin polluted,
Wretched and undone we were,
All we saw and heard was suited
Only to produce despair;

Ours appear'd a hopeless case,
Such it had been, but for grace.

2 As we lay expos'd and friendless,
Needing what no hand could give,
Then the Lord (whose praise be endless)
Passēd by, and bid us live;
This was help in time of need,
This was grace, 'twas grace indeed.

3 When he came, he found us guilty,
We had broken all his laws;
When he look'd, he saw us filthy,
All corrupt our nature was;
Ours appear'd a hopeless case,
'Twas the time to shew his grace.

4 Yes, 'twas grace beyond all measure,
When he bid such sinners live,
Laid aside his just displeasure,
And determin'd to forgive;
But he chose our hopeless case,
With a view to shew his grace.

5 And shall we be found forgetful
Of the Lord, who thus forgave?
Lord, our hearts are most deceitful,
'Tis in thee our strength we have;
Shouldst thou let thy people go,
They'd forget how much they owe.

6 Keep us then, O keep us ever!
While we stand, 'tis in thy strength;
Leave us not, forsake us never,
Till we see thy face at length!
Hold thy helpless people fast,
Save us, Lord, from first to last.

Christ a King.

HYMN CXXI.

"*Hosanna to the Son of David.*"—MATT. xxi. 9.

1 LO! he comes, 'tis Zion's King,
Rejoice ye, whom his grace has savēd;
Let the saints together sing,
"HOSANNA TO THE SON OF DAVID."

2 Though in lowly guise a King,
And long his people were enslavēd;
Freed by him they now may sing,
"HOSANNA TO THE SON OF DAVID."

3 Strike, ye saints, a cheerful string,
Your King for you all dangers bravēd;
Were ye mute, the stones would sing,
"HOSANNA TO THE SON OF DAVID."

4 Though the world no plaudits bring,
The world by Satan still enslavēd;
Yet angelic voices sing,
"HOSANNA TO THE SON OF DAVID."

5 Heav'n's high arches soon shall ring,
While angels join with all the savēd;
And while both together sing,
"HOSANNA TO THE SON OF DAVID."

HYMN CXXII.

"*Great is the Lord.*"—PSALM xlviii. 1.

1 HOW glorious is the King to-day!
How glorious Israel's King!
With truth his people thus may say,
And well his praise may sing.

2 He makes his goodness pass before
His wond'ring people's eyes;
And feeds them with a boundless store
Of satisfying joys.

3 He meets them with a smiling face,
And with a father's voice;
He bids them triumph in his grace,
And in his name rejoice.

4 Their praise with favour he receives,
And hearkens when they pray;
Forgives their sins, their wants relieves,
And leads them in the way.

5 To Israel's God be glory giv'n,
The God whom saints adore,
On earth, and in the highest heav'n,
Both now and evermore.

HYMN CXXIII.

"*The Lord is our King.*"—Isaiah xxxiii. 22.

1 'TIS to thee we owe allegiance,
God our Saviour and our King:
May we render true obedience;
Ev'ry day our tribute bring,
And with rapture,
Of thy love and glory sing.

2 May we bow to thy dominion,
Yielding to thy righteous sway;
Careless of the world's opinion,
May we all thy will obey:
Saviour lead us;
Lead us in the perfect way.

3 Thine is greatness never-wasting:
High thou art, with glory crown'd:
Thine a kingdom everlasting:
Grace and Truth thy throne surround;
While all others
Vanish, and no more are found.

4 Happy they whom thou dost govern!
Great their peace, their honour great;
Thee beholding, thee their Sov'reign,
Thee enthron'd in royal state:
Happy people,
Who before thee ever wait!

5 O may we, through grace unbounded,
Reach that place, that honour share!
Thou, on whom our hopes are founded,
See us needing all thy care:
O preserve us!
Thee we serve, and thine we are.

HYMN CXXIV.

"*Hail! King of the Jews.*"—JOHN xix. 3.

1 JESUS, we hail thee Israel's King;
To thee our tribute, Lord, we bring;
Nor do we fear to bow the knee;
They worship God, who worship *thee*.

2 Hail, Israel's King, enthron'd in light,
Whose glory never shone more bright,
Than when, by trembling friends betray'd,
Thy foes insulting homage paid.

3 Then did admiring angels see
Divine forbearance, Lord, in thee;
With emphasis pronounc'd thee *good*;
And heav'n and earth contrasted stood.

4 An object of contempt beneath,
And judg'd by men to suffer death:
By angels own'd, admir'd, ador'd,
The great, the everlasting Lord!

5 Reign, mighty King, for ever reign!
Thy cause throughout the world maintain;
Let Israel's God his triumphs spread,
And crowns of glory wreathe his head.

Christ a High Priest.

HYMN CXXV.

"*Having an high priest over the house of God.*"—HEB. x. 21.

1 TH' atoning work is done,
The victim's blood is shed;
And Jesus now is gone,
His people's cause to plead:
He stands in heav'n their great High Priest,
And bears their names upon his breast.

2 He sprinkles with his blood
The mercy-seat above;
For justice had withstood
The purposes of love;
But justice now objects no more,
And mercy yields her boundless store.

3 No temple made with hands
His place of service is;
In heav'n itself he stands,
An heav'nly priesthood his:
In him the shadows of the law
Are all fulfill'd, and now withdraw.

4 And though awhile he be
Hid from the eyes of men,
His people look to see
Their great High Priest again:
In brightest glory he will come,
And take his waiting people home.

Christ a Prophet.

HYMN CXXVI.

"*Him shall ye hear.*"—Acts vii. 37.

1 GREAT Prophet of the ransom'd church,
Command the light to shine;
For stores of wisdom let us search,
Thy word the sacred mine.

2 Jesus, sole oracle of truth,
O may we learn of thee!
Receive true wisdom from thy mouth,
And live from error free.

3 Of future things content to know
As much as thou hast taught;
Not idly curious here below,
In things that profit not.

4 One great event, by thee foretold,
Teach us to keep in view;
Thy coming!—when we shall behold,
And share thy glory too.

5 Till then, let all thy people here,
Walk with increasing light;
And when thy glory shall appear,
Welcome the joyful sight.

HYMN CXXVII.

"*This is, of a truth, that Prophet which should come into the world.*"—JOHN vi. 14.

1 "THIS is, of a truth, the Prophet"
Promis'd to the church of old;
Proofs I see sufficient of it,
Jesus is that one foretold;
He whom all are call'd to hear,
He whom all are bound to fear.

2 All who hear him not shall perish
'Tis the purpose of the Lord;
Vain the hope that many cherish,
While unmindful of his word:
One decree there is for all,
They who hear him not must fall.

3 Glorious Prophet! long expected,
Come to bless the church at last;
May we walk, by thee directed,
Till our pilgrimage is past!
Then, from sin and sorrow free,
Dwell eternally with thee.

Christ a Shepherd.

HYMN CXXVIII.

"*The Lord is my Shepherd.*"—PSALM xxiii. 1.

1 JESUS is the Lord my Shepherd,
Then let fear be far away;
From the lion, and the leopard,
And from ev'ry beast of prey,
He will guard his helpless sheep;
Jesus loves his own to keep.

2 When the foe desir'd to have me,
Jesus said—"this sheep is mine,"
And resign'd his life to save me:
Jesus! what a love is thine!
All-victorious in its course,
Nothing can withstand its force.

3 In the path of life he leads me,
By the stream that gently flows;
In the verdant pasture feeds me,
Where no plant injurious grows:
There I hear the Shepherd's voice,
There he bids my soul rejoice.

4 When through death's dark valley going,
Fearful though the way appear,
I will dread no evil, knowing
Thou, my Shepherd, still art near:
When I see thy rod and staff,
Then I know thy sheep is safe.

HYMN CXXIX.

"*I am the good Shepherd.*"—John x. 10.

1 JESUS, the Shepherd of the sheep,
Thy "little flock" in safety keep,
The flock for which thou cam'st from heav'n,
The flock for which thy life was giv'n.

2 Thou saw'st them wand'ring far from thee,
Secure, as if from danger free;
Thy love did all their wand'rings trace,
And bring them to "a wealthy place."

3 O guard thy sheep from beasts of prey!
And keep them that they never stray;
Cherish the young, sustain the old,
Let none be feeble in thy fold.

4 Secure them from the scorching beam,
And lead them to the living stream;
In verdant pastures let them lie,
And watch them with a shepherd's eye.

5 O may thy sheep discern thy voice!
And in its sacred sound rejoice;
From strangers may they ever flee,
And know no other guide but thee.

6 Lord, bring thy sheep that wander yet,
And let the number be complete;
Then let thy flock from earth remove,
And occupy the fold above.

HYMN CXXX.

"*The good Shepherd giveth his life for the sheep.*"—JOHN x. 11.

1 SHEPHERD of the chosen number,
They are safe whom thou dost keep;
Other shepherds faint and slumber,
And forget to guard the sheep:
Watchful Shepherd!
Thou dost wake while others sleep.

2 When the lion came, depending
On his strength, to seize his prey,
Thou wast there, the sheep defending,
And didst then thy pow'r display:
Mighty Shepherd!
Thou didst turn the foe away.

3 When the Shepherd's life was needful,
Or the sheep must else be lost,
Not of thine own safety heedful,
But of theirs alone thou wast:
Thou didst save them!
But no tongue can tell the cost.

HYMN CXXXI.

"*And when he hath found it, he layeth it on his shoulders, rejoicing.*"—LUKE XV. 5.

1 WHILE I wander'd, Jesus sought me,
This was love, 'twas love indeed:
To his fold the Shepherd brought me,
With his sheep to live and feed.

2 While the Shepherd was pursuing,
Still the foolish sheep would fly,
Bent upon its own undoing,
And that foolish sheep was I.

3 When the foolish sheep was flying,
And was still resolv'd to stray,
What could save the sheep from dying,
Had the lion found his prey?

4 But the lion and the leopard
Were not with such terror view'd,
As the good and gracious Shepherd,
Who to save the sheep pursued.

5 Yet the Shepherd, constant ever,
Came and bore the sheep away;
Happy sheep! but never, never,
From the Shepherd henceforth stray..

HYMN CXXXII.

"*I lay down my life for the sheep.*"—JOHN X. 15.

1 WE'LL sing of the Shepherd that died,
That died for the sake of the flock;
His love to the utmost was tried,
And immoveable stood as a rock.

2 When the blood of a victim must flow,
The Shepherd, by kindness, was led
To stand between them and the foe,
And willingly died in their stead.

3 Our song then for ever shall be
Of the Shepherd who gave himself thus;
No subject so glorious we see,
And none so affecting to us.

4 We'll sing of this subject alone,
No other our tongues shall employ;
But better his love will be known,
In yonder bright regions of joy.

5 'Tis there that we hope we shall be,
Among the redeem'd to appear;
From sin and infirmity free,
We'll sing as we cannot do here.

The Church of God.

HYMN CXXXIII.

"*And ye shall be my sons and daughters, saith the Lord Almighty.*"—2 Cor. vi. 18.

1 THERE is a family on earth,
Whose Father fills a throne!
But though a seed of heav'nly birth,
To men they're little known.

2 Whene'er they meet the public eye,
They feel the public scorn;
For men their fairest claims deny,
And count them basely born.

3 But 'tis the King who reigns above,
That claims them for his own;
The favour'd objects of his love,
And destin'd to a throne.

4 The honours that belong to them,
By *men* are set at nought;
Whatever shines not *they* contemn,
Unworthy of a thought!

5 But ah! how little they reflect!
For mark th' unerring word,
"That which with men has most respect,
Is odious to the Lord."

6 Were honours evident to sense,
Their portion here below,
The world would do them reverence,
And all their claims allow.

7 But when the King himself was here,
His claims were set at nought:
Would *they* another lot prefer?
Rejected be the thought!

8 No! they will tread, while here below,
The path their Master trod;
Content all honour to forego,
But that which comes from God.

9 And when the King again appears,
He'll vindicate their claim;
Eternal honour shall be theirs,
Their foes be fill'd with shame.

HYMN CXXXIV.

"*For the Lord hath chosen Zion.*"—Psalm cxxxii. 13.

1 YE who love the cause of Zion,
Though despis'd of men, and few,
Arm'd with boldness like the lion,
Fear not all that men can do:
What though all the world oppose,
God is stronger than her foes.

2 Friends of Zion, mark the promise—
"Zion shall become a praise;"
Earth and hell would wrest it from us,
But in vain, our Saviour says—
Zion's King is "Lord of lords;"
His are true and faithful words.

3 Zion's foes may all assemble,
But their counsel cannot stand;
Soon the stoutest heart will tremble,
When the Lord shall raise his hand:
Who to her would ruin bring,
First must vanquish Zion's King.

4 Now, ye people, walk around her,
View her walls, and count her tow'rs;
See how God, her King and founder,
Keeps her safe from hostile pow'rs:
Zion's children live secure;
God has made their "dwelling sure."

5 See her firm and deep foundation,
Zion stands upon a rock;
God hath call'd her walls "Salvation,"
Form'd to stand each adverse shock:
Strength and beauty here unite:
Zion is the Lord's delight.

6 Foes of Zion, fight no longer;
Here submission will be gain:
Zion's King will prove the stronger,
And with pow'r her cause maintain:
He secures her gates and walls:
'Tis on you the ruin falls.

HYMN CXXXV.

"*For the Lord hath chosen Zion; he hath desired it for his habitation.*"—PSALM cxxxii. 13.

1 ZION is Jehovah's dwelling;
There "the King of kings" appears:
Hers is glory far excelling
All the worldling sees or hears.
Zion's walls are everlasting,
Form'd through endless years to shine;
Strength and beauty never-wasting,
Show their origin divine.

2 Zion claims peculiar honour:
High distinction marks her lot:
Light eternal shines upon her;
Hers a sun that faileth not.
Zion's city hath foundations:
God himself has rais'd her walls:
She survives the wreck of nations:
Zion stands, whatever falls.

3 Happy they who now discerning
Zion's glory, thither move!
Earth with all its honours spurning,
Zion is the place they love.
There the Lord, his face disclosing,
Fills his people's hearts with joy;
While, from all their toils reposing,
Bliss is theirs without alloy.

[illegible]

HYMN XXXVI.

"As the mountains are round about Jerusalem, so the Lord is round about his people from henceforth even for ever."
Psalm cxxv. 2.

Zion stands with hills surrounded,
Zion kept by power divine;
All her foes shall be confounded,
Though the world in arms combine.
Happy Zion,
What a favour'd lot is thine!

Every human tie may perish;
Friend to friend unfaithful prove;
Mothers cease their own to cherish;
Heaven and earth at last remove;
But no changes
Can attend Jehovah's love.

Zion's Friend in nothing alters,
Though all others may and do;
His is love that never falters,
Always to its object true.
Happy Zion,
Crown'd with mercies ever new.

4 If thy God should shew displeasure,
'Tis to save, and not destroy:
If he punish, 'tis in measure;
'Tis to rid thee of alloy.
Be thou patient;
Soon thy grief shall turn to joy.

5 In the furnace God may prove thee,
Thence to bring thee forth more bright;
But can never cease to love thee:
Thou art precious in his sight:
God is with thee,
God thine everlasting light.

HYMN CXXXVII.

"*The portion of Jacob is not like them . . . the Lord of Hosts is his name.*"—JER. x. 16.

1 "JACOB'S portion is the Lord;"
What can Jacob more require?
What can heaven more afford?
Or a creature more desire?

2 "Jacob shall not now wax pale;"
His is sure a pleasant lot;
Jacob's portion cannot fail;
'Tis the Lord who changes not.

3 Jacob need not look to earth,
Since his portion is THE LORD:
Worldly care and worldly mirth,
With his choice would ill accord.

4 Others may their gods display,
Tell what pleasures they afford;
Jacob smiles at all they say;
"Jacob's portion is the Lord."

5 Heav'n and earth shall flee away,
Sinners with their idols fall;
Jacob shall survive the day;
Jacob's God is Lord of all.

6 Happy Jacob! fear not thou;
Triumph when the Lord appears!
He who is thy portion now,
Will be thine through endless years.

HYMN CXXXVIII.

"And it shall come to pass in the last days, that the mountain of the Lord's house shall be established in the top of the mountains, and shall be exalted above the hills, and all nations shall flow unto it."—Isaiah ii. 2.

1 SEE that mountain high exalted;
'Tis the mountain of the Lord;
Much expos'd and oft assaulted,
Lov'd of God, by man abhorr'd:
Now it stands above the hills:
Now its destin'd place it fills.

2 O ye mountains, vast and tow'ring,
Boast no more, nor triumph now;
Zion's head, sublimely soaring,
Leaves your summits far below:
Know ye, this is God's own hill:
Here Jehovah loves to dwell.

3 Hark! a cry among the nations—
"Come, and let us seek the Lord:
"Vain our former expectations;
"Vain the idols we ador'd:
"Zion's King is God alone:
"Let us bow before his throne."

4 See! from ev'ry quarter flowing,
Joyful crowds assemble round:
Love in ev'ry heart is glowing;
Praise is heard in ev'ry sound.
While Jehovah shows his face,
Glory fills the sacred place.

5 Weapons meant for mutual slaughter,
Now are instruments of peace:
They who taste the living water,
Learn from war and strife to cease.
Jesus reigns—the earth is still,
All the nations do his will.

HYMN CXXXIX.

"*By whom shall Jacob arise?*"—AMOS vii. 2.

1 "BY whom shall Jacob now arise?"
For Jacob's friends are few;
And (what should fill us with surprise)
They seem divided too.

2 "By whom shall Jacob now arise?"
For Jacob's foes are strong:
I read their triumph in their eyes;
They think he'll fail ere long.

3 "By whom shall Jacob now arise?"
Can any tell by whom?
Say, shall this branch that wither'd lies,
Again revive and bloom?

4 Lord, thou canst tell—the work is thine;
The help of man is vain:
On Jacob now arise and shine,
And he shall live again.

HYMN CXL.

"*Their Redeemer is strong; the Lord of Hosts is his name: he shall throughly plead their cause.*"—JER. l. 34.

1 WHO shall protract his people's stay?
The day is come, the joyful day,
When God shall set them free:
In vain would man his work oppose,
For God is stronger than his foes,
And what he wills shall be.

2 Long had his people borne the yoke,
Long bow'd beneath th' oppressor's stroke,
Their foes had long prevail'd;
A hard captivity was theirs,
Their bread was water'd with their tears,
They mourn'd, and refuge fail'd.

3 Their harps remain'd without a string;
Amidst their foes how could they sing,
Their unrelenting foes?
Who used their pow'r with cruel rage,
Whom no submission could assuage,
Who scoff'd at Isra'l's woes.

4 Rememb'ring Zion, oft they wept,
Her solemn feasts no longer kept,
Her sabbaths now no more;
On better days they thought with grief,
Nor could they hope to find relief,
Till God's appointed hour.

5 But, lo! the day, the happy day
Is come, and now they haste away,
In spite of all their foes;
The day of liberty is come,
With singing they regain their home,
And think no more of woes.

6 Again they see the happy land,
On Zion's mount again they stand,
Again the temple raise;
Once more the ruin'd walls they build,
And now again is Zion fill'd
With rapture and with praise.

HYMN CXLI.

"*For the house which I am about to build shall be wonderful great.*"—2 CHRON. ii. 9.

1 BEHOLD the temple of the Lord!
The work of God, by man abhorr'd,
Appearing fair and splendid;
It lifts its head in spite of foes,
And though a hostile world oppose,
The work will yet be ended.

2 A building this, not made with hands;
On firm foundations, lo! it stands,
For God himself has laid them:
The workmanship of God alone;
The rich materials all his own;
'Twas he himself that made them.

3 He builds it for his glory's sake;
Its solid frame no force can shake,
However men despise it:
And time, that other works destroys,
'Gainst this in vain its pow'r employs,
The work of God defies it.

4 From age to age his work goes on,
The stones collected one by one,
Ere long it will be finish'd:
And when he works his grand design,
The temple will for ever shine
With lustre undiminish'd!

HYMN CXLII.

"*The joy of our heart is ceased.*"—LAM. v. 15.

1 WHY *sleeps the harp of Judah now,*
Whose notes were once so sweet, so loud?
Why left unheeded on the bough
That overhangs Euphrates' flood?

2 *Why sleeps the harp of Judah now?*
Will no one touch its silent strings?
Are all restrain'd by solemn vow,
That none will praise the "King of kings?"

3 *Why sleeps the harp of Judah now?*
Let Zion's children answer why:
"We cannot sing, while here we bow
Beneath the yoke, and inly sigh.

4 "Our foes insulting ask a song;
And of their captives mirth demand;
But who can sing, their foes among,
Or smile, when in a foreign land?

5 "From Zion far, we mourn and pine;
Our hearts are sad, our tongues are dumb;
No prophet have we now, or sign;
No friend, no guide, no king, no home."

6 And is that arm of pow'r bereft,
That wonders wrought in ages past?
Jehovah's people, are they left
To sorrows that for ever last?

7 The Lord from exile will recall
His people to their native shore;
'd Babylon's proud walls shall fall
'n ruins, to arise no more.

8 Then let the harp of Judah ring
With sounds of joy; the day is near
When Zion shall behold her King,
No more to weep, no more to fear.

HYMN CXLIII.

"How shall we sing the Lord's song in a strange land?"—
PSALM cxxxvii. 4.

1 SILENT on a foreign shore,
Judah's harp is heard no more,
See, it hangs on yonder bough,
No one cares to touch it now:
Whence this silence, whence this sadness?
Where's the voice of joy, of gladness?

2 Can the pining captive sing?
Can he wake the silent string?
Can the exile, far from home,
Aught express but grief and gloom?
Hence this silence, hence this sadness!
Hence the want of joy and gladness.

3 Yet the exile's day will come,
When he shall regain his home:
Zion's children shall return,
And for ever cease to mourn:
Whence this silence, whence this sadness!
Where's the voice of joy and gladness.

4 Zion's sons, though far from home,
Yet may live on joys to come:
Mighty their Redeemer is,
And his people's cause is his:
Whence this silence, whence this sadness?
Where's the voice of joy and gladness?

5 Let the harp of Judah now
Hang no more on yonder bough;
Wake its silent strings again:
Hope has its peculiar strain:
Hope is not allied to sadness;
Hope is full of joy and gladness.

Israel a Type.

HYMN CXLIV.

FIRST PART.

"*O give thanks unto the Lord . . . to him that smote Egypt in their first-born . . . and brought out Israel from among them.*"—
PSALM cxxxvi. 1, 10, 11.

1 ISRA'L serv'd a cruel master,
One in whom no pity dwelt;
When they cried, he bound them faster,
Careless he what Isra'l felt:
Thus the tyrant,
As with slaves, with Isra'l dealt.

2 But the Lord, with all his wonders,
Came to make their bondage cease;
With a voice like many thunders,
He demanded their release;
"Let my people
Serve me where, and how I please."

3 Long the tyrant strove to hold them,
Long resisted the demand;
All their hopes were vain, he told them,
None should save them from his hand:
They should never
[illegible]ak their chains, and leave his land.

4 But no pow'r could hold them longer,
When the Lord proclaim'd them his;
Soon he prov'd himself the stronger,
For his arm almighty is;
Now he summon'd
Friends and foes to witness this.

5 By his awful signs amazēd,
Lo! the tyrant yields his prey;
While the Lord, with arm upraisēd,
Leads his ransom'd hosts away:
Thus Jehovah
Shews his pow'r, and wins the day.

6 Isra'l now, whose chain is broken,
Hastens from the tyrant's land;
Thus, what God before had spoken,
Is accomplished by his hand;
And the tyrant
Forc'd to yield to his demand.

SECOND PART.

"*To him which divided the Red Sea into parts . . . and made Israel to pass through the midst of it . . . but overthrew Pharaoh and his host in the Red Sea.*"—PSALM cxxxvi. 13, 14, 15.

1 WELL might Isra'l, filled with wonder,
Sing in that triumphant hour,
When they saw their foes brought under,
When the Lord display'd his pow'r;
And the tyrant
Vanquish'd sunk, to rise no more.

2 When they saw their foes pursuing,
Ev'ry heart was fill'd with fear;
In their front the waters viewing,
Armed thousands in their rear;
Terror seiz'd them,
And they thought destruction near.

3 Vain their fear; for he who gave them
Freedom from the tyrant's pow'r,
Was at hand, again to save them,
In the dark and trying hour:
God their Saviour,
God, his people's strength and tow'r.

4 By his arm the sea dividing,
Lo! he leads his people on;
Through the deep their footsteps guiding,
Where no foot of man had gone:
Thus he sav'd them,
Thus he made his glory known.

5 'Twas not so with those who follow'd,
'Twas their awful doom to die;
By the mighty waters swallow'd,
In the deep behold they lie;
None could save them
From the God that reigns on high.

6 Well may Isra'l tell the story
Of that day, that wondrous day,
When the Lord display'd his glory,
Op'ning through the deep a way;
"When he worketh,
Who his mighty arm shall stay?"

THIRD PART.

"*To him which led his people through the wilderness.*"—
PSALM CXXXVI. 16.

1 RESCU'D from the hand of strangers,
Isra'l through the desert goes;
Many are his toils and dangers,
Many too are Isra'l's foes;
But Jehovah
All his wants and dangers knows.

2 Isra'l's heart is found deceitful,
Prone to murmur and complain;
Isra'l too is oft forgetful
Of the hand that broke his chain;
But Jehovah
Turns him to himself again.

3 Through a trackless desert going,
Isra'l proves the Saviour's love;
Lo! a cloud before him shewing
When, and whither he should move;
Isra'l's journeys
Are directed from above.

4 Though the desert be unfruitful,
Yet is favour'd Isra'l fed;
His supplies are never doubtful,
God provides his daily bread;
And his table
Through the wilderness is spread.

5 Where no pleasant streams are flowing,
In a parch'd and thirsty land,
Lo! the rock, its Maker knowing,
Pours a stream at his command;
And his people
Wond'ring own his mighty hand.

6 When the foe, of numbers boasting,
Leads his armies to the fight,
Isra'l in the promise trusting,
Puts his num'rous foes to flight;
And goes forward
In the Lord Jehovah's might.

FOURTH PART.

"Understand therefore, that the Lord thy God giveth thee not this good land to possess it for thy righteousness."—

DEUT. ix. 6.

1 ISRA'L, were thy numbers greater
Than the nations all around?
Wast thou wiser, wast thou better,
That thy mercies thus abound?
No: thou knowest,
Weak and worthless thou wast found.

2 When a cruel lord enslav'd thee,
And refus'd to set thee free,
'Twas not thine own arm that sav'd thee,
He had been a match for thee;
'Twas Jehovah
Forc'd him to resign his prey.

3 'Twas not thine own arm that brought thee
Safely through the midst of foes;
'Twas not thine own wisdom taught thee
How their numbers to oppose;
God was with thee
When thine enemies arose.

4 Yea, the Lord would shew his glory,
He would make his wonders known,
That the world might hear the story,
And confess what he had done:
Not to Isra'l,
To the Lord be praise alone.

FIFTH PART.

"*And surely it floweth with milk and honey.*"—NUMB. xiii. 27.

1 ISRA'L'S conflicts now are ended,
All his toils have reach'd a close;
Isra'l, by his God befriended,
Has subdued his num'rous foes;
Isra'l's portion
Henceforth shall be sweet repose.

2 Vanish'd is the cloud that led him,
By the way, so many years;
Gone the manna too that fed him,
Useless now, it disappears;
Happy Isra'l
Needs no guide, no famine fears.

3 There, where Isra'l has his dwelling,
Fruits of ev'ry kind are found;
Trees all other trees excelling,
Rise spontaneous from the ground;
Milk and honey
In the happy land abound.

4 Isra'l sav'd looks back with pleasure
On his conflicts now no more;
Isra'l's triumph knows no measure,
While he stands on Canaan's shore;
Now possessing
All his soul desir'd before.

5 Far remov'd from foes and strangers,
Favour'd Isra'l dwells alone;
Past his toils, and past his dangers,
All his work for ever done;
Peace his portion,
Peace, by prosp'rous warfare won.

6 Happy people! blest for ever!
Isra'l, who like thee is found?
Whom the Lord was pleas'd to sever
From the nations all around;
Happy people!
Sav'd, and now with glory crown'd!

Prayer.

HYMN CXLV.

"*The fruit of the Spirit is love.*"—Gal. v. 22.

1 LORD, let thy Spirit from above
Descend, and fill our hearts
With holy joy, and peace, and love,
The gifts which he imparts.

2 We feel our emptiness of good,
And ask for a supply;
We cannot do the thing we would:
Lord, hear our earnest cry.

3 We cannot love thee as we ought,
Nor can we love at all,
Unless by thine own Spirit taught;
Then hear, O hear our call!

4 We cannot serve thee as we should,
With reverence and fear;
We cannot do it, if we would;
But thine it is to hear:

5 To hear thy people, when they cry
For power to do thy will;
Then hear us now; our wants supply:
Be near thy people still.

6 Inspire our hearts, O Lord, with love;
With earnest love, and pure;
That we may live, and faithful prove;
And to the end endure.

HYMN CXLVI.

"*My soul thirsteth for God.*"—PSALM xlii. 2.

1 THE Spirit, coming in his pow'r,
Is welcome to our waiting hearts;
We look for the refreshing show'r;
We ask for all that love imparts.

2 Lord, let the windows opened be,
By which thy blessings came at first:
For thee, O Lord, we thirst for thee;
For thee, the living God, we thirst.

3 The cisterns that our hands have made
Are broken all, and nothing hold:
From thee, the fountain, we have strayed;
And this has been our way of old.

4 The two-fold evil we lament,
Without thy grace we cannot live:
Our sinful folly we repent;
Thy pardon and thy blessing give.

5 Ashamed, and griev'd, and wiser grown,
We come to thee to make us bless'd;
'Tis fellowship with thee alone
Can satisfy, and give us rest.

HYMN CXLVII.

"Oh! that thou wouldest rend the heavens."—ISAIAH lxiv. 1.

1 COME, O Lord, the heavens rending,
On our barren souls descending,
Grace and greatness sweetly blending;
Come, O Lord!

2 Thou from guilt and curse hast freed us;
With the bread of heaven feed us;
In the path of wisdom lead us;
Lead us, Lord!

3 From thy throne of mercy hear us;
With thy holy presence cheer us;
Now and always be thou near us,
When we call.

HYMN CXLVIII.

"The Spirit . . . . of power and of love."—2 TIM. i. 7.

1 GRANT us, Lord, thy Holy Spirit,
Spirit he of power and love,
Hear us, through the Saviour's merit,
Hear us from thy throne above;
Take away "the stony heart;"
"Heart of flesh," instead, impart:
Take, oh! take us,
Lord, and make us
Such as thou would'st have us be,
Meet to dwell in heav'n with thee.

HYMN CXLIX.

"*Your body is the temple of the Holy Ghost.*"—1 COR. vi. 19.

1 LORD, we plead thy promise giv'n;
Let the Spirit come from heav'n;
Ours to ask, and thine to grant:
Lord, supply thy people's want.

2 Kindle in our hearts a flame,
Pure and vehement—the same
As of old thy people felt,
Those in whom thy Spirit dwelt.

3 At thy feet thy servants see;
Good it is to wait on thee:
Good to wait, and good to pray,
Send us not unblest away.

4 Be our bodies thine abode,
Temples of the Lord our God;
Living, dying, let us be
Consecrated, Lord, to thee.

HYMN CL.

"*Save, Lord: let the King hear us, when we call.*"—PSALM XX. 9.

1 SAVIOUR, when we call, O hear us;
In the trying hour be near us,
Lest the foe should prove too strong:
To thy mercy we betake us;
Never leave us, nor forsake us;
Power and grace to thee belong.

2 Other help than thine we have not;
Other help than thine we crave not;
'Tis enough if we have this:
This from ev'ry ill secures us;
Ev'ry blessing this ensures us;
More than life thy favour is.

3 Keep us on thy strength relying,
In thy name the foe defying;
Till thy coming brings us peace.
O how sweet the thought, and cheering,
In the day of thine appearing,
Trouble shall for ever cease!

HYMN CLI.

"*Thy blessing is upon thy people.*"—PSALM iii. 8.

1 SAVIOUR, send a blessing to us,
Send a blessing from above:
All thy truth and mercy shew us,
Be thou here, in pow'r and love,
Grant thy presence,
Be it ours thy grace to prove.

2 Art thou here! then have we blessing,
Art thou not! we nothing have;
All our good in thee possessing,
For thou only, Lord, canst save;
Be thou present,
This is what thy people crave.

3 Nothing have we, Lord, without thee,
But thy promise is our stay:
And thy people must not doubt thee,
Saviour, now thy pow'r display,
And let gladness
Fill thy people's hearts to-day.

4 Gladness, Saviour, such as they have,
They, whose treasure is above;
This is what thy people may have;
Truth is theirs, and faith and love.
Theirs a treasure
That the world knows nothing of.

HYMN CLII.

"*Wait on the Lord.*"—PSALM xxvii. 14.

1 'TIS good, 'tis sweet, 'tis passing sweet,
To join with those who wait and pray;
Who sit at the Redeemer's feet,
To hear what God the Lord will say.

2 The privilege of doing so
Is great, we know; exceeding great;
But we should feel, as well as know,
That we are blest, when at his feet.

3 To us, O Lord, reveal thy love,
While at thy feet we lowly fall;
Descend in power from above,
And bless us now, O bless us all.

4 O teach us, Lord, to watch and pray;
And should the day of trial come,
Be near us then, our guide and stay,
Nor leave us, till we reach our home:

5 That home, where all thy people meet.
Tho' scatter'd here, they meet above;
With welcomes loud each other greet,
And sing the praise of him they love:

6 Of him who wash'd them with his blood;
Of him who sav'd them by his grace;
Who made them kings and priests to God,
And brought them to behold his face.

HYMN CLIII.

"*Come boldly unto the throne of grace.*"—HEB. iv. 16.

1 MEET thy people, Saviour, meet us,
Meet us at thy throne of grace;
And with signs of welcome greet us,
'Tis thine own appointed place,
Where thy people
Hear thy voice, and see thy face.

2 Cause us, Lord, to feel compunction,
"Godly sorrow" for our sin;
And impart thy holy "unction,"
Life, and peace, and joy within.
This our object,
Christ to serve, and Christ to "win."

3 Let us wait for thine appearing;
Wait, and look, and long to see,
Him who, then our nature wearing,
Judge of quick and dead will be.
O what glory,
Lord, will then be given to thee.

4 Let the prospect cheer and move us,
Move us, Lord, to live to thee;
And, when trials come to prove us,
May thy strength our safety be;
Till thy glory
In the heav'n of heav'ns we see.

HYMN CLIV.

"*My soul cleaveth unto the dust.*"—PSALM cxix. 25.

1 OUR souls, they cleave unto the dust:
O quicken us, or cleave they must,
For ever: 'tis thy power, O Lord,
And thine alone, can help afford.

2 A force with which we cannot cope,
Withstands us, and forbids the hope
That we should rise, except by thee:
This knowing, to thy pow'r we flee.

3 The thing that we can never do,
Is easy, Lord, to thee, we know;
We cast ourselves before thy feet,
O hear us from thy mercy seat.

4 Exert the pow'r exerted then,
What time the Saviour rose again;
Ascended up above the sky,
And took his destin'd place on high.

5 The pow'r that wrought and triumph'd then,
Exert, O Lord, exert in us;
And let thy people quicken'd be,
To holy zeal, and love to thee.

6 Let things above our thoughts employ,
Let peace be ours, and holy joy;
Till, brought to yonder glorious place,
We bless thy name, and see thy face.

HYMN CLV.

"*Whom the Father will send in my name.*"—John xiv. 26.

1 THY precious gift, O Lord, impart,
Thy Holy Spirit give,
That he may dwell in every heart;
'Tis thus thy people live.

2 Of blessings this the blessing is,
'Tis fraught with pow'r and grace;
To be "the Comforter" is his,
To fill the Saviour's place.

3 To take of his and make it known,
Till he appears again;
Till he appears to bless his own,
And judge the rest of men.

4 To us the Holy Spirit be
Both Guide and Comforter,
Till, conflicts past, thy face we see,
No more from truth to err.

5 No more to sin against thy love,
No evils to deplore,
But, dwelling with thy saints above,
To live for evermore.

HYMN CLVI.

"*The Lord make his face shine upon thee.*"—NUMB. vi. 25.

1 WHEN the Saviour shines upon us,
Then we know what gladness is;
Then, if all the world should shun us,
Need we grieve because of this?
They are blessed,
Whom the Saviour owns as his.

2 Are we his, then what can harm us?
What above, or what below?
He for ev'ry conflict arms us,
Keeps us safe from ev'ry foe:
Nor forsakes us,
Till we see the end of woe.

3 Shine thou, then, O Lord, from heaven,
'Tis on thee we call, on thee;
Sweet the sense of sin forgiven:
Sweet the hope of joys to be,
When thy glory
'thout clouds in heav'n we see.

HYMN CLVII.

"*The Lord will bless his people.*"—PSALM xxix. 11.

1 LORD, be present now to bless us,
  Joy and peace to all impart;
Meet it is thou should'st possess us,
  Reign, O Lord, in ev'ry heart:
Slaves to sin we would not be,
Thou alone canst set us free!

2 We are free, thy laws obeying,
  'Tis the truth that makes us free;
O preserve us, Lord, from straying
  From the path mark'd out by thee;
Keep us walking in the way
Leading to eternal day.

3 We are helpless, Lord, without thee,
  To the foe an easy prey;
But we must not, will not, doubt thee,
  Thou wilt be our guide and stay:
This may well our spirits cheer,
And we need no evil fear.

4 Yes, the thought is sweet and cheering;
  When his people's strength is gone,
Then it is the Lord, appearing,
  Cheers and leads his people on:
Be it so with us, O Lord;
Be our shield and our reward.

HYMN CLVIII.

"*And I will take away the stony heart.*"—EZEK. xxxvi. 26

1 THE promise, Lord, that thou hast giv'n
  Emboldens us to seek thy face;
O send thy Spirit now from heaven,
  The Spirit he of pow'r and grace.

2 When he awakens life, we live
When he enlightens, then we see;
We have what we from him receive,
Without him nothing good can be.

8 Lord, send thy Spirit, send him now,
And let us feel a present pow'r;
Before thy throne, behold, we bow,
Be this to us a blessed hour.

4 "The heart of stone," O Lord, remove,
Replace it with "a heart of flesh;"
Now manifest to us thy love,
And by thy grace our souls refresh.

5 Lord, hear us from thy throne above,
And now thy Holy Spirit give,
That we may learn to walk in love,
And henceforth to thy glory live.

HYMN CLIX.

"Another Comforter, that he may abide with you for ever."—
JOHN xiv. 16.

1 "THE Spirit of the Truth" is he
Whom thou, O Lord, appointed hast
To fill thy vacant place, and be
Thy people's teacher to the last.

2 To comfort sent, and sent to bless,
When he is present so art thou;
Thy saints are never "comfortless,"
They never were, nor are they now.

8 Nor shall thy people ever be
Without a comforter and guide;
The Spirit sent from heav'n by thee,
Shall with them to the end abide.

4 The word of promise makes it sure,
No pledge but this we have or need;
Possessing this we feel secure,
For faithful is thy word indeed.

5 This privilege be ours, O Lord,
The presence of "the Comforter;"
Expounder of the sacred word,
Without him we are sure to err.

6 Of unity the source alone,
Inspirer he of peace and love;
His presence and his pow'r we own,
The holy and pacific Dove.

7 'Tis his, O Lord, to take of thine,
And show it to thy people here;
'Tis his upon their souls to shine,
And bring the word of promise near.

8 The sacred office that he bears,
A pledge of ev'ry blessing is:
In all their troubles and their fears,
Thy people may rejoice in this.

9 To us the Comforter be given,
With all his grace and all his pow'rs;
An earnest of the joys of heaven;
This grace we ask, this grace be ours.

HYMN CLX.

"He shall receive of mine, and shall shew it unto you."—
JOHN xvi. 14.

1 NOW may the Spirit's power be felt,
The pow'r that without limit is;
And cause our frozen hearts to melt,
The office and the work are his.

2 We nothing know unless he teach,
Or if we know we do not feel;
'Tis his to bless us all and each,
The love of Jesus to reveal.

3 When he expounds the sacred page,
What light upon the truth is cast!
The teacher he, from age to age,
The church's teacher to the last.

4 To those who "ask," thy word declares
"The Holy Spirit" will be giv'n;
Then hear us, Lord, O hear our pray'rs,
And send the Spirit down from heav'n.

5 'Tis he creates the life within,
The vital air we breathe is his;
He frees us from the pow'r of sin,
His presence life and blessing is.

HYMN CLXI.

"*But if I depart, I will send him unto you.*"—JOHN xvi. 7.

1 SEND thy Spirit, Lord, from heaven,
Promis'd comforter and guide;
Pledge on earth of sins forgiven,
O be not our suit denied.

2 'Tis thy promise brings us here,
This our warrant is to pray;
When we cry, O Lord, draw near;
Send us not unheard away.

3 Let thy Spirit come in pow'r,
Come to teach, and come to bless;
Let us all be glad this hour,
nd, with joy, thy name confess.

4 Teach us at thy feet to bow,
And to fall before thy throne;
Bless us all, O bless us now,
Be to us thy goodness known.

5 Goodness that no tongue can teach,
Words unequal are to this;
Goodness that no thought can reach,
Without limit, Lord, it is.

6 O our Lord, our Saviour thou,
What thy people ask for grant;
Send thy Spirit, send him now,
Having him we nothing want.

7 He unfolds the sacred page,
And applies it by his pow'r;
He the same, from age to age,
Now, and to the final hour.

8 Led by him, thy people go
Safely through the trackless waste;
Led by him, they meet the foe,
And they gain their home at last.

HYMN CLXII.

"*He is like a refiner's fire.*"—MAL. iii. 1.

1 NOW may the Spirit, sent from heav'n,
Baptize us with his fire;
Consuming all unhallow'd leav'n;
Be this our soul's desire.

2 The temples of the living God
Should consecrated be;
"The unclean thing" and his abode
In nothing can agree.

3 His work it is, who dwells within,
To purify the place;
He only can contend with sin,
For pow'r is his, and grace.

4 We look to him, to him we cry,
Expel the evil, Lord;
Thine habitation purify,
According to thy word.

5 Let no unholy thing remain
Thy temple to pollute;
Remove the guilt, remove the stain,
O cast the evil out.

HYMN CLXIII.

"*Praying always with all prayer.*"—EPH. vi. 18.

1 PRAY'R is the new-born infant's cry,
The sign of entrance into life;
'Tis trouble not unmix'd with joy;
'Tis peace, though in the midst of strife.

2 Pray'r is the winged messenger
That bears his sighs from earth to heav'n;
That brings them to his Father's ear,
Nor thence returns till grace is giv'n.

3 Pray'r is the vanquished rebel's cry,
When sounds of mercy reach his ear,
"O save me, save me, lest I die!"
A cry of mingled hope and fear.

4 Pray'r is a voice that sweetly pleads
For saints, beneath the Father's rod;
The Spirit's voice that intercedes
"According to the will of God."

5 Pray'r is a weapon sent from heav'n,
Employing which the saints prevail,
Prevail with him, by whom 'tis giv'n;
A weapon this that cannot fail.

6 Of temper proof, it stands the test,
The test of ev'ry trying hour;
And they who know its value best,
Admire the most its wondrous pow'r.

7 Then let us pray, and never faint,
The pray'r of faith can all things do;
Employing this, the feeble saint
Can meet and vanquish ev'ry foe.

HYMN CLXIV.

"*The Lord is my light and my salvation.*"—Psalm xxvii. 1.

1 O THOU God of our salvation!
Jesus, now enthron'd in light,
Look from thine exalted station,
Look from yonder glorious height;
Save thy people,
Put their enemies to flight.

2 Thou wast once, like us, assaulted,
Once a "man of sorrows" here;
Now to heav'n with joy exalted,
Thou art first and highest there:
Yet thy people
Know their pray'rs will reach thine ear.

3 Sing, ye saints, for ye have reason,
Jesus is your glorious chief;
In affliction's sharpest season,
Think on this, 'twill bring relief;
Sing with gladness,
Jesus knows, and shares your grief.

4 Earthly things are transitory,
Empty all the world can yield;
Jesus gives us grace and glory,
Jesus is our sun and shield:
Fair our portion,
Ours a cup with blessings fill'd.

5 Saviour, make thy people humble,
Full of love, and full of trust;
Then let these "vile bodies" crumble,
And return again to dust:
Fairer mansions
Shall be ours among the just.

HYMN CLXV.

"*In my distress I called upon the Lord.*"—Psalm xviii. 6.

1 JESUS, my Lord, to thee
In my distress I flee,
Hear thou my call;
Jesus, the name I love,
Jesus, all names above,
Jesus, whose grace I prove,
Jesus, my all.

2 Lord, when I fly to thee,
Be a defence to me
In the dark hour;
Strong, because thou art strong,
When foes around me throng,
Be thou my boast and song,
Be thou my tow'r.

3 When thou my Lord art nigh,
Foes I may well defy,
Strong is thine arm;

Mercy and truth are thine,
Wisdom and love divine;
Triumph and peace be mine,
Nothing shall harm.

4 Nothing shall greatly move
Those who thy kindness prove,
Blessed alone:
Strong their Redeemer is,
Greatness and grace are his,
This, and far more than this,
Lord, is thine own.

5 Lord, let thy favour be
Dearer than life to me,
Be thy name dear;
When foes against me fight,
Then raise thine arm of might,
Then save thy worm from flight,
Save him from fear.

HYMN CLXVI.

"*In the Lord put I my trust.*"—Psalm xi. 1.

1 LORD, I trust in thee, O never
Let my soul be put to shame;
Sweet thy promise is, and ever
May its sweetness prove the same:
They alone, whose trust in thee is,
Safe are found, and happy too;
Good, O Lord, thy word to me is,
Source of joys for ever new.

2 Love there is not such as thine is,
Love so constant, love so strong;
But how cold, how languid mine is!
Could thy patience bear so long?

Couldst thou bear with one so froward?
Couldst thou bear with one like me?
In the cause of truth a coward,
And forgetful, Lord, of thee.

3 Yes, of thee, my Lord, forgetful,
In the hour of trial faint;
When corrected, proud and fretful,
Nor abstaining from complaint:
Had my provocations mov'd thee,
I had been consum'd ere this,
For if ever sinner prov'd thee,
He that speaks, that sinner is.

4 Now, my Saviour, mov'd by kindness,
Pardon all my sin anew;
O remove my wicked blindness,
And my stubborn will subdue:
Make, O make me what I should be!
Thou canst break the heart of stone;
What thou wilt is what I would be,
Happy then, and then alone.

HYMN CLXVII.

"*Seek peace.*"—PSALM xxxiv. 14.

1 WHILE contests rend the Christian church,
O may I live the friend of peace!
The sacred mine of Scripture search,
And learn from man, vain man, to cease.

2 O teach me, Lord, *thy truth* to know!
And separate from all beside;
This I would guard from ev'ry foe,
Nor fear the issue to abide.

3 But keep me, Lord, from party zeal,
That seeks its own, and not thy praise;
This temper I would never feel,
Or, when I do, would own it base.

4 Be mine to recommend thy grace,
That sinners may believe and live;
That they who live may run the race,
And then a crown of life receive.

5 Lord, search thy servant, search him through,
Detect, destroy what's not thine own;
Whene'er I speak, whate'er I do,
O may I seek thy praise alone!

HYMN CLXVIII.

"*And the vineyard which thy right hand hath planted.*"—
PSALM lxxx. 15.

1 SEE the vineyard lately planted
By thine hand, O Lord of Hosts;
Let thy people's prayer be granted,
Keep it safe from hostile boasts;
Many think thy work to mar,
O remove the danger far.

2 'Tis thine own, thine hand has made it,
Hide it from the wintry blast;
Let no foot of beast invade it,
No rude hand its beauty waste;
Hear thy people when they pray,
Keep thy vineyard night and day.

3 Drooping plants revive and nourish,
Let them thrive beneath thine hand;
Let the weak grow strong and flourish,
Blooming fair at thy command;
Let the fruitful yield thee more,
Laden with a richer store.

HYMN CLXXI.

"*If ye love me, keep my commandments.*"—JOHN xiv. 15.

1 LORD, let the people of thy love
Be zealous in thy cause;
In ev'ry instance let them prove
Obedient to thy laws.

2 The people thou hast made thine own
Should listen to thy voice,
Should look to thee, and thee alone,
And in thy will rejoice.

3 'Tis thus they glorify thy name,
And prove their origin;
'Tis thus they put their foes to shame,
And silence foolish men.

4 O! teach us, Lord, to walk with thee,
As children of the light;
Unspotted from the world to be,
And pleasing in thy sight.

5 Let all our walk directed be
By thine unerring word:
'Tis meet that we should live to thee,
Our Saviour and our Lord.

HYMN CLXXII.

"*The only wise God, our Saviour.*"—JUDE 25.

1 THE Lord, "the only wise," is he,
Who died on yonder cross for me,
For me, a wretch, and thousands more,
Whose place he took, whose guilt he bore.

2 I wonder when I think on this;
I wonder much that love like his
Should fail to move a heart of stone,
A heart as stubborn as my own.

3 With love like this before my eyes,
That fills an angel with surprise,
My heart, with grief and shame I own,
Is still too like a heart of stone.

4 O Lord, thy Spirit's pow'r alone
Can take away this "heart of stone;"
And in its room another place,
"A heart of flesh," that owns thy grace.

5 Then let thy promis'd grace be giv'n,
The earnest of a future heav'n;
Where all who love thee, there shall be
For ever happy, Lord, with thee.

6 To thee I look, to thee alone;
To thee, to whom all hearts are known;
To walk with thee my soul aspires,
O satisfy my soul's desires.

HYMN CLXXIII.

"*O Lord, rebuke me not in thy wrath.*"—PSALM xxxviii. 1.

1 DEAL gently with thy servant, Lord,
And if the rod should needful be,
Thy seasonable aid afford;
My soul in trouble flies to thee.

2 Thy frown is terrible to bear,
But grace a spring of hope supplies;
Thine anger more than death I fear,
Thy favour more than life I prize.

3 But much I fear, lest in some hour
Of sore temptation, I may fall;
And yielding to the tempter's pow'r,
May faithless prove, and give up all.

4 Lord, save thy worm, for thou alone
Canst keep me in the trying hour;
Thy help I trust to, not my own;
Thy love, thy wisdom, and thy pow'r.

5 When chastisement shall needful be,
Correct thy worm, but not in wrath;
A father's hand I fain would see;
A father's rod no terror hath.

HYMN CLXXIV.

"*Humble yourselves in the sight of the Lord.*"—JAMES iv. 10.

1 'TIS meet that we should humbled be;
'Tis meet we should confess to thee;
To thee, O Lord, how vile we've been,
Confess the greatness of our sin.

2 To thee, O Lord, we ought to cleave,
To thee alone we ought to live;
To thee, O Lord, we have not cleaved,
To thee, alas! we have not lived.

3 We ought, as children of the light,
To walk by faith and not by sight;
But that which should be, has not been;
We have not looked at things unseen.

4 Too much, O Lord, we walk by sight,
And hence are weak when called to fight;
We tremble in the trying hour;
We fall before the tempter's power.

5 We cry to thee for mercy, Lord;
Thine help in time of need afford;
O make us what we ought to be,
And grant us grace to live to thee.

HYMN CLXXV.

"*I acknowledged my sin unto thee.*"—PSALM xxxii. 5.

1 SAVIOUR, 'tis to thee
In my grief I flee;
And to thee alone,
Filling yonder throne.
'Tis a throne of grace, I know;
Near it else I dare not go.

2 Let me tell thee all,
Be it great or small,
All I feel or fear;
Thine it is to hear.
Sin and shame belong to me;
Love and pity, Lord, to thee.

3 Foolish I have been;
Loving what is seen.
No defence have I:
Nothing to reply.
Nothing but the sinner's plea;
Nothing else will do for me.

4 At thy feet I bow;
Hear, O hear me now;
All my sin forgive;
Let the sinner live;
Let the past forgiven be;
Henceforth let me live to thee.

HYMN CLXXVI.

"*The desire of our soul is to thy name.*"—ISAIAH xxvi. 8.

1 YES, I love the name that is
First in heav'n, and soon will be
First on earth. The name is his,
His who hung on yonder tree,
And became a curse for others;
His is love beyond a brother's.

2 Without measure is his love;
Something that we cannot know;
Higher than the height above,
Deeper than the depth below.
Tell its breadth and length we cannot,
'Tis what they in heaven scan not.

3 Love that no beginning has,
Never ends, nor never can;
Always will be, always was,
Who has pow'r this love to scan?
What created tongue can show it?
What created mind can know it?

4 But enough unfolded is
Peace and holy joy to give;
When the Saviour makes us his,
Then do we begin to live.
'Tis his people taste of glàdness,
Other mirth is only madness.

5 Saviour, to our souls reveal
More of thy mysterious love;
All its influence let us feel,
Drawing us to things above;
Make us, Lord, what thou wouldst have us,
Thine it is to bless and save us.

HYMN CLXXVII.

"*Sinners, of whom I am chief.*"—1 TIM. i. 15.

1 BASE among the base,
 Lord, I cry to thee;
Save me by thy grace,
 Set the pris'ner free.
Hear the vanquish'd rebel's cry,
Save, me, save me, else I die.

2 'Twas to save the lost
 That thou cam'st from heav'n;
They will love thee most,
 Who have most forgiv'n.
Hear me, then, O hear my cry,
Who must love thee more than I?

3 Who can have more cause?
 Who could further be,
Further than I was,
 Lord, from heaven and thee?
Hear me, then, O hear my cry,
Who will owe thee more than I?

4 No blasphemer I,
 Nor of sin the slave;
I believ'd a lie,
 But I still was grave.
I was earnest and devout,
And the future thought about.

5 But I thought "as men,"
 And I knew not thee;
Good was evil then,
 Evil good to me.
Lord, I knew not of thy love,
And against thy law I strove.

6 Often did I say,
Would that it were night;
Evil was the day
When I saw the light.
Evil seem'd the day to me,
When I first began to be.

7 'Tis no longer so;
Praise to God for this.
He is blest, I know,
Who forgiven is.
He, and he alone has rest;
He, and he alone is blest.

8 Saviour, all I want
Is to be forgiv'n:
This one favour grant,
Lord of earth and heav'n.
When thy people meet on high,
Who will louder sing than I?

HYMN CLXXVIII.

"[illegible]"—1 Tim. i. 15.

1 [illegible] sinners, Lord, am I:
[illegible] in myself I find:
[illegible]
[illegible]
[illegible] and [illegible]
[illegible]
[illegible]?

2 [illegible]
[illegible]
[illegible]
[illegible]
[illegible]
[illegible]
[illegible] hour.

3 This will be enough for me;
Having this, I'm free within;
Free from guilt, from bondage free,
Vilest bondage, that of sin.
Having this, I've all I need;
Having this, I'm free indeed.

4 Chief of sinners, Lord, am I,
But thy grace sufficient is;
Being so, I shall not die;
This I know—I rest in this.
Matchless grace! who needs it more?
Lord I wonder, and adore.

HYMN CLXXIX.

"*It is the Lord.*"—1 SAM. iii. 18.

1 'TIS the Lord, I know it is;
Let him all his pleasure do;
'Tis enough if I am his;
Safe his people are, I know.
What can harm his people? what!
His they are who changes not.

2 Trials are the lot of all,
Whom the Saviour owns as his:
Mine have been but few and small;
Yet my heart, how weak it is!
Ever ready to repine;
O what patience, Lord, is thine!

3 Thy compassion does not fail;
Therefore I am suffer'd still;
Why this grace to one so frail?
This I know not—'tis thy will.
'Tis thy will it should be so;
This is all I ask to know.

4 Sure I am, beyond a doubt,
If what I deserve were mine,
From thy presence, Lord, cast out,
Far from thee, and far from thine;
I should live, and I should be,
Wretched through eternity.

5 Let not thy compassion fail,
Till the end of strife I see;
Still let grace and love prevail,
And thy name a refuge be,
Till I reach the happy shore
Where thy saints offend no more.

HYMN CLXXX.

"[illegible] himself."—Matt. xvi. 24.

1 [illegible] self-indulgence prone,
I [illegible] help, O Lord, to thee;
The help that comes from thee alone,
That help, O Lord, afford to me.

2 [illegible] me to deny,
[illegible] will, and not my own;
The [illegible] help, O Lord, supply,
[illegible] from his throne.

3 [illegible] spare,
[illegible] how to kill;
[illegible] I cannot bear,
[illegible] dispute thy will.

4 [illegible] with the dust,
[illegible] of thy throne;
[illegible] come down it must,
[illegible] thine alone.

5 Nor can I rest, though I should see
This idol prostrate on the ground,
A mutilated trunk; while he,
Ev'n thus within thy shrine is found.

6 His presence would pollute the place,
Though stunn'd, he might arise once more;
Resume its throne, and O disgrace!
Be worshipp'd as he was before.

7 The idol from thy temple cast,
No fragment of his body spare;
Nor let a trace be found at last,
To tell that he had once been there.

Praise.

HYMN CLXXXI.

"*I will sing of mercy.*"—Psalm ci. 1.

1 SING we praise to God above,
God our Saviour full of grace;
Sing how Jesus, moved by love,
Came from yonder glorious place,
And with men abode a season;
Sing aloud, for we have reason.

2 Let us sing how Jesus came;
Came in mercy, came to save;
Saw the cross, despis'd its shame,
Lay with mortals in the grave;
And in death appear'd victorious:
Sing aloud, the theme is glorious.

3 Yes, the Lord triumphant rose;
Tell, ye saints, his victory;
How he vanquished all his foes,
Captive led captivity;
And to heav'n returned with glory;
Tell, ye saints, the joyful story.

4 Soon we hope to be with him,
Soon to see him as he is:
And renew the wondrous theme,
In a place remote from this;
And with spirits never-wasting,
Sing of mercy everlasting.

HYMN CLXXXII.

"*I will sing, and give praise.*"—PSALM cviii. 1.

1 LET *sinners sav'd give thanks, and sing,*
Of mercies past, of joys to come:
The Lord their Saviour is, and King;
The cross their hope, and heav'n their home.

2 *Let sinners sav'd give thanks, and sing,*
Salvation theirs, and of the Lord:
They draw from heav'n's eternal spring,
The living God their great reward.

3 *Let sinners sav'd give thanks, and sing,*
Sweet is the subject of their song,
Who, made the children of a king,
Expect to sing in heav'n ere long.

Let sinners saved give thanks, and sing;
The Lord has kept in dangers past;
And, O sweet thought! the Lord will bring
His people safe to heav'n at last.

5 *Let sinners sav'd give thanks, and sing,*
Of Jesus sing, through all their days:
In heav'n their golden harps they'll string,
And there for ever sing *his* praise.

HYMN CLXXXIII.

"*Praise him all ye people.*"—PSALM CXVII. 1.

1 TO God our Saviour and our King
Let saints their voices raise:
The people of the Lord should sing,
Since he accepts their praise.

2 Yes, he on whom the angels gaze
With wonder, love, and fear,
Disdains not to accept the praise
His people offer here.

3 On yonder throne, exalted high,
He reigns, his people's head:
He knows their wants, he hears their cry,
And gives them all they need.

4 How sweet to know his name who reigns
Supreme on yonder throne!
His love supplies, his pow'r sustains,
His love and pow'r alone.

5 The source from whence we draw our store
Is full, and overflows;
It yields its treasures to the poor,
Enriching freely those.

6 We'll praise the name of him who gives
What worlds could never buy:
He once was dead, but now he lives!
He lives no more to die.

Was ever love like his?
Stronger than death it is;
Was ever sight like this?
His be the crown.

3 Jesus the curse sustain'd,
Bitter the cup he drain'd,
Happy for us:
Angels were fill'd with awe,
When their own King they saw
Honour his holy law,
Honour it thus.

4 Rich is the grace we sing,
Poor is the praise we bring,
Not as we ought:
But when we see his face,
In yonder glorious place,
Then shall we sing his grace,
Sing without fault.

5 Sing we e'en here of him,
Jesus our lofty theme,
Jesus we'll sing;
Glory and pow'r are his,
His too the kingdom is;
Triumph, ye saints, in this,
Jesus is King.

6 Hail our eternal King!
Jesus, whose name we sing,
Heav'n is thy throne;
Heav'n, where thine angels are,
Where all is bright and fair;
Reign thou for ever there,
Reign thou alone.

HYMN CXC.

"Him hath God exalted . . . . to be a Prince and a Saviour."
ACTS v. 31.

1 OF Jesus we'll sing,
The Saviour and King
Of all who on earth are redeem'd:
No name is so great,
No name is so sweet,
However by men disesteem'd.

2 How high was his seat,
His glory how great,
When sitting on yonder bright throne!
The object above
Of wonder and love,
The object of worship alone.

3 But see, from his place,
In infinite grace
He comes, and appears here below;
He leaves all his store,
And stoops to be poor,
Submitting to want and to woe.

4 No love is like his,
Unequall'd it is
By that of a mother or friend:
What tongue cannot teach,
What thought cannot reach,
'Tis love without measure or end.

5 To Jesus alone,
Who sits on the throne,
Be glory, dominion, and pow'r:
To Jesus be giv'n
All honour in heav'n,
By angels and saints evermore.

HYMN CXCI.

"O God, my heart is fixed; I will sing and give praise."—
PSALM cviii. 1.

1 GRACIOUS Lord, my heart is fixēd,
Sing I will, and sing of thee;
Since the cup that justice mixēd,
Thou didst drink, and drink for me:
Great deliv'rer!
Thou hast set the pris'ner free.

2 Lute and harp awake to praise him!
All my pow'rs your tribute bring!
Though no praise can higher raise him,
(What can higher raise our King?)
Were I silent,
Ev'n the stones would rise and sing.

3 Many were the chains that bound me,
But the Lord has loos'd them all:
Arms of mercy now surround me,
Favours these, nor few nor small:
Saviour, keep me,
Keep, O keep me, lest I fall.

4 Fair the scene that lies before me,
Life eternal Jesus gives:
While he waves his banner o'er me,
Peace and joy my soul receives:
Sure his promise!
I shall live because he lives.

5 When the world would bid me leave thee,
Telling me of shame and loss,
Saviour, guard me, lest I grieve thee,
Lest I cease to love thy cross:
This is treasure:
All the rest I know is dross.

HYMN CXCII.

"*Worthy is the Lamb.*"—Rev. v. 12.

1 YE saints, come and join in the praise of the Lamb,
The theme inexhausted of angels above:
They dwell with delight on the sound of his name,
And gaze on his glory with rapture and love.

2 See, see to what honours the Saviour is rais'd;
He sits on a throne—'tis the throne of the sky:
Come let us adore him who ought to be prais'd,
And learn with the angels in glory to vie.

3 They sing of the Lamb, who to save us was slain;
We'll take up the theme which we cannot improve;
And "Worthy the Lamb" cry again and again,
Till our hearts are inflam'd with the fire of his love.

4 All glory to Jesus, who sits on the throne;
Let angels and saints spread the sound of his fame:
We bow to the Lamb, who is worthy alone,
And give him the praise that belongs to his name.

HYMN CXCIII.

"*Let the children of Zion be joyful in their King.*"—
Psalm cxlix. 2.

1 COME and let us praise our King!
He is worthy to be prais'd:
Should his saints refuse to sing,
How would angels stand amaz'd?
O exalt the sinner's friend!
Let his praises never end.

2 There he dwells whom angels sing;
Once he bore the cross below;
Jesus, heav'n's eternal King,
Liv'd on earth a man of woe:
Now he reigns, and reigns above,
Jesus reigns the God of love.

3 Hail, immortal King of heav'n!
Endless praise surround thy throne;
Lamb of God for sinners giv'n,
"Thou art worthy," thou alone:
Thee we serve, and thee we sing;
Jesus, hail, eternal King.

HYMN CXCIV.

"*Come before his presence with singing.*"—PSALM c. 2.

1 NOW raise a solemn, cheerful strain,
The noblest, sweetest theme invites;
'Tis he who bore our sin and pain,
And in our welfare now delights.

2 'Tis Jesus high upon his throne,
The praise of all the hosts above;
Who rules the universe alone,
The God of everlasting love.

3 'Tis Jesus in the form of man,
And lower than the angels made,
To execute the gracious plan
In God's eternal purpose laid.

4 'Tis Jesus hanging on the cross,
(Mysterious spectacle of woe!)
For whom his people count but loss
The richest portion here below.

5 'Tis Jesus risen from the dead,
 And now in heav'n "both Christ and Lord,"
His people's advocate and head;
 Their joy, their crown, their blest reward.

6 Ah! Lord, how feeble is our song!
 How much below thy matchless love!
But by thy grace we hope, ere long,
 To raise a nobler strain above.

HYMN CXCV.

"*Praise is comely for the upright.*"—PSALM xxxiii. 1.

1 HOW pleasant is the sound of praise!
 It well becomes the saints of God;
Should they refuse their songs to raise,
 The stones would tell their shame abroad.

2 For him who wash'd you in his blood,
 Ye saints, your loudest songs prepare;
He sought you wand'ring far from God,
 And now preserves you by his care.

3 One string there is of sweetest tone,
 Reserv'd for sinners saved by grace;
'Tis sacred to one theme alone,
 And touch'd by one peculiar race.

4 Though angels may with rapture see
 How mercy flows in streams of blood,
It is not theirs to prove, as we,
 The cleansing virtue of this flood.

5 While angels praise the heav'nly King,
 And worship him as God alone,
The saints with exultation sing—
 "He wears our nature on the throne."

6 Sweet truth! it yields unceasing cause
Of wonder and of praise above;
That man, who late accursed was,
Should be the object of such love.

7 Great King of angels and of saints!
(Whose matchless glories far outshine
What eye beholds, or fancy paints,)
Let everlasting praise be thine.

HYMN CXCVI.

"*O God, my heart is fixed; I will sing and give praise, even with my glory.*"—Psalm cviii. 1.

1 AWAKE our souls! awake our tongues!
The subject is divine:
A Saviour's love demands our songs,
Let all his people join.

2 This Saviour is the mighty God
Who fills the throne above;
Reveal'd in flesh he shed his blood,
And thus declar'd his love.

3 Jesus, thy love exceeds our thought,
But this we're giv'n to see,
That they who feel its pow'r are taught
To part with all for thee.

4 And though thy love be faintly seen,
What's seen demands our praise;
Without this view we still had been
Engag'd in folly's ways.

5 But when we lay this flesh aside,
And gain the realms of light,
Obscuring clouds no more shall hide
Thy glory from our sight.

6 Then to the praise of love divine
We'll strike our golden lyres;
With heart and voice we'll sweetly join
The everlasting choirs.

HYMN CXCVII.

"*Thou art worthy, O Lord, to receive glory.*"—Rev. iv. 11.

1 ENDLESS praises
To our Lord!
Ever be his name ador'd!

2 Angels crown him,
Crown the Lamb!
He is worthy—praise his name.

3 Saints adore him,
Sound his fame,
You he saves from endless shame.

4 Saints and angels
Jointly sing,
Glory, glory to our King.

HYMN CXCVIII.

"*In the midst of the throne . . . . stood a Lamb.*"—Rev. v. 6.

1 HOPE in Christ our Lord possessing,
Let us raise a cheerful psalm;
Glory, honour, pow'r, and blessing,
Be for ever to the Lamb!
In the midst of yonder throne,
Lo! he stands, he reigns alone.

2 PRAISE THE LAMB—his love unbounded
Is the theme of praise in heav'n:
On his death our hopes are founded,
Yes, we know his life was giv'n;
And we trust that by his blood
We are reconcil'd to God.

3 PRAISE THE LAMB—ye saints adore him,
You he saves from endless shame:
See, how angels fall before him,
How they triumph in his name;
His the sceptre, his the crown,
His yon bright eternal throne.

4 PRAISE THE LAMB—repeat his praises;
'Tis a theme, ye saints, for you;
When our Lord to heav'n shall raise us,
There the subject we'll renew:
And in yonder glorious place,
We shall see the Saviour's face.

5 There, with all who liv'd as strangers
While on earth, we hope to be;
Free from toils, from fears, from dangers,
Happy through eternity;
There we hope to see the Lamb,
And for ever praise his name.

HYMN CXCIX.

"*Thou art worthy, O Lord, to receive glory.*"—REV. iv. 11.

1 GLORY, glory everlasting
Be to him who bore the cross!
Who redeem'd our souls, by tasting
Death, the death deserv'd by us;
Spread his glory,
Who redeem'd his people thus.

2 His is love, 'tis love unbounded,
Without measure, without end;
Human thought is here confounded,
'Tis too vast to comprehend:
Praise the Saviour!
Magnify the sinner's friend.

3 While we hear the wondrous story
Of the Saviour's cross and shame,
Sing we "Everlasting glory
Be to God, and to the Lamb:"
Saints and angels,
Give ye glory to his name.

HYMN CC.

"*Sing aloud unto God our strength.*"—PSALM lxxxi. 1.

1 SING *aloud to God, our strength;*
He has brought us hitherto;
He will bring us home at length,
This the Lord our God will do:
Doubt not, for his word is stable;
Fear not, for his arm is able.

2 *Sing aloud to God, our strength;*
Sing with wonder of his love;
Who can tell its breadth and length?
Who below, or who above?
Who its depth and height can measure?
'Tis a rich, unbounded treasure!

3 *Sing aloud to God, our strength;*
He is with us where we go;
Fear we not the journey's length,
Fear we not the mighty foe:
All our foes shall be defeated,
And our journey be completed.

HYMN CCI.

"*Praise ye the Lord.*"—PSALM cxiii. 1.

1 LET us sing, for we have reason;
Let us join with those above;
Praise is never out of season;
Let us praise the God of love:
We indeed have cause to sing,
Jesus is our glorious King.

2 He whom angels view with wonder,
He whom angels always sing,
He who wields the awful thunder,
Is himself our glorious King:
O how blest his people are!
Blest who in his glory share.

3 When we reach the full enjoyment
Of the state where sorrows end,
Praise will be our sweet employment,
We shall praise the sinner's friend;
Him who wash'd us with his blood,
Sav'd, and brought us nigh to God.

4 But how diff'rent then our praises
From the praise we render now!
Well our coldness may amaze us,
When we think how much we owe;
But no coldness will remain,
When that glorious state we gain,

5 Yet our Lord accepts our praises,
Ev'n the praise we offer here;
He, on whom th' archangel gazes
With delight and holy fear,
Hears his people when they sing,
And accepts the praise they bring.

6 Sing we then our Saviour's praises,
Sing the praise of him we love;
When our Lord to heav'n shall raise us,
Then we'll join with those above;
Then, like them, unwearied sing,
Glory, glory to our King.

HYMN CCII.

"*Who loved me, and gave himself for me.*"—GAL. ii. 20.

1 WE sing of him who died,
Who died in love to us;
The Lord of life was crucified;
He saved his people thus.

2 This proof of love he gave;
No greater could be giv'n;
He shed his precious blood to save
And bring his saints to heav'n.

3 Redeem'd from earth and hell,
And made the heirs of heav'n;
How much they owe, what tongue can tell,
Whose sins are all forgiv'n?

4 A glorious hope they have;
A hope that grace supplies;
A hope that looks beyond the grave,
Of joy that never dies.

5 Exalt we then his name,
Whom all in heav'n adore;
And let us join to praise the Lamb,
The Lamb for evermore.

HYMN CCIII.

"*The love of Christ, which passeth knowledge.*"—EPH. iii. 19.

1 JESUS gave his life, to save us
From the foe who else would have us:
Such the proof of love he gave us,
Proof indeed!

2 Love exceeding that of brothers;
Love beyond the love of mothers;
Love surpassing far all others;
Love itself!

3 Praise we then his name for ever;
His is love that changes never;
And from him no force can sever
Those he loves!

HYMN CCIV.

"*Sing unto the Lord, O ye saints of his.*"—PSALM XXX. 4.

1 TO heaven's eternal King,
The praise of saints be giv'n;
His name, his glorious name, we sing,
Who fills the throne of heaven.

2 He once was found with men,
A man of sorrows he;
He bore his people's sentence then,
He bore it on the tree.

3 He suffered in their stead;
He saved his people thus;
The curse that fell upon his head
Was due, by right, to us.

4 'Twas love that brought him down,
The purest, strongest love;
He bore the cross, he won the crown,
And now he reigns above.

5 The praise of saints be giv'n
To him who worthy is;
He died on earth, he lives in heav'n;
Eternal praise be his.

HYMN CCV.

"*Sing unto the Lord, bless his name.*"—PSALM xcvi. 2.

1 WE sing of him who came from heav'n,
Who came to seek and save the lost;
And blest are they to whom 'tis giv'n,
To know him best and love him most.

2 No name in heav'n or earth like his,
'Tis one of grace, and power, and love;
How precious to the soul it is!
How far all other names above!

3 And yet, how little do we taste
Its sweetness, or its virtue prove!
O Lord our God, forgive the past,
And let us henceforth feel thy love!

4 To taste the sweetness of thy name,
To feel its sanctifying power,
Be this our one desire and aim,
Both now and to our dying hour.

5 And when that awful hour arrives,
Support and strength thy name supplies;
To those who nothing have, it gives
Assurance of eternal joys.

HYMN CCVI.

"*He that is our God is the God of salvation.*"—Psalm lxviii. 20.

1 PRAISE the God of our salvation;
Praise him, men of every nation;
Praise him, all in every station,
Who are his!

2 With a price the Lord has bought us,
Claimed us as his own, and taught us;
To himself the Lord has brought us;
Good he is!

3 In the day of his appearing,
Mourning ends, and doubt, and fearing;
Sweet the prospect is, and cheering;
Think on this!

HYMN CCVII.

"*The Lord reigneth; he is clothed with majesty.*"—Ps. cxiii. 1.

1 THE Lord Jehovah reigns,
His kingdom glorious is;
The world that he sustains
Is his, and only his.
His angels sing;
They praise their King:
They sing of him who lives for ever,
They sing of him who changes never.
The sight is resplendent,
The glory transcendent.
Come hither, ye ransom'd, your song be it heard,
The song to all others in heaven preferr'd;
The Lamb is its burthen, the Lamb that was slain;
The Lamb who redeem'd us, is worthy to reign;
The kingdom is his, and the glory and pow'r;
Let angels and saints sing his praise evermore.

HYMN CCVIII.

"*O come, let us sing unto the Lord.*"—PSALM XCV. 1.

1 SING of him who came to save us,
Bore our sin, and then forgave us;
Him who died and rose again:
Who can tell how much we owe him?
Where's the grateful love we shew him?
'Tis not thus we deal with men.

2 Saviour, had we dealt with others,
Be they friends or be they brothers,
As we know we've dealt with thee,
We had lost their love for ever:
Thine is love that changes never;
Who can owe thee more than we?

3 While we feel and mourn our coldness,
Still we would draw nigh with boldness
To thy throne, thy throne of grace:
There it is thy people find thee,
And of promises remind thee;
'Tis a safe and blessed place.

4 'Tis a place to sinners suited;
There it is that, though polluted,
We can converse hold with thee:
From it Satan fain would drive us,
And of good would thus deprive us,
But it must not, will not be.

5 Satan's power and purpose knowing,
Lord, behold thy people bowing,
Bowing low before thy throne.
Thine it is, O Lord, to save us,
When the mighty foe would have us;
And to thee we look alone.

6 From thyself let nothing take us;
Never leave us, nor forsake us,
Till we see thy face above:
Thither, when thy power shall raise us,
Then we look to sing thy praises,
Then to sing thy matchless love.

HYMN CCIX.

"*While we were yet sinners, Christ died for us.*"—ROM. v. 8.

1 WE praise and bless the Saviour's name,
His work is wondrous in our eyes;
From heav'n, in love to man, he came,
And on the cross for man he dies.
We know no other love like this;
No other love can equal his.

2 For man, the rebel and the foe,
He bore the curse upon the tree:
When sunk in guilt, and sunk in woe,
When all was lost, or seem'd to be.
'Twas then the Saviour saw his case;
'Twas then the Saviour shew'd his grace.

3 The theme is sweet, 'tis lofty too:
'Tis far too high for thought to scan;
For who is he can fully know
The love of God to guilty man?
Eternity alone will prove
Sufficient to unfold his love.

4 'Tis there the Saviour will unfold
The love that brought him down from heav'n;
Will tell what could not here be told;
Will give what could not here be giv'n,
How blest are they he owns as his!
Their spring of joy eternal is.

HYMN CCX.

"*Redeemed . . . with the precious blood of Christ.*"—1 Pet. i. 19.

1 SING of him, the Lord, who
Bought us with his blood,
And his name record, who
Stemm'd the mighty flood,
That which would have swept us
Into hell's abyss;
Sing of him who kept us
From a death like this.

2 Full it is of wonder,
This his work of love.
'Tis not here but yonder,
In his courts above,
All will be made known that
Now mysterious is;
Then his saints will own that
Power and love are his.

3 Happy day, when he will
Bring his people near;
What they are to be, will
Then to all appear;
"Sons of God" they are not
Own'd on earth or known;
Scorn'd of men, they care not,
Christ will bless his own.

4 Good it is to drink of
Christ's own cup below.
This will make them think of
Where they are to go,
There to be for ever,
With him where he is,
And to sorrow never,
There's a charm in this.

5 Better this, far better,
Than the worldling's mirth:
Sweeter, too, far sweeter,
Than the joys of earth:
They who love their master,
Will approve of this;
They will hold the faster,
To himself and his.

6 They will think more gladly,
Of their home above;
They will part less sadly
With the friends they love,
In their walk more steady
While they live below;
And, when called, more ready
To their Lord to go.

7 Sing of him, and spare not,
Join the blessēd throng;
Sing of him, and care not,
Who may blame your song.
Sing of him victorious,
Prophet, Priest, and King,
Sing of him, for glorious
Is the name we sing.

HYMN CCXI.

"*Praise ye the Lord.*"—PSALM cl. 1.

1 "PRAISE the Lord," 'tis meet we should,
He is great, and he is good,
He has brought salvation nigh,
Praise the Lord, we shall not die;
'Tis a work of sov'reign mercy,
Such beyond all controversy.

2 "Praise the Lord;" much cause we have,
Who but he, the Lord, could save?
Save us from the wrath to come,
Bring us to a blessēd home,
Where all good for ever centres,
Where no evil ever enters.

3 "Praise the Lord;" O shame it is,
That, professing we are his,
We produce so little fruit,
In his praises all but mute;
Lord, thy patience still endures us,
And thy mercy re-assures us.

4 "Praise the Lord;" his wonders tell.
From the lowest depths of hell,
We are sav'd by sov'reign grace,
And we hope to see his face.
Sing of him the Father gave us,
Sing of him who died to save us.

5 "Praise the Lord" with thankful songs,
Praise to him alone belongs;
Praise his right, and his alone,
His who sits upon the throne;
Praise by all to him be given,
All in earth, and all in heaven.

HYMN CCXII.

"*For I am a great King, saith the Lord of Hosts.*"—MAL. i. 14.

1 TO him who reigns in heaven above,
The God of grace, of pow'r, and love,
Let all his saints their tribute bring,
To him, their Saviour and their King.

2 His way is in the sea—his path
In waters deep its being hath.
His footsteps, who is he can trace?
Who search the wonders of his grace?

3 The theme is large, the theme is sweet:
For those who know the Saviour meet.
The grace it treats of suits their case:
'Tis grace indeed, 'tis sov'reign grace.

4 By grace alone his people stand:
They feel his love, they own his hand.
'Tis grace that makes them what they are:
The Saviour's crown, the Saviour's care.

5 How holy should his people be!
From care, from strife, from hatred free;
Oppos'd to sin, to every sin;
To that without, and that within.

6 Their work, to serve their master here,
With reverence, and godly fear;
Their hope, to see him as he is;
And dwell in heaven, with him and his.

HYMN CCXIII.

"*That he might destroy him that had the power of death.*"—
HEB. ii. 14.

1 SING of him, who left a throne,
His a throne all thrones above;
Sing of him, who stood alone,
With "the pow'rs of darkness strove,
Met them in the fearful fight,
Scatter'd all their proud array;
"Not by power, not by might,"
'Tis not thus he wins the day.

2 'Tis no strife of pow'r with pow'r;
Short the struggle, were it so;
Patient suff'ring suits this hour,
'Tis by death he deals the blow.
When he yields his latest breath,
Then the foe perceives his fall,
He who had the pow'r of death,
Vanquish'd lies, and gives up all.

3 He who late was seen to bow
On the cross, behold he lives!
Then a victim, victor now,
Lo! eternal life he gives,
Fruit of that mysterious hour,
When he seem'd as though he fell,
Yielding to superior pow'r,
Yet victorious, strange to tell.

4 Knowing this, his people can
Look on Death, without alarm;
Vanquish'd by "the Son of Man,"
He has lost his pow'r to harm.
Ye who have "in bondage been,
Through the fear of Death," be glad,
He who bore the guilt of sin,
Conquer'd Death, then be not sad!

HYMN CCXIV.

"*God so loved the world that he gave his only-begotten Son.*"—
JOHN iii. 16.

1 WE sing of him, and so we should,
The "only wise," the only good,
Of him who doeth all things well;
But who his wondrous deeds can tell?

2 The wonders that his arm has wrought,
Can any tell them as he ought?
His deeds below, his deeds above,
But chief the wonders of his love?

3 The love of God to fallen man,
Declare it as he ought, who can?
A depth it has, we cannot teach,
A height above, we cannot reach.

4 A breadth it has, a length too vast
For us to measure here below;
But wait the trumpet's final blast,
What's now unknown, we then shall know.

5 But can we ever fully scan
What "passeth knowledge?" He alone
Who all things knows, he only can,
Conceive the love he bears his own.

6 But let us not repine at this,
Enough is known, if known aright;
To bring us where our master is:
Where all is pure, and all is bright.

7 To him we gladly leave the rest,
To him, the Lord of earth and heaven;
He gives himself, of gifts the best;
With this all good is freely giv'n.

HYMN CCXV.

"*Greatly to be praised.*"—PSALM xlviii. 1.

1 PRAISES more than we can render,
More than men or angels can;
Be to Jesus, good and tender,
Who to rescue fallen man,
Came from yonder throne on high,
Came to suffer, bleed, and die!

2 Who can tell in earth or heaven,
What that bitter cup contain'd,
Which to Jesus then was given,
Which he drank, and which he drain'd?
Death itself was found therein,
Death, the full desert of sin.

3 But who knows the fearful meaning
Of that word? or who can tell
How the Saviour felt when screening
Sinners from the pains of hell?
'Tis a theme with wonder fraught,
One too high for human thought.

4 But enough is told, to bind us
To the cross, and keep us bound:
Those who seek us, there will find us,
There at least we *should* be found;
Waiting at the Saviour's feet,
'Tis the place for sinners meet.

HYMN CCXVI.

"*Sing unto the Lord, bless his name.*"—PSALM XXVI. 2.

1 SING of Jesus, sing for ever,
Of the love that changes never.
Who or what from him can sever
Those he makes his own?

2 With his blood the Lord has bought them;
When they knew him not, he sought them,
And from all their wand'rings brought them,
His the praise alone.

3 Through the desert Jesus leads them,
With the bread of heav'n he feeds them,
And through all the way he speeds them,
To their home above.

4 There they see the Lord who bought them,
Him who came from heaven, and sought them,
Him who by his Spirit taught them,
Him they serve and love.

5 Let his people sing with gladness,
Other mirth than this is madness,
Mirth it is that ends in sadness,
Be it far away.

6 'Tis the saints have solid treasure,
They can sing with holy pleasure,
And their joy will know no measure,
In the final day.

HYMN CCXVII.

"*Praise him for his mighty acts.*"—PSALM cl. 2.

1 TO him whose name is "love,"
Who left his throne above,
And dwelt, himself a man, with men:
To him who died to save,
Who slept within the grave,
And took the life he gave again.

2 To him, to whom is giv'n,
All pow'r in earth and heav'n,
Who sits at God's right hand above;
To him who intercedes,
Who for his people pleads,
Whom angels serve, whom angels love.

3 To him we soon shall see
In glorious majesty,
Appearing in the clouds of heav'n:
To him whose name we sing,
Our Saviour and our King,
Everlasting praise be giv'n.

HYMN CCXVIII.

"*Sing praises to our King.*"—PSALM xlvii. 6.

1 TO our Lord a throne is giv'n,
His the highest place in heav'n;
On his vesture shine the words,
"King of kings, and Lord of lords."

2 Heir of all things, rightful heir,
In the honour none can share;
Fruit of toil, and strife, and pain,
Hard the warfare, rich the gain.

3 Saviour, all is now thine own,
Sway the sceptre, fill the throne;
Thine the suff'ring and the toil,
Thine the glory and the spoil.

4 We, thy ransom'd people, sing,
Glory, glory to our King;
Strangers here, and far from home,
Thee we look for, soon to come.

5 Then, and only then, shall we
Gain our rest, and happy be;
Thus then should thy people pray,
Hasten, Lord, the glorious day.

HYMN CCXIX.

"*The Lord is good.*"—NAHUM i. 7.

1 SING of him who bore our guilt,
And for us the curse sustain'd:
'Tis on him our hope is built,
Bitter was the cup he drain'd:
Sing of him, 'tis meet we should,
Say ye, that "the Lord is good."

2 When we lay beneath our load;
When no arm but his could save;
Then the Lord his mercy shew'd,
Then the Lord our sin forgave:
Sing of him, 'tis meet we should,
Say ye, that "the Lord is good."

3 Blessed is his people's lot,
Happy they who bear his name:
God, their God, forgets them not,
Faithful he, and still the same.
Sing of him, 'tis meet we should,
Say ye, that "the Lord is good."

4 Forward look, a day is near,
When "the trump of God" shall sound,
Then will Jesus re-appear,
And his people's joy abound.
Sing of him, 'tis meet we should,
Say ye, that "the Lord is good."

HYMN CCXX.

"*Hallelujah.*"

1 COME praise the Lord, exalt his name,
Our Saviour and our King;
'Tis meet we should his love proclaim,
And hallelujah sing.

2 The theme is high, the work is sweet;
Your harps for concert string:
'Tis blessed thus in love to meet,
And hallelujah sing.

3 How great, how precious is his name!
How poor the praise we bring!
His people still should own his claim,
And hallelujah sing.

4 Sustain'd by faith, and upward borne,
As if on eagle's wing,
We praise our Lord, forget to mourn,
And hallelujah sing.

5 A day will come, its dawn we greet,
When heav'n itself shall ring;
When all the saints with joy shall meet,
And hallelujah sing.

HYMN CCXXI.

"*His great love wherewith he loved us.*"—EPH. xi. 4.

1 THE praise of heav'n to him is due,
To him who died, ye saints, for you:
Mysterious is the Saviour's love,
It brought him down from heav'n above.

2 There's something here we cannot teach;
'Tis something that we cannot reach;
'Tis deep as the abyss below,
'Tis high as heav'n, what can we know?

3 But sweet it is to taste this love,
'Tis far all other joys above;
'Tis more than we can well express,
'Tis peace, and joy, and blessedness.

4 What else but love, mysterious love,
Could bring the Saviour from above?
Could make him lay his glory by,
And come to suffer, and to die?

5 This love we sing, and so we ought,
This love surpassing human thought:
Th' unfolding of this love will be
The work that fills eternity.

HYMN CCXXII.

"*Hosanna to the Son of David.*"—MATT. xxi. 9.

1 YE who know the Lord, draw nigh:
Be ye fill'd with holy joy;
Sing of him who came to die,
Hosanna to the Son of David.

2 Sing of him the Father gave,
Sing of him who died to save,
Vanquish'd death, and burst the grave.
Hosanna, &c.

3 Sing the Saviour's grace and love,
Things the world knows nothing of;
Sing the name all names above.
Hosanna, &c.

4 Jesus, 'tis thy name we sing,
Thine, our Saviour and our King,
Heav'n with triumph soon shall ring.
Hosanna, &c.

5 Here 'tis faith, but there 'tis sight,
All in heav'n is pure and bright:
Praise his name who gives us light.
Hosanna, &c.

HYMN CCXXIII.

"*Washed us from our sins in his own blood.*"—REV. i. 5.

1 TO him who wash'd them in his blood,
The praise of saints is due;
'Tis he who brings them back to God,
He gives them glory too.

2 The Lord with clouds will soon appear:
We cannot tell the day;
There's nothing pure or stable here,
The whole must pass away.

3 New heav'ns, new earth, will then arise,
Where saints shall happy be;
"The King," reveal'd before their eyes,
"In beauty" they shall see.

4 A blessed sight! 'Tis wondrous too,
'Tis passing strange, that *we*,
That sinners should be favour'd so,
Be giv'n the Lord to see.

5 To see him as he is in heav'n;
And in his glory share;
To sing of grace, of sin forgiv'n,
With all his people there.

6 Then let us raise our thankful songs,
To him who "worthy" is;
Eternal praise to him belongs,
Eternal praise be his.

HYMN CCXXIV.

"*Take a psalm.*"—PSALM lxxxi. 2.

1 GLORY to God above;
Object and source of love,
Ever the same.
Maker of all he is,
Heaven, earth, and hell are his:
Glory, ye saints, in this,
Praise ye his name.

2 They who forgiven are,
They who his favour share,
Joyful may be.
Joyful in him they love:
Joyful in him they prove,
Gracious all thought above;
Blessēd is he.

3 Praise our exalted Lord;
Praise him with one accord;
Praise him with songs.
Hymns to his honour sing,
Joyful your tribute bring,
To our eternal King,
Honour belongs.

HYMN CCXXV.

"*Forget not all his benefits.*"—Psalm ciii. 2.

1 SING of him who gives us
More than worlds could buy:
When we come, receives us,
Answers when we cry.
Sing of him for ever;
Who is like to him?
Good, and changing never,
Glorious is the theme.

2 Sing of his appearing,
Welcome be the day;
Hope is sweet, and cheering,
Lord, make no delay.
Come from heav'n, we pray thee,
End our toil and strife;
Lord, let nothing stay thee,
Bring us endless life.

HYMN CCXXVI.

"*Trust thou in him.*"—JOB xxxv. 14.

1 SING the Saviour's praises,
Joyful is the theme;
He to glory raises
Those who trust in him.
Trust in him for ever,
They are blest who do;
Jesus changes never,
Good he is and true;
Sing the Saviour's praises evermore.

HYMN CCXXVII.

"*Ye shall be free indeed.*"—JOHN viii. 36.

1 NOW praise we, and bless we, the Lord who has sav'd us,
Has bought us, and freed us from him who enslav'd us,
How glorious this liberty is!
While men, in their folly, refuse and despise it,
The people who have it, know well how to prize it,
No freedom is equal to this.

2 Redeem'd with a price, that more precious than gold is,
A price, one whose value too great to be told is,
The blood of "the Lamb" that was shed.
When the ransom requir'd was his life, and no other,
A friend he was found, loving more than a brother,
And offer'd himself in our stead.

3 This love is so strange, that no language can teach it,
So deep and so high, that our thought cannot reach it,
We wonder, O Lord, and adore.
Let us live to his glory, who died to redeem us,
Devotion, and zeal, and exertion beseem us:
'Tis meet we should loiter no more.

4 Enable us, Lord, for thou only canst do it,
Our strength is but weakness, our master, we know it,
For such we have proved it to be.
Forgive us, our Saviour, forgive us what past is,
Sufficient thy grace, we are sure, to the last is,
Henceforth let us glorify thee.

HYMN CCXXVIII.

"*O Lord, I will praise thee.*"—ISAIAH xii. 1.

1 PRAISE the Saviour, ye who know him,
Who can tell how much we owe him?
Gladly let us render to him,
All we are and have.

2 Jesus is the name that charms us,
That for conflict fits and arms us;
Nothing moves, and nothing harms us,
When we trust in him.

3 Trust in him, ye saints, for ever,
He is faithful, changing never;
Neither force nor guile can sever
Those he loves from him.

4 Keep us, Lord, O keep us cleaving
To thyself, and still believing,
Till the time of our receiving
Promis'd joy in heav'n.

5 Then we shall be where we would be,
Then we shall be what we should be;
That which is not now, nor could be,
Will be then our own.

HYMN CCXXIX.

" *Thine is the kingdom, and the power, and the glory.*"—
MATT. vi. 13.

1 TO him alone, whose name is love,
To him who left his throne above,
To him who liv'd, and died for men,
Was in the grave. and rose again.

2 To him who is gone up on high,
Beyond the clouds, beyond the sky,
" In heav'n itself" to intercede,
And with his blood for men to plead.

3 To him who soon will come again,
To bless his people, blessed then;
To him be honour, praise, and power:
To him be glory evermore.

HYMN CCXXX.

" *His own self bare our sins.*"—1 PET. ii. 24.

1 EXALT the name of him who bore
The sentence pass'd on us;
Exalt his name for evermore,
Who sav'd his people thus.

2 'Tis strange, 'tis passing strange, that he
Who reigns in heav'n above,
Should bear our curse upon the tree:
But thus he shows his love.

3 The love that without measure is,
The love of God to man;
No love can be compared to his,
'Tis vast, too vast to scan.

4 We praise the name of him who shed
His precious blood to save;
Of him who lay among the dead,
Lay buried in the grave.

5 Of him who rose again, and lives,
Who lives in heav'n above;
Of him who grace and glory gives,
The God of power and love.

6 Of him who soon from heav'n will come,
In pow'r and majesty,
And take his waiting people home,
With him in heav'n to be.

HYMN CCXXXI.

"*I live for ever.*"—Deut. xxxii. 40.

1 SING of him who lives for ever,
Praise his name who changes never,
This our aim, and our endeavour,
Him to serve.

2 Him who set his love upon us,
Strange to tell it, woo'd and won us,
Makes us blest, though all should shun us,
Sing of him.

3 Praise his name, for ever praise it,
'Tis too high for us to raise it;
Strong his arm, there's nothing stays it;
Nothing can.

4 Royal majesty his own is,
That whereon he sits, a throne is;
And the kingdom his alone is—
His alone.

5 His is glory never wasting;
His a throne for ever lasting;
This endures. The rest are hasting
To their fall.

6 Happy they whose God the Lord is;
Though their hope by man abhorr'd is;
God himself their great reward is—
Great indeed.

HYMN CCXXXII.

"Who shall separate us from the love of Christ?"—
ROM. viii. 35.

1 BLESSED be the Lord for ever!
Blessed be his glorious name;
Nothing from his love shall sever
Him he owns. Nor sword, nor flame,
Nor life, nor death, nor that which is,
Nor that to come; these all are his.

2 Blessed be the Lord for ever!
"Full of grace and truth" is he;
Let us cleave to him, and never
Shrink from duty, though it be
To nature hard, and full of pain,
The Lord his people will sustain.

3 Blessed be the Lord for ever!
He has rais'd us from the pit
Where we lay, without endeavour
To relieve ourselves, and fit
For ruin. This was love, indeed;
Relief it was in time of need.

4 Blessed be the Lord for ever!
What his love has here begun,
He will perfect. He will never
Leave his work in part undone.
The Lord will keep us by his pow'r,
Will keep us to the final hour.

5 Then his work will be completed,
When the people of his love
(Conflicts past, and foes defeated)
Shall obtain their place above.
Until it comes, O keep us, Lord;
Thine help in time of need afford.

HYMN CCXXXIII.

"*Salvation to our God which sitteth upon the throne, and unto the Lamb.*"—Rev. vii. 10.

1 TO him that sits upon the throne,
And to the Lamb, be glory given;
'Tis here we bow, and here alone,
And here we join the praise of heav'n.

2 The Lamb is worthy to receive
The tribute of his people's songs;
By him it is his people live,
To him it is their praise belongs.

3 Their robes that were so stained before,
Are white as snow, tho' washed in blood—
The blood of him who meekly bore
Their curse, when in their place he stood.

4 The everlasting crown be his,
Whose blood upon the cross was shed—
The Lord, who only worthy is,
Who liveth now, who once was dead.

5 To him that sits upon the throne,
And to the Lamb, be glory giv'n.
This song be ours, and this alone,
This song on earth, and this in heav'n.

HYMN CCXXXIV.

"*If these should hold their peace, the stones would immediately cry out.*"—Luke xix. 40.

1 HE whom all the prophets told of,
In the temple stands;
Him the elders would lay hold of,
With unhallow'd hands.

2 But the children, taught to know him
As their rightful King,
Offer loyal homage to him,
And hosannas sing.

3 When they saw the Lord, they could not
But confess their King;
If they could, then others would not,
For the stones would sing.

4 "Son of David," reign for ever;
"Heir of all things" thou.
Thine a kingdom ending never;
All to thee shall bow.

5 To "the Son of David" sing we;
Loud hosannas sing;
And our loyal tribute bring we,
This is Israel's King.

6 Join we the celestial chorus,
Praise our common Lord;
Praise we him who suffer'd for us;
Be his name ador'd.

HYMN CCXXXV.

"*And he came and took the book out of the right hand of him that sat upon the throne.*"—Rev. v. 7.

1 TO him who left his throne,
And dwelt with man below;
To him who stood alone,
And fought the mighty foe;
To David's Son and Lord,
Who reigns in earth and heav'n;
To him, th' incarnate Word,
Eternal praise be giv'n.

2 He worthy is alone,
To take the awful book
From him who fills the throne,
Or on its page to look.
'Tis he who breaks the seals,
Unfolds the sacred roll;
And what lay hid reveals,
The Lamb, he does the whole.

3 Of him, then, let us sing;
Of him who worthy is;
Our Saviour and our King,
Eternal praise be his.
He shed his precious blood;
He suffer'd death for us;
Who else, or would, or could
Have sav'd a people thus?

HYMN CCXXXVI.

"*Let us exalt his name together.*"—PSALM xxxiv. 3.

1 PRAISE the Lord,
Christ THE WORD,
Praise his name for ever dear;
His is love
Far above
All we know, or can know here.

2 He it was
Bore the cross,
All its pain, and all its shame;
And for us,
Died he thus,
Praise we then his glorious name.

3 'Tis a name
Mark'd with shame,
Here below it ever was;
But above,
All is love,
Love to him who bore the cross.

4 There's a race
Sav'd by grace,
Here below, who love his name;
Theirs it is,
Theirs, as his,
Theirs to meet reproach and shame.

5 Shrink we not,
Base the thought,
Shrink we not from human scorn;
'Tis our lot,
Grieve we not,
Sing ye, who of God are born.

6 Yet a while,
And his smile,
His whose coming draweth near,
Will repay,
Well it may,
All his people suffer here.

HYMN CCXXXVII.

"*The only wise God.*"—1 TIM. i. 17.

1 TO him, "the only wise,"
Who reigns in heaven above;
To him be praise beyond the skies,
To him whose name is "LOVE."

2 Let us, beneath the skies,
To whom his grace is known,
Exalt his name, "the only wise,"
Exalt his name alone.

3 To us this grace is giv'n,
To us on earth who dwell;
That we should be the heirs of heav'n,
Who once were heirs of hell.

4 'Tis blessed so to be,
And, O what thanks are due,
To him who saved and set us free,
Our God and Saviour too.

5 To him our praise be given,
To him who fills the throne;
To him who reigns in earth and heaven,
To him, and him alone.

6 We hope to see his face,
With all his saints to be;
And sing with them a Saviour's grace,
Throughout eternity.

HYMN CCXXXVIII.

"*Sing ye praises with understanding.*"—PSALM xlvii. 7.

1 SING we praise to God above,
"Sing we praise with understanding;"
Praise we him, who, mov'd by love,
All creating, all commanding,
Came from heav'n, that he might save,
And his life for sinners gave.

2 Blessed be the Saviour's name,
Blessed be his name for ever;
His was pain, and grief, and shame,
His the cross. Forget it, never;
His the curse to sinners due,
His to die, ye saints, for you.

3 Sing we praise, to Jesus sing,
"Sing we praise with understanding;"
Let the saints their tribute bring,
His is love their praise demanding;
Love that is, and ever was,
What nor end nor measure has.

4 Sing we praise, for this is right,
"Sing we praise with understanding;"
Soon we hope to take our flight,
And ascend, our wings expanding,
To the place where Jesus is,
There to live with him and his,

5 Then, indeed, the saints shall sing,
Sing they shall "with understanding;"
Then they shall behold their King,
All ordaining, all commanding;
Nothing then shall wanting be
To their full felicity.

HYMN CCXXXIX.

"*Sing praises to God.*"—Psalm xlvii. 6.

1 PRAISE, O Lord, we know becomes us,
Praise to thee, for thou art good;
Sad it is that sin benumbs us,
And we cannot, though we would.
Send thy Spirit from above,
And our hearts will glow with love.

2 When our hearts with love are glowing,
Then our pleasure is in praise;
Come, O Lord, this grace bestowing,
Then our cheerful songs we'll raise;
Then with feeling will we sing,
Glory, glory to our King.

3 When we think how much we owe thee,
Then it is we feel our shame;
Were we such as those who know thee
Should be, how we'd love thy name!
How we'd glory in the cross,
Counting all for it but loss.

4 Lord, how cold our love to thee is,
Cold to what it ought to be;
Yet we know how blessed he is,
He who lives, O Lord, to thee:
He who deeply feels thy love:
He whose joys are from above.

5 Such we know thy people should be;
   Saviour! cause it to be so;
Such we trust thy people would be,
   But the work is thine to do.
Pow'r and grace are thine, O Lord,
Save, according to thy word.

6 All the things that here surround us,
   Fleeting are and vain at best:
Many chains that erewhile bound us,
   Thou hast broken—break the rest:
Ev'ry one that still remains,
Break it, Lord; we loath our chains.

HYMN CCXL.

"*Ye are not your own.*"—1 Cor. vi. 19.

1 WE sing the praise of him who gave
   His precious life for us;
'Twas wonderful at all to save,
   But more, to do it thus.

2 How awful must our state have been,
   When nothing but *his* blood,
Who gave us life, could make us clean,
   And bring us back to God!

3 The more he suffer'd for our sake,
   The more his kindness is;
But, oh! what poor returns we make,
   For grace and love like his!

4 He might expect that we would give
   Our hearts to him alone,
And, bought with blood, that we would live
   As his, and not our own.

5 But we, alas! too oft forget
How great his kindness is;
And, though redeem'd, we wander yet
From him who made us his.

6 For this our hearts are cold and dead,
For this our eyes are dim;
The crown is fallen from our head,
Because we stray from him.

7 Lord, we confess our shame, and mourn
That we have prov'd so base;
To thee again, to thee we turn,
O save us by thy grace!

HYMN CCXLI.

"*Sing praises unto his name, for it is pleasant.*"—
PSALM CXXXV. 3.

1 THE Saviour bears a lovely name,
Of sacred pow'rs possest;
It takes away the sinner's shame,
And gives his conscience rest.

2 No name on earth is half so great,
Howe'er extoll'd by fame;
Nor can celestial tongues repeat
A more exalted name.

3 Though music has the pow'r to please,
(And oft I feel its pow'r,)
The name of Jesus sweeter is,
And captivates me more.

4 However sweet the flow'r that spreads
Its perfume o'er the fields,
His name a richer fragrance sheds,
And more refreshment yields.

5 Sweet name! the sinner's blest relief,
His med'cine, food, and joy!
'Tis help in trouble, ease in grief,
'Tis gold without alloy.

6 Jesus, thy name is dear to me,
It saves me from my foes;
Arm'd with its pow'r, I need not flee,
Though earth and hell oppose.

7 In many painful conflicts past,
Thy name has brought me through;
Nor wilt thou leave the worm at last,
Whom thou hast sav'd till now.

8 No; in thy heav'n I shall appear,
And cease to know "in part;"
My strengthen'd faculties will bear
To see thee as thou art.

9 Then shall my cup of joy o'erflow
With still increasing store;
My only heav'n, thy name to know
And praise thee evermore.

HYMN CCXLII.

"*Who can shew forth all his praise?*"—PSALM cvi. 2.

1 TO God, my Saviour, praise is due,
A debt I never can discharge;
For when I bring the sum to view,
I find it infinitely large.

2 "Goodness and mercy" have pursued
My steps since I have seen the light;
Favours each day have been renew'd,
My sun has shone benignly bright.

3 But since the Saviour's name I've known,
And seen how bright his glories shine,
My mercies centre all in *one*,
That I am his, and he is mine.

4 With other things I can dispense,
The world and all its joys forego;
But oh! my loss would be immense,
If I should cease the LORD to know.

5 This is the central point of bliss,
'Tis all I ask, 'tis all I need;
My soul is rich, possess'd of this,
Without it, I am poor indeed.

6 Nor need I grieve because I owe
A debt that may the world amaze;
Thro' endless years my praise shall flow,
And what is heav'n but endless praise?

HYMN CCXLIII.

"*Bless the Lord, O my soul.*"—PSALM ciii. 1.

1 BLESS, my soul, the name of Jesus,
He is God, and he alone;
All thy wants and thy diseases
Are to him, the Saviour, known:
He forgives and heals them too,
All the praise to him is due.

2 O my soul, how satisfying
Are the joys that spring from truth!
Everlasting strength supplying,
God himself renews thy youth;
Thou shalt mount on eagles' wings,
Far above all earthly things.

3 As a father kind and tender
Pitying views his children here,
God so pities those who render
To his name a filial fear;
They are taught in him to trust,
And he knows they are but dust.

4 Human life is short and wasting,
Happy they whom God forgives!
Mercy is from everlasting,
And to everlasting lives;
They who know his name shall be
Blessed through eternity.

5 Bless the Lord, ye angels, bless him,
Praise him, all ye hosts above;
Ye his saints on earth, confess him,
Objects of his grace and love:
Let the world his love proclaim,
Bless, my soul, the Saviour's name.

HYMN CCXLIV.

"*Which things the angels desire to look into.*"—1 PET. i. 12.

1 ANGELS heard with admiration
How th' eternal counsel ran;
Wonder'd at the great salvation,
Wonder'd at the gracious plan,
Angels wonder'd
At the love of God to man.

2 Angels, with profound amazement,
Saw th' eternal King come down;
In the time of his abasement,
Saw the Saviour stand alone;
Angels saw him
Then deserted by his own.

3 Angels saw the Saviour dying
On the cross, in love to men;
Angels saw his body lying
In the tomb among the slain:
O how awful
Sin appear'd to angels then!

4 Angels saw him rise victorious
From the tomb in which he lay;
Never sight was seen so glorious
As what angels saw that day,
When the Saviour
Rose, and death resign'd his prey.

5 Hark! what bursts of acclamation
Through th' eternal arches ring;
Angels now ascribe salvation
To the everlasting King:
Loud their praises,
"Glory to the LAMB" they sing.

6 Praise the LAMB, ye saints adore him,
Ye for whom he shed his blood;
Bow with angels, bow before him,
Make his glory known abroad:
Saints and angels
Join to praise THE LAMB OF GOD.

HYMN CCXLV.

"*Bound in affliction and iron.*"—PSALM cvii. 10.

1 JOYFUL let us raise our voices,
Pris'ners once, but now set free;
As the bird releas'd, rejoices
And exults in liberty;
So the slaves of sin, when freed,
Feel that they are free indeed.

2 Bound we were with iron fetters,
Galling was the yoke we bore;
Debtors we, insolvent debtors,
Yet unfelt the chains we wore:
Sleep had all our pow'rs opprest,
And we dreamt that this was rest.

3 But, as with a voice of thunder,
Were we roused from sleep profound;
Then our souls were fill'd with wonder,
All was new and strange around:
Grievous then our chains appear'd;
Much we felt, and much we fear'd.

4 Then the voice of mercy sounded
Sweet as music in our ears;
"Grace abounds where sin abounded;"
Grace it is removes our fears;
Grace has power to cheer our hearts,
Grace, a holy joy imparts.

5 Grace we sing, "the grace of Jesus;"
Grace, the spring of hope to man;
Grace, that from our bondage frees us;
Grace, too high for thought to scan;
Grace, the theme that sinners love;
Grace, a theme all themes above.

HYMN CCXLVI.

"*Glory to God in the highest.*"—LUKE ii. 14.

1 GLORY to God on high!
Peace upon earth, and joy!
Good will to man!
Ye who the blessing prove,
Join with the hosts above!
Sing ye a Saviour's love,
Too vast to scan.

2 Mercy and truth unite,
This is a joyful sight!
All sights above.
Jesus the curse sustains;
Bitter the cup he drains;
Nothing for us remains,
Nothing but love!

3 Love, that no tongue can teach;
Love, that no thought can reach;
No love like his:
Heav'n is its blessēd source;
Death could not stop its course;
Nothing can stay its force;
Matchless it is.

4 Join, then, this love to sing;
Join to exalt our King,
Sinners forgiv'n!
To the great One in three,
Honour and majesty
Now and for ever be,
Here and in heav'n.

DOXOLOGIES.

I.

TO the Father praise be giv'n,
To the Son, and to the Spirit;
Thine it is, the God of heav'n,
Isra'l's praises to inherit.
Lord, we own thy claim, and bow;
Manifest thy presence now.
Thine the kingdom, thine the pow'r;
Thine the glory evermore.
Hallelujah! Amen.

II.

TO the Father, to the Son,
To the Spirit praise be giv'n;
One in three, and three in one,
Lord of earth, and Lord of heav'n.
Hallelujah! Amen.

III.

THE Father praise, and praise the Son,
The Spirit praise, the three in one;
To Father, Son, and Spirit be,
Eternal praise, the One in three.
Hallelujah! Amen.

State of Believers, a Warfare.

HYMN CCXLVII.

"*He teacheth my hands to war.*"—PSALM xviii. 34.

1 BELOV'D associates in the strife
That ends in blessed peace,
A life of conflict is our life,
From war we must not cease.

2 The soldiers of the cross must fight,
Till life itself is past;
The foe assails them day and night,
Assails them to the last.

3 But let us still remember this,
To faith it stands disclos'd,
The Lord, who saves us, greater is
Than all who are oppos'd.

4 We need not fly, we need not fear,
Since he who reigns above,
In all our conflicts will be near
The people of his love.

5 Our foes are strong, and many too,
Yet why these doubts and fears?
For while we keep our Lord in view,
Our strength is more than theirs.

6 If thus we face the adverse pow'rs,
If thus we meet the strife,
The victory will then be ours,
And ours a crown of life.

HYMN CCXLVIII.

"*And David put them off him.*"—1 SAM. xvii. 39.

1 HAD David done as Saul advis'd,
And with *his* arms the conflict tried,
His strength might well have been despis'd,
And David, not his foe, had died.

2 So we, when call'd to meet the foe,
All human counsel must refuse;
For man, though wise, can never know
What arms we need, and ought to use.

3 Yet are we apt, too apt to try
What arms supplied by man can do;
But soon we throw such armour by,
As useless, and as cumbrous too.

4 We learn to go as David went,
Confiding in the Lord of Hosts:
A pebble and a sling, when sent
By him, will silence hostile boasts.

5 They who in Israel's God confide
May boldly venture to the field;
The feeblest arms by him supplied
Are better than the sword and shield.

HYMN CCXLIX.

"*He will deliver me.*"—1 Sam. xvii. 37.

1 HE who sav'd us when assaulted
By the lion and the bear,
High on yonder throne exalted,
Stoops to save his people here:
He will save his servants now,
He will lay the giant low.

2 Who is this that thus defieth
Those whom God preserves from harm?
Who is this that thus relieth
On his arm, his own right arm?
Short his arm and feeble is,
Feeble in a strife like this.

3 With a sword he comes to meet us,
With a spear and with a shield;
Thinking quickly to defeat us,
And to chase us from the field:
Vain his boast, his hope is vain,
He shall lie among the slain.

4 In *that* name we come to meet him,
In that name, high over all;
In that name we shall defeat him,
And before it he shall fall:
Vain the shield, the spear, the sword,
Vain his help against the Lord.

5 And his people shall with wonder
Look on him they feared before;
When they see their foe brought under,
When his strength is now no more:
Then shall Israel sing indeed,
When from fear and danger freed.

HYMN CCL.

"*Fight the good fight of faith.*"—1 Tim. vi. 12.

1 CHRISTIANS an arduous fight maintain,
Nor do they hope or *wish* for peace,
Till they their heav'nly mansion gain,
Then, not before, their conflicts cease.

2 Them whom they now account as foes,
They once without a blush obey'd;
And liv'd in amity with those,
Who, while they wore a smile, betray'd.

3 Nor did they see the chains they wore;
Or, if they saw, felt no alarm:
The yoke contentedly they bore,
Till God himself dissolv'd the charm.

4 Awaken'd then as from a sleep,
And taught from whence their danger rose,
They flew to arms, resolv'd to keep
No terms with such deceitful foes.

5 With earth and hell in arms combin'd,
And with a heart as false as they,
Are saints engag'd, nor rest will find,
Till they have reached the realms of day.

6 The fight unequal seems, 'tis true;
It would be so but for *his* grace,
Who arms provides, and courage too,
With which his saints the foe may face.

7 He who appear'd on David's side,
When match'd with his gigantic foe,
Is still the same, and will provide
For all his struggling saints below.

8 And when the last great foe appears,
He'll find them proof against his pow'r;
For God, *their* God, will quell their fears,
And save them in a dying hour.

9 This conflict past, the work is done,
They'll see their enemies no more;
The final victory is won,
And then they reach the heav'nly shore.

10 In robes of white they stand array'd,
The palm's triumphant branch they bear;
Adorn'd with crowns that never fade,
Before their King they all appear.

11 And while they sing before his throne,
The Lamb, the Lamb inspires their songs;
Salvation comes from him alone;
To him eternal praise belongs.

HYMN CCLI.

"*For we wrestle not against flesh and blood, but against principalities, against powers.*"—EPH. vi. 12.

1 HARK, 'tis a martial sound!
To arms, ye saints, to arms!
Your foes are gathering round,
And peace has lost its charms;
Prepare the helmet, sword, and shield,
The trumpet calls you to the field.

2 No common foes appear,
To dare you to the fight,
But such as own no fear,
And glory in their might:
The pow'rs of darkness are at hand;
Resist, or bow to their command.

3 An arm of flesh must fail
In such a strife as this;
He only can prevail,
Whose arm immortal is:
'Tis heav'n itself the strength must yield,
And weapons fit for such a field.

4 And heav'n supplies them too;
The Lord, who never faints,
Is greater than the foe,
And he is with his saints:
Thus arm'd, they venture to the fight,
Thus arm'd, they put their foes to flight.

5 And when the strife is past,
On yonder peaceful shore
They shall repose at last,
And see their foes no more;
The fruits of victory enjoy,
And never more their arms employ.

HYMN CCLII.

"*Hold that fast which thou hast, that no man take thy crown.*"—
Rev. iii. 11.

1 O ISRA'L to thy tents repair!
Why thus secure on hostile ground?
Thy King commands thee to beware,
For many foes thy camp surround.

2 The trumpet gives a martial strain;
O Isra'l! gird thee for the fight;
Arise, the combat to maintain,
And put thine enemies to flight.

3 Thou shouldst not sleep as others do;
Awake! be vigilant! be brave!
The coward, and the sluggard too,
Must wear the fetters of the slave.

4 A nobler lot is cast for thee,
A kingdom thine beyond the skies:
With such a hope shall Isra'l flee,
Or yield, through weariness, the prize?

5 No! let a careless world repose,
And slumber on through life's short day,
While Isra'l to the conflict goes,
And bears the glorious prize away.

HYMN CCLIII.

"*He teacheth my hands to war.*"—PSALM xviii. 34.

1 ARISE, ye saints, arise,
The Lord our leader is;
The foe before his banner flies,
For victory is his.

2 Behold! he leads the way;
We'll follow where he goes;
We cannot fail to win the day,
Since he subdues our foes.

3 Lead on, Almighty Lord,
Lead on to victory;
Encourag'd by the bright reward,
With joy we'll follow thee.

4 We'll follow thee, our guide,
Our Saviour and our King;
We'll follow thee, through grace supplied
From heav'n's eternal spring.

5 We hope to see the day
When toil and strife shall cease;
We then shall cast our arms away,
And dwell in endless peace.

6 This hope supports us here,
It makes our burdens light;
'Twill serve our drooping hearts to cheer
Till faith shall end in sight:

7 Till, of the prize possest,
We hear of war no more;
And, O sweet thought! for ever rest
On yonder peaceful shore.

HYMN CCLIV.

"Help us, O Lord our God! for we rest on thee, and in thy name we go against this multitude."—2 CHRON. xiv. 11.

1 MANY foes our march opposing,
Lord, we turn our eyes to thee,
All our wants and fears disclosing,
Helpless to thy pow'r we flee;
O protect us!
Neither skill nor pow'r have we.

2 See our foes with proud defiance
Call thy people to the fight!
Lord, on thee is our reliance,
Thee whose arm is cloth'd with might:
Saviour, guard us!
Let not thine be put to flight.

3 Not of human armour boasting,
Do we venture to the field;
In defence so feeble trusting,
Soon we would be forc'd to yield:
God of Israel!
Be thyself our sword and shield.

4 On thy faithfulness relying,
We may boldly meet the foe;
All his boasted pow'r defying,
While we come defended so:
God will save us;
This our enemies shall know.

5 Let the fainting soul be cheerful,
Let the timid now be brave:
Why should they be faint or fearful,
Whom the Lord delights to save?
Whom he rescues,
Satan can no more enslave.

HYMN CCLV.

"*He that overcometh shall inherit all things.*"—Rev. xxi. 7.

1 IF our warfare be laborious,
Soon the strife will reach a close:
Rest is sweet, secure, and glorious,
That from prosp'rous warfare flows:
Doubly precious
After labour is repose.

2 Once our choice was peace inglorious,
Then we yielded to our foes;
Warfare now the most laborious,
Ev'n with all its toils we choose:
Glorious warfare!
Leading to secure repose.

3 Are there many foes before us,
Standing to oppose our way?
Yet they shall not overpow'r us;
This with boldness we may say,
Since Jehovah
Keeps his people night and day.

4 Are we blind and prone to error?
God vouchsafes to be our guide;
Are we faint and full of terror?
He himself is on our side;
'Tis sufficient:
God our Saviour will provide.

5 When through him we prove victorious,
Then will strife and labour cease;
Then our triumph will be glorious,
Then his people dwell at ease:
And their portion
Will be everlasting peace.

HYMN CCLVI.

"*For the battle is the Lord's.*"—1 SAM. xvii. 47.

1 YES, "the battle is the Lord's,"
Blessed be his name it is.
These are good and faithful words,
And remember they are his;
'Tis the Lord himself who said it,
Be it ours to give him credit.

2 This can make the timid brave,
This can make the feeble strong.
He who able is to save,
He to whom the worlds belong,
Says, his people's cause his own is,
And to conquer his alone is.

3 Yes, "the battle is the Lord's,"
Well for us that so it is;
Strength and courage this affords,
All is ours, if we are his;
who timid are be cheerful,
should God's elect be fearful?

4 Yet we often fearful are;
Often do we sheath the sword;
Peace we think of then, not war,
And we thus offend the Lord:
Then he lets the foe assail us,
And our strength and courage fail us.

5 No, we must not think of peace,
Never, till the day is won;
Then it is our conflicts cease;
Then it is our work is done;
Then we may put off our armour,
But till then resist the charmer.

HYMN CCLVII.

"*Be strong and of a good courage.*"—DEUT. xxxi. 6.

1 COURAGE, ye who fighting are,
With a foe ye feel, but see not.
'Tis the Lord conducts the war,
Of his work forgetful be not:
Follow him, and nothing fear,
Comrades, there's a blessing here.

2 That in vain we labour not,
Here we have a sweet assurance;
Hardship is the soldier's lot,
Ours be patience and endurance:
For the day of conflict ends,
And the triumph makes amends.

3 Yours the prize will be ere long,
For the final day at hand is;
"Quit yourselves like men," "be strong,"
This our master's own command is;
Be like men who will not yield,
Men who will not quit the field.

4 Let us not forget 'tis he,
He, and he alone, that makes us
Strong for fight, if strong we be;
Lost we are, if he forsakes us;
Feeble in ourselves we are,
And unequal to the war.

5 Gracious is the Lord to hear,
And his arm is nothing shorten'd;
Why, then, should his people fear?
Why grow pale, like men dishearten'd?
Strong the Lord is, strong to save,
And in him our strength we have.

6 Fellow-soldiers, fear we not,
Though the passes all be guarded;
Fight we must, and fight we ought,
Though oppos'd, and though retarded,
Yet we shall prevail at last,
And with joy review the past.

HYMN CCLVIII.

"*The Captain of their salvation.*"—Heb. ii. 10.

1 THE Saviour leads his people on,
To combat and to conquest leads,
The soldiers and their chief are one,
The fruit is theirs, and his the deeds.

2 His royal banner when he waves,
A shout is heard through all his host;
The arm is then display'd that saves,
The arm in which his people boast.

3 They shrink not from the conflict then,
Though timid and though feeble too,
His people "quit themselves like men,"
With confidence they meet the foe.

4 His arm, they know, sufficient is,
Though foes unnumber'd should appear;
They know the people that are his,
May follow him and nothing fear.

5 They smile at danger when they see
Their chief advance to meet the foe,
A surer pledge of victory
His presence is, than sword or bow.

6 At sight of him, opposing hosts
Are fill'd with terror and dismay,
His presence quells their proudest boasts,
By him his people win the day.

7 And when the mortal strife is past,
The peace and joy of heav'n succeed;
'Tis peace that will for ever last,
'Tis joy unmix'd, 'tis joy indeed.

HYMN CCLIX.

"*Kept by the power of God.*"—1 Pet. i. 5.

1 SPAR'D a little longer,
May our souls grow stronger,
To maintain the arduous fight of faith.

2 Many foes surround us,
Hoping to confound us,
But the Lord himself is our defence.

3 We have hearts deceitful,
And of truth forgetful,
Yet our gracious Lord his people spares.

4 Pilgrims here, and strangers,
Who can tell our dangers?
But our Lord will save us from them all.

5 He has dearly bought us,
Hitherto has brought us,
And will lead us to himself at last.

6 By his eye directed,
By his arm protected,
We shall gain the presence of our God.

HYMN CCLX.

"Let not him that girdeth on his harness boast himself as he that putteth it off."—1 Kings xx. 11.

1 FELLOW soldier, where's thine armour?
Is it time to put it off?
Hast thou listen'd to the charmer?
Dost thou fear the worldling's scoff?
Brother, has thy courage fail'd?
Has the wily foe prevail'd?

2 Thou art not what once I knew thee,
Well equipp'd for battle then.
Since the world began to woo thee,
Thou hast been like other men;
Be again what once thou wast,
Stop! O stop! ere all be lost.

3 Know'st thou what the foe is doing?
Know'st thou what a foe he is?
Baffled often, still pursuing,
Bent upon his prey to seize.
Brace thine armour on again:
Brother, who can harm thee then?

4 Proof it is; when tried it fails not;
Temper'd by unerring skill.
Here the fiery dart avails not,
Strike it may, it cannot kill.
Be it thine again to wield
Faith's impenetrable shield.

5 Shun this place, for death is in it;
This is not a place for thee.
Rich the prize: if thou wouldst win it,
Be as thou was wont to be.
To the battle-field repair,
Thou wilt gather trophies there.

6 'Tis a prize well worth the winning:
One beyond all others far;
So thou thoughtest when beginning
In the mortal strife to share.
Then didst thou esteem the cross
Wealth indeed—all else but lost.

7 Thou hast sinn'd, but know the Lord is
Willing all to pardon still;
Sweet and full of grace his word is,
Let him come, whoever will;
Many wonders here are found,
Brother, this is holy ground.

8 Here is all that thou hast need of,
That which takes thy sin away;
But in time to come take heed of
That which led thee far astray.
Evil shun, and evil men,
Never leave the Lord again.

HYMN CCLXI.

"*And the shout of a King is among them.*"—NUMB. xxiii. 21.

1 THOUGH others be sad,
Let Isra'l be glad,
For "the shout of a King is among them;"
The Lord, whose they are,
Will make them his care;
And who shall be able to wrong them?

2 Though many the foes
That stand to oppose
Their passage to yonder bright regions,
The arm of the Lord
(Their shield and their sword)
Will scatter their numberless legions.

3 How happy are they
Who truly can say,
The Lord is our portion for ever!
The Lord, whom we trust,
A Saviour, yet just,
Of grace and of glory the giver.

4 Though theirs is a life
Of trouble and strife,
No weapon that's raised up against them
Shall ever prevail;
Their foes shall all fail,
For God with his favour has fenc'd them.

5 The men of his choice
May well then rejoice,
Since the shout of a King is among them;
The name that they love
For ever shall prove
A terror to all who would wrong them.

HYMN CCLXII.

"*O Lord, what shall I say when Israel turneth their backs before their enemies?*"—JOSHUA vii. 8.

1 WHEN Joshua saw the hosts give way,
And fly before their conqu'ring foe,
His soul was struck with deep dismay,
He never look'd to see it so.

2 Shall Isra'l fear, shall Isra'l yield?
  Oh, who can bear the mournful sight?
Shall Isra'l vanquish'd leave the field,
  And God's own host be put to flight?

3 Ah! Lord, behold thy people flee!
  The people whom thine arm redeem'd;
Thy vanquish'd host retreating see,
  Invincible till now esteem'd.

4 Encourag'd by this fatal day,
  How will the nations gather round!
Thy people will become their prey,
  And Isra'l's name no more be found.

5 O let that hour be far remov'd!
  For how will then the heathen boast;
Will they not say thine arm has prov'd
  Too feeble to protect thine host?

6 Return, return, O God, our King,
  Remember, Lord, thy glorious name;
O let thy presence vict'ry bring!
  And Isra'l's foes be put to shame.

HYMN CCLXIII.

"*Whom resist stedfast in the faith.*"—1 PET. v. 9.

1 OUR strife is mortal with the foe,
  Or he or we must yield;
'Twould ruin be to us, we know,
  If we should quit the field.

2 And what are we that we should meet
  A mighty foe like this;
The world itself is at his feet,
  Its "Prince," its "God" he is.

3 And yet we must encounter one
With titles such as these;
Nor must there be, the fight begun,
Or peace, or truce, or ease.

4 The foe we fight with, watchful is;
He sleeps not day or night;
A fearful pow'r to hurt is his,
With guile or else with might.

5 "A roaring lion" now he is,
And "seeking to devour;"
An angel's form anon is his,
As suits the present hour.

6 Destruction only is his aim,
He lives but to destroy;
His purpose evermore the same,
For evil is his joy.

7 Our help, it cometh from the Lord,
Whose arm almighty is;
And glad we know, the faithful word
We rest upon, is his.

HYMN CCLXIV.

"*Be vigilant, because your adversary, the devil . . . walketh about.*"—1 Pet. v. 8.

1 HAPPY he who has his quiver
Full of arrows sharp and bright;
And his bow beside him ever,
Fit for use. This man is right.
Should the watchful foe appear,
He is safe, and need not fear.

2 Woe to him, whose empty quiver
Proof is of a mind unwise;
What is he to do, whenever
Sudden danger bids him rise.
Can he meet the coming foe?
Can he ward the deadly blow?

3 'Tis no time to look around him,
When the danger pressing is;
Without arms the foe has found him,
And the 'vantage all is his.
He who watches not will know
That he has a watchful foe.

4 O how like the case to mine is!
I have acted even so;
Saviour, all the glory thine is,
That I have escaped the foe.
'Twas not I that wrought, but thou,
Else I had been lost ere now.

HYMN CCLXV.

"*I beheld Satan as lightning fall from heaven.*"—LUKE x. 18.

1 THE fight is done;
The day is won,
The foe is forc'd at length to yield.
Be no more sad;
Be glad, be glad;
For Satan vanquish'd quits the field.

2 His reign was long,
For he was strong;
He reigned until "one stronger" came.
No more he reigns;
But he remains
Unchanged—his purpose still the same.

3 From heav'n cast out,
He goes about;
On earth his aim is to devour.
Nor force nor guile
He spares, nor toil;
He knows the limit of his pow'r.

4 "Be sober," then;
"Behave as men,"
As those who have a watchful foe.
It cannot be
That we should flee;
'Twere shame and death if it were so.

5 But why this fear
When he is near,
The Lord, on whom our care is cast?
Then valiant be:
The Lord is he
Who fights our battles to the last.

State of Believers, a Pilgrimage.

HYMN CCLXVI.

"*For here have we no continuing city, but we seek one to come.*"—
Heb. xiii. 14.

1 "WE'VE no abiding city here,"
This may distress the worldling's mind;
But should not cost the saint a tear,
Who hopes a better rest to find.

2 "We've no abiding city here,"
Sad truth, were this to be our home;
But let the thought our spirits cheer,
"We seek a city yet to come."

3 "We've no abiding city here,"
Then let us live as pilgrims do;
Let not the world our rest appear,
But let us haste from all below.

4 "We've no abiding city here,"
We seek a city out of sight,
Zion its name,—the Lord is there,
It shines with everlasting light.

5 "We've no abiding city here;"
Methinks I hear the worldling say,
"Your hope is vain, ye fools, forbear,
For pleasure lies another way."

6 No wonder men should reason thus,
And count our expectation vain;
But did they know the truth like us,
They would adopt another strain.

7 Did they, like us, by faith discern
The glorious city of our God,
They too, like us, would quickly learn
To walk in Zion's heav'nly road.

8 Zion!—Jehovah is her strength!
Secure she smiles at all her foes;
And weary travellers at length
Within her sacred walls repose.

9 O! sweet abode of peace and love,
Where pilgrims freed from toil are blest!
Had I the pinions of the dove,
I'd fly to thee, and be at rest.

10 But hush, my soul, nor dare repine!
The time my God appoints is best:
While here, to do his will be *mine*;
And *his* to fix my time of rest.

HYMN CCLXVII.

"*For they that say such things declare plainly that they seek a country.*"—HEB. xi. 14.

1 FROM Egypt lately come,
Where death and darkness reign,
We seek our new, our better home,
Where we our rest shall gain.
Hallelujah!
We are on our way to God.

2 To Canaan's sacred bound
We haste with songs of joy;
Where peace and liberty are found,
And sweets that never cloy.
Hallelujah! &c.

3 Our toils and conflicts cease
On Canaan's happy shore;
We there shall dwell in endless peace,
And never hunger more.
Hallelujah! &c.

4 But hark! those distant sounds
That strike our list'ning ears—
They come from Canaan's happy bounds,
Where God our King appears.
Hallelujah! &c.

5 There, in celestial strains,
Enraptur'd myriads sing;
There love in every bosom reigns,
For God himself is King.
Hallelujah! &c.

6 We soon shall join the throng,
Their pleasures we shall share;
And sing the everlasting song,
With all the ransom'd there.
Hallelujah! &c.

7 How sweet the prospect is!
It cheers the pilgrim's breast;
We're journeying through the wilderness,
But soon shall gain our rest.
Hallelujah! &c.

HYMN CCLXVIII.

"*There remaineth, therefore, a rest to the people of God.*"—
HEB. iv. 9.

1 THE people of the Lord
Are on their way to heav'n,
They there obtain their great reward,
The prize will there be giv'n.

2 'Tis conflict here below,
'Tis triumph there, and peace;
On earth we wrestle with the foe,
In heav'n our conflicts cease.

3 'Tis gloom and darkness here,
'Tis light and joy above;
There all is pure, and all is clear,
There all is peace and love.

4 'Tis snares and dangers here,
But when we reach our home,
Then danger is no more, nor fear,
Our joys are yet to come.

5 There rest shall follow toil,
And ease succeed to care,
The victors there divide the spoil,
They live in triumph there.

6 Then let us joyful sing,
The conflict is not long;
We hope in heav'n to praise our King
In one eternal song.

State of Believers, a Voyage.

HYMN CCLXIX.

"*So he bringeth them unto their desired haven.*"—Ps. cvii. 30.

1 THE Christian navigates a sea
Where various forms of death appear;
Nor skill, alas! nor pow'r has he,
Aright his dang'rous course to steer.

2 Why does he venture then from shore,
And dare so many deaths to brave?
Because the land affrights him more
Than all the perils of the wave.

3 Because he hopes a port to find,
Where all his toil will be repaid;
And though unskilful, weak, and blind,
Yet Jesus bids him nothing dread.

4 But though *his* faithful word is giv'n,
Who does not change, and cannot lie;
Yet when his bark by storms is driv'n,
He doubts, and fears destruction nigh.

5 Sometimes there lies a treach'rous rock
Beneath the surface of the wave;
He strikes, but yet survives the shock,
For Jesus is at hand to save.

6 But hark! the midnight tempest roars,
He seems forsaken and alone,
But Jesus, whom he then implores,
Unseen preserves and leads him on.

7 On the smooth surface of the deep,
Without a fear he sometimes lies;
The danger then is lest he sleep,
And ruin seize him by surprise.

8 His destin'd land he sometimes sees,
And thinks his toils will soon be o'er;
Expects some favourable breeze
Will waft him quickly to the shore.

9 But sudden clouds obstruct his view,
And he enjoys the sight no more;
Nor does he now believe it true
That he had ever seen the shore.

10 Though fear his heart should overwhelm,
He'll reach the port for which he's bound;
For Jesus holds and guides the helm,
And safety is where he is found.

11 Methinks I view him now at last
Safe anchor'd in the haven of joy;
He thinks no more of conflicts past,
Wonder and love his heart employ.

12 He *wonders* much at all he sees;
He *loves* the author of his bliss;
And cries, while he the scene surveys,
"O! what a glorious land is this!"

HYMN CCLXX.

"These see the works of the Lord, and his wonders in the deep."
PSALM cvii. 24.

1 WE'RE bound for yonder land,
Where Jesus reigns supreme;
We leave the shore at his command,
Forsaking all for him.

2 'Twere easy, did we choose,
Again to reach the shore;
But this is what our souls refuse,
We'll never touch it more.

3 We know the state of those
Who still continue there;
And fly, that we may shun the woes
That else our portion were.

4 The perils of the sea,
The rocks, the waves, the wind,
Are small, whatever they may be,
To those we leave behind.

5 Nor have we cause to fear;
The God who rules the sea,
In ev'ry danger will be near,
And our protector be.

6 The Lord himself will keep
His people safe from harm;
Will hold the helm, and guide the ship
With his almighty arm.

7 Then let the tempests roar,
The billows heave and swell;
We trust to reach the peaceful shore,
Where all the ransom'd dwell.

8 And when we gain the land,
How happy shall we be!
How shall we bless the mighty hand
That led us through the sea!

HYMN CCLXXI.

"*What manner of man is this, that even the wind and the sea obey him?*"—Mark iv. 41.

1 WHY those fears? behold 'tis Jesus
Holds the helm, and guides the ship:
Spread the sails, and catch the breezes
Sent to waft us through the deep,
To the regions
Where the mourners cease to weep.

2 Could we stay where death was hov'ring?
Could we rest on such a shore?
No, the awful truth discov'ring,
We could linger there no more:
We forsake it;
Leaving all we lov'd before.

3 Though the shore we hope to land on
Only by report is known,
Yet we freely all abandon,
Led by that report alone;
And with Jesus
Through the trackless deep move on.

4 Led by that, we brave the ocean;
Led by that, the storms defy;
Calm amidst tumultuous motion,
Knowing that our Lord is nigh:
Waves obey him,
And the storms before him fly.

5 Render'd safe by his protection,
We shall pass the wat'ry waste;
Trusting to his wise direction,
We shall gain the port at last;
And with wonder,
Think on toils and dangers past.

6 O! what pleasures there await us!
There the tempests cease to roar:
There it is that those who hate us
Can molest our peace no more:
Trouble ceases
On that tranquil, happy shore.

HYMN CCLXXII.

"*Arise ye, and depart; for this is not your rest.*"—
MICAH ii. 10.

1 COME weigh the anchor, put to sea,
It is not safe to tarry here;
The land polluted is, and we
Must part from all we hold most dear:
This moment let us quit the shore,
And never let us touch it more.

2 The sea we have to pass is wide
And deep, with rocks on either hand;
The thought of this, and much beside,
May make us loth to quit the land;
It matters not, we must away,
Or perish here—'twere death to stay.

3 The die is cast, our gallant ship
Is moving from the fatal shore;
We soon shall reach the mighty deep,
To see the land we left no more.
The present is a trying hour,
But trust we him with whom is pow'r.

4 If we had put off our flight
  But one short day, then all was lost;
For turn ye to the fearful sight,
  The fatal fire has reach'd the coast,
And with a force no man can stay,
Will burn till all is burnt away.

5 Then hasten hence, away! away!
  Too near the fatal shore we are;
May he whom waves and winds obey,
  Our vessel deign to make his care,
And never leave us till we stand
Secure within the happy land.

6 But see, the clouds are gathering round,
  The storm is coming, reef the sails;
We hear it in the distant sound,
  And, as it comes, our courage fails:
But he to whom belongs the pow'r,
Will save us in the trying hour.

7 The storm is past; to him be praise,
  Who brought us thro' the dreary night;
To him our thankful song we raise;
  To him whose arm is cloth'd with might;
To him whom storms and waves obey;
His name we praise, and well we may.

8 The Lord will bring his people through
  The many perils of the sea;
Will safety give, and courage too;
  Their guardian and their guide will be,
Till landed on the happy shore,
They hear the storms and waves no more.

HYMN CCLXXIII.

"*These see the works of the Lord.*"—PSALM cvii. 24.

1 WE'RE going to embark
For yonder happy shore;
We sail in hope; but, hark!
The tempest seems to roar;
At sea there's much to fear,
'Twere wise to tarry here.

2 Away the thought! away!
'Tis one that's full of woe;
This day, this very day,
This moment let us go;
For here we must not stay;
To work! the anchor weigh.

3 'Tis a polluted land,
No rest for us is here;
We go, at his command,
Who bids us nothing fear.
The tempest and the wave
At his command we brave.

4 And well we may, for his
The sea is, and the land;
The world, and all that is,
All bows to his command;
His will it is presides,
His arm it is that guides.

5 O Lord, at thy command,
We leave our native shore,
Nor shall we touch the land,
Or ever see it more,
Till, safely moor'd at last,
The anchor holds us fast.

6 With wonder, then, and joy,
We shall survey the place,
Where good without alloy
Abounds, the fruit of grace;
While sense of dangers past,
Enhances joy at last.

HYMN CCLXXIV.

"*So he bringeth them unto their desire'd haven.*"—
PSALM CVII. 30.

1 HALF a wreck, by tempests driven,
Yet this feeble bark survives;
Dash'd against the rocks, and riven,
In the midst of death it lives;
See it press'd on ev'ry side;
See it still the storm outride.

2 Can a bark, like mine, so shatter'd,
Ever reach yon friendly shore?
Tempest-toss'd so long, and batter'd,
Can it stand one conflict more?
Should another storm assail,
Mast and planks and all must fail.

3 So they would, but One that's greater
Than the storms and waves is here;
He it is, whose name is sweeter
Far than music to my ear;
He preserves my shatter'd bark,
He makes light when all is dark.

4 Jesus is the Lord, who hears me
When the tempest roars around;
He it is whose presence cheers me,
When I hear the dreadful sound;
Trusting to his grace and pow'r,
Need I fear the darkest hour?

5 What though ev'ry plank is starting,
Waves are running mountain high,
Thunders rolling, lightnings darting,
And no saving hand seems nigh?
Let me still no danger fear,
Jesus, though unseen, is near.

HYMN CCLXXV.

" *Which hope we have as an anchor of the soul.*"—Heb. vi. 19.

1 HOPE is the anchor of the soul;
It enters that within the vail;
And though the waves of trouble roll,
The anchor holds, and will not fail.

2 The night is dark, the sea runs high,
The mast before the tempest bends;
A shore bestrew'd with wrecks is nigh,
And on the anchor all depends.

3 The vessel drifts, if that gives way,
And founders on the fatal shore,
Where death and night maintain their sway;
Where light and life are seen no more.

4 At such a time, in such a state,
A single anchor holding all,
No wonder that our fear is great,
No wonder that our hope is small.

5 But one sweet word dispels our fear,
The word of him who cannot lie;
His truth is pledg'd, his pow'r is near;
His truth and pow'r all ills defy.

6 Hope, O my soul, thine anchor is,
Both sure and steadfast; be thou strong:
The word that makes thee bold is his,
Who reigns yon shining host among.

HYMN CCLXXVI.

"*Escape for thy life.*"—Gen. xix. 17.

1 NOW weigh the anchor, clear the land,
Depart we from the fatal shore.
Depart we, 'tis our Lord's command;
And we must never touch it more.

2 Though many things we leave behind,
Are pleasant to the eye, and dear;
Depart we still, resolv'd in mind,
Before us better things appear.

3 A pleasant land before us lies,
Where all is bright, and all is fair.
The Lord is there, "the only wise,"
The Lord we love and serve is there.

4 Between this land and us, 'tis true,
An ocean lies, both deep and broad:
And perils, that no man can view,
Or think of, with a mind unaw'd.

5 But he who bids us put to sea,
And brave the perils of the deep,
Our guide by day and night will be;
He slumbers not, nor does he sleep.

6 When he is nigh, then all is well,
Though neither sun nor stars appear;
Though tempests rage, and billows swell:
Ev'n then no cause there is for fear.

7 One greater than the storms and waves
Is with us, and our vessel steers.
When all seems lost, 'tis then he saves,
And shows how causeless were our fears.

8 His mild rebuke, "Why did ye doubt?"
Should teach us not to doubt again.
The "evil heart," O Lord, cast out,
And we shall learn to trust thee then.

HYMN CCLXXVII.

"*What manner of man is this?*"—Mark iv. 41.

1 "WHO is this that calms the ocean?"
Thus they cried, who were on board,
When they saw the wild commotion
Cease, as Jesus spoke the word;
When the sudden calm they saw,
Wonder fill'd their minds, and awe.

2 He, who bids the tempest riot
On the deep, and makes it swell,
He alone the storm can quiet,
Saying to it, "peace, be still:"
He, whose pow'r to all gives birth,
All in heav'n, and all in earth.

3 He who calms the sea when raging,
Stills the tumult of the soul;
By his word the storms assuaging,
Storms no other can control:
But *he* binds them with his hand,
And they cease at his command.

4 Ye who, all your hope deriving
From yourselves, have labour'd long
To allay the storm by striving,
But have found the storm too strong,
From the hopeless labour cease,
Jesus gives the troubled peace.

HYMN CCLXXVIII.

"*This is not your rest.*"—MICAH ii. 10.

1 HOMEWARD bound, the way is dreary,
Through the ocean wide and deep.
Fearful we, and often weary;
Watching, too, while others sleep.
But our trouble ends at last;
Sweet the thought of evils past.

2 We have seen the billows swelling
Till they seem'd to reach the sky.
We have felt our vessel reeling
"To and fro," now low, now high.
But our Lord was always near,
And his presence calm'd our fear.

3 We have been in perils many,
Passing through the mighty deep.
None have sunk us, nor will any,
For the Lord his own will keep.
Though their way through danger is,
They are safe, for they are his.

4 'Tis the Lord's, and not our doing,
We have neither pow'r nor skill;
He it is that saves us going
Through the deep: he can and will
Keep us safe from first to last:
His the future as the past.

5 Kept by him, no harm can reach us;
Kept by him, no ill befall;
'Tis a truth the past may teach us,
In our trials, great or small.
Still the Lord has been the same;
And "a tow'r of strength" his name.

6 Homeward bound—the thought is cheering;
Soon we hope the land to see:
Ev'ry day the haven nearing,
Where at length we hope to be.
When we reach it, then we rest;
And his people then are blest.

7 Saviour, be thou near us ever;
Keep us by thy mighty arm;
Never leave us, never, never;
Nothing then can do us harm.
Land us on the happy shore,
Where thy people weep no more.

HYMN CCLXXIX.

"*So he bringeth them unto their desired haven.*"—
PSALM cvii. 30.

1 WE'RE bound for yonder pleasant land,
Where all are safe, and all are blest;
Where hostile foot can never stand;
Where nought can injure or molest.

2 The perils of the deep we brave,
At his command, who bids us fly.
The master he of wind and wave,
We need not fear when he is nigh.

3 The land we hope to reach is his;
And he appears in glory there;
We hope to see him as he is,
And in his glory then to share.

4 How blessēd, after dangers past,
To reach the port, the friendly port!
And there to be secure, at last,
From ills, all ills of ev'ry sort.

5 To know that nothing can molest,
Or ever do us harm again.
Our rest an everlasting rest;
How blessed are his people then!

6 'Tis blessedness no tongue can tell;
For thought itself a joy too great.
To toil and suffer now is well;
'Tis after these that rest is sweet.

A State of Trial.

HYMN CCLXXX.

"*Now no chastening for the present seemeth to be joyous, but grievous.*"—HEB. xii. 11.

1 TRUE, no chast'ning for the present
Bringeth joy, but bringeth grief;
Pain has nothing in it pleasant;
But the saints obtain relief,
Knowing that their Father sends
Ev'ry rod, and good intends.

2 Were his people free from trials,
They might doubt their royal birth;
They might justly fear the vials
Destin'd for the sons of earth:
Trials are a fruit of love,
Sent in mercy from above.

3 Yes, the true-born sons of heaven
Feel the chast'ning hand of God;
Though accepted and forgiven,
Yet they need their Father's rod;
Nor, if they should bid him spare,
Would he hearken to their pray'r.

4 Full of pity, full of kindness,
Yet he makes his children prove,
Nothing of paternal blindness
Ever mixes with his love:
When the rod must be applied,
Truth and wisdom are his guide.

5 In affliction's darkest season,
When their trials sharpest prove,
Saints may smile, for they have reason
To confess their Father's love:
All is needful, nothing vain;
Present loss is future gain.

6 Trials prove and strengthen patience,
Trials purge the dross away,
Trials sweeten expectations
Of a bright and glorious day;
When from sin and suff'ring freed,
Saints shall gain their rest indeed.

7 Trials thus, though often bitter,
Yet are needful in their place;
Rend'ring ev'ry promise sweeter,
Adding strength to ev'ry grace:
Thus, whatever grief they bring,
Blessed fruits from trials spring.

HYMN CCLXXXI.

"*I will also leave in the midst of thee an afflicted and poor people, and they shall trust in the name of the Lord.*"—ZEPH. iii. 12.

1 "POOR and afflicted," Lord, are thine,
Among the great unfit to shine;
But though the world may think it strange,
They would not with the world exchange.

2 "Poor and afflicted"—yes, they are;
They're not exempt from grief and care;
But he who sav'd them by his blood,
Makes ev'ry sorrow yield them good.

3 "Poor and afflicted"—'tis their lot;
They know it, and they murmur not;
'Twould ill become them to refuse
The state their Master deign'd to choose.

4 "Poor and afflicted"—yet they sing,
For Jesus is their glorious King;
"Through suff'rings perfect," now he reigns,
And shares in all their griefs and pains.

5 "Poor and afflicted"—but, ere long,
They'll join the bright, celestial throng;
Their suff'rings then will reach a close,
And heav'n afford them sweet repose.

6 And while they walk the thorny way,
They're often heard to sigh and say—
"Dear Saviour, come, O quickly come!
And take thy mourning pilgrims home."

HYMN CCLXXXII.

"*For our light affliction, which is but for a moment, worketh for us.*"—2 Cor. iv. 17.

1 YES, 'tis a rough and thorny road
That leads us to the saints' abode;
But when our Father's house we gain,
'Twill make amends for all our pain.

2 And though we feel our present grief,
In hope we find a sweet relief;
For hope anticipates the day
When all our griefs shall pass away.

3 And what is all we suffer now,
Or all we can endure below,
To that bright day when Christ shall come,
And take his weary pilgrims home?

4 Then let us walk, without complaint,
The thorny road, and never faint;
Though now by weariness opprest,
The end is everlasting rest.

5 And when we gain the saints' abode,
We'll oft look back upon the road;
The recollection of the past
Will sweeten our repose at last.

HYMN CCLXXXIII.

"*Thy blessing is upon thy people.*"—Psalm iii. 8.

1 LORD, if thy people suffer grief,
Yet are their comforts great;
Nor are they left without relief,
Thy time is never late.

2 If, when affliction's waves run high,
Deliv'rance should be slow,
Thy purpose is their faith to try,
And make their patience grow.

3 In sorrow's sev'n-fold furnace tried,
This thought may yield them joy;
Thou, Lord, art walking by their side,
Nor can the fire destroy.

4 Yea, ev'n the flames' destructive pow'r,
Directed, Lord, by thee,
Shall nothing but their bands devour,
And leave their bodies free.

5 All this I know; but in the hour
Of trial, then I faint;
And feel that nothing but thy pow'r
Can keep me from complaint.

6 Howe'er a mother loves her own,
I know, beyond a doubt,
Her love by thine is far outdone,
Thy love that changes not.

7 Whatever light in man may shine,
And guide a father's care,
'Tis but a shadow, Lord, of thine;
Thy wisdom cannot err.

8 Of this convinc'd, I would "be still,
And know that thou art God;"
Would give up my rebellious will,
And kiss thy chast'ning rod.

9 O teach thy worm, whate'er his state,
Therewith to be content;
Thine hand to bless, thy time to wait,
And leave to thee th' event.

HYMN CCLXXXIV.

"*Thy testimonies that thou hast commanded are righteous and very faithful.*"—PSALM cxix. 138.

1 GOOD and faithful are thy words,
"King of kings, and Lord of lords;"
In the time of grief and care,
Sweet, and full of grace, they are.

2 When thy people are distress'd,
Harass'd by the foe, and press'd,
Whither should thy people flee,
Whither, Saviour, but to thee?

3 Words that spirit are, and life,
Cheer them in their mortal strife;
When thy people are opprest,
Then do they afford them rest.

4 Then it is thy words declare
Whence they come, and what they are;
Sinners, in the trying hour,
Know their worth, and feel their pow'r.

5 Why? Because they are thy words,
"King of kings, and Lord of lords;"
And thy spirit gives them pow'r,
Fitted to the trying hour.

6 Whither, then, but unto thee,
Whither should the helpless flee?
Pow'r and grace to thee belong,
Hence our safety, hence our song.

HYMN CCLXXXV.

"*It is good for me that I have been afflicted.*"—Psalm cxix. 71.

1 IS it not God appoints it so?
Then why should I repine or grieve?
From him my trials come I know,
And he can all my pain relieve.

2 He sought and found me when a foe,
He might have cast me down to hell,
But love prevail'd, and well I know
The love of God no tongue can tell.

3 If he could save an enemy,
Adopt and make his foe a child,
What goodness may I hope to see,
When pardon'd thus and reconcil'd?

4 If he should cross my stubborn will,
To wean my heart from earthly things,
Shall I repine and murmur still,
Nor learn the lesson sorrow brings?

5 Forbid it, Lord! I come to thee,
My weakness and my wants thou know'st,
From proud impatience set me free,
And make me like whate'er thou dost.

HYMN CCLXXXVI.

"*My son, despise not thou the chastening of the Lord.*"—
PROV. iii. 11.

1 WHEN the Lord rebukes his servant,
'Tis to save and not destroy;
'Tis to make my spirit fervent,
'Tis to give me real joy;
'Tis to make me better know
That my rest is not below.

2 Shall I then repine at trials
By my Father's love decreed?
What if God had pour'd the vials
Of his wrath upon my head:
Death of sin the wages is,
All is mercy short of this.

3 Since the Lord has giv'n me reason
To expect a place above,
In affliction's sharpest season,
Let me own that God is love;
Let me own that all he does
From paternal kindness flows.

4 Shall I murmur at his dealings?
Shall I not his kindness trust?
Since he knows my frame and feelings,
And remembers I am dust;
Shall I not receive the rod,
And confess the hand of God?

5 Hear me, Lord, in my petition,
O sustain me lest I faint!
Teach me patience and submission,
Keep thy servant from complaint;
And in ev'ry trying hour,
Lord, uphold me by thy pow'r.

A State of Joyful Hope.

HYMN CCLXXXVII.

"*And God shall wipe away all tears from their eyes.*"—
REV. vii. 17.

1 YE saints, whose tears now often flow,
(And will while ye are here below,)
Rejoice that in a few short years,
Your God will wipe away your tears.

2 Your conflicts then will end in peace,
And ev'ry cause of sorrow cease;
The purest joys will fill your hearts,
Such joys as God himself imparts.

3 When landed on the heav'nly shore,
You'll see your enemies no more;
The limit of their pow'r is such,
That sacred place they cannot touch,

4 "An evil heart of unbelief"
Will then no more occasion grief;
And base "desires of flesh and mind"
For ever will be left behind.

5 The world, or lov'd or fear'd before,
Can charm or threaten then no more;
And Satan, baffled in his schemes,
Retires indignant, and blasphemes.

6 'Tis thus the Lord has fix'd a day
To wipe his people's tears away;
Their toils, and griefs, and conflicts past,
He'll bring them to himself at last.

7 O! happy state, where purest joy
For ever reigns without alloy;
O! happy saints, ordain'd to prove
The fulness of this joy above.

HYMN CCLXXXVIII.

"By the rivers of Babylon there we sat down, yea we wept when we remembered Zion."—Psalm cxxxvii. 1.

1 O ZION, when I think on thee,
I wish for pinions like the dove,
And mourn to think that I should be
So distant from the place I love.

2 A captive here, and far from home,
For Zion's sacred walls I sigh;
To Zion all the ransom'd come,
And see the Saviour eye to eye.

3 While here, I walk on hostile ground;
The few that I can call my friends
Are, like myself, with fetters bound,
And weariness our steps attends.

4 But yet we shall behold the day,
When Zion's children shall return;
Our sorrows then shall flee away,
And we shall never, never mourn

5 The hope that such a day will come
Makes ev'n the captive's portion sweet;
Though now we wander far from home,
In Zion soon we all shall meet.

HYMN CCLXXXIX.

"If I prefer not Jerusalem above my chief joy."—
PSALM CXXXVIII. 6.

1 THE breezes that from Zion blow,
Sweeter than aromatic gales,
Refresh me while I walk below,
And cheer my spirit when it fails.

2 And still as I approach the ground
Where consecrated pleasure reigns,
A richer fragrance breathes around,
To soothe the weary trav'ller's pains.

3 Such earnests of the joys to come
Support the pilgrim as he goes,
And make him long to reach his home,
Where all his toils for ever close.

4 Zion, how fair thy dwellings are!
Beyond what man admires the most;
To me they seem more lovely far
Than all that fancy's realms can boast.

5 Nor would I change the hope I have,
That I shall reach thy blest retreats,
For all that fame or wealth e'er gave,
Or all the store of earthly sweets.

HYMN CCXC.

"*For from the top of the rocks I behold him.*"—NUMB. xxiii. 9.

1 METHINKS I stand upon the rock
Where Balaam stood, and wond'ring look
Upon the scene below:
The tents of Jacob goodly seem,
The people happy I esteem,
Whom God has favour'd so.

2 The sons of Isra'l stand alone,
Jehovah claims them for his own,
His cause and theirs the same:
He sav'd them from the tyrant's hand,
Allots to them a pleasant land,
And calls them by his name.

3 Their toils have almost reach'd a close,
And soon in peace they shall repose
Within the promis'd land:
Ev'n now its rising hills are seen,
Enrich'd with everlasting green,
Where Israel soon shall stand.

4 O Isra'l, who is like to thee?
A people sav'd, and call'd to be
Peculiar to the Lord!
Thy shield! he guards thee from the foe;
Thy sword! he fights thy battles too;
Himself thy great reward!

5 Fear not, though many should oppose,
For God is stronger than thy foes,
And makes thy cause his own:
The promis'd land before thee lies,
Go up, and take the glorious prize
Reserv'd for thee alone.

6 In glory there the King appears;
He wipes away his people's tears,
And makes their sorrows cease:
From toil and strife they there repose,
And dwell secure from all their foes,
In everlasting peace.

7 Fair emblem of a better rest,
Of which believers are possest,
Beyond material space!
Methinks I see the distant shore,
Where sin and sorrow are no more;
And long to reach the place.

8 Nor shall I always absent be
From him my soul desires to see,
Within the realms of light;
Ere long my Lord will rend the veil,
And not a cloud shall then conceal
His glory from my sight.

9 Sweet hope! it makes the coward brave;
It makes a freeman of the slave,
And bids the sluggard rise;
It lifts a worm of earth on high,
It gives him wings, and makes him fly
To worlds beyond the skies.

HYMN CCXCI.

"*For all things are yours.*"—1 COR. iii. 21.

1 EV'RY good possessing
In our Saviour's blessing,
Let us live to celebrate his grace!

2 Mean the worldling's treasure!
Short his boasted pleasure!
They alone are blest who know the Lord.

3 Sweet the scene before us!
We shall join the chorus
Of the saints and angels round his throne.

4 Let the prospect cheer us;
Here our LORD is near us,
But in heav'n we see him as he is.

5 Till we reach our station,
Let his great salvation
Be the glorious subject of our songs!

HYMN CCXCII.

"*Whom having not seen, ye love.*"—1 PET. 1. 8.

1 WE have not seen the Saviour's face,
Nor shall we until life shall end;
But yet we love him for his grace,
We love an unseen, absent friend.

2 The glorious work he wrought, endears
The Saviour to his people's hearts;
In hope they wait till he appears,
And hope a present joy imparts.

3 They hope to see their Lord that day
Descend with all the hosts of heav'n;
The Lord, who bore their sins away,
The Lord, thro' whom they stand forgiv'n.

4 They hope that what they now believe,
They then with joyful eyes shall see;
No more to doubt, no more to grieve,
But with their Lord himself to be.

5 Till that bright day we'll think of him,
And may our love with fervour glow;
An unseen Lord be all our theme,
Till with him hence to heav'n we go.

HYMN CCXCIII.

"*For the Egyptians whom ye have seen to-day, ye shall see them again no more for ever.*"—EXOD. xiv. 13.

1 WHEN we pass through yonder river,
When we reach the further shore,
There's an end of war for ever,
We shall see our foes no more;
All our conflicts then shall cease,
Follow'd by eternal peace.

2 After warfare, rest is pleasant;
O how sweet the prospect is!
Toil and strife are for the present,
Let us not repine at this;
Toil, and pain, and conflict past,
All endear repose at last.

3 When we enter yonder regions,
When we touch the sacred shore,
Blessed thought! no hostile legions
Can alarm or trouble more;
Far beyond the reach of foes,
We shall dwell in sweet repose.

4 O that hope, how bright! how glorious!
'Tis his people's blest reward;
In the Saviour's strength victorious,
They at length behold their Lord;
In his kingdom they shall rest;
In his love be fully blest.

5 When the sight of war alarms us,
Let us to call to mind our friend;
He who for the conflict arms us,
Will be with us to the end:
'Tis enough, the war is his;
God our King and leader is.

HYMN CCXCIV.

"*While we look not at the things which are seen, but at the things which are not seen.*"—2 COR. iv. 18.

1 AS much of heav'n as earth affords,
To those who "walk by faith" is known;
They hear the Saviour's gracious words,
And hope to see him on his throne.

2 In hope, they now enjoy a taste
Of future happiness above,
And sav'd from low desire, they haste
To regions of eternal love.

3 Cast down they may be oft, and are,
Who is not while on hostile ground?
Who is not when from home so far,
Whom snares beset, whom foes surround?

4 But hope of heav'n outweighs them all,
It brings the distant object near,
It makes our greatest trials small,
And boldness gives where all was fear.

5 In hope we taste of heav'n to come,
To know our Lord is heav'n below;
But when we reach the pilgrim's home,
As we are known, we then shall know.

6 We then shall be as angels are,
Like them shall love, like them obey;
In all their pleasures we shall share,
As happy and as pure as they.

HYMN CCXCV.

"*Beloved, now are we the sons of God.*"—1 JOHN iii. 2.

1 WE boast an origin divine,
God is our father, heav'n our home;
In yonder world we hope to shine,
Where sin and sorrow never come.

2 As Jesus, whom we worship, was,
'Tis thus we are, and wish to be;
We glory only in his cross,
And who on earth so blest as we?

3 We wait the coming of our Lord,
Nor do we wait that day in vain;
We cannot doubt his faithful word,
That tells us he will come again.

4 Come then, dear Lord, O come and take
Thy people to their heav'nly home;
The scorn they suffer for thy sake,
Sweetens the hope of joys to come.

5 They long to see thee as thou art,
They long to mix with those above,
To meet where they shall never part,
And sing thine everlasting love.

HYMN CCXCVI.

"*In that day there shall be a fountain opened . . . . for sin and for uncleanness.*"—ZECH. xiii. 1.

1 BLESSED fountain, full of grace!
Grace for sinners, grace for me;
To this source alone I trace
What I am, and hope to be:

2 What I am, as one redeem'd,
Sav'd and rescued by the Lord;
Hating what I once esteem'd,
Loving what I once abhorr'd:

3 What I hope to be, ere long,
When I take my place above;
When I join the heav'nly throng;
When I see the God of love,

4 Then I hope like him to be,
Who redeem'd his saints from sin,
Whom I now obscurely see,
Through a cloud that stands between.

5 When I see him as he is,
No corruption can remain;
Such their portion who are his,
Such the happy state they gain.

6 Blessed fountain, full of grace!
Grace for sinners, grace for me;
To this source alone I trace
What I am, and hope to be.

HYMN CCXCVII.

"*But ye see me.*"—JOHN xiv. 19.

1 AN absent Lord I serve and love;
His image I with joy survey;
He reigns a King; he reigns above;
The hosts of heav'n confess his sway.

2 How blest are they who see his face,
And gaze upon his glory near!
Their nature pure, and heav'n their place;
They feel no want, they know no fear.

3 A day, I hope, will come, when I,
Ev'n I, though now so base and vile,
Shall see the Saviour's glory nigh,
And prove that heav'n is in his smile:

4 Till then I would his image trace,
And copy what I deem so fair;
In heav'n I hope to see his face;
His people will be like him there.

5 But still a doubt will oft arise,
An anxious doubt, if one like me
Shall ever gain so rich a prize,
Or ever with the Saviour be.

6 O thou, whose favour I prefer
To life itself, thy Spirit send:
Be mine the promised Comforter,
Be mine his presence to the end.

7 An earnest to my soul be given
Of joys unspeakable above;
An earnest of the joys of heav'n,
The joys of everlasting love.

HYMN CCXCVIII.

"*O death, where is thy sting?*"—1 COR. xv. 55.

1 DEATH has lost its terror;
Praise the Lord, ye saints, with me:
While I liv'd in error,
This could never, never be.
Till the Saviour found me,
And reveal'd his grace and love,
All was dark around me;
All below and all above.

2 Now the prospect bright is;
Brighter far than words can tell,
In the place where light is,
There it is I hope to dwell.
There to be for ever,
With the Lord, whose grace I prove.
To rejoice, and never
From his presence to remove.

3 Such a hope possessing,
Shall I live as once I did,
When without the blessing?
No! I answer, "God forbid!"
Be it my endeavour
Him to please whose own I am.
This my song for ever,
Praise to God, and to the Lamb.

4 But I am not able,
Lord, to do the thing I would:
Helpless and unstable,
Prone to evil, void of good.
Such I am; O take me;
Thou hast pow'r the dead to raise.
What I should be, make me:
Thine the work, and thine the praise.

HYMN CCXCIX.

"*I wot that he whom thou blessest is blessed.*"—NUM. xxii. 6.

1 THE stream that from the fountain flows,
The fountain of eternal love,
Imparts its virtue as it goes;
A gift all other gifts above.
'Tis life and peace divinely giv'n,
'Tis mercy coming down from heav'n.

2 How blessed to enjoy the gift,
To taste of mercy here below;
In humble thankfulness to lift
Our hearts to him who saves us so!
To know his love, how great it is,
To own and feel that we are his.

3 How blessed is the hope of good,
The good that without measure is,
Of seeing him who shed his blood
To save us, and to make us his!
Redeem'd by blood, and sav'd by grace,
We look to see the Saviour's face.

4 We look to see him as he is;
This honour to his saints is giv'n,
To see the glory that was his,
Before the world, while yet in heav'n;
To see his face, to share his throne,
And give the praise to him alone.

A State of Security.

HYMN CCC.

"*He that dwelleth in the secret place of the Most High, shall abide under the shadow of the Almighty.*"—PSALM xci. 1.

1 HAPPY they who trust in Jesus!
Sweet their portion is, and sure;
When the foe on others seizes,
He will keep his own secure.
Happy people!
Happy, though despis'd and poor.

2 Ye whom God has sav'd from error,
Ye "who know the joyful sound,"
Fear ye not the nightly terror;
Arms of mercy close you round:
Dread no evil;
God will all your foes confound.

3 Since his love and mercy found you,
Ye are precious in his sight;
Thousands now may fall around you,
Thousands more be put to flight;
But his presence
Keeps you safe by day and night.

4 Lo! your Saviour never slumbers,
Ever watchful in his care;
Though ye cannot boast of numbers,
In his strength secure ye are:
Sweet their portion,
Who our Saviour's kindness share.

5 As the bird beneath her feathers
Guards the objects of her care,
So the Lord his children gathers,
Spreads his wings, and hides them there;
Thus protected,
All their foes they boldly dare.

HYMN CCCI.

"*Unto thee lift I up mine eyes.*"—PSALM cxxiii. 1.

1 LORD, to thee I turn my eyes,
This has been my comfort long,
I am foolish, thou art wise,
I am weak, but thou art strong.

2 Strength, thy helpless worm has none,
Yet he need not fear his foes,
Since thy strength, and not his own,
Is the strength in which he goes.

3 Thus prepar'd, thy worm defies
Hostile force, and hostile art;
Strong, though weak, though foolish, wise,
Thou his strength and wisdom art.

4 More than conqu'ror at the last,
Through thy grace he hopes to prove,
And the final conflict past,
Then to dwell with thee above.

HYMN CCCII.

"*It is not in man that walketh to direct his steps.*"—Jer. x. 23.

1 IT is not we who can direct
Our steps, where many snares abound;
It is not we who can protect
Ourselves, when many foes surround.

2 The Lord, our leader, goes before,
Sufficient he, and none beside;
And were the dangers many more,
We need not fear with such a guide.

3 Thro' snares, thro' dangers, and thro' foes,
He leads, whose arm almighty is;
What, then, if earth and hell oppose!
We need not fear, if we are his.

4 All things are ours, if we are his,
All things on earth, and all in heav'n;
And high the destination is
Of those to whom this grace is giv'n.

5 Tho' many are their foes, and strong,
Tho' fears are great, and strength is small,
Tho' sharp their warfare is, and long,
Yet heav'n will make amends for all.

6 Their conflicts there for ever cease;
No warfare is, where all are friends;
There all is love, and all is peace,
And joy is there that never ends.

HYMN CCCIII.

"*My grace is sufficient for thee; for my strength is made perfect in weakness.*"—2 COR. xii. 9.

1 THY promise, Lord, just suits my case,
I sought assurance from thy mouth,
That one like me, so poor and base,
Would persevere to keep thy truth.

2 When inward, Lord, I turn my eyes,
I see but motives to despair;
Whatever charm the world supplies,
It finds a kindred temper there.

3 Sufficient ground *thy promise* yields,
On which a worm may rest his hope;
And he who on thy promise builds,
May give his confidence full scope.

4 Thy strength in weakness is display'd,
My soul this truth can relish now;
A worm upon thy pow'r is stay'd,
The weaker *he*, the greater *thou*.

5 If of myself I henceforth speak,
'Tis of infirmity alone;
I know that I am strong though weak,
My strength is Christ, the mighty one.

6 On everlasting arms I lean,
These only can sustain my hope;
These have till now my refuge been,
And these thro' life will hold me up.

7 I can look forward now with joy,
Though in myself a feeble worm;
For Jesus will his pow'r employ,
And save my soul in ev'ry storm.

HYMN CCCIV.

"*And if children, then heirs.*"—ROM. viii. 17.

1 THE mighty God our father is,
We call him thus, though worms of dust;
Happy the people who are his,
Who place in him a filial trust.

2 His children's wants are well supplied,
Their Father gives them angels' food;
No favour is by him denied,
That, granted, will promote their good.

3 He saves them from their enemies,
From snares by night, and force by day;
He sees the arrow as it flies,
And turns its course another way.

4 He smiles himself, and with his smile
The bright inheritance is giv'n:
What matter if the world revile,
When God is pleas'd, and smiles from heav'n?

5 The heirs of heav'n may well forego
The world's applause, nor feel the loss;
The gold is theirs, and well they know
The world's applause is worthless dross.

6 The sons of God, by heav'nly birth,
A rich inheritance is theirs;
For this, the highest throne on earth
To them a place too low appears.

7 Their souls aspire to nobler things,
Beyond the world their portion lies;
Their father is the King of kings,
And gives them everlasting joys.

HYMN CCCV.

"*But now, O Lord, thou art our father.*"—Isaiah lxiv. 8.

1 OUR Father sits on yonder throne,
Amidst the hosts above;
He reigns throughout the world alone,
He reigns, the God of love.

2 He knew us when we knew him not,
Was with us, though unseen;
His favour came to us unsought,
His love has wondrous been.

3 He keeps us now, securely keeps,
(Whatever foe assails,)
With vigilance that never sleeps,
With pow'r that never fails.

4 He gives us hope that we shall be
Ere long with him above;
That we shall all his glory see,
And celebrate his love.

5 Then let us, while we dwell below,
Obey our Father's voice;
To all his dispensations bow,
And in his name rejoice.

6 How sweet to hear him say at last,
"Ye blessed children, come;
The days of banishment are past,
And heav'n is now your home."

HYMN CCCVI.

"*They that wait upon the Lord shall renew their strength*."—
ISAIAH xl. 31.

1 THEY that wait upon the Lord,
As on eagles' pinions mounting,
Shall arise, (so says his word,)
All on earth beneath them counting;
They shall rise from earthly things,
God himself will give them wings.

2 They that wait upon the Lord,
Shall not faint and fail like others;
God will needful help afford,
God, whose love is more than mothers';
This may fail, however strange,
His is love that cannot change.

3 They that wait upon the Lord,
Ev'ry day their strength renewing,
Shall his grace with songs record,
Ev'ry day their foes subduing;
They shall go from strength to strength,
Till they meet in heav'n at length.

HYMN CCCVII.

"*Thou wilt keep him in perfect peace*."—ISAIAH xxvi. 3.

1 HAPPY man! he trusts in Jesus,
Therefore has he peace within;
While dismay on others seizes,
Lo, he wears a smile serene.

Ev'ry sound is full of terror,
  With a conscience ill at ease,
For we know the path of error
  Cannot be the path of peace.

2 Nothing now can greatly move him,
  For the Lord upholds his steps:
Trials may be sent to prove him,
  But the Lord his servant keeps.
Though he lives on earth a stranger,
  Press'd by many foes and fears,
God will keep in time of danger,
  And at last dry all his tears.

HYMN CCCVIII.

"*Come, my people, enter thou into thy chambers.*"—
ISAIAH xxvi. 20.

1 "COME, my people, to your chambers,
  Lo! the day of wrath draws nigh;"
Thus the Lord his saints remembers,
  Bidding them from danger fly:
When he comes in indignation,
  Comes to scourge a guilty land,
Then his people, from their station,
  See, but do not feel his hand.

2 Happy people, thus protected!
  Happy, whom the Lord secures!
O ye saints, by man rejected,
  Sing for joy, this lot is yours.
Though the worldling's hope should fail him,
  Yours is one that never will;
When ten thousand fears assail him,
  You may trust, and fear no ill.

3 Yea, in that more awful season,
When the heav'ns shall pass away,
Saints, ev'n then, shall have no reason
For confusion or dismay:
He who sought them here, and found them,
Will secure them from alarm;
And while nature flames around them,
They shall then sustain no harm.

4 O may we be found among them,
Now, and when the Lord appears;
Tho' the world should slight and wrong them,
One there is who counts their tears:
Pilgrims now on earth and strangers,
Yet the saints are truly blest;
God will save them here from dangers,
And in heav'n will give them rest.

HYMN CCIX.

"He giveth power to the faint."—ISAIAH xl. 29.

"HE giveth power to the faint,"
A blessed truth, and sweet when known,
How welcome to the trembling saint!
He knows his strength is not his own.

O man, whose hope is in the Lord,
When thou art weak, then art thou strong;
Be sure of this, nor doubt his word,
And thou shalt sing his praise ere long.

... man who trusts in him is strong,
God's own pow'r can make him so;
... who trusts in him, ere long,
... he himself is known, shall know.*

4 Our strength is he, whose hand has made
Both earth and heav'n, and all therein;
His people need not be afraid;
To doubt his faithful word is sin.

5 It matters not how weak we are;
We cannot fail, since he is strong;
Confiding in his love and care,
We hope to see his face ere long.

6 Let all the praise to him be giv'n,
Of what we have, or hope to have;
To him alone who came from heav'n,
Was on the cross, and in the grave,

7 Who rose again, and took his place
Beside the majesty in heav'n;
To God our Saviour, full of grace,
To him eternal praise be giv'n.

HYMN CCCX.

"*For the fashion of this world passeth away.*"—1 COR. vii. 31.

1 THOUGH all these things substantial seem,
The world itself is but a dream,
And soon must pass away;
The things that variously employ,
That yield us either grief or joy,
Must see their final day.

2 How sweet to have our portion there,
Where sorrow never comes, nor care,
And nothing will remove:
We now may hear without a sigh,
The world's destruction to be nigh,
Our treasure is above.

3 How sweet to know the Saviour's name,
The Saviour who in mercy came,
And vanquish'd all our foes;
On him, as on a solid rock,
Our hope is built, and stands the shock,
Of ev'ry storm that blows.

4 Then let a world of shadows go.
It matters not, his people know
Their treasure still is sure.
'Tis laid up there where nothing fades,
No rust consumes, no thief invades,
And there it is secure.

Christian Intercourse.

HYMN CCCXI.

"*Touching the King.*"—PSALM xlv. 1.

1 THE Saviour's people, when they meet,
With wonder and with joy may sing;
For lofty is their theme, and sweet;
It touches heav'n's eternal King.

2 It touches him, who mov'd by love,
Though prais'd by yonder shining host,
In mercy left his throne above,
And stoop'd to save what else were lost.

3 It touches him who suffer'd pain,
And shame, and death, that they might live;
That they might grace and glory gain,
And all that God himself can give.

4 The theme is sweet and lofty too;
It moves our wonder and our love:
The theme is great, and ever new;
It yields unceasing joy above.

5 It animates the soul with hope,
With hope, the spring of many joys;
It holds the fainting spirit up,
And ev'ry day new strength supplies.

6 Preserv'd through grace in wisdom's ways,
May we with yonder shining host
At length be join'd, and sing the praise
Of him who came to save the lost.

HYMN CCCXII.

"*Lord, lift thou up the light of thy countenance upon us.*"—
PSALM iv. 6.

1 BLEST intercourse! when Christians meet,
And speak of him who died for them;
They sit at the Redeemer's feet,
And care not if the world condemn.

2 The world knows nothing of the joys
That Christian fellowship supplies;
Enamour'd of their glittering toys,
Our hope seems nothing in their eyes.

3 But we can witness what we know,
And speak aloud, nor care who hears;
Our joys from heav'nly sources flow,
And would be ill exchang'd for theirs.

4 One day in wisdom's sacred ways
Is better than a thousand, spent
As thoughtless worldlings spend their days,
From pleasure far, and sweet content.

5 We envy not the great and wise;
We count ourselves more blest than they:
We're taught their honours to despise,
And from their joys to turn away.

6 'Twill soon appear who serve the Lord,
And who are they that serve him not;
Then let us hold his faithful word,
And ours shall be a glorious lot.

HYMN CCCXIII.

"*Then they that feared the Lord spake often one to another.*"—
MAL. iii. 16.

1 WHY should believers, when they meet,
Not speak of Christ, the King they own,
Who gives them hope that they shall sit
With him for ever on his throne?

2 Is any other name so great
As his who bore the sinner's load?
Is any subject half so sweet,
So cheering as the love of God?

3 'Tis this that charms reluctant man,
That makes his opposition cease;
Beholding love's amazing plan,
He drops his arms, and sues for peace.

4 'Twas so with us; we once were foes—
Were foes to him who gave us breath;
But he, whose mercy overflows,
Has sav'd us from eternal death.

5 We look with hope to that great day,
When Jesus will with clouds appear;
A sight of him will well repay
Our labours and our sorrows here.

6 Of him then let us speak and sing,
Whose glory we expect to share;
In heav'n we hope to see our King,
And yield a nobler tribute there.

HYMN CCCXIV.

"Thou hast put gladness in my heart, more than in the time that their corn and wine increased."—Psalm iv. 7.

1 FAR from us be grief and sadness,
Farther still unhallow'd mirth;
Zion's sons may sing with gladness,
Theirs are joys of heav'nly birth:
Jesus owns them:
He is Lord of heav'n and earth.

2 All the worldling's mirth is madness;
All his labour fruitless toil;
'Tis the saints that taste of gladness,
Though the world their choice revile:
Sweet their portion!
Life is in the Saviour's smile.

3 Worlds would seem as nothing to us,
Balanc'd with a Saviour's love;
Since the Lord in mercy drew us,
Drew our souls to things above,
Earthly objects
Can no longer greatly move.

4 Once the world was all our treasure,
Then the world our hearts possest;
Now we taste sublimer pleasure,
Since the Lord has made us blest:
And can witness
Jesus gives his people rest.

HYMN CCCXV.

"*Let your speech be alway with grace.*"—Col. iv. 6.

1 SWEET and solemn be the season,
When the friends of Jesus meet;
Let the worldling boast his reason,
While he fills the scorner's seat:
Heav'nly wisdom
Leads us to the Saviour's feet.

2 Far be idle jesting from us!
Sacred themes to us belong:
Ours the cross, and ours the promise,
Subjects these for endless song;
Subjects worthy
To employ the Christian's tongue.

3 Time is precious, we'll improve it,
Worldlings talk of worldly things;
Leave the world to those who love it,
'Tis not thence our comfort springs:
Jesus owns us,
Jesus is the King of kings.

HYMN CCCXVI.

"*Exhorting one another, and so much the more as ye see the day approaching.*"—Heb. x. 25.

1 WHILE in the world we still remain,
We only meet to part again;
But when we reach the heav'nly shore,
We then shall meet to part no more.

2 The hope that we shall see that day
Should chase our present griefs away;
A few short years of conflict past,
We meet around the throne at last.

3 Then let us here improve our hours,
Improve them to a Saviour's praise,
To him with zeal devote our pow'rs,
And run with joy in wisdom's ways.

4 Let all our meetings now be made
Subservient to each other's good;
For worldly joys must quickly fade,
Nor can they yield substantial food.

5 Whene'er required to part from those
With whom the truth unites us here,
We'll call to mind the joyful close,
When Christ the Saviour will appear.

6 Then shall his saints all meet again,
For so his word of promise says,
With him for ever to remain,
And sing his everlasting praise.

HYMN CCCXVII.

"*Unto you therefore which believe, he is precious.*"—1 Pet. ii. 7.

1 If worldly thoughts so much employ,
And worldly themes yield so much joy,
While God is yet unknown,
With what delight we now should speak
Of him who came from heav'n to seek,
And claim us as his own!

2 From us his glory long lay hid,
We lov'd the world as others did,
No portion else had we;
But he who first sent forth the light,
The Lord remov'd our mental night,
He gave us eyes to see.

3 His love supplies a boundless theme,
Then let us think and speak of him,
Who saves his people thus;
He came in mercy from above,
He came upon the wings of love,
And gave himself for us.

4 Dear Saviour, let us never be,
Before the world asham'd of thee,
Nor shrink from duty's call:
Our work to do thee service here,
Our hope in glory to appear,
Where thou art all in all.

HYMN CCCXVIII.

"*Nor foolish talking nor jesting, which are not convenient.*"—
EPH. v. 4.

1 ENAMOUR'D of their golden dreams,
Let worldlings talk on worldly themes;
This should not be when Christians meet,
The world should lie beneath their feet.

2 And do *they* want a nobler theme,
Whom Jesus suffer'd to redeem?
The love that bore the cross should throw
A shade on ev'ry thing below.

3 The cross!—its burden, O how great!
No strength but his *could* bear its weight;
No love but his *would* undertake
To bear it for the sinner's sake.

4 His saints can never want a theme,
How can they, when they think of him?
For love like his, so rich, so strong,
Is theme enough for endless song.

5 Come then, and let us talk of him,
Who died the sinner to redeem;
The joyful theme we'll still pursue,
'Tis sweet, 'tis rich, 'tis ever new.

6 Let idle jests be far from us,
It suits us not to trifle thus;
We'll leave it to the sons of earth,
And meet for profit, not for mirth.

HYMN CCCXIX.

"*Unto you therefore which believe, he is precious.*"—1 Pet. ii. 7.

1 WE'LL speak of Christ, nor heed we who
Should disapprove the theme;
When he is precious in our view,
'Tis sweet to speak of him.

2 And he is precious in the sight
Of all who know his voice;
'Twas he who brought them to the light,
And taught them to rejoice.

3 'Tis he who cheers them by his smile,
And guards them by his pow'r,
Who keeps them safe from force and guile,
In ev'ry trying hour.

4 'Tis he who will conduct them home,
Beyond the reach of ill,
Where all the ransom'd people come,
Where saints for ever dwell.

5 Let glory wreathe his sacred head,
Who once was crown'd with thorns;
Whose blood upon the cross was shed,
Whom man reviles and scorns.

6 And let his people make their boast
Of him, and him alone,
Who came from heav'n to save the lost:
The praise be all his own.

HYMN CCCXX.

"*What do ye more than others?*"—MATT. v. 47.

1 AND do we hope to be with him
Who on the cross resign'd his breath;
Who died a victim to redeem
His people from eternal death?

2 Then should the question oft recur,
What do we more than others do?
How do we show that we prefer
The things above to those below?

3 Where is that holy walk that suits
The name and character we bear?
And where are seen those heav'nly fruits
That shew we're not what once we were?

4 Allied to him who bore the cross,
And call'd the people of the Lord,
The world to us should seem but loss,
And worthless all it can afford.

5 As pilgrims on their journey home,
'Tis thus his people should be found;
Who seek a city yet to come,
And cannot rest on earthly ground.

6 'Tis thus his people prove their birth,
'Tis thus they glorify their Lord;
To others they resign the earth,
And hasten to their bright reward.

HYMN CCCXXI.

"*They shall speak of the glory of thy kingdom.*"—
PSALM cxlv. 11.

1 SUBJECTS of the King of heaven,
We can talk on glorious themes;
Happy they to whom 'tis given
To despise the worldling's dreams!
Subjects of the King of kings,
We can speak of real things.

2 Of his kingdom, and his glory,
We can speak since we are his;
Mighty kingdoms famed in story,
Nothing are compared to this:
All that makes a kingdom great,
Here alone is found to meet.

3 Other thrones, however splendid,
Yield to time's destructive pow'r;
Human glory soon is ended,
God appoints its final hour;
But the throne at which we bow,
Time can never overthrow.

4 While the kingdoms round us vanish,
(What that's human can endure?)
Ev'ry sad reflection banish,
God has made *his* kingdom sure;
Other thrones may shake and fall,
But *his* throne survives them all.

5 Good it is for us and pleasant,
To converse on themes like these;
When with God his saints are present,
Then they see him as he is;
Till that day we'll talk of him,
Heav'n supplies no richer theme.

HYMN CCCXXII.

"*I have set the Lord always before me.*"—Psalm xvi. 8.

1 OH! how many subjects draw us
    From that sweet, that sacred theme,
Of his love, who, when he saw us
    In our sins, and far from him,
Form'd a wondrous plan to save,
And himself for sinners gave!

2 Were the Saviour, as he should be,
    Always set before our eyes,
This would never be, nor could be,
    Other themes we should despise;
What our hearts desire and seek,
'Tis of that we love to speak.

3 Saviour, let thy great salvation
    Be the theme of our delight,
Subject of our meditation,
    Till our faith shall end in sight;
Till before thee we appear,
And behold thy glory near.

HYMN CCCXXIII.

"*And he said, Come in, thou blessed of the Lord.*"—
Gen. xxiv. 31.

1 WELCOME hither, friends beloved,
    Ye to whom our Lord is dear;
They who are by him approved,
    Ever shall be welcome here:
'Tis our privilege to know
Those who serve our Lord below.

2 Welcome, brethren, welcome hither,
In our Saviour's name we meet;
While we now remain together,
May our fellowship be sweet:
We will speak of things above,
All our theme a Saviour's love.

3 Thanks to him, by whose permission,
We can meet without alarm;
Free from human opposition,
Sav'd from ev'ry hostile arm:
Though our foes are all around,
Jesus makes our peace abound.

4 'Tis to him we owe our treasure,
All we have, and hope to have;
Come, ye saints, unite with pleasure,
Sing of Jesus, strong to save:
Join the happy hosts above,
Celebrate the God of love.

Evangelical Alliance.

HYMN CCCXXIV.

"*Behold, how good and pleasant it is for brethren to dwell together in unity.*"—Psalm cxxxiii. 1.

1 NOW let us all, with one accord,
Invoke the presence of our Lord;
For ever hallowed be his name,
To-day, as yesterday, the same.

2 The same for ever; his it is,
To touch the heart. To bless is his:
To visit us from heaven above;
To fill our souls with holy love.

3 His presence consecrates the place;
'Tis blessed when we see his face;
And when we hear his sacred voice,
'Tis then our very souls rejoice.

4 At strife too long, O Lord, we've been,
We own and we abjure our sin;
And now we look for better things,
The very hope a blessing brings.

5 Forgive the past, forgive it all,
And let us now obey the call;
For such it is, or seems to be,
A call to love and unity.

6 We bless thee that thy people seem
As if awakened from a dream;
Resolved henceforth from strife to cease,
And "follow things that make for peace."

7 The holy purpose, Lord, we hail;
But what will human strength avail?
This precious truth we're given to see,
That power, O Lord, belongs to thee.

8 To thee, then, Lord, we raise our cry,
The blessed season bring it nigh;
Let strife among thy people cease,
And love succeed, and holy peace.

HYMN CCCXXV.

"*The Lord hath done great things for us.*"—PSALM cxxvi. 3.

1 FOR such a season, Lord, as this,
We bless thy name; 'tis meet we should;
The air we breathe refreshing is,
To mingle thus, we feel is good.

2 We never look'd to see it so,
Thine arm was shorten'd as we thought;
We fear'd thine ear was heavy too,
We did thee wrong, thou changest not.

3 Thy hallow'd presence is to us
The pledge that we are doing right;
We feel assur'd that acting thus,
We do what's pleasing in thy sight.

4 So strange is what we witness here,
That we are like to those that dream;
It may illusion prove, we fear,
What real is not, though it seem.

5 But why those fears? the work is thine,
Without thy power it could not be;
Its very strangeness is the sign,
That it belongs, O Lord, to thee.

6 In holy fellowship we meet,
The bond of union that we own,
Is love to thee. The thought is sweet,
This bond sufficient is alone.

7 We bless the day, when taught by thee,
As we believe, this work of love
We first began; and glad we see,
How many now the work approve.

8 'Tis meet we should commit to thee
The work thus happily begun;
No wisdom, Lord, nor pow'r have we,
Thy will, we pray, not ours be done.

9 We do not wish it to succeed,
Unless it owes its birth to thee;
Against, not for it, would we plead,
If man's device or work it be.

10 We deem it thine, and we exhort
Each other to be true to thee;
"Through evil and through good report,"
Thy faithful witnesses to be.

11 Where thou wilt lead, we do not know,
To know it, Lord, we do not need;
Implicit faith be ours, to go
Wherever 'tis thy will to lead.

The Gospel.

HYMN CCCXXVI.

"*Blessed are the people that know the joyful sound.*"—
PSALM lxxxix. 15.

1 SWEET sounds of grace are heard abroad,
The sinner is surpris'd and charm'd;
He feels the conqu'ring pow'r of God,
He feels it, and is straight disarm'd.

2 Till now to vain desire a prey,
Nor peace nor pleasure could he find;
But see, old things are past away!
New objects occupy his mind.

3 A Saviour's love, a Saviour's death,
(Fit themes for sinful man to hear,)
Not heard before, or not in faith,
Now captivate his list'ning ear.

4 The world no longer keeps his heart,
His chains dissolve before the cross;
His choice is now the better part,
And former gain appears but loss.

5 'Tis thus the Gospel wins its way;
It brings good tidings to the poor;
And those who nothing have to pay,
Are welcome to its richest store.

HYMN CCCXXVII.

"*I will sing of mercy.*"—Psalm ci. 1.

1 I HEAR a sound that comes from far,
It fills my soul with joy and love;
Not seraphs' voices sweeter are,
That echo through the courts above.

2 'Tis mercy's voice that strikes my ear.
From Calvary it sounds abroad;
It soothes my soul and calms my fear,
It speaks of pardon bought with blood.

3 And is it true that many fly
The sound that bids my soul rejoice;
And rather choose with fools to die,
Than turn an ear to mercy's voice?

4 Alas for those! the day is near
When mercy will be heard no more;
Then will they ask in vain to hear
The voice they would not hear before.

5 With such I own I once appear'd,
But now I know how great their loss;
For sweeter sounds were never heard,
Than mercy utters from the cross.

6 But let me not forget to own
That if I differ aught from those,
'Tis due to sov'reign grace alone,
That oft selects its proudest foes.

HYMN CCCXXVIII.

"*Sinners, of whom I am chief.*"—1 Tim. i. 15.

1 THE Gospel comes with welcome news
To sinners lost like me;
Their various schemes let others choose,
Saviour! I come to thee.

2 Of sinners sure I am the chief,
But grace is rich and free;
This welcome truth affords relief
To *sinners*, ev'n to me.

3 Of merit now let others speak,
But merit I have none;
For merit 'tis in vain to seek;
I'm sav'd by grace alone.

4 'Twas grace my wayward heart first won,
'Tis grace that holds me fast;
Grace will complete the work begun,
And save me to the last.

5 Then shall my soul with rapture trace
What God has done for me,
And celebrate redeeming grace
Throughout eternity,

HYMN CCCXXIX.

"*And the truth shall make you free.*"—John viii. 32.

1 WELCOME news the Gospel brings,
Welcome news from heav'n above,
Tidings from the King of kings,
Tidings full of grace and love.

2 O ye sons of men, give ear!
Listen to the "joyful sound,"
Better news ye cannot hear:
In the Gospel truth is found.

3 Truth, that makes the simple wise,
Truth, on which the hungry feed,
Truth, the source of many joys,
Truth, that makes us free indeed.

4 Welcome news the Gospel brings,
Welcome to the poor and vile,
Gladden'd by these glorious things,
Guilt and poverty may smile.

HYMN CCCXXX.

"*We hanged our harps upon the willows.*"—PSALM cxxxvii. 2.

1 MY harp on yonder willow lies,
Silent, neglected, and unstrung;
My cheerful songs are turn'd to sighs,
Sad is my heart, and mute my tongue.

2 Once I could sound the note of praise;
As loud as others I could sing;
But retrospect of former days
No help in present grief will bring.

3 Unfaithfulness, my God, to thee,
Has chill'd my heart, and seal'd my tongue;
Thy smiling face no more I see,
No wonder then my harp 's unstrung;

4 But why should I give way to grief?
I see my remedy at hand;
The words of grace, they bring relief
To such as self-convicted stand?

5 Yes, 'tis a faithful cheering word,
That Jesus came to save the lost!
This truth with richest grace is stor'd,
And to the vilest yields the most.

6 Here, then, let all my sadness end,
I'll take my harp again and sing;
My theme shall be the sinner's friend,
Jesus, my Saviour and my King.

HYMN CCCXXXI.

"*O Lord, how manifold are thy works!*"—PSALM civ. 24.

1 NOT from the azure vault we see,
With glowing stars profusely sown,
Though ev'ry star a world should be,
The character of God is known.

2 The heav'ns indeed his praise declare;
They shew his wisdom and his might;
But sinners see no token there
Of mercy, to refresh their sight.

3 That sun, which climbs the height of heav'n,
And like a strong man runs his race,
No notice brings of sins forgiv'n;
To guilty man, no news of grace.

4 How welcome, then, the news must be,
That in the sacred page is found!
The news of mercy, rich and free!
Proclaim it to the world around.

5 Where'er yon sun, in all its round,
Declares his praise, who sends him forth;
Proclaim ye there "the joyful sound,"
From west to east, from south to north.

6 'Tis meet the people of the Lord
   Should wide unfold the sacred page;
And spread throughout the world that word
   That shines a light to every age.

HYMN CCCXXXII.

"*Behold upon the mountains the feet of him that bringeth good tidings.*"—NAHUM i. 15.

1 SEE! he comes upon the mountains,
   Bringing news of heav'nly birth!
Mercy opens all her fountains,
   And directs the streams to earth;
This is news to cheer the sad,
This is news to make us glad.

2 Sing of mercy, sing with gladness,
   Let the theme our tongues employ;
Talk no more of gloom and sadness,
   Mercy is a theme of joy;
They, we're sure, who know not this,
Do not know what mercy is.

3 But for this all-cheering subject,
   What a waste the earth would seem!
Mercy now on ev'ry object
   Seems to shed a cheerful beam;
Till we knew "the joyful sound,"
All was dark and waste around.

4 Mercy lightens all our crosses,
   Mercy mitigates our pains,
Makes amends for all our losses,
   And gives worth to what remains;
All our joys from mercy spring,
Let us then of mercy sing.

HYMN CCCXXXIII.

"*Of whom I am chief.*"—1 Tim. i. 15.

1 Of sinners the chief,
But finding relief,
In the Gospel, the word of thy grace:
I come to thee, Lord,
Thy blessing afford,
And shew me the light of thy face.

2 How blessed is he,
Who clearly can see,
Thy mercy reveal'd in the word!
He dries up his tears,
Dismisses his fears,
And trusts in the name of the Lord.

3 "The things that are seen,"
Had hitherto been
The things that engross'd every thought.
'Tis not as before;
The charm is no more:
He now by the Spirit is taught.

4 He looks for the day,
When Jesus will say,
"Enter into the joy of thy Lord."
Ev'n here is there giv'n,
A foretaste of heav'n,
His people rejoice in his word.

5 Then what will it be,
When Jesus they see,
The Lord whom, tho' unseen, they love!
What language can paint
The joy of the saint,
When he enters the mansions above!

HYMN CCCXXXIV.

"*And in sin did my mother conceive me.*"—PSALM li. 5.

1 BORN in sin, and doom'd to die,
Such are you, and such am I.
Nothing we can say or do,
Will or can make this untrue.
Bitter is the cup we drink of;
Sad it is—'tis sad to think of.

2 But how sad the case would be—
Sad for you, and sad for me,
Were it not for news from heav'n—
News of grace, of sin forgiv'n!
This can take away our sadness;
This can fill our hearts with gladness.

3 Grace it is—'tis grace indeed,
When "a child of wrath" like me
Is from guilt and ruin freed,
And at length is brought to see,
Him whose voice is in the thunder—
Him whom angels view with wonder.

4 Grace, "the grace of God" it is;
His in act, in purpose his.
Wonder, O ye heavens, with me,
And thou earth, astonish'd be.
Grace is what for sinners meet is;
Grace is what to sinners sweet is.

HYMN CCCXXXV.

"*Good tidings.*"—LUKE ii. 10.

1 NEWS we have, 'tis news from heaven,
News to make a sinner glad;
News of grace, of sin forgiven,
Henceforth why should we be sad?

2 Were the news of doubtful credit,
'Twould not be the cause of joy;
But the book in which we read it,
Is *his* book, who cannot lie.

3 Were the grace that there we read of,
Less, it would not reach our case:
'Tis the grace that we have need of,
Rich, abounding, sov'reign grace.

4 Did the Saviour's invitation,
One except of Adam's race;
Could we say that his salvation,
Then would reach the sinner's case?

5 But the Lord excepts not any;
Not the vilest of mankind:
All may come, however many,
All who come will pardon find.

6 Welcome, then, the news from heaven.
Fit it is to make us glad;
Sing of grace, of sin forgiven,
And be never henceforth sad.

Addresses to Unbelievers.

HYMN CCCXXXVI.

"*A prudent man foreseeth the evil, and hideth himself; the simple pass on, and are punished.*"—PROV. xxii. 3.

1 TO the ark away, or perish,
Sinners, to the ark away;
Vain the hope, that thousands cherish,
Of deliv'rance in that day,
When destruction
Cometh, that no arm can stay.

2 Sinners, be advised, and haste ye
To the ark that open lies;
Why, O why, in folly waste ye
Precious time that quickly flies?
Soon your laughter
Will be turn'd to mournful cries.

3 Hear the Lord himself invite you
To his arms, a refuge sure;
O believe him, lest he smite you
With a curse that none can cure:
When he thunders,
Who his anger can endure?

4 They are safe, and none beside them,
Who the Saviour's word obey;
They are safe, for he will hide them
In the dark and gloomy day;
He will hide them
Till the storm has pass'd away.

5 Then a bright and glorious season
Shall succeed, and never end;
Hear him then, for there is reason,
Jesus is the sinner's friend;
Safe his people:
Nothing shall his saints offend.

HYMN CCCXXXVII.

"*Doth not wisdom cry?*"—PROV. viii. 1.

1 SINNERS, hear, for God hath spoken;
'Tis the God that reigns on high,
He, whose law the world has broken,
Sends you tidings of great joy;
Hear his message,
Hear it, sinners, lest ye die.

2 'Tis of Jesus, God's own equal,
Blessed ere the world began;
Sinners, mark th' important sequel,
Cloth'd in flesh, he died for man:
'Tis the Gospel
Brings to light love's gracious plan.

3 Hear the Gospel, sinners hear it,
Joyful news from heav'n it brings;
Here's a fountain, O draw near it!
Open'd by the King of kings:
Living water
Thence in streams eternal springs.

4 Hear the Gospel, slaves of pleasure,
Here are joys that never end;
Ye, whose God is earthly treasure,
Why for nought your labour spend?
Boundless riches
See in Christ the sinner's friend.

5 Ye who with the wise are number'd,
Here may learn what wisdom is;
All by worldly cares encumber'd,
Come and find your rest in this:
'Tis the Gospel
Shews the road to heav'nly peace.

6 Sinners, hear, why will ye perish?
Death to life, O why prefer?
Why your vain delusions cherish?
Why from truth persist to err?
Wisdom calls you,
Happy they who learn of her.

HYMN CCCXXXVIII.

" *Why will ye die?*"—EZEK. xviii. 31.

1 SINNER, wilt thou still go on?
Fear'st thou not eternal death?
Think how ev'ry hope is gone,
When the sinner yields his breath.

2 Did some earthly int'rest call,
Wouldst thou, couldst thou careless be?
Think of thine eternal all,
Sinner, what's the world to thee?

3 Can the world remove thy sin?
Can it set thy conscience free?
Can it give thee peace within?
Sinner, what's the world to thee?

4 Why, ah why provoke the Lord?
Is thine arm omnipotent?
Why despise his gracious word?
Why upon destruction bent?

5 Canst thou still of sin make light,
Nor suppose the danger great?
See the cross! for there's a sight
Well explains thy awful state.

6 See the Lamb of God in pain!
Pain like his has never been;
This, in language clear and plain,
Speaks the true desert of sin.

7 But while justice gives the wound,
Mercy's voice is heard to say,
"See the ransom I have found!
Jesus is the living way."

8 Sinner, here is hope for thee,
Jesus bore the sinner's shame;
This is thy sufficient plea,
Life is in his saving name.

HYMN CCCXXXIX.

"When the poor and needy seek water . . . . I the Lord will hear them."—ISAIAH xli. 17.

1 SINNERS, come, though poor and needy,
Jesus will relieve the poor;
He declares, "All things are ready,"
And what Jesus says is sure:
O believe him!
Take of mercy's boundless store.

2 Hear how God himself beseeches—
"Sinners, be ye reconcil'd;"
Jesus in the Gospel teaches
How a foe becomes a child;
When he suffer'd,
Love prevail'd, and justice smil'd.

3 See his sacred body broken!
Broken on th' accursed tree;
Hear the words the Lord hath spoken—
"Sinners live, beholding me;"
Hopeless sinner,
Thus the Saviour speaks to thee.

4 Should you slight his great salvation,
Can you stand when he appears?
When the Judge shall take his station,
What will then avail your tears?
Seek, O seek him!
While the Lord in mercy hears.

HYMN CCCXL.

"*What will ye do in the day of visitation?*"—ISAIAH x. 3.

1 SINNERS, living without God,
Hear the voice of sov'reign mercy,
Else expect to feel the rod,
In the day of controversy;
When the Saviour comes again,
Comes from heav'n to plead with men.

2 Though conceal'd from mortals now,
Jesus will appear in glory;
God pronounces all below
Fading, vain, and transitory:
All we see at last shall fall,
Destin'd to destruction all.

3 Why then fight with God above?
Why persist your hearts to harden?
O be wise, nor slight his love,
While the Gospel speaks of pardon;
Pardon through a Saviour's blood,
Pardon freely giv'n of God.

HYMN CCCXLI.

"*But when thou makest a feast, call the poor.*"—LUKE xiv. 13.

1 THE King has made a feast,
Where choice with plenty vies,
'Tis furnish'd with the best
His rich domain supplies:
Its varied store
Is for the poor;
Then haste, ye poor, and come away,
The King invites, why then delay?

2 Why should the poor refuse
A banquet spread for them?
Deride the joyful news,
The proffer'd good contemn?
'Tis madness all
To slight his call;
Then haste, ye poor, and come away,
The King invites, why then delay?

3 This King is Lord of all,
And Jesus is his name;
If you neglect his call,
Your portion will be shame;
But they are bless'd
Who share his feast;
Then haste, ye poor, and come away,
'Tis Jesus calls, why then delay?

HYMN CCCXLII.

"Ho, every one that thirsteth, come ye to the waters."—
ISAIAH lv. 1.

1 ADAM'S ruin'd sons and daughters,
Hear the voice of God, and live;
Come ye, come ye to the waters,
Come, for God will freely give:
Here the spring of life is found,
Streams of mercy here abound.

2 Why your substance vainly spending
To procure what is not food?
To the Saviour's voice attending,
Come and find substantial good:
Jesus is the Saviour giv'n,
Jesus is the bread from heav'n.

8 Hear the Saviour, O ye thoughtless!
They who hear him not must fall:
Will ye trust your schemes as faultless,
While the Lord condemns them all?
O be wise, and hear the Lord!
Fight no more against his word.

HYMN CCCXLIII.

"*But now commandeth all men everywhere to repent.*"—
ACTS xvii. 30.

1 WHAT a day of awful terror,
When the Saviour shall appear!
Ye who, led away by error,
See no danger, own no fear,
O bethink you!
Now to wisdom's voice give ear.

2 Simple ones, though oft admonish'd,
Still pass on—no fear have they;
But they learn at length, when punish'd,
What it is to go astray:
Awful lesson!
They can never find the way.

3 See the fatal end of scorning,
The reproof by wisdom sent;
O be wise, and take the warning;
'Tis a voice in mercy meant:
Be admonish'd;
God commands you to repent.

4 Grace and justice meet together
In the Saviour's work of love;
Whither will ye fly, ah, whither,
When he cometh from above,
Should you slight him,
Should his word now fruitless prove?

HYMN CCCXLIV.

"*He shall flee unto one of those cities, and live.*"—DEUT. xix. 5.

1 FLY, O man, thy life's at stake;
Fly from the avenger's blow.
Sleepest thou? Awake, awake:
Now or never shun the foe.
Stay not, for a moment's stay
May be fatal—haste away.

2 Flee thou as a man would flee
From the hungry lion's jaws.
Haste thee, faint though thou shouldst be.
Haste thee, is there not a cause?
Cause to flee, and cause to fear?
Is not the avenger near?

3 Flee thou to the sacred spot,
God's asylum, thither flee;
Till within it, slack thou not;
There alone wilt thou be free,
Free from the avenger's arm,
There thou wilt be safe from harm.

4 Know'st thou what I mean by this?
Thou, O man, a sinner art,
And, as such, thy sentence is,
Death. O lay the truth to heart.
Flee thou from the coming wrath,
Who to meet it courage hath?

5 Can thine heart, O man, endure,
When the Lord from heav'n appears?
Who can then thy life secure?
What will then avail thy tears?
Shouldst thou die unpardon'd, know,
Then comes never-ending woe.

6 Haste thee, then, to him who is
    Strong to save, and willing too;
Grace, and love, and pow'r are his;
    What he pleases, he can do;
'Tis his pleasure, man to save.
Ask of him, and thou shalt have.

7 Thou shalt have what needful is,
    Pardon, peace, and life within;
His the work, the glory his,
    Thine the need, for thine the sin:
Thou a sinner art, but he
Died for sinners: well for thee.

HYMN CCCXLV.

"Ye have taken, and by wicked hands have crucified and slain."
ACTS ii. 23.

1 SEE the Saviour, sinners slew him;
    Yet for sinners he was slain;
Sinners now are welcome to him,
    Such compose the Saviour's train;
Sinners ransom'd by his blood,
Sinners reconcil'd to God.

2 See the holy victim suff'ring,
    Sinners, here's a sight for you;
Here's an all-sufficient off'ring,
    O believe the record true!
See the Lamb, for sinners slain,
Ev'ry other hope is vain.

3 'Tis a true and joyful saying,
    Jesus came to save the lost;
Grace and truth at once displaying,
    God the Saviour, true and just:
Sinners, hear his gracious voice,
In his saving work rejoice.

HYMN CCCXLVI.

"*Come ye, buy wine and milk without money and without price.*"
ISAIAH lv. 1.

1 BRING no money here, nor price,
Here it is not wanted;
God hath spoken once, yea twice;
What is here is granted,
Granted freely to the poor,
Theirs the living waters.
Enter, then, the open door,
Adam's sons and daughters.

2 'Tis the Saviour's gracious call,
His the invitation;
And his message is to all,
All of every station;
'Tis for every clime and age;
"Grace and truth" it teaches;
To the simple and the sage,
Pardon free it preaches.

3 'Tis the word of truth indeed,
And of grace abounding,
Suited to the sinner's need,
Yet our thought confounding;
Masterpiece of him it is,
Him who works his pleasure;
Power, and grace, and wisdom his,
His, but without measure;

4 He it is who leaves his throne,
Leaves his throne, yet fills it.
So it is, and be it known,
So, because he wills it.

Lo! he stoops to raise us up,
  Who of all could think it?
And he drinks a bitter cup,
  Who but he could drink it?

5 Wonder, O ye heav'ns, at this;
  Earth, be thou astonished;
Sons of men, for you it is,
  Be ye then admonished;
Hear the Saviour's voice, and live,
  Mercy 'tis that woos you;
To the message credence give,
  Unbelief undoes you.

Effects of the Gospel.

HYMN CCCXLVII.

"*To turn them from darkness to light.*"—Acts xxvi. 18.

1 BOUNDLESS glory, Lord, be thine!
  Thou hast made the darkness shine;
Thou hast sent a cheering ray;
Thou hast turn'd our night to day.

2 Hither is the Gospel come;
'Tis "the pow'r of God" to some;
O let such in praise unite
To the Lord who gives them light.

3 Darkness long involv'd us round,
Till we knew "the joyful sound;"
Then our darkness fled away,
Chas'd by truth's celestial ray.

4 *They* are bless'd, and none beside,
They who in the truth abide;
Clear the light that marks their way,
Leading to eternal day.

5 Ye who walk this heav'nly road,
Hasting to the saints' abode,
See how bright it shines above!
There appears the God of love.

6 Soon your stronger sight will bear
To behold that glory near;
Light that now would but destroy,
Then will yield sublimest joy.

HYMN CCCXLVIII.

"*And thou shalt speak and say . . . . a Syrian ready to perish was my father.*"—DEUT. xxvi. 5.

1 "READY to perish," Lord, we lay,
And only for destruction meet;
Yet unconcern'd we seem'd to say,
"Disgrace is pleasant, ruin sweet."

2 Foolish in mind, deprav'd in will,
The vilest, basest slaves were we;
And such we had continued still,
Had not thy mercy set us free.

3 Yes, Lord, we'll tell what thou hast done,
And if we boast, we'll boast in thee;
Thine arm the victory has won,
For none were greater foes than we.

4 A light surpris'd us on the way,
When flying we were found of thee;
Thus, Lord, may all thy people say,
But none with greater truth than *we*.

5 And, though we have no perfect rest,
Till we attain our place above,
Yet *here* we count thy people bless'd,
As favour'd objects of thy love.

6 Ev'n here, from Canaan's fertile fields,
Some earnest of the fruits we share;
And if the taste such pleasure yields,
How sweet to be for ever there!

7 Lord, let the years roll swiftly on,
That we may take our place above,
May *there* proclaim what thou hast done,
And sing thine everlasting love.

HYMN CCCXLIX.

"*When the Lord turned again the captivity of Zion, we were like them that dream.*"—PSALM cxxvi. 1.

1 WHEN Jesus broke the chains that bound me,
I hardly could believe it true;
All nature seem'd to smile around me,
And brightest prospects cheer'd my view.

2 It seem'd like some enchanting vision,
That charms awhile, but does not last;
And much I fear'd some sad transition,
Some change that all my hopes would blast.

3 But when my doubts and fears had vanish'd,
I felt a joy unknown before;
Like one restor'd who had been banish'd,
Restor'd, to leave his home no more.

4 Thus ancient Isra'l saw with wonder,
How God had set his people free;
When those who long had kept them under,
At his command resign'd their prey.

5 And now to sin no more a servant,
O may I live to God alone!
Blameless in life, in spirit fervent,
In me may all his will be done.

6 And when my work on earth is over,
The work assign'd me here to do,
In heav'n my Lord will then discover,
His matchless glories to my view.

HYMN CCCL.

"O Lord our God, other lords beside thee have had dominion over us."—ISAIAH xxvi. 13.

1 ONCE to other lords we bow'd,
None were more enslav'd than we;
Once we join'd the thoughtless crowd,
Saviour, now we come to thee.

2 Long, too long, alas! we were
Slaves of sin, and foes to thee;
Now with truth we can declare,
None owe more to grace than we.

3 Lord, we now confess with shame,
How we slighted all thy love;
How we long withstood thy claim,
And against thy mercy strove.

4 Henceforth we desire to be
Thine alone, for ever thine;
Thou hast set the pris'ners free,
Saviour, on thy people shine.

5 Let us walk with thee below,
  Thee on whom our hopes depend,
Then with all thy people go
  Thither, where our conflicts end.

HYMN CCCLI.

"*And Jesus asked him, What is thy name? and he said, Legion.*"
LUKE viii. 30.

1 WELL might he be callēd *Legion*,
  Who my soul did occupy;
Round about through all the region
  None was more possess'd than I:
Satan held me till one stronger
  Came and set the pris'ner free;
Satan then could reign no longer,
  Jesus made him yield his prey.

2 'Mong the dead the Saviour found me;
  There it was I lov'd to dwell;
Solemn vows had often bound me;
  What could bonds like these avail?
As when Samson, rous'd from slumber,
  Broke with ease the chains he wore,
So my vows, whate'er their number,
  Yielded to the tempter's pow'r.

3 They who in my madness knew me,
  Gaze and wonder at the change;
At the Saviour's feet they view me,
  And confess the matter strange:
Many think the change a sad one,
  Look upon it as a curse;
Though the case was once a bad one,
  Yet they think the present worse.

4 Fearful of the world's derision,
Eager, too, to see his face,
Oft I ask'd the Lord's permission,
With himself to take my place;
But whene'er I ask'd this favour,
'Twas his word, or seem'd to be,
"Go and spread the truth's sweet savour,
Tell what God has done for thee."

5 Be it so, since thou hast said it,
Be this world awhile my place;
And may those who hear me, credit
What I tell them of thy grace!
Soon I hope to stand before thee,
Soon to join the hosts above,
There for ever to adore thee,
And proclaim thy matchless love.

HYMN CCCLII.

"*While we look not at the things which are seen, but at the things which are not seen.*"—2 Cor. iv. 18.

1 THINGS unseen engage us now,
Glorious things to faith reveal'd;
Yes, through grace, 'tis ours to know
Things that were before conceal'd;

2 Things of high importance too,
Things connected with our peace;
Yes, from these our comforts flow,
All our chief delights from these.

3 Since we've known his precious name,
Who on earth sustain'd the cross,
Pomp and pleasure, wealth and fame,
All the world is counted loss.

4 Better things appear in view,
Drawing us away from earth;
Shall we stoop then to pursue
Objects of inferior worth?

5 No: we'll leave the world behind,
Once the object of our love,
And be satisfied to find
Rest among the saints above.

HYMN CCCLIII.

"Thou hast turned for me my mourning into dancing."—
PSALM xxx. 11.

1 GOD has turn'd my grief to gladness,
He has made my heart rejoice;
I who lately pin'd in sadness,
Now can raise my thankful voice:
Sweet it is the saints to join,
Sweet to call their Saviour mine.

2 O how short is his displeasure!
As a moment it appears;
But his love is without measure,
Still the same through endless years:
Weeping may the night employ,
But the morning beams with joy.

3 Jesus smiles, and from his favour,
Life and joy are found to flow;
O for faith that does not waver!
Lord, on me this faith bestow:
Since thy promise changes not,
Grant that I may never doubt.

4 Help me now, ye saints, to praise him;
Join, ye angels, while we sing;
Though our efforts cannot raise him,
(What can raise our glorious King?)
Praise should never cease to flow;
'Tis the tribute that we owe.

HYMN CCCLIV.

"*He brought me up also out of an horrible pit.*"—PSALM xl. 2.

1 RESCU'D from the lake infernal,
Sav'd from yonder dark abyss,
Jesus gives us life eternal,
Now we live since we are his;
Now we hope with him to be
Happy through eternity.

2 O how great our former danger,
When we walk'd in folly's ways!
He who lives to God a stranger,
Far from peace and safety strays.
Under guilt, enslav'd by sin,
All is dark and foul within.

3 Long, too long, our hearts were harden'd,
We despis'd the truth of God,
But the Lord our sin has pardon'd,
He has wash'd our souls with blood,
Blood of him who fills a throne,
Blood of Christ, the Holy One.

4 Let us bow and fall before him,
Let us bow before our King;
Lo! the hosts of heav'n adore him,
All above his praises sing:
Much they owe him, more we owe,
Sinners sav'd from endless woe.

Reproach of the Cross.

HYMN CCCLV.

"*I go to prepare a place for you.*"—JOHN xiv. 2.

1 AND art thou, gracious Master, gone,
A mansion to prepare for me?
Shall I behold thee on thy throne,
And there for ever sit with thee?
Then let the world approve or blame,
I'll triumph in thy glorious name.

2 Should I, to gain the world's applause,
Or to escape its harmless frown,
Refuse to countenance thy cause,
And make thy people's lot my own,
What shame would fill me in that day,
When thou thy glory wilt display!

3 And what is man, or what his smile?
The terror of his anger, what?
Like grass he flourishes awhile,
But soon his place shall know him not;
Through fear of such a one, shall I
The Lord of heav'n and earth deny?

4 No: let the world cast out my name,
And vile account me, if they will;
If to confess the Lord be shame,
I purpose to be viler still:
For thee, my God, I all resign,
Content if I can call thee mine.

5 What transport then shall fill my heart,
When thou my worthless name wilt own;
When I shall see thee as thou art,
And know as I myself am known!
From sin, and fear, and sorrow free,
My soul shall find its rest in thee.

HYMN CCCLVI.

"Whosoever therefore shall confess me before men, him will I confess also before my Father."—Matt. x. 32.

1 THEY who confess the Saviour here
Must count upon the worldling's sneer;
Must reckon on his malice too,
Nor fear to stand among *the few*.

2 How many, through the fear of shame,
Refuse to own the Saviour's name!
Lest fools the question should renew,
And cry, "Are ye deceivēd too?"

3 The fear of man thus brings a snare,
For few his frown and scorn can bear,
But men should weigh what Jesus says,
"Them who confess me I'll confess."

4 Ah Lord! with truth we all may tell
That we have lov'd the world too well;
O make us valiant in thy cause!
And careless of the world's applause.

5 While we despise its utmost scorn,
Let all our works thy truth adorn!
And when thy glorious day we see,
O let us be confess'd of thee!

HYMN CCCLVII.

"*Despising the shame.*"—HEB. xii. 2.

1 SHALL I be ashamed of Jesus?
Who so true a friend as he?
He whose offer'd life appeases
Wrath, that else had fall'n on me;
Jesus, when he shed his blood,
Sav'd me from the wrath of God.

2 Few would die to save another,
Yet there might be love like this;
Some, to save a friend or brother,
Might resign their life for his;
But the Lord his kindness shows,
While he dies to save his foes.

3 Others may profess to love us,
And may seem to be our friends;
But when trials come to prove us,
Then alas! their friendship ends:
Jesus *is* what others seem;
Shall I be asham'd of him?

4 Lord thou know'st how oft already
I have been asham'd of thee:
False I've been, and most unsteady,
From the cross too prone to flee:
Yes, my Lord, I tell my shame,
Oft I've blush'd to own thy name.

5 O forgive the past, nor let me
Ever be so base again;
When temptation shall beset me,
Lord, be near, be near me then;
Teach me to confess thy name,
Careless who approve or blame.

Death of Believers.

HYMN CCCLVIII.

"*Thanks be to God, which giveth us the victory.*"—1 COR. XV. 57.

1 COME, look here, ye sons of science,
  Look upon the dying man;
On the cross is his reliance,
  Faith does more than reason can;
Read his triumph in his eyes,
Thus it is the Christian dies.

2 Boast no more, ye sons of science,
  Death was never foiled by you;
To your arms he bids defiance,
  Safe from all that you can do;
Death comes smiling, when he sees
Arms against him such as these.

3 David once, by wisdom guided,
  Threw such arms as yours away,
And with other arms provided,
  Sought the foe, and won the day;
His no sword, nor spear, nor bow,
Yet he laid the mighty low.

4 Israel's God the youth directed
  How to aim the deadly blow,
And with arms by him selected,
  David fought and slew the foe;
Israel's God is still the same,
Saving those who know his name.

5 Happy they, who still confiding
In the strength of Israel's God,
And with arms of his providing,
Meet the haughty foe unaw'd;
Though the conflict prove severe,
They prevail, for God is near.

HYMN CCCLIX.

"We have a building of God, an house not made with hands, eternal in the heavens."—2 Cor. v. 1.

1 THE tedious pilgrimage is past,
The forty years have reach'd a close,
And happy Isra'l now at last
Is destin'd to enjoy repose.

2 Through toils and death their journey lay,
And many did their march oppose;
But he who led them by the way
Was mighty to subdue their foes.

3 He took them from the tyrant's hand,
He led them safely through the deep,
He promis'd them a fruitful land,
And did not God his promise keep?

4 How pleasant, after so much toil,
To see the land where rest is found;
To tread in hope the sacred soil,
With everlasting verdure crown'd!

5 Thus Isra'l stood on Jordan's banks,
And view'd the land on th' other side,
While pleasure spread thro' all his ranks,
And joy was felt, till then denied.

6 And thus the saints, with heav'n in view,
Rejoice and triumph at the last;
Their pilgrimage is ended too,
And all the storms of life are past.

7 This frame dissolves, but well they know
A nobler house is theirs on high;
With pleasure from the world they go,
To meet the Saviour in the sky.

HYMN CCCLX.

"*And deliver them who through fear of death were all their lifetime subject to bondage.*"—Heb. ii. 15.

1 NOW come on, thou king of terrors;
Once I fear'd thy threat'ning frown;
Rescued from my former errors,
Lo! my former fears are gone:
Yes, I may defy thee now,
To thy pow'r no more I bow.

2 Well thou know'st the name of Jesus;
'Tis a sound excites alarm;
His I am, and him it pleases
To defend me from thine arm:
Death, of terrors once the king,
Tell me "where is now thy sting?"

3 When I see the Saviour near me,
Nothing do I fear from thee:
He, I know, will kindly hear me,
He will give me victory:
On his truth my soul relies,
And through him thy pow'r defies.

HYMN CCCLXI.

"*Having a desire to depart, and to be with Christ, which is far better.*"—PHIL. i. 23.

1 WHEN a believer yields his breath,
I follow him with eyes of faith
Where sense can see no more;
Methinks I see him spread his wings,
And soar above material things,
To yon celestial shore.

2 No tongue can tell, no fancy paint,
What transport fills th' enraptur'd saint,
Of paradise possest;
His wants abundantly supplied!
His wishes fully satisfied!
Himself supremely blest.

3 But what occasions so much joy?
Or what can now his pow'rs employ,
That yields him such delight?
'Tis Jesus on his heav'nly throne,
Who sav'd and claim'd him for his own;
What object half so bright?

4 How far is what he saw below,
Or all he had the pow'r to know,
By what he sees, excell'd!
The clouds that interpos'd before
Obstruct his clearer view no more,
And Jesus stands reveal'd.

5 But see! he joins the ransom'd throng,
And swells the grand triumphant song
"Of Moses and the Lamb;"
JESUS, the object of their praise,
The LORD, who deign'd such worms to raise,
Th' unsearchable "I AM!"

6 O may we know the Saviour's grace,
And then in heav'n behold his face,
On wings angelic borne!
For this let men our hope contemn!
Well pleas'd we smile and pity them,
And haste beyond their scorn.

HYMN CCCLXII.

"*O death, where is thy sting? O grave, where is thy victory?*"—
1 Cor. xv. 55.

1 LET reason vainly boast her pow'r
To teach her children how to die,
The sinner, in a dying hour,
Needs more than reason can supply;
A view of Christ, the sinner's friend,
Alone can cheer him in his end.

2 When nature sinks beneath disease,
And ev'ry earthly hope is fled,
What then can give the sinner ease,
And make him love a dying bed?
Jesus, thy smile his heart can cheer,
He's blest ev'n then if thou art near.

3 The Gospel does salvation bring,
And Jesus is the Gospel theme;
In death *redeemēd* sinners sing,
And triumph in the Saviour's name:
"O death, where is thy sting?" they cry,
"O grave, where is thy victory?"

4 Then let me die the death of those
Whom Jesus washes in his blood,
Who on his faithfulness repose,
And know that he indeed is God:
Around his throne we all shall meet,
And cast our crowns beneath his feet.

HYMN CCCLXIII.

"*Lord, now lettest thou thy servant depart in peace . . . . for mine eyes have seen thy salvation.*"—LUKE ii. 29, 30.

1 WHAT pleasure fill'd old Simeon's breast,
While he his infant Lord caress'd,
And gaz'd upon his face!
As he the glorious child survey'd,
He recogniz'd the promis'd seed,
The God of truth and grace.

2 How welcome to his eyes the sight!
But one could yield him *more* delight,
And that he now enjoys;
'Tis Jesus dwelling in the light,
Whose glory infinitely bright
The praise of heav'n employs.

3 "According to thy gracious word,"
He cries, "now take thy servant, Lord,
For I have seen thy grace;
What more can I expect beneath?
O let me cease on earth to breathe,
That I may see thy face!"

4 'Tis thus, hope beaming in his eyes,
The aged saint, before he dies,
Declares his joy aloud;
In death may we prove conqu'rors too,
And after death the Saviour view
Reveal'd without a cloud.

HYMN CCCLXIV.

"*It is sown in dishonour, it is raised in glory.*"—1 COR. xv. 43.

1 WHEN the appointed honr is come
That Jesus takes his people home,
The body sinks to dwell below,
And lets th' imprison'd spirit go.

2 The paradise of God receives
The saint, when he the body leaves;
Where Jesus gives him purest joys,
Till the last trumpet's awful voice.

3 Then shall his body rise again,
Exempt from all disease and pain;
In weakness and dishonour sown,
The Lord will raise it like his own.

4 A pris'n no more, a mansion fair,
And form'd the spirit's joys to share!
In perfect union now they meet,
And dwell in happiness complete.

HYMN CCCLXV.

"*Blessed are the dead which die in the Lord.*"—Rev. xiv. 13.

1 HARK! a voice! it cries from heav'n,
"Happy in the Lord who die!"
Happy they to whom 'tis giv'n
From a world of grief to fly!
They indeed are truly blest,
From their labour then they rest.

2 All their toils and conflicts over,
Lo! they dwell with Christ above;
O what glories they discover
In the Saviour whom they love;
Now they see him face to face,
Him who sav'd them by his grace.

3 'Tis enough, enough for ever,
'Tis his people's bright reward;
They are blest indeed who never
Shall be absent from the Lord;
O that we may die like those
Who in Jesus then repose!

HYMN CCCLXVI.

"And the spirit shall return unto God who gave it."—
ECCLES. xii. 7

1 AWAY! thou dying saint, away!
Fly to the mansions of the blest;
Thy God no more requires thy stay,
He calls thee to eternal rest.

2 Thy toils at length have reach'd a close,
No more remains for thee to do;
Away, away to thy repose,
Beyond the reach of evil go.

3 Away to yonder realms of light,
Where multitudes, redeem'd with blood,
Enjoy the beatific sight,
And dwell for ever with their God.

4 Go, mix with them, and share their joy,
In heav'n behold the sinner's friend;
In pleasures share that never cloy,
In pleasures that will never end.

5 And may our happy portion be,
To join thee in the realms above,
The glory of our Lord to see,
And sing his everlasting love.

HYMN CCCLXVII.

"For what is your life? it is even a vapour."—JAMES iv. 14.

1 WHAT is life? 'Tis but a vapour,
Soon it vanishes away;
Life is like a dying taper,
O my soul, why wish to stay?
Why not spread thy wings, and fly
Straight to yonder world of joy?

2 See that glory, how resplendent!
Brighter far than fancy paints,
There, in majesty transcendent,
Jesus reigns, the King of saints:
Spread thy wings, my soul, and fly
Straight to yonder world of joy.

3 Joyful crowds, his throne surrounding,
Sing with rapture of his love.
Through the heav'ns his praises sounding,
Filling all the courts above:
Spread thy wings, my soul, and fly
Straight to yonder world of joy.

4 Go, and share his people's glory;
'Midst the ransom'd crowd appear;
Thine a joyful, wondrous story,
One that angels love to hear:
Spread thy wings, my soul, and fly
Straight to yonder world of joy.

HYMN CCCLXVIII.

ON THE DEATH OF ONE MUCH BELOVED AND REGRETTED.

"*My flesh also shall rest in hope.*"—PSALM xvi. 9.

1 AWAY! he calls thee hence away,
Before thy Lord with joy appear;
We cannot, do not bid thee stay,
Though loath to part with one so dear.

2 The storm is hush'd, and all is still,
Her conflicts are for ever past;
And now, beyond the reach of ill,
She waits the trumpet's final blast,

3 The signal of our Lord's return,
When all his saints shall rise again,
The mark no more of human scorn,
But glorious like their master then.

4 The people of the Lord may say,
The friends we mourn are gone before,
And soon we hope to see the day,
When we shall meet, to part no more.

5 How sweet, how blessed thus to see
The last great foe bereft of pow'r!
'Tis Jesus sets his people free,
And gilds with light their final hour.

6 O teach us, Lord, to follow those
Who run the heav'nly race, and win!
That when our mortal life shall close,
Our life of glory may begin.

HYMN CCCLXIX.

"*That they may rest from their labours.*"—Rev. xiv. 13.

1 BELOVED one, thy place no more
Is here below; 'tis henceforth there
Where things but dimly seen before,
In all their truth and worth appear.

2 Away! away! thy race is run;
Long hast thou waited for this day.
The work assign'd thee here, is done,
'Tis God that calls thee hence away.

3 Eternal life thy portion is,
The fruit of love, his love who bore
The cross below; the grace is his:
He bears a name all names before.

4 His will is, that his people be
With him above, for ever there;
The glory of their Lord to see,
And (strange to tell) his throne to share.

5 'Tis wondrous all, from first to last;
It first and last applies to what
Had no beginning in the past,
And in the future endeth not.

6 Rejoice, then, happy saint, rejoice!
The door before thee open is;
Thou soon shalt hear the bridegroom's voice,
And take thy place with him and his.

HYMN CCCLXX.

"*Enter thou into the joy of thy Lord.*"—MATT. XXV. 23.

1 AWAY, away! thy work is done!
The day 's thine own, the prize is won.
Away to yonder peaceful shore,
Where storms are felt and heard no more;

2 Where robes made white with blood are worn,
And branches from the palm-tree borne;
The place where harps of gold are strung,
And hymns of praise for ever sung;

3 The place where those at length unite,
Who, like thyself, have fought the fight,
"The fight of faith," and won the prize;
"The holy place" above the skies;

4 The place where God has built his throne,
Himself "the high and lofty One,
·habiting eternity,"
›m none hath seen, whom none can see.

5 Away, away! he calls thee hence,
Away from things of time and sense;
He calls thee to thy place above,
To dwell with him, to sing his love;

6 To see what here thou canst not see;
To be what here thou canst not be;
Without a foe, without a fear,
To drink of joy, but tasted here;

7 To be with him who once was dead,
Of life himself the fountain-head,
Who died to save, who lives to bless,
Away to perfect happiness!

Commencing Public Worship.

HYMN CCCLXXI.

"*Speak, for thy servant heareth.*"—1 SAM. iii. 10.

1 IN thy name, O Lord, assembling,
We, thy people, now draw near;
Teach us to rejoice with trembling,
Speak, and let thy servants hear,
Hear with meekness,
Hear thy word with godly fear.

2 While our days on earth are lengthen'd,
May we give them, Lord, to thee!
Cheer'd by hope, and daily strengthen'd,
May we run, nor weary be,
Till thy glory
Without clouds in heav'n we see.

3 There in worship purer, sweeter,
Thee thy people shall adore;
Tasting of enjoyment, greater
Far, than thought conceiv'd before;
Full enjoyment,
Full, unmix'd, and evermore.

HYMN CCCLXXII.

"*Early will I seek thee.*"—Psalm lxiii. 1.

1 LORD, we come to seek thee early,
Hear, O hear us when we cry!
Thou hast bought thy people dearly,
Thou hast brought the strangers nigh:
God our Saviour!
All thy people's wants supply.

2 Lord, we bless thee, that, invited,
We draw near, and seek thy face;
Once the privilege we slighted,
Ours was then a fearful case:
God our Saviour!
We adore thy sov'reign grace.

3 Through the desert safely guide us,
Cheer us, when by toil opprest;
Though the world around deride us,
Thine, we know, are truly blest;
Soon thy people
Shall from all their labours rest.

4 In the midst of foes and strangers,
Keep thy people safe from harm;
While they pass through toils and dangers,
Hold them with thy mighty arm,
And convey them
There, where foes no more alarm.

HYMN CCCLXXIII.

"*Seek ye me, and ye shall live.*"—AMOS v. 4.

1 TO thee we come, our God, to thee,
We come to seek thy face;
Before thy throne thy people see,
Before thy throne of grace.

2 We bring thy promise, and we plead
Thy mercy and thy name;
To our petitions, Lord, give heed,
And put us not to shame.

3 Subdue the foes that are within,
Our mighty foes subdue;
O! break in us the pow'r of sin,
And make us, Lord, anew.

4 We know, in such a strife as this,
How vain are mortal pow'rs;
No strength but thine sufficient is,
Against such foes as ours.

5 In us thy pleasure, Lord, fulfil,
The work of faith with pow'r;
That we may do and love thy will,
Nor leave thee from this hour.

HYMN CCCLXXIV.

"*Watching daily at my gates.*"—PROV. viii. 34.

1 FEW we are, but though still fewer,
Yet would God incline his ear;
Well we know that we are slower
Far to ask, than he to hear;
Thus encourag'd,
Let us to his throne draw near.

2 Happy they who wait his leisure,
Who in faith and patience wait;
Happy they, to whom 'tis pleasure
To attend at wisdom's gate;
Good awaits them,
And the peace they have is great.

3 They who know not God are strangers
To the joys his people have;
In the midst of fears and dangers,
He is near to help and save;
And his presence
Renders even the coward brave.

4 Let us then in faith and patience
Wait on him who hears our cry;
He fulfils our expectations,
He will all our wants supply;
He will give us
Present and eternal joy.

HYMN CCCLXXV.

"*They that feared the Lord spake often one to another.*"—
MAL. iii. 16.

1 BE with us now, O Lord, and make
Our meeting what it ought to be;
We ask it for thy mercy's sake;
No other plea but this have we.

2 Be with us as thou wast of old,
With those who "thought upon thy name;"
Our minds are dark, our hearts are cold,
We want the light, we want the flame.

3 We kindle sparks, but what's their worth?
Not good but evil comes from this;
The sparks we kindle are of earth,
The fire we want from heaven it is.

4 Thou answerest, O Lord, by fire;
The holy fire that burns within;
That kindles love, and pure desire;
That burns the very root of sin.

5 With what intense desire we should
Entreat for such a gift as this.
We do not, Lord, the thing we would;
Our folly and our shame it is.

6 Forgive, O Lord, our sin forgive;
For thou art gracious, thou art true;
In thee we move, in thee we live;
Without thee nothing can we do.

HYMN CCCLXXVI.

"*O Lord, make haste to help me.*"—PSALM xl. 13.

1 THANKS to him who thus permits us
In his gracious name to meet;
Who for conflict arms and fits us,
Else for such a strife unfit;
In his service
Loss is gain, and pain is sweet.

2 O! our Saviour, be thou near us,
When we join the world again;
In the time of trouble hear us,
Nor forsake thy people then;
O preserve us,
Lest we learn to "walk as men."

3 Thine we are, and thine we would be,
Lord we would be thine alone;
What thou doest is what should be,
This is to thy people known;
Teach us always
Thus to say "Thy will be done."

4 In our way through life supply us,
Lord, with grace to live to thee;
In the hour of death stand by us,
Grant us then the victory,
And hereafter
Let us all thy glory see.

HYMN CCCLXXVII.

"*Hear my prayer, O Lord.*"—PSALM xxxix. 12.

1 THANKFUL for thy kind permission
To appear before thy throne,
Lord, we come with our petition,
Though with claim and merit none;
All we ask for
Is the fruit of grace alone.

2 Yet this grace sufficient ever
For thy people's need is found;
Sweet assurance! never, never
Let us leave this solid ground;
This supports us
When our wants and fears abound.

3 Lord, we plead with thee for pardon;
Who can need it more than we?
Make us as a water'd garden,
Fruitful let thy people be;
'Tis thy pleasure
That thy people live to thee.

4 Keep us in a world of sorrow;
When we call, O hear our pray'r;
Let us trust thee for the morrow,
Free from boasting, free from care;
When they trust thee,
Happy then thy people are.

HYMN CCCLXXVIII.

"*Be of good cheer, it is I.*"—MATT. xiv. 27.

1 LORD, when thou thyself art present,
Then it is thy people say,
"Praise our God, for praise is pleasant,"
Then it is thy people pray;
'Tis thy presence
Turns the darkest night to day.

2 Be thou present then to cheer us,
All thy people ask is this;
We are safe when thou art near us,
Where thou art, there safety is;
Keep thy people,
And no foe shall make them his.

3 Often, Lord, our hearts we harden,
And forget how much we owe;
See, we come to thee for pardon,
Bid us not unblest to go;
For thy favour
Better is than life, we know.

4 Love like thine has pow'r to soften
Hearts like ours, though hard as stone
To thy cross, O! bring us often,
Be its pow'r to us made known;
There thy people
Learn to live, and there alone.

5 From this sight let nothing move us,
From this mournful, joyful sight;
And when trials come to prove us,
Trials, needful all and right,
May they find us
Arm'd, and ready for the fight.

HYMN CCCLXXIX.

"*Waiting at the posts of my doors.*"—PROV. viii. 34.

1 SWEET are the seasons when we wait
To hear what God our Lord will say;
For they who watch at wisdom's gate
Are never empty sent away.

2 Behold us, Lord, a few of thine,
Who hither come to seek thy face;
In mercy on thy people shine,
And let thy presence fill the place.

3 How sweet, how blessed is the thought
That thou dost hear thy people's cries!
And whether thou dost give or not,
'Tis love that grants, and love denies.

4 O teach us, Lord, to wait thy will,
To be content with all thou dost;
For us thy grace sufficient still,
With most supplied when needing most.

5 Till life shall end, thus let it be,
And, O sustain us in that hour;
That conflict past, we hope to see
The Saviour then, but not before.

6 Yes, Lord, we hope to take our part
With yonder host, through trouble brought:
We hope to see thee as thou art,
And then to praise thee as we ought.

HYMN CCCLXXX.

"*Wherefore come out from among them, and be ye separate, saith the Lord.*"—2 COR. vi. 17.

1 LORD, behold us few and weak,
Humbly at thy feet we fall:
See, we come thy face to seek;
Deign, O deign to hear our call.

2 When we lay in sin and death,
Thou didst pass, and bid us live,
Thou didst give thy people faith,
Thou didst all our sin forgive.

3 Jesus, thou didst shed thy blood,
On this rock our hope we raise;
Thou hast brought us nigh to God,
Thine the work, and thine the praise.

4 'Tis thy will that we should be
Separate from all around;
Let our will with thine agree,
Let thy people thus be found.

5 Teach us, Lord, to walk with thee,
Teach us to adorn thy cause;
Let us live in unity,
Foes to pride and self-applause!

6 Let us bear each other's load,
Faithful to each other prove,
Till we gain the saints' abode,
Till we take our place above.

7 There to see without a cloud,
There without fatigue to sing;
Mix with heav'n's triumphant crowd,
And for ever praise our King.

HYMN CCCLXXXI.

"Cause thy face to shine, and we shall be saved."—
PSALM lxxx. 19.

1 LORD, we esteem the favour great,
And give the praise to thee,
That we can thus together meet,
And none to make us flee.

2 But all our meetings barren prove,
Except thou shew thy face;
Come then, dear Saviour, from above,
And consecrate this place.

3 O let the visits of thy love
The purest joys impart!
Let all our deadness now remove,
And zeal fill ev'ry heart:

4 Zeal to confess thy glorious name,
In spite of earth and hell,
Thy loving-kindness to proclaim,
And all thy goodness tell!

5 Lord, let thy people's light so shine,
That all the world may see,
And own its origin divine,
And give the praise to thee.

HYMN CCCLXXXII.

"Where two or three are gathered together in my name, there am I."—MATT. xviii. 20.

1 HOW sweet to leave the world awhile,
And seek the presence of our Lord!
Dear Saviour, on thy people smile,
And come according to thy word.

2 From busy scenes we now retreat,
That we may here converse with thee;
Ah, Lord, behold us at thy feet!
Let this the "gate of heaven" be.

3 "Chief of ten thousand," now appear,
That we by faith may see thy face!
Oh speak, that we thy voice may hear,
And let thy presence fill this place!

4 Lord, thou hast cast a pleasant lot
For those whom thou hast call'd thine own;
'Tis true the world esteems them not,
But thou wilt place them on thy throne.

5 Then let the worldling boast his joys!
We've meat to eat he knows not of;
We count his treasures worthless toys,
While we possess a Saviour's love.

6 Lord, let thy people's views be clear,
And let their hearts be fill'd with love;
O may their light to all appear,
And prove their doctrine from above.

HYMN CCCLXXXIII.

"*And he shall give you another Comforter . . . . even the Spirit of truth.*"—JOHN xiv. 16, 17.

1 JESUS is gone up on high,
But his promise still is here,
He will all our wants supply;
He will send the Comforter.

2 Let us now his promise plead,
Let us to his throne draw nigh,
Jesus knows his people's need,
Jesus hears his people's cry.

3 Who can boast a lot like theirs
  Whom the Lord vouchsafes to own?
Jesus listens to their prayers,
  What they ask in faith is done.

4 Saviour, this is our request,
  "On us make thy face to shine;"
Grant us this, and for the rest,
  All is ours when we are thine.

5 Send us, Lord, the Comforter,
  Pledge and witness of thy love,
Dwelling with thy people here,
  Leading them to joys above.

6 Till we reach the promis'd rest,
  Till thy face unveil'd we see,
Of this blessed hope possest,
  Teach us, Lord, to live to thee.

HYMN CCCLXXXIV.

"*I will instruct thee and teach thee.*"—PSALM xxxii. 8.

1 LORD, behold thy people here
  Come to learn what thou wilt say;
Oh, in mercy now draw near!
  Meet thy people when they pray;
Thou art God, and thou alone,
Lord, we worship at thy throne.

2 Jesus, 'tis on thee we call,
  Isra'l's Saviour, Isra'l's King;
Low before thy feet we fall,
  Thine, whom angels love to sing;
Saviour, lead us in the way,
Only thee would we obey.

3 Teach us what we do not know,
Lord, instruct us in thy will;
What we learn, O may we do!
To thy voice obedient still;
Close to thee may we abide,
Thee, our Saviour and our guide.

HYMN CCCLXXXV.

"*I cried unto the Lord with my voice.*"—PSALM iii. 4.

1 O OUR God! we call upon thee;
Thou art God, and thou alone;
Though the world around us shun thee,
Lord, we bow before thy throne:
They are blessed,
They, to whom thy grace is known.

2 Nothing, Lord, have we to boast of,
Nothing we can call our own;
Strength and wisdom they have most of,
Who depend on thee alone:
God our Saviour!
Lo! we bow before thy throne.

3 Thou art glorious; we are wretchēd;
Yet possess'd of all in thee;
When we see thine arm outstretchēd,
Then our foes in fear we see;
Then a thousand
At the sight of one shall flee.

4 To thy name we now betake us,
To thy name, a refuge sure;
Never leave us nor forsake us,
Us, so helpless and so poor,
Till our trials
End, and foes molest no more.

HYMN CCCLXXXVI.

"*I will instruct thee and teach thee.*"—PSALM xxxii. 8.

1 GRANT us, Lord, thy gracious presence,
While we worship at thy throne;
Teach our souls important lessons,
Lessons learn'd of thee alone.
While we pray, and sing, and hear,
In the midst do thou appear;
Sin reproving,
Fear removing,
Light to all our minds impart,
Love convey to every heart.

HYMN CCCLXXXVII.

"*Where two or three are gathered together in my name, there am I.*"—MATT. xviii. 20.

1 WHEN two or three together meet,
In his great name who reigns above,
The fellowship they have is sweet;
They meet, and they depart in love.

2 The Lord is with his people there,
Wherever they are met to pray;
He listens to their feeble pray'r,
And sends them not unblest away.

3 O be it, Lord, to us this day,
According to thy gracious word!
And send us not unblest away,
But pardon, peace, and strength afford.

4 We nothing have, but all is thine;
While thou art rich, we cannot want;
Thine ear, O Lord, to us incline,
And what thy people pray for, grant.

5 To love and serve thee better, Lord,
This is the favour that we seek;
Thine all-sufficient help afford,
And then we shall be strong, tho' weak.

6 Thus arm'd, to conflict we may go,
And boldly meet the adverse pow'rs;
Thus arm'd, we need not fear the foe,
For everlasting strength is ours.

HYMN CCCLXXXVIII.

"*The Lord shall bless thee out of Zion.*"—PSALM CXXVIII. 5.

1 TO thee, O Lord our God, we come,
For thou art great, and thou art good;
Within thy house we know there's room,
And on thy table richest food.

2 For mercy, Lord, we come to thee,
For grace to help in time of need:
Thy promise is our only plea,
And this with confidence we plead.

3 No goodness, Lord, or strength have we;
We live upon our Saviour's grace;
Nor would we less dependent be;
We do not ask a higher place.

4 'Tis sweet to know, that all we need
Is found in him by whom we live;
Then grant us that for which we plead,
Increase our faith, our sin forgive.

5 Before we go, thy servants bless,
For they whom thou dost bless, are blest;
Of everlasting righteousness,
And everlasting strength possess'd.

HYMN CCCLXXXIX.

"*Surely I will remember thy wonders of old.*"—PSALM lxxvii. 11.

1 WE have heard, and we believe it,
What thou didst, O Lord, of old;
'Tis thy word, and we receive it,
This it is that makes us bold.
What thou didst of old, we pray,
Do the same in this our day.

2 Smite the rock, and let the waters
Flow at thy command, O Lord,
To supply thy sons and daughters;
Pow'r attends thy sovereign word.
Speak, O Lord, and this shall be,
Wonders then our eyes shall see.

3 Speak, and we shall see a table
Cover'd with "the living bread;"
This shall be, for thou art able,
And thy people shall be fed.
Theirs is bread—the bread of heav'n,
Freely by their Father giv'n.

4 Speak, then, and our foes shall tremble,
Strong and many though they be;
When for battle they assemble,
Struck with terror, they shall flee,
While thy people, wond'ring, gaze,
And with gladness sing thy praise.

5 Speak thou, and the waves, obeying,
Shall divide at thy command;
And thy people, at thy saying,
Shall go through, and win the land.
There, at length, thy people rest,
There they live, for ever blest.

HYMN CCCXC.

"*He that eateth me, even he shall live by me.*"—JOHN vi. 57.

1 IN fellowship we meet to-day,
A blessed fellowship it is,
When those who meet can truly say
The Lord is ours, and we are his.

2 Our fellowship be that of love,
Thyself its root and centre, Lord;
What's here below and what's above
Shall mingle then in sweet accord.

3 Thou givest to thy people here,
A foretaste of the joys to come;
When thou in glory shalt appear,
And take them to their final home.

4 The symbols of thy suff'ring be
To us memorials of thy love;
'Tis blessed to remember thee,
Thy mercy and thy truth to prove.

5 Be with us then, O Lord, for good,
Thy spirit to us all impart;
Thyself our life, thyself our food,
Whatever we can want thou art.

HYMN CCCXCI.

"*But he, being full of compassion, forgave their iniquity.*"—
PSALM lxxviii. 38.

1 BEHOLD us, Lord, we come to thee,
Regard us with a father's eye,
That pity hath; thy children see,
Nor let us for our follies die.

2 A thousand and a thousand times,
We have provoked thine anger, Lord;
Thou know'st our follies and our crimes,
And yet we live, though self-abhorr'd.

3 But this we fear—we fear it much,
When musing on the time that's past,
Our future doings may be such,
That thou wilt give us up at last.

4 Forbearance, Lord, is thine, we know,
But such as this we look'd not for;
We fear'd we had offended so,
That pardon was for us no more.

5 But we were wrong: forbearance still,
Divine forbearance still holds out;
And to the end we trust it will,
From what is past we cannot doubt.

6 In future, Lord, O let us be
More circumspect; this grace we crave;
Nor strength nor aught of good have we,
'Tis thine, and thine alone, to save.

HYMN CCCXCII.

"*What is man, that thou art mindful of him?*"—Psalm viii. 4.

1 DESCEND, O Lord, from heav'n descend,
Thy people come to seek thy face:
To our petition, Lord, attend,
And let thy presence fill this place.

2 The heav'n with all its space, we know,
Is not enough, O Lord, for thee,
And how, then, shouldst thou dwell below?
How dwell with us? How can this be?

3 'Tis strange, 'tis passing strange, and yet,
According to thy word, 'tis thus;
If we in thy great name are met,
Thy presence, doubtless, is with us.

4 With us, O Lord, if we are met,
According to thy word, indeed,
Thy promise, never broken yet,
Is ours in every time of need.

5 Believing, we would now draw near,
The word of promise we would plead;
Thy faithfulness will thus appear,
And we shall taste of joy indeed.

HYMN CCCXCIII.

"*Seek the Lord and his strength: seek his face evermore.*"—
PSALM CV. 4.

1 WE come to seek the Lord to-day,
His promised presence to enjoy;
Be with us, then, O Lord, we pray,
And to our waiting souls draw nigh.

2 This chief of blessings let us have—
The chief of blessings here below;
'Tis thine to give, 'tis thine to save,
To do us good is thine, we know.

3 We have thy word, the pow'r we want,
We want to feel as well as know;
This blessing to thy people grant,
To love thee much, for much we owe.

4 Our debt is great; we know it well,
And to confess it, 'fitting is;
How great, eternity will tell;
No other line can fathom this

5 But now enough is known to make
The Saviour precious, and to cause
That we abandon, for his sake,
The thing that once our treasure was.

6 That both in purpose and in deed,
We follow him, tho' scorn'd of men;
Receiving from him all we need,
And waiting till he comes again.

HYMN CCCXCIV.

"And I will commune with thee from above the mercy-seat."—
Exod. xxv. 22.

1 THERE is a throne of grace,
'Tis God's appointed place,
For hearing and for answ'ring prayer;
Where else could this be so?
Where else then should we go?
'Tis safe and blessed to be there.

2 We want to be forgiv'n,
We want the bread of heav'n,
We want the Spirit's pow'r and grace;
For these where we should go,
The Lord has made us know:
'Tis to his own appointed place.

3 With blood it sprinkled is,
"The precious blood" is his,
Who drank the bitter cup for us;
The blood it is that pleads,
And hence our pray'r succeeds,
'Tis blessed that it should be thus.

4 'Tis blessed sure to know,
That we may boldly go,
To him who fills the throne of grace;
May tell him all we need,
And then be blest indeed,
For they are blest who seek his face.

5 Then let us seek his face,
In his appointed place,
And all our wants to him make known;
His arm almighty is,
And those he owns as his,
Are blest indeed, and they alone.

HYMN CCCXCV.

"*Let the king hear us when we call.*"—PSALM XX. 9.

1 LORD, be with us here to-day,
In the midst do thou appear;
When thy people meet to pray,
From thy throne of mercy hear.

2 Thence it is that thou dost speak
To thy people here below;
Lo, we come thy face to seek,
Bid us not unblest to go.

3 Darkly now thy people see,
Thus it is while here below,
Thus it will not always be,
What we know not we shall know.

4 'Tis thy grace that makes it so,
'Tis thy sov'reign grace alone;
This, beyond a doubt, we know,
Be the glory thine alone.

5 Hope is ours, the hope of life,
Life, with joy, that never ends;
Heav'n is free from toil and strife,
There we rest, and all are friends.

6 Happy we, if this be so;
Happy though we suffer here.
They who bear the cross below,
When above, a crown shall wear.

HYMN CCCXCVI.

"*We have fellowship one with another.*"—1 JOHN i. 7.

1 THE fellowship enjoy'd by those
Who know the Lord, is one of love;
With faith it comes, with faith it goes,
Its life, its health, is from above.

2 The element of strife is one
In which it sickens, fades, and dies;
With unity and peace, alone,
It lives, and there imparts its joys.

3 A holy brotherhood is theirs,
Whom Jesus owns; and good it is
When each a brother's burden shares,
Because the Lord accounts him his.

4 When undissembled love is found
Among the people of the Lord,
A proof is given to all around,
That they obey their Master's word.

5 Where this is wanting, all the rest
Is vain pretence, but sound and show:
'Tis *love* the Saviour makes the test,
What he determines, be it so.

6 This test be ours, 'tis meet it should;
What he pronounces right, is right;
What he approves as good, is good;
No darkness here, but all is light.

7 Then follow after love, all ye
Who wish to do your Master's will,
When all the saints in this agree,
The royal law they then fulfil.

Concluding Public Worship.

HYMN CCCXCVII.

"*I cried unto thee, save me.*"—PSALM cxix. 146.

1 GOD of our salvation hear us,
Bless, O bless us, ere we go;
When we join the world, be near us,
Lest thy people careless grow:
Saviour, keep us,
Keep us safe from ev'ry foe.

2 Let us live in view of heaven,
Where we hope to see thy face;
Save us from unhallow'd leaven,
All that might obscure thy grace;
Keep us walking
Each in his appointed place.

3 As our steps are drawing nearer
To the place we call our home,
May our view of heav'n grow clearer,
Hope more bright of joys to come;
And when dying,
May thy presence cheer the gloom.

4 In the day of thine appearing,
When the trump of God shall sound,
May we hear it, nothing fearing,
Though all nature sinks around,
By our Saviour
Rais'd, and then with glory crown'd.

HYMN CCCXCVIII.

"Now the God of hope fill you with all joy and peace."— Rom. xv. 13.

1 GOD of hope and consolation,
Sweeten ev'ry bitter cup;
Thine a great, a free salvation,
Thou canst hold thy people up.
Great thou art in operation,
Thou art rich in grace and love;
Thou art our expectation,
O fulfil our expectation,
Lead us safe to joys above.

2 Never can we taste enjoyment
Pure and full, till thou appear;
Praise thy people's blest employment,
Praise, that day, unmix'd with fear.
When thou comest, Lord, what gladness
Will be felt by all thy friends!
Then they bid adieu to sadness,
Then their night of trouble ends.

3 Through a world of sorrow going,
Keep us from the evil, Lord;
'Tis thine arm we trust to, knowing
This alone can help afford:
When the sharpest trials prove us,
Be thou near, and hold us fast;
Keep us, Lord, let nothing move us,
Till the stormy day is past.

4 Then thy people sorrow never,
Then the storm is heard no more;
Peace and joy are ours for ever,
When we land on yonder shore:
Fear and hope alike are banish'd,
And thy saints are fully blest;
All that caus'd them fear has vanish'd,
All they hop'd for is possess'd.

HYMN CCCXCIX.

"*I will be with thee in trouble.*"—PSALM xci. 15.

1 OH! our Saviour, be thou near us,
While we live, and when we die;
From thy throne of mercy hear us,
When from day to day we cry;
Let our conflicts
End in everlasting joy.

2 Many trials here await us,
'Tis thy people's lot, we know;
In the midst of those who hate us
We shall be while here below;
But thy presence
Cheers us when oppress'd by woe.

3 Precious is thy word of promise,
Precious to thy people here;
Never take thy mercy from us,
O! our Saviour, still be near;
Living, dying,
May thy name our spirits cheer!

HYMN CCCC.

"*For unto us was the Gospel preached.*"—HEB. iv. 2.

1 PRAISE we him, by whose kind favour
Truth from heav'n has reach'd our ears;
May its sweet reviving savour
Fill our hearts, and quell our fears!
TRUTH—how sacred is the treasure!
Teach us, Lord, its worth to know;
Vain 's the hope, and short the pleasure,
Which from other sources flow.

2 What of truth, we've now been hearing,
Lord, to ev'ry heart apply;
In the day of thine appearing,
May we share thy people's joy!
Till thou take us hence for ever,
Saviour, guide us with thine eye;
This our aim, (O leave us never!)
Thine to live, and thine to die.

HYMN CCCCI.

"*Shew me a token for good.*"—PSALM lxxxvi. 17.

1 OF thy love, some gracious token
Grant us, Lord, before we go;
Bless thy word which has been spoken,
Life and peace on all bestow,
When we join the world again,
Let our hearts with thee remain;
O direct us
And protect us!
Till we gain the heav'nly shore,
Where thy people want no more.

HYMN CCCCII.

"*Be of good cheer, I have overcome the world.*"—JOHN xvi. 33.

1 SAVIOUR, be thou with us, going
With the world to mix again;
'Tis thy strength we trust to, knowing
We are weak as other men;
If thou keep us,
We are safe, and only then.

2 Precious is thy word of promise,
Precious to thy people here;
Though the foe would wrest it from us,
Thou hast bid us nothing fear;
In our trials,
Thou hast said thou wilt be near.

3 In thy strength we bid defiance
To the world, its smile or frown;
On thy strength our whole reliance,
On thy strength, and not our own;
Happy are we
When we trust in thee alone.

4 May we thus, till life is over,
Trust in thee, and valiant prove;
Ev'ry day fresh cause discover,
Cause of wonder, joy, and love;
And victorious
To our place in heav'n remove,

5 There to see our Saviour's glory,
There to serve him without fear;
There to tell the wondrous story
Of the grace that found us here;
And for ever
Praise the name to sinners dear.

HYMN CCCCIII.

"*Cause thy face to shine.*"—PSALM lxxx. 3.

1 MAKE thy face to shine upon us,
O! our Saviour and our King;
Then, tho' all should scorn and shun us,
We are blest, and we may sing;
From thy favour
Life, and hope, and gladness spring.

2 Smile thou, and thy people heed not
Though the world around revile:
Smile thou, and thy people need not
Fear, tho' match'd with force and guile;
Foes ten thousand
Cannot harm them if thou smile.

3 Smile thou then, O smile from heaven,
They are blest who wait on thee;
Let this grace to us be given,
Thee to know, and thine to be,
Here to serve thee,
And in heav'n thy face to see.

4 There to tell the wondrous story
Of the grace that made us thine;
There with all thy saints in glory
As the stars of heav'n to shine;
And for ever
In thy praise with angels join.

HYMN CCCCIV.

"*Happy is that people, whose God is the Lord.*"—PS. cxliv. 15.

1 LORD, dismiss us hence with gladness,
Be thy people's lot our choice;
'Tis thy foes have cause of sadness,
But thy people may rejoice;
Who shall harm them,
While they hear and know thy voice?

2 From thy word with food provided,
May we feed thereon and grow;
And by thee, our Saviour, guided,
Through the pathless desert go;
While the Gospel
Wins our hearts from all below.

3 Saviour, keep all evil from us,
Go before us in the way;
Till we reach the land of promise,
Be thy word our guide and stay:
Joy and triumph
Shall be ours in that bright day.

4 Then thy people's griefs are over;
Then thy people cease to fight;
In that day thou wilt discover
All thy glory to our sight:
God our portion,
God our everlasting light.

Public Worship.

MISCELLANEOUS.

HYMN CCCCV.

"*Make us to go in the path of thy commandments.*"—
PSALM cxix 35.

1 KEEP us, Lord, O keep us ever!
Vain our hope, if left by thee;
We are thine, O leave us never,
Till thy face in heav'n we see,
There to praise thee
Through a bright eternity!

2 All our strength at once would fail us,
If deserted, Lord, by thee;
Nothing then could aught avail us,
Certain our defeat would be;
Those who hate us
Thenceforth their desire would see.

3 But we look to thee as able
Grace to give in time of need;
Heav'n, we know, is not more stable
Than the promise which we plead;
'Tis thy promise
Gives thy people hope indeed.

4 Lead us then a way we know not,
Make the darkness round us light;
When thy will thy people do not,
Pardon, cleanse, and set them right,
Till in glory
All in joyful songs unite.

HYMN CCCCVI.

"*For he hath said, I will never leave thee.*"—HEB. xiii. 5.

1 NEVER leave us nor forsake us,
Thou on whom our souls rely;
Till thou shalt for ever take us
To behold that glory nigh,
Which, though distant,
Fills thy people's hearts with joy.

2 They are blest, and none beside them,
They who hope, O Lord, in thee;
They are blest, though all deride them,
They, whom grace and truth make free;
Joys await them:
Where thou art, they hope to be.

3 Joys await them without measure,
Theirs, conferr'd by royal grant;
Rivers of eternal pleasure,
For which now thy people pant,
Shall supply them,
And they then shall feel no want.

4 'Tis the hope of this that charms them
From the love of all below;
Hope of this with boldness arms them
To oppose the mighty foe:
Hope of glory
Sweetens toil, and lightens woe.

HYMN CCCCVII.

"*It is God which worketh in you both to will and to do.*"—
PHIL. ii. 13.

1 SAVIOUR, work in us thy pleasure,
All thy pleasure work, O Lord;
Thine the Spirit, without measure,
Thine the word, the living word;
Sharper is it,
Sharper than a two-edg'd sword.

2 Make us, Lord, what thou wouldst have us;
Meet thy people here to-day.
Thine it is alone to save us;
Hear thy people when they pray.
Saviour keep us
Walking in the "perfect way."

3 While the things remain that now are,
Keep us from the evil free;
Thine the grace, and thine the power;
Safety comes, O Lord, from thee.
In thy kingdom
Evil will not, cannot be.

4 There we hope to be for ever,
Free from sin, and free from fear;
There, at length, to rest, and never
See the foes we fight with here.
Come, Lord Jesus,
Bring the promis'd glory near.

HYMN CCCCVIII.

"*Great is the Lord, and greatly to be praised.*"—Psalm xlviii. 8.

1 PRAISE the Saviour, ye who know him,
Jesus well deserves your praise:
O ye careless, turn ye to him,
Turn from folly's fatal ways;
In the Gospel
Jesus all his grace displays.

2 Saviour, full of love and pity,
Grant repentance to thy foes;
Till thy saints in heav'n are with thee,
Let them on thine arm repose,
And grow stronger,
Till their arduous strife shall close.

HYMN CCCCIX.

"*For thou also hast wrought all our works in us.*"—
Isaiah xxvi. 23.

1 WHAT we should be, Saviour, make us,
'Tis what thou alone canst do;
To thyself we now betake us,
Knowing that thy word is true;
Thou art able,
Saviour, thou art willing too.

2 Willing to do more to bless us
Than we ask thee, Lord, to do;
What could harm or much distress us
If we kept thy grace in view?
Lord, forgive us,
And thy people's strength renew.

3 'Tis thy pow'r alone secures us
From the various ills we fear,
And thy gracious word assures us,
Those who know and trust thee here,
Shall in glory,
With their Lord at length appear.

4 Let the hope of this inspire us,
Lord, with holy love to thee,
Should our foes around require us,
Of the world we're in to be:
Keep us, Saviour,
Keep us "from the evil" free.

HYMN CCCCX.

"*For ye serve the Lord Christ.*"—Col. iii. 24.

1 TEACH us, Lord, to serve thee better
Than we do, or yet have done;
Ours the spirit, not the letter,
Ours a holy course to run.
Lord, be with us;
Perfect what thou hast begun.

2 'Tis thy work, thine hand must do it;
What could we do without thee?
To thyself alone we owe it,
That we live, and hope to be,
Ever living,
Where the saints thy glory see.

3 'Tis thine hand alone that does it,
Does the whole, both first and last;
Guard the crown, else we shall lose it,
'Tis thine hand must hold it fast:
Saviour, guard it,
Now, as in the time that's past.

4 Rich the prize, but sore the strife is,
While it lasts, O leave us not;
Hid with thee thy people's life is;
Happy is thy people's lot;
Guarded by thee,
Who shall do them harm, or what?

5 Soon the strife will end for ever,
And the joyful day begin,
When thy saints shall rest, and never
Sorrow more, nor ever sin.
There abiding,
Where no evil enters in.

HYMN CCCCXI.

"*And the truth shall make you free.*"—John viii. 32.

1 TO thee, O Lord, we turn our eyes;
To thee, O Lord, we raise our hands;
We foolish are, O make us wise;
In fetters still, O break our bands.

2 For liberty it is we plead;
The fetters of the soul, O break;
For then we shall be "free indeed"—
This liberty thy people seek.

3 We once were willing slaves of sin,
We lov'd our prison and our chains;
Then all was dark and foul within;
Tho' changed, much evil still remains.

4 This is the thing we feel, O Lord,
Our burden and our shame to be;
Come, then, according to thy word,
And make thy waiting people free.

5 Enlarge our hearts, that we may run,
With pleasure, in thy holy ways;
And when our race on earth is done,
May sing in heav'n thine endless praise.

HYMN CCCCXII.

"*For in thee, O Lord, do I hope.*"—PSALM xxxviii. 15.

1 FOR the hope we have of life,
Be the name of Jesus blest;
All is conflict here and strife,
But the end is peace and rest.

2 Let us "follow on to know"
Him we love and fain would serve;
In his footsteps ever go,
From his precepts never swerve.

3 'Tis the strength that he imparts,
Makes his people's burthens light;
When his spirit fills their hearts,
Then they think and feel aright.

4 Saviour, let thy spirit be
To thy people largely given.
Lord, we raise our cry to thee,
Send the Comforter from heav'n.

5 His it is, to take of thine;
His to show, and his to teach;
His upon our souls to shine,
His to bless us all, and each.

6 Saviour, hear us from above,
Let the Spirit now descend;
Make us to "abound in love,"
And preserve us to the end.

7 Then with all whom thou hast bought,
Bought with blood, we hope to sing;
Sing thy praise, and as we ought,
Thine, our Saviour and our King.

HYMN CCCCXIII.

"*We walk by faith, and not by sight.*"—2 Cor. v. 7.

1 "WE walk by faith, and not by sight,"
'Tis God who makes us thus to walk;
Himself our guide, himself our light,
Of him we think, of him we talk.

2 His people oft, in days gone by,
Would meet, and talk of him they lov'd;
And when they did, the Lord "drew nigh,"
He heard, he listen'd, and approv'd.

3 He said they should be his that day,
When he his jewels should collect.
Their Father he, his children they,
Such good awaits the Lord's elect.

4 When feeling as they felt of old,
'Tis then we think and talk of him;
But when our love and zeal wax cold,
We change, and choose another theme.

5 They blessed are who nothing see,
But who, believing in the Lord,
Assurance have that they shall be
With him, according to his word.

6 Then let us walk still less by sight,
And more by faith, 'twill all be gain;
The things we see will take their flight,
The things we see not will remain.

HYMN CCCCXIV.

"Who delivered us . . . . and doth deliver: in whom we trust that he will yet deliver."—2 Cor. i. 10.

1 YES, the Lord has thus far led us;
Here our "stone of help" we raise;
He has taught, and he has fed us;
Glorious he in all his ways.
Let us tell it,
Tell it to our Saviour's praise.

2 In the land of slaves he found us;
Grievous was the tyrant's yoke,
Galling were the chains that bound us,
But the Lord our fetters broke;
Strong his arm is,
And the tyrant felt his stroke.

3 He whose arm has thus far brought us,
Will be with us all our way;
With his blood the Lord has bought us;
Trust him, then, for well we may.
What we owe him,
Who in heav'n or earth can say?

4 Bright and blessed regions are there,
Where we hope one day to be;
We shall never hear of war there,
And no foe shall ever see.
Blessed regions,
Free from sin, from trouble free.

HYMN CCCCXV.

"*The Lord shall fight for you, and ye shall hold your peace.*"—
EXOD. xiv. 14.

1 THE battle is the Lord's; 'tis his
Whose power without a limit is;
Then why those fears that make us sad?
As if his word no value had.

2 'Tis ours to stand and prove his might,
To see him put our foes to flight.
The battle is the Lord's, and his
The honour of the triumph is.

3 His foes are ours, and ours are his,
He counts them so, and thus it is,
He makes his people's cause his own,
And all their foes are overthrown.

4 The thing is wondrous in our eyes,
That he who fram'd the earth and skies,
And gave to Nature all its forms,
Should thus ally himself to worms.

5 Yet so it is, "the Holy One,"
Whose place is heav'n's eternal throne,
Is one with those for whom he gave
His Son to die; this grace they have.

6 Of wonders this the wonder is,
No love can be compared to his;
'Tis love with things mysterious fraught,
Too much for words, too much for thought.

7 But what we know not now, will be
Hereafter known, when we shall see
The Lord enthroned in heav'n above;
The Lord himself, whose name is "LOVE."

8 But time will insufficient prove
To tell of "everlasting love;"
Nor can the theme exhausted be:
'Twill occupy eternity.

HYMN CCCCXVI.

"*Is the Lord among us?*"—Exod. xvii. 7.

1 "IS the Lord among us?"
Happy if he is;
Who shall harm or wrong us,
Since the power is his?
He who stands between us
And the foes we fear,
Able is to screen us,
And is always near.

2 Were he not "among us"
In the midst of foes,
Any one might wrong us,
Any one who chose.
Now they may alarm us,
When we see them near;
But they cannot harm us,
Since the Lord is here.

3 'Tis the Lord "among us"
Keeps our foes away;
Thus they cannot wrong us,
Wish it as they may.
Whom the Lord confesses,
Who can do them wrong?
Whom he saves and blesses,
Who forbid their song?

4 Sing we, then, with gladness
Of the Lord our King,
Who removes our sadness,
And who bids us sing;
Who with blood has bought us,
And pronounced us blest,
Through the sea has brought us,
And will give us rest.

HYMN CCCCXVII.

"*By grace are ye saved.*"—Eph. ii. 8.

1 SING of grace, the grace of Jesus;
Sing of grace, for well we may;
Sing the royal grace that frees us,
From the proud usurper's sway.

2 Sing his grace, we owe it to him,
All we are, and hope to be.
"Wicked" were the hands that "slew him,"
Though a willing victim he.

3 No man took his life, nor could he,
'Twas his own, to give or keep;
But he spar'd it not, nor would he,
When requir'd to save "his sheep."

4 Freely did he die to have them
Safe from the destroying foe;
'Twas his life he gave to save them:
What a debt, then, do they owe!

5 Sing his grace, all ye who know it;
'Tis to you a joyful theme.
Ye who have his Spirit, show it;
Live to him, and die to him.

6 Jesus gives us life eternal;
What have men, compar'd to this?
Theirs the husk, but ours the kernel.
Blest his people's portion is.

7 Rich the grace is that we sing of;
Glory to the Saviour be.
What we have, the best we bring of,
Lord, we bring our all to thee.

8 Thou art worthy to receive it.
"All is ours," if we are thine;
'Tis thy word, and we believe it.
Saviour, on thy people shine.

9 This it is removes our sadness,
When our hearts begin to sink.
This imparts a holy gladness;
Saviour, on thy people think.

10 Think of us, our Saviour, think of
Those whom thou hast thus far led;
Nor forsake us, till we drink of
Pleasure at the fountain head.

HYMN CCCCXVIII.

"*If so be ye have tasted that the Lord is gracious.*"—1 Pet. ii. 3.

1 HAVE we known indeed, and tasted
That the Saviour gracious is?
If we have, why have we wasted
Talents not our own, but his?
Why have we unfaithful prov'd?
Why the things "that perish" lov'd?

2 With a price all price exceeding,
Has the Lord his people bought.
Slaves he found them, little heeding;
His was grace, 'twas grace unsought.
'Twas the fruit of boundless love,
Something far our thoughts above.

3 He has burst the chains that bound them:
Blessed is his people's lot;
Arms of mercy now surround them:
His is love that changes not.
They who by his grace are sav'd,
Never more shall be enslav'd.

4 Precious is the blood that bought them,
Far beyond what words can tell;
Marvellous the love that sought them,
This they know, they know full well.
Theirs it is to sing his praise,
Theirs to love his holy ways.

5 Theirs to live in expectation
Of a glorious day to come,
When the God of their salvation
Will return to take them home.
Theirs to see him as he is,
And to live with him and his.

HYMN CCCCXIX.

"*For whom I have suffered the loss of all things.*"—PHIL. iii. 8.

1 LOSS is gain, and pain is pleasure,
In the service of our Lord;
His is love that has no measure;
Be his blessed name ador'd.
Praise the Lord, 'tis meet we should:
"Only wise," and only "good."

2 Happy they who call him "Master,"
And his servants truly are;
Time they wish to move still faster,
While they see his day afar.
Him they look for, and await,
Coming in his royal state.

3 Here they suffer, but object not:
'Tis his people's lot, they know;
Ease and honour they expect not,
Where their master found a foe.
It was *here* their master died,
And by man was crucified.

4 'Tis our shame, O Lord, whenever
We lose sight of things like these;
Yet we do it, and endeavour
An ungodly world to please.
Often we decline the cross:
Thus incurring shame and loss.

5 Yet we would not wish to shun it,
Saviour, we would rather die;
All our hope is founded on it;
'Tis our life, and 'tis our joy.
Though it should a burthen prove,
'Tis the cross of him we love.

6 Only give us strength to bear it:
Strength according to our day;
Then we need not shun or fear it,
Bear it gladly then we may.
'Tis a pleasure, not a pain,
And our loss, indeed, is gain.

HYMN CCCCXX.

"*Two are better than one.*"—ECCLES. iv. 9.

1 "BETTER two than one;"
Who would be alone,
Could he find another?
One to walk the road,
And to share his load,
As a friend or brother.

2 "Better two than one;"
He that walks alone,
May require assistance.
But in time of need,
Who his cry shall heed?
Friends are at a distance.

3 "Better two than one;"
He that walks alone
May be sad or fearful.
Then he feels his need
Of a friend indeed,
One to make him cheerful.

4 Fellowship is good,
'Tis a brotherhood,
Common joys and sorrows.
'Tis to joy increase;
Sorrow it makes less.
Thus it lends and borrows.

5 This be then our care,
Each in turn to share,
That which grieves another.
When 'tis so with us,
We shall prosper thus,
Brother helping brother.

6 Till we reach the place
Where the God of grace
Will his people gather,
There with him to be,
There his face to see,
His, our common Father.

7 There our trouble ends,
There we join our friends,
In his presence meeting.
Nothing will remain,
Nothing causing pain:
Joy and mutual greeting.

8 Then shall heav'n ring,
While his people sing:
Sing of grace for ever.
Him they love they see,
And with him shall be,
Ages ending never.

HYMN CCCCXXI.

"*Go and sit down in the lowest room.*"—LUKE xiv. 10.

1 WHAT for us is more befitting,
Than with those to take our place,
Who, the least, are lowest sitting,
Debtors, like ourselves, to grace.
Grace that beyond hope abounds;
Grace that dazzles and confounds.

2 Can it be that such as we are,
Should in heav'n obtain a place?
Pure and holy, such as they are
Who behold the Saviour's face.
Shall we be with him and his?
Shall we see him as he is?

Never can we rest, no never,
Till the day when he appears,
Then we cease from sin for ever,
And he wipes away our tears.

3 Then we shall be what we should be,
Which, till then, can never be;
Then we shall be where we would be,
Dwelling, Lord, in heav'n with thee.
What a hope! To be for ever
In thy presence, Lord, above;
To behold thee there, and never
Cease to sing thy grace and love.

4 With a hope like this, we would be
What thy people ought to be;
And we would not, if it could be,
Shun the cross—'twere unlike thee.
Grace we ask for, grace to bear it;
Thou alone canst give the pow'r.
Be it ours with thee to share it,
And await the final hour.

HYMN CCCCXXIV.

"This is life eternal, that they might know thee."—
JOHN xvii. 3.

1 'TIS a blessed thing to know
Him from whom all good proceeds;
Blessed at his throne to bow,
Blessed to rehearse his deeds.

2 Deeds of power and deeds of grace,
Deeds of wonder and of love;
His "the high and holy place,"
His a throne all thrones above.

3 Saviour, who is like to thee?
As thou doest who can do?
Meet it is that we should be
Full of love and wonder too.

4 Much we owe thee, but how much,
Who can tell, or who can know?
Sinners bought with blood, as such,
At thy feet behold we bow.

5 Hadst thou in that fearful day
When "in agony" thou wast,
Hadst thou put the cup away,
All was lost, for ever lost.

6 But thy purpose was to save,
All must be endur'd for this;
Hence the cross, and hence the grave,
O that love! how great it was!

7 Saviour, help us to take up,
And to bear the cross for thee;
Thou for us didst drain the cup,
Thine our hearts, our homage be.

HYMN CCCCXXV.

"*Be not afraid.*"—MATT. xiv. 27.

1 MUCH there is to harm us
In the path we tread,
This should not alarm us,
Since the Lord has said,
He will never leave us
Till the day shall come,
When he will receive us
To our blessed home.

2 Why should they be fearful
Whom the Lord befriends?
Should they not be cheerful,
Whom his arm defends?
Who or what can harm them,
Objects of his love?
What, then, should alarm them,
Shielded from above?

3 If his arm were shorten'd
That it could not save,
We might be dishearten'd—
Cause we then should have,
Were he deaf, and could not
Hear his people's pray'r,
Were he chang'd, and would not,
Then we might despair.

4 But he changes never—
Still the same he is;
Trust him, then, for ever,
Well assur'd of this.
He with strength provides us;
He, from first to last;
He from danger hides us
Till the storm is past.

HYMN CCCCXXVI.

"*If God be for us, who can be against us?*"—Rom. viii. 31.

1 "GOD is for us;" if it be so,
Whom or what have we to fear?
Why, then, do his people flee so?
Flee as if no friend were near,
Or, if present,
Could not save, or would not hear.

2 Is the arm that saves us shorter
Than it was in ages past?
Is it to some other quarter
We must go at last?
Saviour, help us,
Thou alone the power hast.

3 Lord, thine arm is nothing shorten'd,
Sad it would be were it so;
Hence we need not be dishearten'd,
Hence we need not fear the foe;
Those thou keepest,
Nothing have to fear, we know.

4 In thy keeping happy are we,
Then alone from evil free;
If thy strength is ours, what care we,
Who or what oppos'd may be,
While possessing
"Everlasting strength" in thee.

HYMN CCCCXXVII.

"*Thou hast the words of eternal life.*"—John vi. 68.

1 YES, Lord, thou hast the words of life,
"Eternal life." To whom should we
Or others go, for rest from strife,
For inward peace, but unto thee.

2 Thy words of grace and truth can quell
The inward storm, and make it cease;
And when the billows heave and swell,
Thy words are heard, and all is peace.

3 When thoughts impure arise within,
And passions that defy control,
Thy words are found a match for sin,
They force the demon from the soul.

4 Thy words a living power have,
A "spirit" that is theirs alone;
Thy words can cure, thy words can save,
Thy words can break the heart of stone.

5 Thy words can heal the broken heart,
And take the sense of guilt away;
Can peace and holy joy impart,
And hope, that hails the coming day.

6 All this thy words can do, we know,
And more, our thoughts surpassing far;
To whom, then, Saviour, should we go,
But to thyself, whose words they are?

HYMN CCCCXXVIII.

"*I go to prepare a place for you.*"—JOHN xiv. 2.

1 WE look for joys to come,
We seek another home,
Where all the saints together dwell,
A blessed home it is;
The Lord is there and his.
The thought of such a home is sweet.

2 But sweet to those alone
To whom the Lord is known;
To whom the Saviour's name is dear.
And why to them so sweet?
Because they hope to meet
The Saviour, whom they trust to here.

3 They hope to see his face,
To sing his pow'r and grace
With all the ransom'd saints above.
To see him as he is,
To be with him and his,
And never, never to remove.

4 The prospect blessed is,
No hope can equal this,
To be for ever with the Lord,
Who died that we might be
From sin and sorrow free,
Himself his people's great reward.

5 But this the wonder is,
That with a hope like this
Our minds should still so carnal be.
Forgive, O Lord, forgive,
And suffer us to live,
And henceforth let us follow thee.

6 Our strength, O Lord, renew,
And let us keep in view
The home where all thy people meet.
When safe arrived at last,
The thought of dangers past
Will serve to render home more sweet.

HYMN CCCCXXIX.

"*More to be desired than gold .... sweeter also than honey.*"—
PSALM xix. 10.

1 BETTER is thy word than money:
Better than the finest gold;
Sweeter is thy word than honey;
Sweeter, Lord, a thousand fold.
In this treasure
Things we have both new and old.

2 Let us profit when we read it;
Be thy spirit, Lord, our guide.
Grant his teaching, for we need it,
Better he than all beside;
By his teaching
We shall in the truth abide.

8 Let thy word appear more precious,
And its truths be better known;
Let its promises refresh us,
And by faith become our own;
And thy statutes
Be they learn'd, and be they done.

HYMN CCCCXXX.

"*Did not our heart burn within us?*"—LUKE xxiv. 32.

1 NOW may the Spirit from above
Impart his holy fire!
And cause our hearts to glow with love,
And vehement desire.

2 The sweet desire of holy things,
That finds its element
In converse with the King of kings,
With nought but this content.

3 The pledge of sacred joys to come,
Anticipation bless'd
Of heav'n, our everlasting home;
Of heav'n, our place of rest.

4 A feeling not to be express'd,
But sweetly known to those
Who lean upon the Saviour's breast,
Who on his truth repose.

5 To us the Comforter be giv'n,
Whose presence better is
Than life itself, than all but heav'n;
The grace we ask is this.

For a Revival.

HYMN CCCCXXXI.

"*My word . . . shall not return unto me void.*"—ISAIAH lv. 11.

1 SAVIOUR, follow with thy blessing
Truths deliver'd in thy name,
Thus the word, thy pow'r possessing,
Shall declare from whence it came:
Mighty let the Gospel be,
All subduing, Lord, to thee.

2 Let the word be food to nourish
Those whom thou hast call'd thine own;
Let thy people's graces flourish,
Flourish to thy praise alone:
Thou who mad'st the sinner live,
Further life alone canst give.

3 Let the sinner see his danger,
Shew him, Lord, his fearful state,
While he lives to thee a stranger,
Loving what his soul should hate;
Let him now thy truth receive,
Let him now repent and live.

HYMN CCCCXXXII.

"*The sure mercies of David.*"—ISAIAH lv. 3.

1 SOUNDS of mercy come from heaven,
In the Gospel strike our ears;
Happy he to whom 'tis given
To believe the truth he hears!
Then the Saviour
Precious in his sight appears.

2 O our God! let thousands hearing
Of thy love in every place,
Though till now as foes appearing,
Foes to thee, the God of grace,
Turn them to thee,
And begin to seek thy face.

3 Lord, remove the sinner's blindness,
Give him eyes that he may see;
And let many, won by kindness,
Leave the world to follow thee;
Mighty Saviour,
Set the captive sinner free.

HYMN CCCCXXXIII.

" *The entrance of thy word giveth light.*"—PSALM cxix. 130.

1 O MAY the Gospel's conqu'ring force
Be felt by all who hear its sound!
So shall it prove its heav'nly source,
And praise shall to our God redound.

2 Lord, let thy mighty voice be heard,
Speak in the word, and speak with pow'r,
So shall thy glorious name be fear'd
By those who never fear'd before.

3 O pity those who lie in sin!
Preserve them from the sinner's doom;
Open the ark and take them in,
And save them from the wrath to come.

4 So shall thy people joyful be,
The angels too will louder sing,
And both ascribe the praise to thee,
To thee, the everlasting King.

HYMN CCCCXXXIV.

"*He sendeth out his word.*"—Psalm cxlvii. 18.

1 SAVIOUR, bless the word to all,
Quick and powerful let it prove;
O let sinners hear thy call!
And thy people grow in love.

2 Thine own gracious message bless,
Follow it with pow'r divine,
Give the Gospel great success,
Thine the work, the glory thine.

3 Saviour, bid the world rejoice,
Send, O send thy truth abroad!
Let the nations hear thy voice,
Hear it, and return to God.

HYMN CCCCXXXV.

"*For our Gospel came not unto you in word only, but also in power.*"—1 Thess. i. 5.

1 MAY the pow'r that brings salvation,
Still exerted in the word,
By its quick'ning operation,
Life impart and joy afford!
Life to sinners,
Joy to those who know the Lord.

2 Hark the voice of love proclaiming
Mercy through a Saviour's blood!
Vain the schemes of human framing,
This alone is own'd of God;
'Tis the Gospel
Points to heav'n, and shows the road.

HYMN CCCCXXXVI.

"*For God, who commanded the light to shine out of darkness, hath shined in our hearts.*"—2 Cor. iv. 6.

1 THOU who didst command the light
First upon the world to shine,
Put the shadows, Lord, to flight,
By the beams of truth divine;
Let the sinner turn to thee,
Let him now thy glory see.

2 Darkness reigns till thou art known;
Darkness can no longer reign;
Vain delusive hope is gone,
When the joyful truth is seen;
Sweet the hope the Gospel gives,
Blest the sinner who believes.

3 Saviour, all our prayer fulfil,
Let thy people too be blest,
On their hearts more deeply still
Let the truth be now imprest;
Let them go from strength to strength,
Till they come to heav'n at length.

HYMN CCCCXXXVII.

"*The Lord openeth the eyes of the blind.*"—Psalm cxlvi. 8.

1 SAV'D ourselves by Jesu's blood,
Let us now draw nigh to God;
Many round us blindly stray,
Mov'd with pity let us pray,
Pray that they who now are blind,
Soon the way of truth may find.

2 Lord, awaken all around,
Let them know the joyful sound;
Slaves to Satan heretofore,
Let them now be slaves no more;
Lord, we turn our eyes to thee,
Set the captive sinner free.

3 Glorious things of thee are told,
What thine arm has wrought of old;
Thousands once its pow'r confess'd,
O for seasons like the past!
Lord, revive the former days,
Thine the pow'r, and thine the praise.

HYMN CCCCXXXVIII.

"*Let all that be round about him bring presents unto him that ought to be feared.*"—PSALM lxxvi. 11.

1 SINNERS we, but sinners savēd,
(Praise to sov'reign grace alone!)
Now approach thee, Son of David,
Thee who fill'st yon heav'nly throne:
When we turn our eyes around us,
Thousands perishing we see;
Thou who brak'st the chains that bound us,
Set our friends and neighbours free.

2 Though we can't but fear for many,
So unthinking they appear,
Why should we despair of any,
When we know what once *we* were?
Bound with twice ten thousand fetters,
Thou hast set thy servants free;
Sure there's none can greater debtors
Be to sov'reign grace than we.

3 What thou hast for us effected
Shows us what thy pow'r can do;
We, whom grace has thus selected,
Would have others savēd too!
Thoughtless sinners, Lord, awaken,
Let them see their fearful state,
Lest their souls be snar'd and taken,
And they mourn at length too late.

4 Grant thy people too a blessing,
Lord, revive thy work in them;
Peace and joy in thee possessing,
Let them glorify thy name:
Still of thee, their Master, learning,
Let them grow in mutual love;
And the world, their grace discerning,
Own the power from above.

HYMN CCCCXXXIX.

"*For the word of God is quick and powerful, and sharper than any two-edged sword.*"—HEB. iv. 12.

1 "QUICK and powerful is the word,
Sharper than a two-edg'd sword;"
In the Lord Jehovah's hand,
Nothing can its force withstand.

2 How its pow'r was felt of old,
They who felt its pow'r have told;
Many were the wonders wrought,
Multitudes were fed and taught.

3 Mighty God, whose word it is,
Hear our pray'r, and grant us this,
What thy pow'r has done before,
Now descend and do once more.

4 Give the word, let many speak,
Many hear, and many seek,
Seek thy face, whom angels praise,
Love thy truth and learn thy ways.

5 Happy days when God descends!
When his pow'r the word attends,
Then the truth its beauty shows,
Charms and conquers all its foes.

HYMN CCCCXL.

"*Awake, as in the ancient days.*"—ISAIAH li. 9.

1 AWAKE, awake, O arm of God!
Awake, as in the days of old;
"Put on thy strength," and take thy rod,
Thy former works are not untold.

2 O be, as thou wast wont to be,
When thou didst "wound the dragon's head."
As when thou didst divide the sea,
And through it did the people lead.

3 O do, as thou wast wont to do,
What time the smitten rock obey'd;
And struck, into a fountain grew,
Thy mighty pow'r was then display'd.

4 "Awake, awake, O arm of God!"
That man may learn, and cease to mock;
The word of truth, be this thy rod,
And man's proud heart the smitten rock.

5 Let streams of "godly sorrow" flow
From hearts that never felt before;
Thy mighty power we thus shall know,
"O arm of God," thy mighty power.

HYMN CCCCXLI.

"*He was lost and is found.*"—LUKE XV. 24.

1 WE were lost, but God has found us,
God, who seeks and saves the lost;
Let us pray for those around us,
Thousands by the world engross'd;
Though they seem from God to fly,
God has pow'r to bring them nigh.

2 Lord, behold the sinner wand'ring
Far from thee, and far from peace:
All his precious substance squand'ring
In pursuit of earthly bliss;
Show him, Lord, that none can be
Truly blest till brought to thee!

3 Let thy word go forth with power,
Spread abroad "the joyful sound;"
O our light, our strength, our tower,
Make thy glory known around;
Let the truth's resistless force
Stop the sinner in his course.

4 Of their Master's honour jealous,
Let thy people plead thy cause,
In thy service bold and zealous,
Let them scorn the world's applause;
Whether men approve or blame,
Let them own thy glorious name.

Lord's Day.

HYMN CCCCXLII.

"*Then were the disciples glad, when they saw the Lord.*"—
JOHN xx. 20.

1 COME, let us all rejoice to-day,
The day the Saviour rose,
And sent confusion and dismay
Among his vanquish'd foes.

2 His people's fears unfounded prov'd,
(Though much his people fear'd,)
But all their doubts were straight remov'd,
When he again appear'd.

3 Their joy was great, 'twas greater then
Than had they felt no dread,
To see their Master's face again
Was joy, 'twas joy indeed.

4 If we are his. and hear his voice,
As they did, so we do;
We think like them, like them rejoice,
Like them we suffer too.

5 Like them, too, we shall see a day
When grief and labour end,
When heav'n and earth shall pass away,
And Jesus shall descend:

6 Descend, and bear his people hence
To dwell with him above,
Where they shall see his face, and whence
They never shall remove.

HYMN CCCCXLIII.

"*Make thee two silver trumpets . . . that thou mayest use them for the calling of the assembly.*"—NUMB. x. 2.

1 THE day of rest once more comes round,
A day to all believers dear;
The silver trumpets seem to sound,
That call the tribes of Isra'l near;
Ye people all
Obey the call,
And in JEHOVAH's courts appear.

2 Obedient to thy summons, Lord,
We to thy sanctuary come;
Thy gracious presence here afford,
And send thy people joyful home.
Of thee, our King,
O may we sing,
And none with such a theme be dumb!

3 O hasten, Lord, the day when those
Who know thee here shall see thy face;
When suff'ring shall for ever close,
And they shall reach their destin'd place;
Then shall they rest,
Supremely blest,
Eternal debtors to thy grace.

HYMN CCCCXLIV.

"*And shalt honour him, not doing thine own ways.*"—
ISAIAH lviii. 13.

1 EV'RY thought should be directed
Heav'nward through this hallow'd day;
Worldly themes should be rejected,
Themes that draw the soul away;
'Tis the day of sacred rest,
'Tis the day the Lord has blest.

2 O what glorious themes invite us,
When we look on mercy's plan!
These are themes may well delight us,
Themes of joy to guilty man;
Full of sweetness, full of grace,
Suited to the sinner's case.

3 Why should we grow weary thinking
Of the Saviour's grace and love?
From these springs his people drinking,
Get a taste of joys above;
O 'tis good the Lord to know!
'Tis our heav'n begun below.

HYMN CCCCXLV.

"This is the day the Lord hath made, we will rejoice and be glad in it."—PSALM CXVIII. 24.

1 ANOTHER week begins,
This day we call the Lord's;
This day he rose, who bore our sins,
For so his word records.

2 Hark how the angels sing!
Their voices fill the sky;
They hail their great victorious King,
And welcome him on high.

3 We'll catch the note of praise,
Their joys in part we feel;
With them our thankful song we'll raise,
And emulate their zeal.

4 We cannot sing too loud,
Whom God has deign'd to call;
To other gods we lately bow'd,
But he has pardon'd all.

5 Come then, ye saints, and sing
Of Christ, our risen Lord;
Of Christ, the everlasting king,
Of Christ, th' incarnate word.

6 This is the sacred theme
On which the angels dwell;
How pleasant should the subject seem
To sinners sav'd from hell?

7 Hail, mighty Saviour, hail!
Who fill'st the throne above;
Till heart and flesh together fail,
We'll sing thy matchless love.

8 And when these tongues no more
On any theme can move,
We hope to sing thy love and pow'r
With other tongues above.

HYMN CCCCXLVI.

"*And call the Sabbath a delight, the holy of the Lord, honourable.*"—Isaiah lviii. 13.

1 I FAIN would love the day of rest,
Would still esteem this day the best,
But oft, alas! I've need to say,
"How barren is my soul to-day!"

2 True, I frequent the house of pray'r,
I go and sit with others there;
I hear, and sing, and seem to pray,
But oft my mind is call'd away.

3 I fain would see the Saviour near,
Of him would think, and speak, and hear;
[illegible] vain and sinful thoughts intrude,
[illegible]raw my soul from what is good.

4 Redeem'd from earth by Jesus' blood,
I fain would give the day to God;
But, seldom to my purpose true,
'Tis mine to plan, but not to do.

5 Of sinners, Lord, I am the chief;
O bring thy worthless worm relief!
Revive thy work within my soul,
And all my thoughts and pow'rs control.

HYMN CCCCXLVII.

"*For a day in thy courts is better than a thousand.*"—
PSALM lxxxiv. 10.

1 WHEN I can see the Saviour's grace,
And call the Saviour mine,
I feel content in ev'ry place,
The darkness seems to shine.

2 In such a frame I greatly prize
The day the Saviour claims;
Nor envy then the great and wise,
Their joys and golden dreams.

3 With those who love the Saviour's name
I choose to have my part;
And, if my portion should be shame,
I'll bind it to my heart.

4 With saints I'll sanctify the day
The Lord has call'd his own;
I'll go where they are wont to pray,
And worship at his throne.

5 And O! may ev'ry Sabbath prove
An earnest of that rest,
Of which, when we arrive above,
We hope to be possess'd.

HYMN CCCCXLVIII.

" *Hitherto hath the Lord helped us.*"—1 SAM. vii. 12.

1 ANOTHER week is past and gone,
  Rejoice, we're nearer home,
Our gracious Lord has led us on;
  And thus far have we come.

2 Our Ebenezer here we'll raise:
  The Lord our help has been:
We'll publish, to our Saviour's praise,
  The things our eyes have seen.

3 We've seen our foes before us flee,
  They turned and fled apace:
To God alone the glory be;
  We'll sing his pow'r and grace.

4 We've seen the timid lose their fears,
  And valiant wax in fight;
We've seen the mourners dry their tears,
  And put their griefs to flight.

5 We've seen the pris'ners burst their chains,
  And walk at liberty;
We've seen the guilty lose his stains,
  And without blemish be.

6 All this we've seen, and more than this,
  "The goings of our King:"
The praise be his, and only his,
  Whose pow'r and grace we sing.

7 His word, on which we rest, is true,
  Himself a faithful friend:
And he, who kept us hitherto,
  Will keep us to the end.

HYMN CCCCXLIX.

"*But now is Christ risen from the dead.*"—1 Cor. xv. 20.

1 THIS is the day, the sacred day
When Jesus left the grave:
Of him we sing, and well we may,
His arm is strong to save.

2 'Tis sweet to know that by his death
We live—this grace is sweet:
The Saviour, with his dying breath,
Proclaim'd his work complete.

3 He lives, he reigns the God of love,
He reigns for evermore:
His throne, all other thrones above;
His name, all names before.

4 To him who died and rose again,
The Lord of earth and heav'n:
To him, by angels and by men,
Be endless glory giv'n:

5 The glory due to him alone,
Who reigns in heav'n above;
Who fills the everlasting throne;
The God of grace and love.

HYMN CCCCL.

"*There remaineth therefore a rest to the people of God.*"—
Heb. iv. 9.

1 SWEET day of rest! for thee I'd wait,
Emblem and earnest of a state
Where saints are fully blest
For thee I'd look, for thee I'd sigh;
I'd count the days till thou art nigh,
Sweet day of sacred rest!

2 But oft (with shame I will confess)
My privilege my burden is,
No joy, alas! have I;
When I would take my harp and sing,
I find it oft without a string,
And lay it coldly by.

3 But while I thus confess my shame,
'Tis right that I should praise *his* name,
Who makes me sometimes sing;
Yes, Lord, (I'll speak it to thy praise,)
My cheerful song I sometimes raise,
And triumph in my King.

4 O! let the case be always so,
My song no interruption know,
Till death shall seal my tongue;
In heav'n a nobler strain I'll raise,
And rest from ev'ry thing but praise,
My heav'n an endless song.

HYMN CCCCLI.

"*I was in the spirit on the Lord's day.*"—Rev. i. 10.

1 SACRED be the hours to-day!
Sacred to our risen Lord;
He has borne our sins away:
Ever be his name ador'd.

2 Sweet it is to think of him,
Sweet to speak, and sweet to sing;
Never can we want a theme,
Since our Lord himself is King.

3 This is he who reigns above;
This is he who reigns below:
And his people, mov'd by love,
To his royal sceptre bow.

4 Glad this day, the first of sev'n,
  Glad we sing, "the Lord is ris'n;"
Christ our King, the Lord from heav'n,
  Rose this day, and left his pris'n:

5 Left the grave, a while his pris'n,
  Left it, to return no more:
Sing we then, "the Lord is ris'n,"
  Sing his name, whom saints adore.

6 Since he rose, his saints shall rise;
  Since he lives, his saints shall live:
Theirs are everlasting joys,
  All is theirs that grace can give.

HYMN CCCCLII.

"*Not forsaking the assembling of ourselves together.*"—
HEB. x. 25.

1 ON this day the first of seven,
  Sinners we, through grace forgiven,
Come before the God of heaven:
  Saviour, let us hear thy voice.

2 From our hearts remove all sadness;
Fill us, Lord, with holy gladness:
All the worldling's mirth is madness;
  But thy people should rejoice.

3 Of thy love for ever tasting,
Theirs are pleasures ever lasting;
Theirs a treasure never wasting,
  Which nor moth nor rust destroys.

4 Trusting to thy faithful promise,
Joy and gladness well become us:
Who shall wrest the blessing from us,
  Who that force or guile employs?

HYMN CCCCLIII.

"*It is Christ that died; ye, rather, that is risen again.*"—
Rom. viii. 34.

1 THERE'S joyful news for us to-day,
The Lord is ris'n indeed;
The surety bore our sins away,
And we from guilt are freed.

2 It well becomes us then to sing,
For who such reason have?
Ascribe ye glory to our King;
His arm is strong to save.

3 Through death he vanquish'd him who had
The power of death before;
And now he makes his people glad:
They live for evermore.

4 How glorious is our risen Lord!
His conflict finished is:
And now he goes to his reward,
The crown and sceptre his.

5 Ascribe ye glory to our King;
Your hearts and voices raise;
Let all the saints their tribute bring,
The tribute of their praise.

HYMN CCCCLIV.

"*And upon the first day of the week, when the disciples came together to break bread.*"—Acts xx. 7.

1 THE week's first day is that on which
The Saviour left the grave:
We sing of him in mercy rich;
His arm is strong to save.

2 He drank a bitter cup for us,
How bitter, who can tell?
'Twas thus he paid our debt, and thus
He saved our souls from hell.

3 We hail the day, the week's first day,
The day the Saviour rose:
The Lord, he bore our sins away;
From this our comfort flows.

4 From this there flows a rich supply
Of all we can require;
'Tis pardon, peace, and holy joy:
What more can we desire?

5 What more, but that we may sustain,
Untired, the holy strife;
And then, with all the victors, gain
A crown, the crown of life?

HYMN CCCCLV.

"*If Christ be not raised, your faith is vain.*"—1 Cor. xv. 17.

1 THE day that Jesus rose should be
Remembered by his friends;
Upon his rising, all agree,
Their hope of heaven depends.

2 If Jesus rose not from the dead,
His people's hope is vain;
He then would have no pow'r to save,
Nor should they live again.

3 But now is Jesus ris'n indeed,
And he "the first-fruits" is;
The first-fruits of the ransomed seed,
Of those he claims as his.

4 As he has ris'n, so they shall rise;
As he lives, so shall they:
A dwelling theirs beyond the skies,
And theirs a glorious day:

5 That day when Jesus shall appear,
And take his saints to heav'n;
To dwell with him for ever there:
This grace to saints is giv'n.

HYMN CCCCLVI.

"*Sing unto the Lord a new song.*"—PSALM xcvi. 1.

1 BLESSĒD day, the first of sev'n!
Blessēd day when Jesus rose;
And, with him, the heirs of heav'n:
Blessēd day, when saints repose.

2 Blessēd day, when brethren meet,
Breaking bread in peace and love;
Sitting at the Saviour's feet,
Drawing comforts from above.

3 Jesus died and rose again;
Jesus took his place above:
Heaven was filled with rapture then;
All was wonder, joy, and love.

4 Sing we then of him who died,
Him who rose again and lives;
Sing of Jesus glorified,
Him who all our sin forgives;

5 Him who saves us by his grace,
Keeps us till the final day;
Gives us then a glorious place:
Sing of him, for well we may.

HYMN CCCCLVII.

"*O come, let us sing unto the Lord.*"—PSALM XCV. 1.

1 JOYFUL be the hours to-day;
Joyful let the season be.
Let us sing, for well we may;
Jesus, we will sing of thee.

2 Should thy people silent be,
Then the very stones would sing.
What a debt we owe to thee,
Thee, our Saviour and our King.

3 Meet it is that we should own
What thy grace has done for us;
Sav'd we are by grace alone,
And we joy to have it thus.

4 'Tis thy grace alone can save;
Ev'ry blessing comes from thee;
All we have, and hope to have,
All we are, and hope to be.

5 Thine the name to sinners dear;
Thine the name all names before;
Blessed here and everywhere,
Blessed now and evermore.

HYMN CCCCLVIII.

"*Let us keep the feast.*"—1 COR. V. 8.

1 GLAD we keep the feast to-day,
And the leaven we remove;
Thus it is that we obey
Him we serve and him we love.

2 But our love, how cold it is,
When compar'd with what we owe;
Lord, we mourn because of this;
'Tis our shame to have it so.

3 Let *our* love rekindled be,
When we meditate on *thine;*
Let us learn to live to thee,
And to thee our cares consign.

4 Let the broken bread we see
Lead us to the bread unseen.
Saviour, let us think of thee,
Thee, whose love has wondrous been.

5 Let the cup we drink of, bring
To our minds remembrance sweet
Of thy love, the love we sing.
Blessed theme! for sinners meet.

6 Let thy Spirit, Lord, descend;
His it is to teach, we know.
Saviour, keep us to the end,
Then a crown of life bestow.

HYMN CCCCLIX.

"*This do in remembrance of me.*"—1 Cor. xi. 24.

1 WELCOME be the day of rest,
When "the children" breaking bread,
Prove that they alone are blest
Who with meat from heav'n are fed.

2 Welcome be the day that brings
To our minds remembrance sweet
Of the things, the glorious things,
Touching him whose flesh we eat;

3 Touching him whose blood we drink;
Him who died and rose again;
Him of whom 'tis sweet to think;
Glorious, though "despis'd of men."

4 Feed us, Lord, O feed us now;
Let us have the living bread.
Saviour, at thy feet we bow,
Praying, waiting to be fed.

5 From the flesh no profit is;
By the spirit life is giv'n:
His the pow'r, the blessing his,
His to make us meet for heav'n.

6 Think we, then, of him who died:
Bore our sins upon the tree;
Let us live to self denied,
And to him devoted be.

HYMN CCCCLX.

"*But I will see you again, and your heart shall rejoice.*"—
JOHN xvi. 22.

1 WE ought to sing for joy to-day,
The day on which the Lord arose;
'Twas he who bore our sins away,
And thence his people's comfort flows.

2 "The Lord is ris'n indeed!" How sweet,
How blessed to be sure of this!
To know his work to be complete;
To have our part with him and his.

3 To have a hope that we shall see
The Lord in heav'n with all his train;
With him that we shall ever be;
With him to live, with him to reign.

4 The people who with him are one,
Arise with him, ascend, and reign;
Their destiny to fill a throne.
What is there more than this to give?

5 All this is ours, if we are his;
His people then may sing to-day:
The pledge his resurrection is,
"The first-fruits" he, the harvest they.

6 As he arose, his people shall
Themselves, when he appears, arise:
Not one be missing. They shall all
Ascend, and meet him in the skies.

7 "The end is then;" the day is won;
The Lord himself has won the day.
"The mystery of God" is done;
But what is after, who can say?

8 'Tis that "which doth not yet appear;"
Not seen, not heard, not dreamt of yet.
'Tis what there's no possessing here;
'Tis joy and blessedness complete.

HYMN CCCCLXI.

"*He is not here, but is risen.*"—LUKE xxiv. 6.

1 WE sing with joy to-day:
The day the Saviour rose.
"The Lord is risen indeed," we say,
That friends may hear, and foes.

2 His friends have joy indeed,
That no man takes away.
'Tis joy to see the surety freed,
Then hail the happy day.

3 The awful debt is paid;
The debt to justice due:
Atonement ample has been made
For you, ye saints, for you.

4 Then let his people sing:
The people of the Lord,
And raise, in honour of their King,
A psalm, in full accord.

5 Let praise to him be giv'n,
Who liveth and was dead;
The Lord of earth, the Lord of heav'n,
Let glory wreathe his head.

6 His precious blood it is
That makes our garments white;
The grace by which we live is his,
And his our saving light.

7 His people well may sing,
And hail with joy the day
When he will come, the Lord their King,
And bear them hence away;

8 And take them to their home,
Their destin'd place of rest,
Where aught that harms can never come,
Where all are fully blest.

HYMN CCCCLXII.

"*But now is Christ risen from the dead.*"—1 Cor. xv. 20.

1 TO-DAY the Saviour rose,
No day like this there is;
A blessed day it is to those
The Saviour owns as his.

2 They hail the great event,
And joyfully they sing;
They sing of him the Father sent,
Their Saviour and their King.

3 His resurrection gives
Assurance of their own;
Because the Saviour rose and lives,
They know his work is done.

4 Then hail, our risen Lord!
The power is all thine own.
Of strife and pain the great reward,
'Tis thine, and thine alone.

5 For ever hallow'd be
Thy name, to sinners dear;
We hope, ere long, thy face to see,
Remote from foe and fear.

6 We hope to sing thy grace
When time shall cease to be,
In yonder holy, happy place,
Throughout eternity.

HYMN CCCCLXIII.

"*The love of Christ, which passeth knowledge.*"—EPH. iii. 19.

1 WE sing with joy to-day,
And meet it is we should;
We sing of him, and well we may
Who bore his people's load.

2 What love is like to his?
The love that saves a foe!
We wonder when we think of this;
'Tis strange it should be so.

3 'Tis passing strange that he
Who fills the throne above,
Should here on earth a victim be;
What tongue can tell this love?

4 Can any tongue declare
How deep, how high it is?
Its breadth and length, how vast they are,
What tongue can tell us this?

5 But this we know, and this
To know is good we deem,
That "God is love," and blessed is
The man that trusts in him.

6 In him, then, let us trust,
He gives us blessed hope;
These bodies will return to dust,
But he will raise them up.

7 A glorious day will come,
When we shall see our King;
He then will take his people home,
His praise in heav'n to sing.

HYMN CCCCLXIV.

"*Ye do show the Lord's death till he come.*"—1 Cor. xi. 26.

1 THE week's first day is come again,
The chief of all the sev'n;
'Tis precious to believing men,
This day belongs to heav'n.

2 Of him who died, of him we sing;
Who died and rose and lives;
Of lords the Lord, of kings the King,
Eternal life he gives.

3 The death he died, we shew it forth,
Until he comes again:
All other things are little worth:
They all must perish then.

4 But joy to those who know the Lord,
They nothing have to fear,
They know, according to his word,
'Tis JESUS will appear.

5 The same whose body broken was,
Whose life for us was giv'n;
The same who died upon the cross,
'Tis he will come from heaven.

6 Will come, to take his people hence,
That they may dwell above;
Their place is there prepar'd, and thence,
They never shall remove.

HYMN CCCCLXV.

"*Wait upon the Lord.*"—PSALM xxvii. 14.

1 GLAD this day we meet, to seek
Him we love and fain would see;
Lord, behold us faint and weak,
"All our springs" are found in thee.

2 Hail, our risen gracious Lord!
Thou hast fought, and won the day!
Thine the victor's great reward,
Thee we sing, and well we may.

3 Thine we are, and thee we serve;
Let us be a faithful band;
Keep us, Lord, nor let us swerve
From thy way, on either hand.

4 Better is thy service far,
Than the freedom prais'd so much;
They are free, no others are,
Whom thy grace has render'd such.

5 Saviour, cause thy face to shine;
Nothing lack we, when thou dost;
And the praise be ever thine,
Father, Son, and Holy Ghost.

HYMN CCCCLXVI.

"*I was glad when they said unto me, Let us go into the house of the Lord.*"—PSALM cxxii. 1.

1 GLAD I was to-day
When I heard them say,
Let us now repair
To the house of prayer;

2 There to meet the Lord,
There to hear his word,
There our songs to raise
To the Saviour's praise.

3 Though of saints the least,
There to keep the feast,
And renew our strength;
Hoping that, at length,

4 When the Lord appears
He will dry our tears;
And in heav'n above
Shew us all his love.

5 There his people rest:
There are fully blest;
And for ever sing
Glory to their king.

New Year.

HYMN CCCCLXVII.

"*And he answering said, Lord, let it alone this year also.*"—
LUKE xiii. 8.

1 ANOTHER year has reach'd a close,
And though mere cumb'rers of the land,
Our Saviour deigns to interpose,
And we're permitted yet to stand.

2 But while we humbly own our fault,
And praise him for another year,
We've need to tremble at the thought,
The hand of justice may be near.

3 Long has the Lord been seeking fruit,
But ah! how little has he seen!
Nor blame to *him* can we impute,
The cause with *us alone* has been.

4 Lord, we acknowledge all our shame,
Our privileges have been great;
The greater they, the more our blame,
That we have done so little yet.

5 The sweetest truths that angels know,
It is our privilege to hear;
And yet we seem to come and go,
As if the whole a fable were.

6 Lord, melt our hearts to mourn the past,
And let us henceforth faithful be;
And if this year should be our last,
O may our souls repose with thee!

HYMN CCCCLXVIII.

"*As for man, his days are as grass.*"—PSALM ciii. 15.

1 SWIFT fly the years, and, swift as they,
The fleeting life of man;
With truth the moralist may say,
"His life is as a span:"

2 But here the moralist may stop,
And sad his word appears;
"If in the world alone there's hope,
O give me length of years!"

3 'Tis thus with pain the worldling sees
That time makes no delay;
One year and then another flees,
And steals his life away.

4 Not so the man who hopes to be
With Jesus where he is;
Time's flight unruffled *he* may see,
For endless life is his.

5 Ah! Lord, if we be thine indeed,
Why love those earthly toys?
Why do our gross affections plead
For sublunary joys?

6 O send thy Spirit from above,
And set thy people free!
Our glorious calling let us prove,
By leaving all for thee.

7 And as the circling years revolve,
We'll hasten on the day
When thou these bodies wilt dissolve,
And bear our souls away.

HYMN CCCCLXIX.

"*Suffered he their manners.*"—ACTS xiii. 18.

1 LORD, we desire to praise thy name,
That, spar'd, another year we see;
To us belongeth only shame,
But love and faithfulness to thee.

2 Reflecting on what we've deserv'd,
It moves our wonder and our praise,
That such as we should be preserv'd,
And still be walking in thy ways.

3 How oft, like Israel of old,
Have our vile hearts turn'd back from thee!
To idols base, to calves of gold,
How oft, alas! we've bow'd the knee!

4 We've sinn'd against the clearest light,
We've sinn'd against the greatest love;
We stand convicted in thy sight;
Shouldst thou condemn, we must approve.

5 Nor can we use the suppliant's plea:
"Henceforth thy pleasure we'll fulfil;"
It suits us not to *vow*, but *pray*,
"Lord, teach us to perform thy will."

HYMN CCCCLXX.

"*He hath not dealt with us after our sins.*"—PSALM ciii. 10.

1 SPAR'D, through grace, another year,
Good it is to praise the Lord;
Good to meet our Saviour here;
Good his mercies to record.

2 Foes we have, unseen and seen,
Foes too strong for us to meet;
But the Lord our strength has been,
And our foes have found defeat.

3 When our foes we greatly fear'd,
When we seem'd an easy prey,
Then it was the Lord appear'd,
Then he drove our foes away.

4 Now he seems to ask us why,
When the foe appear'd in view,
We should fear, and he so nigh?
We should doubt, and he so true?

5 Saviour, all our sin forgive,
Make us what we ought to be;
Let us by thy mercy live,
And in heav'n thy glory see.

The Lord's Supper.

HYMN CCCCLXXI.

"*This do in remembrance of me.*"—Luke xxii. 19.

1 YES, Lord, we must remember thee,
While memory keeps its place;
'Tis meet we should, for thou art he
Who saves us by his grace.

2 Thy body broken on the tree,
Thy blood for sinners shed,
Remove their guilt, and blest are they
For whom the victim bled.

3 To thee, O Lord, we look and pray,
Who hast provided food
For all thy people on the way
To yonder blest abode.

4 O grant us, Lord, the living bread,
That we may live and grow,
And bless the table thou hast spread,
To feed us here below.

5 In mercy, all our sins forgive,
And on thy people shine;
In sweet communion may we live
With thee, O Lord, and thine.

6 And when we leave the world below,
May this our portion be,
With all thy happy saints to go,
And live in heav'n with thee.

HYMN CCCCLXXII.

[illegible] our passover is sacrificed for us."—1 Cor. v. 7.

[illegible] passover is offer'd up,
[illegible] bread we break his body is;
[illegible] was shed to fill the cup,
[illegible] was ever love like his?

[illegible] the feast has said,
[illegible] to remove;
[illegible] th' unleaven'd bread
[illegible], and love.

[illegible]
[illegible] his name;
[illegible] above,
[illegible]

HYMN CCCCLXXIII.

"*I am that bread of life.*"—JOHN vi. 48.

1 IN fellowship we meet around
The table of our Lord;
Let joy and thankfulness abound,
For faithful is his word.

2 The people whom the Lord appoints
The heirs of glory here,
He saves, and by his grace anoints,
And bids them nothing fear.

3 The food they eat is meat indeed,
The choicest heav'n affords;
The bread of God is living bread,
His words are living words.

4 Then let our thankful songs abound,
Our privilege is great;
Our Father's table we surround,
And eat of children's meat.

HYMN CCCCLXXIV.

"*But I said, How shall I put thee among the children?*"—JER. iii. 19.

1 AND is there room for us
Among the favour'd few?
Are we permitted thus
The Saviour's death to shew?
And say by this,
That we are his?
Come, then, obedient to his word,
And eat the supper of our Lord.

2 'Tis true, we nothing have
Deserving his regard;
But Jesus came to *save*,
He came not to *reward:*
Reflection sweet,
For sinners meet!
Come, then, &c.

3 For them the table 's spread,
Who make his name their hope;
Theirs is the living bread,
And theirs salvation's cup.
Saviour, thou know'st
Thy name 's our boast.
Come, then, &c.

HYMN CCCCLXXV.

"*This do in remembrance of me.*"—LUKE xxii. 19.

1 OBEDIENT to our dying Lord,
Who bid us thus remember him,
O let us now surround his board,
His flesh our food, his love our theme!

2 Let others feast on sensual sweets,
We are supplied with richer food;
When Jesus thus his people meets,
They want not what the world calls good.

3 Sweet feast! here love and union reign,
An earnest of the joys above;
And, meanest of the Saviour's train,
We celebrate his dying love.

4 O may that love, by pow'r divine,
To all our hearts be better known;
Dear Saviour, on thy people shine,
The people thou hast made thine own.

2 Love is cherish'd and augmented,
While we keep our Saviour's laws;
And his people are contented
To forego the world's applause:
Should they suffer,
Pain is sweet in such a cause.

3 Saviour, hear thy people praying,
Hear us from thy throne of grace;
O be here, thy love displaying,
Let thy people see thy face;
'Tis thy presence
Renders sacred ev'ry place.

4 Let us here have sweet communion
With each other and with thee;
Truth the sacred bond of union,
Truth, that makes thy people free;
Heav'n in prospect,
Heav'n, where saints thy glory see.

HYMN CCCCLXXVIII.

" *Ye do shew the Lord's death till he come.*"—1 Cor. xi. 26.

1 BEHOLD our table! 'tis the Lord's,
Prepar'd for Jacob's seed;
The choicest meat that heaven affords,
Is that on which we feed.

2 While we enjoy a feast like this,
On husks let others feed;
Our cup "the cup of blessing" is,
Our meat, "the living bread."

3 Our Saviour's death is here display'd,
The death endured for us;
On Jesus all our sin was laid,
He bore it on his cross.

4 And now in heav'n his people's names
Upon his breast appear;
For them eternal life he claims,
Whose sin he cancels here.

5 We hope, with all the ransom'd crowd,
Ere long to see his face;
To testify our joy aloud,
In songs of endless praise.

HYMN CCCCLXXIX.

"*He hath filled the hungry with good things.*"—LUKE i. 53.

1 BRETHREN, come, our Saviour bids us,
Bids us to a feast of love;
Bless the Lord, whose bounty feeds us
With provision from above;
Ye, for whom his life was giv'n,
Come, and eat the bread of heav'n.

2 Let us think of him who bought us,
'Tis the Saviour's own command;
When we wander'd, Jesus sought us,
Now he leads us by the hand;
Now he gives us hope, and says,
We shall sing his endless praise.

3 O how much his people owe him,
For the love so freely shewn!
Well may we surrender to him
All that once we call'd our own:
Lord, we give ourselves to thee,
Thou our guide, our master be.

HYMN CCCCLXXX.

"*The bread which we break, is it not the communion of the body of Christ?*"—1 Cor. x. 16.

1 IN blessed union here we meet,
We sit at the Redeemer's feet,
And eat the bread of heav'n;
How highly privileg'd are we,
And O! how thankful should we be,
To whom this grace is giv'n!

2 To join in fellowship, how sweet,
With those who in the Saviour meet,
Enlighten'd from above!
How excellent the pleasure is
That flows from such a feast as this,
When all are join'd in love!

3 But if such joy is found to flow
From sacred fellowship below,
Then what must heaven be?
Where all the Saviour's friends shall meet,
And dwell in happiness complete,
Throughout eternity.

HYMN CCCCLXXXI.

"*In breaking of bread.*"—Acts ii. 42.

1 OURS is a rich, a royal feast,
Provided by the King of heav'n;
How privileg'd are they and bless'd,
To whom the bread of life is giv'n!

2 We worship him who bore the cross,
We glory in his death alone;
The world itself appears but loss
To those to whom his name is known.

3 We celebrate the great event
On which our peace and hope depend;
And leave an empty world, content
To know the Lord, the sinner's friend.

4 The blood he shed supplies a stream
That washes all our sins away;
How precious then the Lord should seem,
Whose death we celebrate to-day!

5 O that his great, his precious name,
May charm our hearts from all below!
Our love become an ardent flame,
And brighter, purer, daily grow!

HYMN CCCCLXXXII.

"*When the disciples came together to break bread.*"—Acts xx. 7.

1 MEETING in the Saviour's name,
"Breaking bread" by his command,
To the world we thus proclaim
On what ground we hope to stand,
When the Lord shall come with clouds,
Join'd by heav'n's exulting crowds.

2 From the cross our hope we draw,
'Tis the sinner's blest resource;
Jesus magnified the law,
Jesus bore its awful curse;
What a joyful truth is this!
O how full of hope it is!

3 Jesus died, and then arose,
Yes, he rose, he lives, he reigns;
Jesus vanquish'd all his foes,
Jesus led them all in chains;
His the triumph and the crown,
His the glory and renown.

4 Sing we then of him who died,
Sing of him who rose again,
By his blood we're justified,
And with him we hope to reign;
Yes, we hope to see our Lord,
And to share his bright reward.

HYMN CCCCLXXXIII.

"*And Jesus said unto them, I am the bread of life.*"—JOHN vi. 35.

1 LET the world, its joys partaking,
Boast how excellent they prove;
In the bread we've now been breaking,
We have meat they know not of.
Jesus is the living bread,
'Tis by this his friends are fed;
Saints adore him,
Bow before him;
Join the kindred hosts on high;
Let his praise fill earth and sky.

HYMN CCCCLXXXIV.

"*My flesh is meat indeed.*"—JOHN vi. 55.

1 IN sacred fellowship we meet,
To celebrate our Saviour's death;
His blood we drink, his flesh we eat,
His people feed on him by faith.

2 How blest the people who are his!
To them the bread of life is giv'n;
How fair, how rich their portion is!
They hope to see their Lord in heav'n.

3 Till he appears, his death shall be
Their spring of hope, their theme of joy;
And when in heav'n their Lord they see,
His praise shall all their pow'rs employ.

HYMN CCCCLXXXV.

"*O give thanks unto the Lord!*"—PSALM CXXXVI. 1.

1 OH! how pleasant, thus united,
To surround the sacred board!
While the hosts above, delighted,
Sing the praises of our Lord;
Let us join them;
Be the Saviour's name ador'd.

2 When he died, the cup was finish'd,
That which he was call'd to take;
Yes, he drank it undiminish'd,
Drank it for his people's sake;
Jesus drain'd it;
Nothing could his purpose shake.

3 Let us thank him, let us praise him,
Let us sing, though well we know
Nothing that we do can raise him:
No, nor all that angels do;
Yet his people
Should confess how much they owe.

HYMN CCCCLXXXVI.

"*Yet the dogs eat of the crumbs which fall from their master's table.*"—MATT. XV. 27.

1 NOT of crumbs, that from the table
Of the children fall, we eat;
It were mercy, were we able,
This, and nothing more, to get;
But our Father
Lets us have the children's meat.

2 Bread we have, the bread of heaven;
God has sent it from above:
They to whom this grace is given
Well may sing a Saviour's love;
Joy possessing,
Joy the world knows nothing of.

3 Of this bread, Lord, give us ever;
Eating this, we shall not die!
We are thine, O leave us never:
All our various wants supply,
Till our conflicts
End in everlasting joy.

HYMN CCCCLXXXVII.

"*Herein is love, not that we loved God, but that he loved us.*"—
1 JOHN iv. 10.

1 WE celebrate his love,
Who came from heav'n to save;
'Tis far, 'tis far above
What friends or mothers have;
Maternal love is weak to this,
No other love can equal his.

2 He died, and thence our hope,
He bought his people thus;
He drain'd the bitter cup
That justice mix'd for us;
Sound, sound his glorious name abroad,
Praise, ev'ry voice, THE LAMB OF GOD.

3 To save his foes he died,
For them he shed his blood,
And sinners, justified
Through him, draw nigh to God;
THE LAMB, THE LAMB shall be our theme,
Eternal honour be to him.

4 His work most glorious is,
Most precious is his name;
We leave the world for this,
Preferring loss and shame;
Nor do we ask a higher grace
Than to behold the Saviour's face.

HYMN CCCCLXXXVIII.

" *We are all partakers of that one bread.*"—1 Cor. x. 17.

1 AT our Father's table meeting,
All our sins by him forgiv'n;
Children's bread together eating,
Bread that cometh down from heav'n;
Let us banish
Hence the old unhallowed leav'n.

2 Blessed is the name we think of,
When together breaking bread;
Blessed is the cup we drink of,
Type of blood for sinners shed:
Happy are we,
Quicken'd by the Lord, and fed.

3 Let us walk in love, united
To our living head above;
Let us sing his praise, delighted,
Sing the praise of him we love:
Saviour, bless us!
Let us all thy goodness prove.

4 Standing in the Saviour's merit,
We have peace, and we are blest;
Taught and guided by the Spirit,
We have hope of future rest:
This we wait for,
And the Saviour's time is best.

HYMN CCCCLXXXIX.

"*Purge out therefore the old leaven.*"—1 COR. v. 7.

1 PUT away the leaven,
Put it all away,
'Tis the King of heaven
Meets us here to-day.
This a holy feast is,
Holy to our Lord;
Happy then the least is,
Round the sacred board.

2 O how blessed is it,
That the Lord should come,
And his people visit!
Shall we then be dumb?
Ill it would become us,
To refuse to sing.
Shall the heirs of promise
Fail to praise their King?

3 Lord, be gracious to us,
Let us see thy face.
All thy glory show us,
All thy truth and grace.
Blessed is our table,
When thou present art.
Thou alone art able
Blessing to impart.

HYMN CCCCXC.

"*It is iniquity, even the solemn meeting.*"—ISAIAH i. 13.

1 WHEN coming to thy table, Lord,
We ask ourselves, or ask we ought,
Does what we feel within, accord
With what's without, or does it not?

2 A form, without its spirit, Lord,
Is hateful, well we know, to thee:
The same by us should be abhorr'd;
Our thoughts as thine the same should be.

3 We would not willingly offend;
To do thy will is our desire.
Then let the Spirit now descend:
Baptize us, Lord, with holy fire.

4 The same that in the time of old,
Within thy people liv'd and burn'd,
As in the word of truth is told,
And we believe what we have learn'd.

5 At thy command, it issues forth;
Impell'd by thee, it takes its course;
Or east, or west, or south, or north:
And works with a resistless force.

6 Then give the word, and bid it burn
The thing we hate, yet cherish still.
To thee we look, to thee we turn:
We ask the grace to do thy will.

7 This very hour, let fire descend;
The holy fire that burns within.
O hear our prayer, the heavens rend;
The mountains melt; consume our sin.

HYMN CCCCXCI.

"*I will take the cup of salvation.*"—PSALM cxvi. 13.

1 "THE cup of salvation," the cup that we drir
Is sweet to the taste, and is life to the s
All honour and blessing to him whom we thin
Who only was worthy to open the roll.

2 And worthy was he, because he had offer'd
Himself for his people, and died in their stead.
Mysterious the death on the cross that he suffer'd:
All value above, was the blood that he shed.

3 The people he died for, are gather'd from out of
All kindreds, and nations, and tribes here below.
Be thankful, be joyful, his people, nor doubt of
The one that is stronger than death, as we know.

4 All honour to him who in earth and in heaven,
Alone was found worthy to open the seals,
To spread out the roll, and to whom it was given
To publish the wonderful things it reveals.

5 How blessed is he, and how glorious his name is!
The name above all to be lov'd and ador'd!
That we love and adore it so little, our shame is.
Forgive us, forgive us, our merciful Lord.

6 Thy name be it honour'd by angels in heaven,
By all who on earth and beneath it who live.
The power to thee, and the glory, be given,
What thou hast ordain'd that all beings should
give.

HYMN CCCCXCII.

"*This is my body, which is broken for you.*"—1 COR. xi. 24.

1 BROKEN was his body; broken
For his people's sake it was.
Hear we, for the word has spoken,
Love the motive, sin the cause.

2 Shed his blood was; shed for those who
To the shepherd's fold belong.
Good the Lord is, and he knows who
Trust in him, and he is strong.

3 He is able to take care of
Those who put their trust in him.
This his people are aware of:
And their portion happy deem.

4 What we live on, from above is:
This it is that makes us glad.
And our hope the fruit of love is:
Love that no beginning had.

5 Love we sing of, everlasting:
All our good we trace to this,
Never changing, never wasting,
For the love of God it is.

6 Sing of love, then, sing for ever;
'Tis the theme all themes above:
Ever new, it wearies never:
Sing of everlasting love.

HYMN CCCCXCIII.

"*Evermore give us this bread.*"—JOHN vi. 34.

1 MEETING at the sacred table,
By our Father's bounty spread,
We rejoice that he is able
Richly to supply our need.
When we ask him,
He will grant us children's bread.

2 "Children's bread!" we beg to have it:
Bread that cometh down from heaven;
"Children's bread!" O Lord, we crave it,
Let this bread to us be giv'n;
Feed we on it,
Pure it is, and free from leav'n.

3 Lord, we cannot live without it:
Life it gives, and life sustains.
Grant thou wilt, we cannot doubt it,
Grant our pray'r: this faith obtains.
Ours to praise thee,
Praise thee, though in humble strains.

4 Good it is that we should praise thee;
Meet it is that we should sing;
Though our praises cannot raise thee,
(What can raise the eternal King?)
Praise becomes us,
Praise, the tribute that we bring.

HYMN CCCCXCIV.

"If any man eat of this bread, he shall live for ever."—John vi. 51.

1 WERE it only ours to gather
Crumbs that from the table fall
Of the children, theirs whose father
Lives and reigns the Lord of all,
Thankful should we be for this,
But our portion better is.

2 Bread we have, the bread of heaven,
And this bread is meat indeed;
Pure it is, unmix'd with leaven,
That on which "the children" feed;
Living bread that God supplies,
He that eats it never dies.

3 Feed us, Lord, O feed us ever,
Be this living bread our food;
Never let us want it, never
Till we reach the saints' abode;
There we hope to see thy face,
And for ever sing thy grace.

HYMN CCCCXCV.

"*Lord, evermore give us this bread.*"—JOHN vi. 34.

1 GRANT us bread to eat, O Lord,
Bread that comes from heaven,
Meat indeed, the living bread,
Pure and without leaven;
Hear thy people when they pray,
Manifest thy power to-day.

2 Let thy people deeply feel,
Feel how much they owe thee;
When thou dost thyself reveal,
Then thy people know thee;
Lord, vouchsafe thy presence now,
While before thy throne we bow.

3 Met together in thy name,
We surround thy table;
Saviour, thou art still the same,
To supply us able;
Thou canst give thy people food,
Thou canst do thy people good.

Morning.

HYMN CCCCXCVI.

"*Cause me to hear thy loving kindness in the morning.*"—
PSALM cxliii. 8.

1 SAVIOUR, let thy loving kindness
In the morning be our joy;
Save us, Lord, from mental blindness,
Let thy praise our tongues employ;
Sweet it is to praise thy name,
Angels testify the same.

2 Angels, without intermission,
Sing thy praises day and night;
Here we meet with opposition,
None can sing thy praise aright;
Unbelief and weariness
Check our songs, our joy repress.

3 Saviour, take thy people to thee,
Raise them to their destin'd place,
Where with angels we shall view thee,
And with angels sing thy grace;
Many things distress us here,
All is light and glory there.

HYMN CCCCXCVII.

"*O thou preserver of men!*"—JOB vii. 20.

1 THROUGH all the dangers of the night
Preserv'd, O Lord, by thee,
Again we hail the cheerful light,
Again we bow the knee.

2 O! may the beams of truth divine,
With clear convincing light,
In all our understandings shine,
And chase our mental night.

3 Preserve us, Lord, throughout the day,
And guide us by thine arm;
For *they* are safe, and *only* they,
Whom thou preserv'st from harm.

4 Let all our words and all our ways
Declare that we are thine,
That so the light of truth and grace
Before the world may shine.

5 Nor let us turn away from thee,
Dear Saviour, hold us fast,
Till with immortal eyes we see
Thy glorious face at last.

HYMN CCCCXCVIII.

"*Thou shalt keep them, O Lord.*"—Psalm xii. 7.

1 THROUGH the night by thee preservēd,
Lord, we come to own thy care;
Hadst thou done as we deservēd,
Death and wrath our portion were:
Saviour, pardon all our sin,
Let this day with thee begin;
Thine we should be,
Thine we would be,
Thine with ev'ry talent giv'n,
Thine on earth, and thine in heav'n.

Evening.

HYMN CCCCXCIX.

"*Thou shalt not be afraid for the terror by night.*"—
Psalm xci. 5.

1 ONCE more the cheerful sun 's withdrawn,
And darkness comes again:
How many, since the morning dawn,
Have left th' abodes of men!

2 They who had known the Saviour's name
Are present with the Lord;
But theirs is misery and shame,
Who fought against his word.

2 [illegible]

3 We bless thee, Lord, that yet we live
To see another day;
Our many trespasses forgive,
And keep us in thy way.

4 When we shall close our eyes in sleep,
Preserve us safe from harm;
From deadly foes our dwelling keep,
And guard us with thine arm.

5 And should we sleep to wake no more,
Till the last trumpet sound;
May we, in that decisive hour,
Among thy sheep be found.

HYMN D.

"I will both lay me down in peace, and sleep: for thou, Lord, only makest me dwell in safety."—Psalm iv. 8.

1 THROUGH the day thy love has spar'd us,
[illegible] we lay us down to rest,
[illegible] the silent watches guard us,
[illegible] our peace molest;
[illegible] our guardian be,
[illegible] to trust in thee.

[illegible]ers on earth, and strangers,
[illegible]g in the midst of foes,
[illegible]urs preserve from dangers,
[illegible]e arms may we repose!
[illegible] life's sad day is past,
[illegible] thee in heav'n at last.

HYMN DI.

"*Boast not thyself of tomorrow.*"—PROV. xxvii. 1.

1 THROUGH the dark and silent hours
Of the night, preserve us, Lord!
Safely keep both us and ours,
Peace and confidence afford;
We are bold, in thee confiding,
Safe beneath thy shade abiding.

2 Should we never rise again,
Till the morning of that day,
When thy glory shall be seen,
When the world shall pass away,
May we stand by thee confessēd,
And with all thy saints be blessēd.

3 Since we cannot tell to-day
What to-morrow's dawn may bring,
Saviour, draw our hearts away
Far from ev'ry earthly thing;
Make us in thy service steady,
Always for thy coming ready.

HYMN DII.

"*Neither shall any plague come nigh thy dwelling.*"—
PSALM xci. 10.

1 GOD of Isra'l, we adore thee!
Thou hast kept us through the day;
Thus preserv'd, we come before thee,
Ours the new and living way!
Safely keep us through the night,
Guard us till the morning light,
Nor forsake us
Till thou take us
Far from earth to dwell with thee,
Through a bright eternity.

The Bible.

HYMN DIII.

"*Thy word have I hid in mine heart.*"—PSALM cxix. 11.

1 GLAD I am to have thee,
Book of God! I am;
And the Lord, who gave thee,
Blessed be his name!
Of the blessings given,
This precedence hath;
For it points to heaven,
And it shews the path.

2 Book of books! I love thee,
Not as I should do;
Though I daily prove thee,
Sweet and precious too.
Once I could refuse thee,
Choosing worthless things:
Now I would not lose thee,
For the wealth of kings.

3 Wealth of kings, what is it?
Saints have better things;
And they never miss it,
Leaving it to kings.
Book of books! in thee is
All that's worth a thought.
This enough for me is:
So, at least, it ought.

4 "Key of knowledge!" what will
Those who hide thee do?
Judgment comes, and that will
Be the time of woe.

Tremble, ye who do it,
Yours a fearful state;
Stop, or ye will rue it,
Soon 'twill be too late.

5 Book of books! I have thee,
And the Lord, who gave,
For a blessing gave thee,
This I trust I have.
Had I lov'd thee better,
And less sought my own;
Where I feel a fetter,
I should now feel none.

6 Make me what I should be,
Saviour, make me such;
This is what I would be,
Though I fail so much.
Never leave me, never,
Till the final day,
When thou wilt for ever
Bear me far away.

HYMN DIV.

"*How sweet are thy words unto my taste.*"—PSALM cxix. 103.

1 I LOVE the sacred book of God,
No other can its place supply;
It points me to the saints' abode,
It *gives* me wings, and *bids* me fly.

2 Sweet book! in thee my eyes discern
The image of my absent Lord;
From thine illumin'd page I learn
The joys his presence will afford.

3 In thee I read my title clear
To mansions never to decay;
My Lord! O when will he appear,
And bear his pris'ner far away!

4 Then shall I need thy light no more,
For nothing shall be then conceal'd;
When I have reach'd the heav'nly shore,
The LORD himself will stand reveal'd.

6 When midst the throng celestial plac'd,
The bright original I see,
From which thy sacred page was trac'd,
Sweet book! I've no more need of thee.

6 But while on earth, thou shalt supply
His place, and tell me of his love;
I'll read with faith's discerning eye,
And get a taste of joys above.

7 I know his spirit breathes in thee,
To animate his people here;
May thy sweet truths prove life to me,
Till in his presence I appear.

HYMN DV.

"*The entrance of thy words giveth light.*"—PSALM cxix. 130.

1 UNFOLD, O Lord, to us unfold
The wonders of the sacred page;
The things by prophets sung of old,
And handed down from age to age;
The things that Jesus said and did,
And all that from the world lies hid.

2 The spirit, not the letter, Lord,
Is what we ask. 'Tis thine to give
The spirit of the sacred word:
By this it is thy people live.
The letter kills: we know it does;
'Twas always, and is ever thus.

3 Be ours the spiritual mind,
That apprehends the hidden sense,
The truth that wise men cannot find,
To whom the cross is an offence.
They see no grandeur in the scheme
By wisdom plann'd: 'tis lost on them.

4 The child-like spirit, Lord, impart,
That with implicit faith receives
The living word, and in the heart
Deposits that which it believes,
There, Lord, to work thy sov'reign will,
And all thy pleasure to fulfil.

HYMN DVI.

"*My tongue shall speak of thy word.*"—PSALM cxix. 172.

1 PRECIOUS volume! what thou doest,
Other books attempt in vain.
Plainest, fullest, sweetest, truest,
All our good from thee we gain!
How thy living words refresh us!
Words of truth and grace they are;
Than the finest gold more precious,
Than the honey sweeter far.

2 What lay hid from ancient sages,
What they sought, but fail'd to find,
This, unfolded in thy pages,
Now appears to all mankind.
Far too high for man to reach it,
'Tis reveal'd from heav'n above;
God himself alone could teach it:
'Tis the mystery of love.

3 Why the angels, once in heaven,
Were allow'd to fall, and fell;
Why no angel is forgiven,
Who but God himself can tell?
Why is man the favour'd being?
This resolve us, ye who can,
Favour'd above others, seeing
Christ the Lord has died for man.

4 Precious volume! all revealing,
All that we have need to know:
Nothing from our view concealing,
That can profit here below.
Hope we have: this hope is cheering,
That the things we know not now,
In the day of his appearing,
Christ will to his people show.

5 Book of books! by him indited,
Him who reigns, "the only wise,"
How art thou despis'd and slighted!
Small thy work in human eyes.
I did once myself, profanely,
Leave thy sacred page unread,
And for wisdom sought, but vainly,
In the works of man instead.

Receiving a Member.

HYMN DVII.

"And he said, Come in, thou blessed of the Lord."—
GEN. xxiv. 31.

1 "COME in, thou blessed of the Lord,"
Enter in Jesu's precious name;
We welcome thee with one accord,
And trust the Saviour does the same.

2 Thy name, 'tis hop'd, already stands
Mark'd in the book of life above;
And now to thine we join our hands,
In token of fraternal love.

3 Those joys which earth cannot afford,
We'll seek in fellowship to prove;
Join'd in one spirit to our Lord,
Together bound by mutual love.

4 And while we pass this vale of tears,
We'll make our joys and sorrows known;
We'll share each other's hopes and fears,
And count a brother's case our own.

5 Once more our welcome we repeat,
Receive assurance of our love;
And may we all together meet
Around the throne of God above!

HYMN DVIII.

"And the Lord added to the church daily such as should be saved."—ACTS ii. 47.

1 LET joy and thankfulness be felt,
That Jesus still subdues the foe;
He makes the frozen heart to melt,
He lets the hopeless pris'ner go.

3 Speed on the wings of love,
Jesus, who reigns above,
Bids us to fly;
They who his message bear
Should neither doubt nor fear,
He will their friend appear,
He will be nigh.

4 When on the mighty deep,
He will their spirits keep
Stay'd on his word;
When in a foreign land,
No other friend at hand,
Jesus will by them stand,
Jesus their Lord.

5 Ye who, forsaking all
At your lov'd Master's call,
Comforts resign;
Soon will your work be done,
Soon will the prize be won,
Brighter than yonder sun
Then shall ye shine.

HYMN DXI.

"*We cannot but speak the things which we have seen and heard.*"
ACTS iv. 20.

1 WE have heard the joyful news,
Now let others hear it;
Bear the tidings to the Jews,
To the nations bear it:
They who know the joyful sound
Never should conceal it,
'o all the world around
ınd wide reveal it.

2 Joyful news the Gospel is,
  And to thought confounding;
Wonder, O ye heav'ns, at this,
  Sing of grace abounding:
Grace like this was never known,
  God our nature wearing,
Making human guilt his own,
  And our sorrows bearing.

3 Spread abroad the joyful sound,
  Fly in all directions;
Speak to men the world around,
  Men of all complexions:
All are sinners needing grace,
  God's own word has said it,
Go with speed to ev'ry place,
  And unwearied spread it.

4 And may he, whose grace it is,
  Give the word a blessing,
Make the conquer'd nations his,
  Ev'ry ill redressing;
May he take the veil away
  All the earth o'erspreading,
And his mighty pow'r display,
  All our hopes exceeding.

HYMN DXII.

"*To proclaim liberty to the captives.*"—Isaiah lxi. 1.

1 NOW let the trumpet's cheerful sound
    Make known the welcome news abroad,
  And to the world's remotest bound
    Proclaim the jubilee of God;
      The day appears,
      To dry all tears;
    The day to break th' oppressor's rod.

2 Ye slaves throughout the world, give ear,
Ye who have sold yourselves for nought,
In Zion's sacred gates appear,
And see what Zion's King has wrought;
Behold he reigns!
He breaks your chains,
And sends you liberty unsought.

3 Come home, ye wand'rers, now come home,
Receive th' inheritance you sold;
The year of jubilee is come,
The year by prophets long foretold;
The truth believe,
The gift receive:
'Tis yours again, unbought with gold.

4 And now let cheerful songs arise
From th' utmost limits of the earth:
The jubilee a theme supplies,
A joyful theme of heav'nly birth;
Let songs abound
The world around,
The season calls for sacred mirth.

HYMN DXIII.

"*This day is a day of good tidings.*"—2 KINGS vii. 9.

1 SPREAD the news, go spread it wide,
Spread the joyful story;
Tell how Jesus liv'd and died,
Spread the victor's glory:
He is now by angels crown'd,
He, whom man rejected;
Tell to all the nations round
What he has effected.

2 Having heard the joyful news,
Let us not conceal it;
Rather let his people choose
Boldly to reveal it:
'Tis the joyful news, when known,
Takes away our sadness;
This it is, and this alone,
Fills the heart with gladness.

3 Let us then with zeal engage
In a work so glorious;
Knowing, though the foe should rage,
Truth will prove victorious.
'Tis a cause that must prevail,
Let who may desert it,
Since the arm that cannot fail
Will with pow'r assert it.

HYMN DXIV.

"*We also believe, and therefore speak.*"—2 Cor. iv. 13.

1 ARISE, ye saints, arise and tell
The joyful news come down from God;
Arise, and with devoted zeal,
Convey th' intelligence abroad.

2 To sit at ease would ill become
The people whom the Lord has bless'd;
Let those who make the world their home,
Be silent, and remain at rest.

3 But let us rise, and speak aloud,
And tell the world the things we know,
How God the heav'ns in mercy bow'd,
And liv'd a man of grief below.

4 O yes! the God who reigns above,
Was once on earth a man of grief;
Ye nations, hear it, "God is love,"
And brings a ruin'd world relief.

5 In streams of blood his mercy flows,
The blood of him who bore the cross,
Who suffer'd death, and then arose,
And lives to plead the sinner's cause.

6 Now let the idols fall around,
And be the Saviour's name ador'd;
His Gospel through the world resound,
And all the nations call him Lord.

HYMN DXV.

"*Because they came not to the help of the Lord.*"—JUDGES v. 23.

1 YE people away,
Nor talk of delay;
The time for exertion is come;
The summons is giv'n,
The Lord calls from heav'n:
Let no man now tarry at home.

2 The Lord, in his might,
Is gone to the fight;
And if we should shrink from the toil,
The day will be won,
The work will be done,
And others will gather the spoil.

3 And should we decline,
His standard to join.
Our slackness will meet its reward;
A woe they will find,
Who tarry behind,
Nor go to the help of the Lord.

4 Then cast off delay,
"To arms," and away;
To arms—'tis the Lord gives the word:
With sword and with shield,
Away to the field;
"Away to the help of the Lord."

HYMN DXVI.

"*Shall receive a hundred-fold.*"—MATT. xix. 29.

1 YE "who know the joyful sound,"
Make it known the world around:
If the Lord has giv'n to you,
Freely give to others too:
Men of God, fulfil your mission,
Awful is the world's condition.

2 Ye whom God the Spirit moves,
Whose delaying he reproves,
Up and leave your pleasant home,
Leave it for the joys to come.
They who go where Jesus sends them,
Nothing want, for he befriends them.

3 Does the peril, does the toil,
Make your heart with fear recoil?
Does it worse than death appear,
To abandon all that 's here?
Still, if Jesus calls you, shrink not:
That he will desert you, think not.

4 He who calls you far away,
Will the sacrifice repay;
Friends and home will still be yours,
This his promise well secures.
Go, then, on his word relying,
In his name all ills defying.

5 Soon the final trumpet's sound
Will be heard the world around:
What will friends and home avail,
In the day when all will fail?
All but that which changes never,
That which will endure for ever.

6 Glorious then will they appear,
They who follow Jesus here:
Follow, without fear or shame,
Through the flood, and through the flame:
They may glory in his coming,
Honours theirs for ever blooming.

HYMN DXVII.

"Say among the heathen, that the Lord reigneth."—
PSALM xcvi. 10.

1 SEND the Gospel to the heathen:
Let them hear "the joyful sound;"
Honour'd will our master be then:
Honour'd all the world around.
Wherefore is our love so cold?
Why are we so little bold?
Why are we so slow to offer?
Why are we so loath to suffer?

2 Were we acting as we should do,
How the word of God would run;
Were we doing what we could do,
Then the Gospel, like the sun,
Round the world would run its race,
Giving light to every place;
From the heart removing sadness,
Through the nations spreading gladness.

3 Let us work, the night is near us:
Work we while there yet is day;
Saviour, from thy dwelling hear us:
Hear thy people when they pray;
Spring of life and health thou art,
Life and health to us impart.
Let us love thee as we should do,
Let us serve thee as we would do.

HYMN DXVIII.

"*Cry aloud, spare not.*"—ISAIAH lviii. 1.

1 "CRY aloud, and spare not,"
'Tis the Lord's command;
Should they blame you, care not;
Cry to ev'ry land.
Let not any nation,
All the world around,
Of the great salvation,
Ignorant be found.

2 Ill it would become us,
Favour'd as we are
With a gracious promise,
To decline the war.
Mighty as the foe is,
We have more than he;
Vain his strength and prowess.
Victors we shall be.

3 Yes, the Lord will make us
Victors in the fight;
He will not forsake us,
Nor withhold his might.

What we do, we do it
  To our Master's praise;
And he is, we know it,
  True in all his ways.

4 Onward then—good reason
  Have we to go on;
To retreat were treason;
  Bid the thought begone.
Strong and valiant be then,
  Jesus leads the way,
His to rule the heathen,
  His to win the day.

HYMN DXIX.

"*The Lord is thy keeper.*"—Psalm cxxi. 5.

1 BLEST, whom Jesus keeps;
    Blest they are for ever;
Jesus never sleeps,
  Never slumbers, never.
Safe whom he defends,
  Though beset with dangers;
Blest whom he befriends,
  Though midst foes and strangers.

2 Sing of him, then, sing;
  Other mirth is madness;
When we praise our King,
  There is "joy and gladness."
This is lawful mirth,
  Such as saints may share in;
Free it is from earth,
  And from all things therein.

3 His the kingdom is;
His the pow'r and glory,
Tell the world of this;
Tell the wondrous story.
Tell how he came down
From his lofty station,
Died, and won the crown;
Tell of his salvation.

4 Spread the news abroad;
Through the nations spread it;
They are blest of God,
They who give it credit.
Nothing leave undone,
Till the great salvation,
Like yon glorious sun,
Visits ev'ry nation.

5 Who the blessing share,
Zealous let them still be,
Till the kingdoms are
What we know they will be;
Till the Lord we own,
Proves himself the stronger,
And a hostile throne
Shall exist no longer.

ENCOURAGEMENT TO MISSIONARY WORK.

HYMN DXX.

"*Be glad in the Lord, and rejoice.*"—PSALM xxxii. 11.

1 'TIS a joyful day we live in,
God is doing wondrous things;
See the foe before him driven,
Hark! the ransom'd captive sings;
Sings with gladness,
Glory to the King of kings.

2 Favour'd spot, the spot we live in,
Mercies in our lot abound;
Chiefly that to us 'tis given
To convey the joyful sound,
To convey it
To the nations all around.

3 They to whom this grace is granted,
Should be strong, should valiant prove,
In the face of foes undaunted,
Full of zeal, and full of love;
God is with them,
God, who reigns supreme above.

4 Though a hostile world oppose it,
God's own cause must yet prevail;
True this is, and he who knows it
May persist, when others fail;
May be valiant,
When the rest through fear grow pale.

5 "God is with us:" this may cheer us
In the darkest day that is;
"God is with us," and will hear us,
For the cause we plead is his;
"God is with us,"
All we need is found in this.

HYMN DXXI.

"Lo, I am with you alway."—MATT. xviii. 20.

1 LET the friends of Jesus boldly
Plead the cause he owns as his,
Ill it would become them coldly
To maintain a cause like this;
He who owns it
Lord of life and glory is.

2 They who plead the cause of error,
Labour in the work they love;
And shall they, who know the terror
Of the Lord, less zealous prove;
And less gladly
In their Master's service move?

3 Long we were as those who cared not,
While the nations went astray;
Or as those, we seem'd, who dared not
Meet the foe and take the prey;
Henceforth zealous,
Let us mourn the long delay.

4 Though the world around be strangers
To the truth, and will oppose;
Let us go, nor shrink from dangers,
Though we meet ten thousand foes;
'Tis sufficient;
Jesus with his people goes.

HYMN DXXII.

"*Worship him, all ye gods.*"—PSALM xcvii. 7.

1 FALL, ye idols, fall before him,
Lo, the living God appears;
All ye gods around, adore him,
Tremble, and confess your fears;
Prostrate, from your places hurl'd,
Own the God that made the world.

2 Long he seem'd as one forgetting,
Or as one who lay asleep,
Or as one who cared not, letting
All the nations stray like sheep;
Only seem'd: he slumber'd not,
Nor was heedless, nor forgot.

8 But he seems to sleep no longer,
Lo, he comes to meet his foes;
Soon to prove whose arm is stronger,
His, or theirs who dare oppose;
When his arm is lifted up,
Who or what his work shall stop?

HYMN DXXIII.

"When thy judgments are in the earth, the inhabitants of the world will learn righteousness."—ISAIAH xxvi. 9.

1 LET those who are agreed
That Jesus is THE LORD,
The sinner's hope indeed,
His people's blest reward,
Unite in one
To make him known,
And spread abroad, in ev'ry place,
The tidings of a Saviour's grace.

2 What day like this has been,
So promising and fair?
How many signs are seen,
That shew the season rare!
And bid us fly
With eager joy,
To spread abroad, in ev'ry place,
The tidings of a Saviour's grace.

3 The judgments of our God,
That shew his mighty arm,
Are in the earth abroad,
And fill it with alarm;
A time like this
Propitious is,
To spread abroad, in ev'ry place,
The tidings of a Saviour's grace.

4 The doors now open stand,
That lately all were barr'd,
Unlock'd at his command,
To whom no work is hard;
He points the way,
Let us obey,
And spread abroad, in ev'ry place,
The tidings of a Saviour's grace.

HYMN DXXIV.

"*I shall give thee the heathen for thine inheritance.*"—
PSALM ii. 8.

1 A BRIGHT day it is that we live in,
A promise to cheer us there is;
To our Lord shall the heathen be given,
The ends of the earth shall be his.
Awake, then, ye saints, and be doing,
The work of the Lord is begun;
The word of his grace is pursuing
Its course, round the earth, like the sun.

2 We may not draw back, 'twould be treason;
Go forward we will, nay, we must;
The will of the Lord is our reason,
His grace and his promise our trust.
His people need not be dishearten'd,
Whatever before them they see;
The arm of the Lord is not shorten'd,
Unchang'd and unchangeable he.

3 Go forth, then, ye men who are ready
For Jesus to give up your lives;
Who, counting the cost, will be steady,
Whenever the moment arrives,

To bring to the proof your pretension.
Then go, whom the Lord has ordain'd,
Of his name and his truth to make mention:
Go forth, by his power sustain'd.

4 No peril, no foe, no disaster,
Nor things that appal other men,
Need move you, because of your Master,
Who knows how to succour, and when.
His pow'r is at hand, and, when needed,
Will help you, of this be ye sure:
Your cry will be never unheeded,
Your interests with him are secure:

5 'Tis blessed to suffer for Jesus,
Whatever the suff'ring may be;
He knows us, we're sure, and he sees us,
All-knowing, all-seeing is he;
The griefs of his people, he makes them
His own, and his burthen they are;
His people, he never forsakes them:
His treasure they are, and his care.

MISSIONARY WORK A DUTY.

HYMN DXXV.

" *Ye are the light of the world.*"—MATT. v. 14.

1 SALVATION! what a blessed sound!
Convey it all the world around.
Wherever men are known to dwell,
The tidings of salvation tell.

2 On you, the people of the Lord,
This work devolves, to spread his word.
Convey it then from shore to shore,
A light to those unblest before.

3 "A city set upon a hill,"
His people are, and 'tis his will
They should be seen; remember this.
An unseen people are not his.

4 To spread the knowledge of his name,
Their mission is; and O what shame
Would theirs be, should they not fulfil
Their trust, and do their Master's will!

5 A mighty voice is heard abroad,
A voice by which the world is awed.
"Men's hearts are failing them for fear,"
Lest things, thought distant, should be near.

6 Arise, then, ye whose mission is
To preach the truth; the work is his,
Who reigns below, who reigns above,
A work of power, a work of love.

7 And ye whom God the Lord may call
To part from home, and friends, and all,
Let nothing stay you, nothing here,
However good, however dear.

8 And ye who for the present live,
Who having much, but little give,
O think of him who died to save,
To make you his, and all you have.

9 They little give, who little love;
Their hearts are here, and not above.
For where the treasure is, the heart
Will always be. They never part.

10 Now may the Spirit give us pow'r
To love our Lord; and from this hour
May all we are, and all we have,
Be his who came from heav'n to save.

HYMN DXXVI.

"*Their line is gone out throughout all the earth.*"—PSALM xix. 4.

1 AROUND the globe, this world of ours,
The idol reigns, of God abhorr'd.
Your work it is: ye saints, 'tis yours,
To spread the knowledge of your Lord.
The lamp is meant a light to be
To all around, that all may see.

2 Then lose no time, and spare no pains,
Nor any sacrifice too great esteem,
If made on his account whose veins
Supplied the rich and copious stream,
That cancels guilt, that cancels yours,
And pardon, peace, and life procures.

3 We must not sleep upon our post,
But to our Master's will give heed;
They serve him best, who love him most,
And love gives value to the deed.
Then think we of the cross and shame,
'Tis this that fans the holy flame.

4 Come on, then, and let nothing damp
Our ardour in the Saviour's cause;
Nor fear we, though an host encamp
Around, 'tis thus it always was.
The cause we plead has many foes,
And ever ready to oppose.

5 Then spread around this world of ours,
With holy zeal, the truth of God;
'Tis this subdues the adverse powers;
Then send the word of life abroad,
And be ye sure that it will prove
A power the world itself to move.

6 In doing so, we only own
Our common Master's power and grace.
Then let us, when before his throne,
Entreat him that in ev'ry place
The missionary may be found,
Imparting light to all around.

PRAYER FOR SUCCESS.

HYMN DXXVII.

"*But thou art the same.*"—PSALM cii. 27.

1 NOW may the mighty arm awake,
That wonders wrought in ancient days,
That Babylon's proud walls may shake,
And God his own fair temple raise.

2 Art thou not still the same, O God,
The same to hear, the same to save,
As when thy servant mov'd his rod
At thy command, and cleft the wave?

3 Is any thing too hard for thee,
For thee, whose arm is cloth'd with might?
Then let thy waiting people see
Thy pow'r display'd, a wondrous sight!

4 The pow'r that sets the pris'ner free,
That wipes the mourner's tears away;
The pow'r that makes the blind to see,
And turns the darkest night to day.

5 Shine, Lord, upon the world around,
To sinners let thy grace be giv'n;
So shall thy people's songs abound,
And angels feel new joy in heav'n.

HYMN DXXVIII.

"*Behold, the Lord's hand is not shortened.*"—ISAIAH lix. 1.

1 LORD, arise, and crush the foe,
Conqu'ring and to conquer go;
See thy people wait and pray,
Looking for a promis'd day;
Yes, thy people wait with reason,
Looking for a glorious season.

2 Where is now thy gracious ear,
Is it deaf and cannot hear?
Where the arm that smote the wave,
Is it weak and cannot save?
Lord, arise, thy people pray thee:
When thou workest, who shall stay thee?

3 Lord, arise, the pow'r is thine,
Let thy light from Zion shine;
Glorious thou in all thy ways,
Work as in the ancient days,
When thine arm thy people guided
Through the sea, for them divided.

4 As when in a thirsty land,
Water flow'd at thy command,
Water to refresh thine own,
Water from the flinty stone;
And thy people saw with wonder
Rocks and mountains cleft asunder.

5 God of Isra'l, still the same,
For the glory of thy name,
Let thy people now behold
Mighty works like those of old;
Works of pow'r, the mountains moving,
Works of grace, thy kindness proving.

HYMN DXXIX.

"*Let God arise.*"—Psalm lxviii. 1.

1 LET God arise,
The only wise,
And let his foes before him fly;
At his command,
Let ev'ry land
Be fill'd with light and sacred joy.

2 The dawning ray
Of that bright day
Whose sun shall gladden ev'ry place,
A light imparts,
That cheers our hearts,
And bids us toil and danger face.

3 The Lord has said
His truth shall spread,
And all the earth his glory see;
Arise, O Lord,
Fulfil thy word,
And thine alone the honour be.

4 Thy people wait
With hope elate;
Not distant far the day appears,
When war shall cease,
And heav'nly peace
Shall wipe away ten thousand tears.

5 Then Abrah'm's seed,
From bondage freed,
Shall taste of liberty and joy;
From home long driv'n,
But now forgiv'n,
The waster shall no more destroy.

6 This day is light,
But far more bright
The day when Jesus will return;
He'll wipe away
All tears that day,
His people never more shall mourn.

HYMN DXXX.

"Then thou shalt say in thine heart, Who hath begotten me these?"—Isaiah xlix. 21.

1 "GIVE us room that we may dwell,"
Zion's children cry aloud;
See their numbers how they swell,
How they gather like a cloud;
Go and tell the joyful story,
'Tis the day of Zion's glory.

2 O how bright the morning seems!
Brighter from so dark a night;
Zion is like one that dreams,
Fill'd with wonder and delight;
Zion's night of grief is ended,
Zion of her God befriended.

3 Zion, now arise and shine,
Lo! thy light from heav'n is come;
These that crowd from far are thine,
Give thy sons and daughters room;
Sorrow from thy cup is taken,
Thou shalt be no more forsaken.

4 Lo! thy sun goes down no more,
God himself will be thy light;
All that caus'd thee grief before
Buried lies in endless night:
Earthly pomp is short and wasting,
Thine is glory everlasting.

HYMN DXXXI.

"*Let the earth hear.*"—ISAIAH xxxiv. 1.

1 O 'TIS a sound should fill the world!
The sound of mercy through the LAMB;
Lo! Satan from his seat is hurl'd,
Unable to withstand *his* name;
From heav'n like lightning see him fall,
Struck by the arm that conquers all.

2 Lord, give the word!—and wak'd by thee,
Let many tongues thy vict'ry tell;
That hopeless sinners now may see
That thou hast vanquish'd death and hell:
Sound, sound the joyful truth abroad!
Let sinners now draw nigh to God.

3 And thou, victorious Lord, all hail!
Immortal honours shade thy brow!
When death and hell thy friends assail,
They find in thee a refuge now;
Thy name shall furnish them with arms,
And free their souls from all alarms.

HYMN DXXXII.

"*Gird thy sword upon thy thigh, O most mighty, with thy glory and thy majesty.*"—PSALM xlv. 3.

1 JESUS, immortal King, go on,
The glorious day will soon be won;
Thine enemies prepare to flee,
And leave a conquer'd world to thee.

2 Gird on thy sword, victorious chief!
The captive sinner's sole relief;
Cast the usurper from his throne,
And make the universe thine own.

3 Thy footsteps, Lord, with joy we trace,
And mark the conquests of thy grace;
Finish the work thou hast begun,
And let thy will on earth be done.

4 Then shall contending nations rest,
For love shall reign in every breast;
Weapons for war design'd shall cease,
Or then be implements of peace.

5 Hark! how the hosts triumphant sing,
"The Lord omnipotent is King;"
Let all his saints rejoice at this,
The kingdoms of the world are his.
Hallelujah! Amen!

HYMN DXXXIII.

"*For a great door and effectual is opened unto me.*"—
1 COR. xvi. 9.

1 NOW let "a great effectual door"
Be open'd to our labours, Lord!
That open'd shall be shut no more,
A door of entrance to thy word.

2 O touch their lips with hallow'd fire,
Who to the world unfold thy plan;
Their hearts with sacred love inspire,
The love of God, the love of man.

3 O animate thy servants, Lord,
With zeal that nothing can repress;
And while they seek to spread thy word,
Their counsels and their labours bless.

4 O send thy Spirit from above,
Nor let his holy influence cease,
Till hatred ends in mutual love,
And strife in universal peace.

HYMN DXXXIV.

"*God reigneth over the heathen.*"—PSALM xlvii. 8.

1 KING of Zion, give the order,
Send thy light and truth abroad,
O let Zion stretch her border,
Zion favour'd of her God.

2 Thou canst form the zealous preacher,
Thou canst light and love impart;
Send thy word to ev'ry creature,
Send it to the sinner's heart.

3 O let many now be ready
To go forth, at thy command,
Men of faith, approv'd and steady,
Leaving all at thy command.

4 Send thy truth to ev'ry region,
Let the distant people hear;
Let them turn from false religion,
And to truth alone give ear.

5 Thou art God: who would not fear thee,
Who that knows thy glorious pow'r?
O that all the world may hear thee,
And be slaves of sin no more.

HYMN DXXXV.

"*And the desert shall rejoice.*"—ISAIAH xxxv. 1.

1 SEE! the wilderness rejoices,
Lately 'twas a barren spot;
Let us raise our thankful voices,
Let us own what God has wrought:
Who could think of such a thing,
God has made the waste to sing!

2 Here, where nought but thorns and briers
Lately grew and wildly spread,
Lo! the cedar now aspires,
Lo! the cypress lifts its head;
Lord, we own the work divine,
All the glory, Lord, be thine.

3 See the trees thine hand has planted,
Watch them with a constant care;
O let our request be granted,
Make them fruitful, make them fair;
Keep, O keep them still in view,
Let them live and flourish too!

4 Further, Lord, 'tis our desire,
(Turn not thou away thine ear,)
Root out ev'ry thorn and brier,
In their place let *trees* appear;
Thus from plants injurious freed,
Shall the desert smile indeed.

HYMN DXXXVI.

"*I have considered the days of old.*"—PSALM lxxvii. 5.

1 WHERE'S the mighty arm, where is it?
Where the arm that wrought of old?
When will God his church revisit,
And his glorious plans unfold?
Long expected,
And by prophets long foretold.

2 Will the Lord cast off, and never
Shew his pow'r as heretofore?
Is his mercy gone for ever?
Will the Spirit come no more,
As when thousands
Yielded to his quick'ning pow'r?

3 God of Isra'l, hear, O hear us!
Hear the feeble cry we raise;
Let the Spirit come to cheer us,
Come as in the ancient days,
When thy people
Saw thy pow'r, and sang thy praise.

4 Let thy word, with force resistless,
Urge its course, nor hinder'd be;
Let thy Spirit rouse the listless,
Let the blind begin to see;
And the pris'ners,
Send them glorious liberty.

HYMN DXXXVII.

"*Then the Lord awaked as one out of sleep.*"—Psalm lxxviii. 65.

1 AWAKE, O Lord, as one from sleep,
The foe is proud, the foe is strong;
For this do those who love thee weep,
And tempted are to ask "How long,
How long, O Lord," wilt thou refrain?
How long shall the usurper reign?

2 Thou sleepest not, we know it, Lord;
Nor dare we utter thoughts like these,
Unless instructed by thy word;
But, taught by this, we bend our knees,
And cry, "Awake, O Lord, awake,"
And hear us, for thy mercy's sake.

3 This favour, Lord, we ask of thee,
That thy salvation may go forth,
And "as a lamp that burneth" be
From east to west, from south to north,
Imparting light to every place,
The holy light of truth and grace.

4 And they who are not called to leave
Their native land, to spread the truth:
Let them with more affection cleave
To him, the common Lord of both,
To him, the same in every place,
The same in truth, in power, in grace.

HYMN DXXXVIII.

"*To proclaim liberty to the captives.*"—Isaiah lxi. 1.

1 SEEST thou yonder vessel borne
On the broad Atlantic wave?
Sent she is to those that mourn,
To the captive, to the slave;
Touch her not, ye men that war,
Deal not with her as a foe;
Goods she has that sacred are,
Let her unmolested go.

2 Know ye whither she is bound?
Know ye what her errand is?
Where the idol keeps his ground,
Where all hearts and hands are his:
Thither does she steer her course,
Bent upon the idol's fall,
Arm'd with Truth's resistless force,
Truth, *that* Truth that conquers all.

3 Speed her, Lord, O speed her way,
Speed her through the mighty deep,
Bring her to her port, we pray,
Save the cargo, save the ship;
Waft her to the distant shore
Whither she is bound, O Lord;
Open for thy word a door,
Let the idol be abhorr'd.

4 Bring her back again, we pray,
Safely from the distant land
Whither now she bends her way,
Guided by thine unseen hand;
Often let her sail again,
Thus commission'd from above:
Bearing to the sons of men
Tidings of redeeming love.

HYMN DXXXIX.

ON THE VESSEL CALLED "THE DOVE," WHEN ABOUT TO SAIL.

"*And the dove came in to him . . . and lo! in her mouth was an olive leaf.*"—GEN. viii. 11.

1 SEE how many vessels yonder
Ready are to quit the shore,
Some for trade, and some for plunder,
Man it is that covets more.
Soon the land will be lost sight of,
Nothing seen but sea and sky,
Yet the peril he makes light of,
As if death were not so nigh.

2 But there is a vessel floating
In the midst, with sails unfurl'd,
And she bears a name denoting
She belongs not to this world.
Yes, her goodly name "The Dove" is,
And the olive branch her sign;
Her commission from above is,
And the Lord says, "This is mine."

3 Speed her through the mighty ocean,
Be her guide, and be her guard;
When the waves, in wild commotion,
Rage, and foam, and threaten hard,

Then the time, O Lord, for thee is,
To appear, and save thine own,
Save the vessel then, for she is
Thine, and power is thine alone.

4 What a precious cargo hers is!
'Tis the word of God she bears,
Teeming with a thousand mercies,
Drying up the source of tears.
Nor forgotten is the preacher,
Faithful partner of the word,
Its example and its teacher,
Leaving all to serve his Lord.

5 When she gains her destination,
And her cargo puts on shore,
Bless the word of thy salvation,
Saviour, bless it more and more.
Often going and returning,
May she long a blessing be;
And the distant people learning,
From thy word, thy glory see.

HYMN DXL.

"*And the isles shall wait for his law.*"—ISAIAH xlii. 4.

1 SHINE, Lord, on this dark land of ours,
Forth from thy sanctuary shine;
Send out thy word with all its pow'rs,
And make this people henceforth thine.

2 Where superstition's iron chain
Has long been worn with deep disgrace,
ʼet glorious liberty now reign,
ʼuch liberty as saints possess.

3 Let men anointed from above,
Faithful, affectionate, and bold,
Go through the land, proclaim thy love,
And bring the wand'rers to thy fold.

4 Though many obstacles appear,
Since nothing can withstand thy pow'r,
We'll look in hope, and wait in pray'r,
Till thou shalt bring the glorious hour.

5 Then shall this happy island smile,
When truth's fair light shall shine from heav'n,
When Satan shall no more beguile,
Nor spread abroad his fatal leav'n.

HYMN DXLI.

"*And in thy majesty ride prosperously.*"—PSALM xlv. 4.

1 PROSP'ROUS be thy way, O Lord,
Ride thou on and win the day;
Thine the Spirit's conqu'ring sword,
Who thy mighty arm can stay?

2 Ride thou on, as in the day
When the tyrant own'd thy pow'r,
And, though loath, resign'd his prey;
Ride thou on, as in that hour.

3 Or as when, beneath the wave,
He and his lay buried all.
Whom thou judgest, who can save?
Who or what can stay his fall?

4 Ride thou on, as in the day
When thou didst thy people guide
Through the desert, in a way
By the foot of man untried.

5 Or as when, led on by thee,
Isra'l gain'd the promis'd land.
When thou mad'st their foes to flee;
When thou led'st them by the hand.

6 As it was, so be it still,
Shew thy faithfulness and love,
Ancient promises fulfil,
Shed thy blessings from above.

HYMN DXLII.

"*Awake, why sleepest thou, O Lord?*"—Psalm xliv. 23.

1 AWAKE, O Lord, why sleepest thou?
Or seem'st to us to sleep?
Awake, and show thy wonders now:
Thy wonders in the deep.

2 Awake, as in the days of old,
For thou art still the same;
Thy purposes of love unfold,
And manifest thy name.

3 We look to see a glorious day,
Nor do we look in vain;
Rely upon thy word we may,
Thou wilt thy cause maintain.

4 Thy word throughout the earth shall spread,
Thy word of truth and grace:
Thy quick'ning pow'r shall raise the dead;
The same in ev'ry place.

5 Thine is the word, the pow'r is thine,
The work is thine alone.
O Lord, upon the nations shine,
And make the world thine own.

HYMN DXLIII.

"*Thy will be done in earth, as it is in heaven.*"—MATT. vi. 10.

1 "FROM the rising of the sun
To the going down thereof,"
Let thy will, O Lord, be done,
As it is by those above.

2 Let thy people strive and pray,
That thy word may freely run;
Through the world may win its way;
And thy will on earth be done.

3 Be thy banner, Lord, unfurl'd:
"Grace and truth" its motto be,
Till the kingdoms of this world
All belong, O Lord, to thee.

4 Thine they are, by right, we know;
Thou wilt soon assert thy claim;
Thou wilt seize and bind the foe;
Thine the victor's deeds and fame.

5 Bright that day, but brighter still,
Brighter far the glorious day,
When, thy promise to fulfil,
Thou wilt bear thy saints away.

6 Bear them to their place above,
Where the "many mansions" are:
There to sing thy matchless love,
Free from sin, from error far.

7 In the prospect of that day,
Ev'n now, thy saints are blest:
Come thou, then, thy people say,
Come, and take them to their rest.

THANKS FOR SUCCESS.

HYMN DXLIV.

"*What have I to do any more with idols?*"—Hosea xiv. 8.

1 SEE, how many lately bowing
To their idols, wood and stone,
Now a blessed change avowing,
Bow before the Saviour's throne,
And with gladness
Praise the Saviour's name alone.

2 This is cause of joy and wonder,
God has set the captives free,
He has burst their bonds asunder,
Happy they and glorious he.
God our Saviour!
Who can be compar'd to thee?

3 When thou workest, who shall stay thee?
Who shall stay the work begun?
Lord, go on, thy people pray thee,
Till the glorious day is won:
And the gospel
Takes its circuit like the sun.

HYMN DXLV.

ON HEARING THE LATE HAPPY NEWS FROM THE SOUTH-SEA ISLANDS.

"*I will talk of thy doings.*"—Psalm lxxvii. 12.

1 JOY to all the friends of Zion!
Joy to thousands, joy to us!
He whose promise we rely on,
Wondrous is, and wonders does;
Praise our Saviour,
Who revives his people thus.

2 Tidings from a distant quarter,
Full of joy, demand our praise;
Is Jehovah's arm now shorter
Than it was in ancient days?
Or his mercy,
Is it less, the fall'n to raise?

3 Joyful let us raise our voices;
God, our God, is still the same,
Still in mercy he rejoices,
Still he puts his foes to shame;
And his people
Still have cause to bless his name.

4 Still the same and doing wonders;
In the whirlwind, in the flame,
In the storms, and in the thunders,
In the still small voice the same;
Sing with gladness,
Hallow'd be our Saviour's name.

5 What his arm has wrought already,
Shews us what his pow'r can do;
Zealous in his cause and steady,
Let his people onward go;
So our Saviour
Greater wonders yet will shew.

HYMN DXLVI.

"*Sing unto the Lord.*"—ISAIAH xii. 5.

1 HARK! how the distant nations sing,
The mountains and the valleys ring;
And while they welcome Jacob's star,
With joy we listen from afar.

2 'Tis Jacob's star that sheds its light
On lands till now involv'd in night,
And gives the promise of a day,
Whose glories never fade away.

3 For joy of this, the people sing,
For joy of this, the mountains ring;
A cheerful and a blessed sound,
'Twill spread, ere long, the world around.

4 A day of promise such as this,
The cause of joy and wonder is;
We wonder, and we praise the Lord,
We own the triumphs of his word.

5 The God of Isra'l glorious is,
The kingdom and the pow'r are his;
While foes, ere long, must own his claim,
His friends shall triumph in his name:

6 Shall triumph in his name that day,
When heav'n and earth shall pass away.
God's chosen and appointed heirs,
The bright inheritance is theirs.

HYMN DXLVII.

"*And the tongue of the dumb sing.*"—ISAIAH XXXV. 6.

1 HARK! the sound of distant voices,
Sweet and solemn is the strain;
'Tis the savage—he rejoices,
Not as once, with joy profane;
'Tis the Saviour's praise he sings,
"Glory to the King of kings."

2 Whence this change, so great so blessēd,
Tell it through the world abroad;
'Tis the work of God confessēd,
God himself, the living God;
He has wrought a work so strange,
He has made this wondrous change.

3 Ye who thought the arm contracted,
That was wont to save of old,
Now behold! a scene is acted,
Such as God's own word has told;
Yes, a mighty work is done,
And the hard fought day is won.

4 Ye who, round his throne assembling,
Long have look'd for such a day,
Now rejoice, "rejoice with trembling,"
Be not proud, but "watch and pray:"
Much is done, but much remains,
Ere our Lord his right obtains.

5 Though the foe has now retreated,
Soon he'll come with strength renew'd,
Foil'd in fight and oft defeated,
Hostile still and unsubdued;
They who fight with such a foe,
Must not sleep as others do.

6 Yet rejoice, the cause is glorious,
His it is who reigns in light,
And his arm will prove victorious,
For his arm is cloth'd with might.
Soon the foe will lose his pow'r,
Soon will fall to rise no more.

EFFECT OF MISSIONARY WORK AT HOME.

HYMN DXLVIII.

"*Thy light is come.*"—ISAIAH lx. 1.

1 THE friends of truth unite, resolv'd,
By grace from heav'n, to spread the light
Throughout the world, too long involv'd
In deepest shades of mental night.

2 The night was dark, but now a ray
Is sent to cheer us with its light,
It comes, the harbinger of day,
'Tis day begun—a blessed sight.

3 Rejoice, ye people far away;
Ye islands of the sea, be glad!
The day is come, the joyful day,
The day that God himself has made.

4 A light by you unseen, unknown,
Unheard of, comes to you from far:
Celestial light! that never shone
On you before—THE MORNING STAR.

5 The long dark night has clos'd at length,
Auspicious is the early dawn;
The sun shall soon, in all its strength,
Arise, and be no more withdrawn.

6 The objects of a Saviour's love,
Though now divided, shall unite
-onder distant world above;
- Lord, their everlasting light.

7 Then joy to you on whom the morn
Already sheds its dawning ray;
And joy to thousands yet unborn,
Whose eyes shall see the "perfect day."

HYMN DXLIX.

"*Blessed are the eyes which see the things that ye see.*"—
LUKE X. 23.

1 THE day is come, the golden day,
That prophets long foretold should be;
And we who see it well may say,
We see what others wish'd to see.

2 We've seen the Spirit like a dove,
(Or seem'd to see) with placid wings
Descend, inspiring peace and love,
An earnest of still greater things;

3 Perhaps an earnest of that day,
When all the people of the Lord,
In ev'ry place at length shall say,
"We'll seek our God with one accord;"

4 When party strife, now too much known,
Shall yield to love's pacific sway,
And all the saints on earth shall own
At length, one Lord, one faith, one way.

EFFECT OF MISSIONARY WORK ABROAD.

HYMN DL.

"*But the word of God is not bound.*"—2 TIM. ii. 9.

1 THE word of God now runs indeed,
'Tis glorified in ev'ry place,
And captives, from their bondage freed,
Now sing of grace, of sov'reign grace.

2 We hear the song, or seem to hear,
It comes from earth's remotest bound,
It sweetly vibrates on the ear,
A solemn and a cheerful sound:

3 A sound of praise, the praise of him
Who came from heav'n to save the lost.
A Saviour's love their only theme,
A Saviour's death their only boast.

4 How glorious is our King to-day!
At his approach the idols fall;
The distant people own his sway,
And join to crown him "LORD OF ALL."

5 This day a day of triumph is,
Of triumph to the Saviour's friends;
The joy is ours, the glory his,
The Saviour's kingdom never ends.

6 His scatter'd people soon shall be
Collected round his throne above,
They then shall all his glory see,
And sing his everlasting love.

HYMN DLI.

"*It shall blossom abundantly.*"—ISAIAH XXXV. 2.

1 PROPHETIC vision is fulfill'd,
The long neglected soil is till'd,
A skilful and a mighty hand
Is breaking up the fallow land.

2 Beneath its culture, yet awhile,
The desert shall be seen to smile;
And where the thorns and briers spread,
The rose shall soon its fragrance shed.

3 Where all is dry, and all is dead,
The cypress soon shall rear its head;
Where plants injurious flourish now,
The myrtle and the pine shall grow.

4 A thousand springs, at God's command,
Shall bless the dry and thirsty land;
And streams of living water flow,
Where all is parch'd and wither'd now.

5 Go on, thou God of pow'r and grace,
Go on, and gladden every place;
Nor let a spot, the world around,
Untill'd, or without fruit be found.

HYMN DLII.

"*The isles and the inhabitants thereof.*"—ISAIAH xlii. 10.

1 HARK! the sounds of gladness
From a distant shore;
Like relief from sadness,
Sadness, now no more:
'Tis the Lord has done it,
He has won the day,
His own arm has won it,
Joyful let us say.

2 Idols lately bow'd to,
Lie by all abhorr'd;
And the people crowd to
Temples of the Lord:
What a change! how glorious!
Lord, thine arm is strong,
Thou hast prov'd victorious,
Though the fight was long.

3 Our voices we'll raise,
We'll sing and give praise
To him, who from yonder bright throne
Dispenses his grace
In every place,
We'll sing of his glory alone.

4 How glorious is he!
How blessed are we,
Ascribing salvation to him!
His footsteps we trace,
His triumphs of grace,
And joyfully dwell on the theme.

5 To Jesus alone,
Who sits on the throne,
Salvation and glory belong;
All hail the blest name!
For ever the same,
Our boast, and the theme of our song.

HYMN DLV.

"How beautiful upon the mountains are the feet of him that bringeth good tidings."—Isaiah lii. 7.

1 On the mountain's top appearing,
Lo! the sacred herald stands;
Welcome news to Zion bearing,
Zion long in hostile lands;
Mourning captive!
God himself will loose thy bands.

2 Has thy night been long and mournful?
Have thy friends unfaithful prov'd?
Have thy foes been proud and scornful,
By thy sighs and tears unmov'd?
Cease thy mourning;
Zion still is well belov'd.

3 God, thy God will now restore thee:
He himself appears thy friend:
All thy foes shall flee before thee,
Here their boasts and triumphs end;
Great deliv'rance
Zion's King vouchsafes to send.

4 Enemies no more shall trouble,
All thy wrongs shall be redress'd;
For thy shame thou shalt have double,
In thy Maker's favour bless'd;
All thy conflicts
End in everlasting rest.

HYMN DLVI.

"*And they caused great joy unto all the brethren.*"—
ACTS XV. 3.

1 GLAD we hear, from day to day,
What the Lord is doing,
How the Gospel wins its way,
Through the nations going:
What a glorious work it is!
Work, for ever lasting;
Ev'ry other work but this
Fading is and wasting.

2 While the judgments of the Lord
Heav'n and earth are shaking,
Rous'd from slumber by his word,
Thousands are awaking:
Swiftly flies "the joyful sound,"
"Grace and truth" declaring,
To a guilty world around,
News of pardon bearing.

8 Saviour, let thy message run,
Message of salvation,
Take its circuit like the sun,
Visit every nation.
Earth has long been overspread,
Overspread with sadness;
Let the day-spring come with speed,
Bringing light and gladness.

HYMN DLVII.

"*In that day there shall be a fountain opened . . . for sin and for uncleanness.*"—ZECH. xiii. 1.

1 SEE, from Zion's sacred mountain,
Streams of living water flow;
God has open'd there a fountain,
That supplies the world below;
They are blessed,
Who its sov'reign virtues know.

2 Through ten thousand channels flowing,
Streams of mercy find their way;
Life, and health, and joy bestowing,
Making all around look gay;
O ye nations!
Hail the long-expected day.

3 Gladden'd by the flowing treasure,
All-enriching as it goes,
Lo, the desert smiles with pleasure,
Buds and blossoms as the rose;
Ev'ry object
Sings for joy where'er it flows.

4 Trees of life, the banks adorning,
Yield their fruit to all around;
Those who eat are sav'd from mourning,
Pleasure comes, and hopes abound:
Fair their portion,
Endless life with glory crown'd.

HYMN DLVIII.

"*How beautiful upon the mountains are the feet of him that bringeth good tidings!*"—ISAIAH lii. 7.

1 BEAUTIFUL upon the mountain
Are the feet of him who brings
Tidings of the cleansing fountain
Open'd by the King of kings:
Blessed tidings!
Hearing this, the mourner sings.

2 Yes, he puts away his sadness,
When he knows "the joyful sound;"
'Tis to him the voice of gladness,
Sweeter far than music found:
All is transport;
Ev'ry object smiles around.

3 Well it may, for great the pleasure
That the news of pardon brings;
Then the soul, relieved from pressure,
Rises, and expands her wings;
Then she rises,
And forgets all earthly things.

4 Pardon to the rebel granted
Brings a new and strange delight;
All around appears enchanted,
Like some vision to the sight:
Blessed vision!
True, yet past expression bright.

5 Welcome then is his appearing,
Who unfolds the wondrous plan,
News of grace from heaven bearing,
News of grace to guilty man;
Grace mysterious!
Grace too high for thought to scan.

MISSIONARY LABOURERS.

HYMN DLIX.

"*For his name's sake they went forth.*"—3 JOHN 7.

1 WHO are those that go with gladness,
Far from friends and native land?
By the world 'tis counted madness,
But they do not understand:
God is with them,
And they go at his command.

2 These are citizens of Zion,
Once they lov'd the world alone;
Now his promise they rely on,
Who has claim'd them as his own;
And he bids them
Go, and make his mercy known.

3 Theirs are toils and theirs are dangers,
While they traverse land and sea;
Far from home, midst foes and strangers,
Is their lot ordain'd to be,
While they publish
Grace to sinners, rich and free.

4 Grace be with them, truth and mercy,
In the work they have to do;
Theirs an awful controversy,
Awful and yet glorious too:
Grace be with them,
To whatever clime they go.

5 Blessings from the Saviour speed them,
And make ev'ry burthen light;
May the hand of mercy lead them
Safe to yon celestial height,
Where for ever
All is pure and all is bright.

HYMN DLX.

"*Because that for his name's sake they went forth.*"—3 JOHN 7.

1 WHILE in the general joy we share,
And learn the Lord to bless,
Who makes our native land his care,
And gives her arms success:

2 On other deeds we fix our eyes,
On deeds of higher boast,
On deeds whose mem'ry never dies,
Whose good is never lost.

3 On those we look, who, distant far
From friends and native land,
To meet the pow'rs of darkness dare,
At God's supreme command.

4 They face the perils of the wave,
The perils of the land,
The perils of the clime they brave,
A chosen faithful band.

5 A voluntary service theirs,
Their work a work of love;
'Tis love that dissipates their fears,
And makes them constant prove.

6 The world knows nothing of their deeds,
Or, if it knows, disdains;
But God above, their labour heeds,
And shares in all their pains.

7 Be patient, then, ye champions bold,
Nor weary in the strife;
Your Master you will soon behold,
And gain a crown of life.

HYMN DLXI.

"*Cry aloud, spare not.*"—Isaiah lviii. 1.

1 MEN of God, go take your stations,
Darkness reigns throughout the earth;
Go, proclaim among the nations
Joyful news of heav'nly birth;
Bear the tidings
Of the Saviour's matchless worth.

2 Of his Gospel not ashamēd,
As "the pow'r of God to save,"
Go, where Christ was never namēd,
Publish freedom to the slave!
Blessed freedom!
Such as Zion's children have.

3 What though earth and hell united
Should oppose the Saviour's plan?
Plead his cause, nor be affrighted,
Fear ye not the face of man;
Vain their tumult,
Hurt his work they never can.

4 When expos'd to fearful dangers,
Jesus will his own defend;
Borne afar midst foes and strangers,
Jesus will appear your friend,
And his presence
Shall be with you to the end.

HYMN DLXII.

"These see the works of the Lord, and his wonders in the deep."
PSALM cvii. 24.

1 SPEED thy servants, Saviour, speed them,
Thou art Lord of winds and waves;
They were bound, but thou hast freed them,
Now they go to free the slaves;
Be thou with them:
'Tis thine arm alone that saves.

2 Friends, and home, and all forsaking,
Lord, they go at thy command;
As their stay thy promise taking,
While they traverse sea and land;
O be with them!
Lead them safely by the hand.

3 Speed them through the mighty ocean,
In the dark and stormy day;
When the waves in wild commotion
Fill all others with dismay,
Be thou with them,
Drive their terrors far away.

4 When they reach the land of strangers,
And the prospect dark appears,
Nothing seen but toils and dangers,
Nothing felt but doubts and fears,
Be thou with them:
Hear their sighs, and count their tears.

5 When they think of home, now dearer
Than it ever seem'd before,
Bring the promis'd glory nearer;
Let them see that peaceful shore,
Where thy people
Rest from toil, and weep no more.

6 Where no fruit appears to cheer them,
And they seem to toil in vain,
Then in mercy, Lord, draw near them,
Then their sinking hopes sustain:
Thus supported,
Let their zeal revive again.

7 In the midst of opposition,
Let them trust, O Lord, in thee;
When success attends their mission,
Let thy servants humbler be;
Never leave them,
Till thy face in heav'n they see:

8 There to reap in joy for ever,
Fruit that grows from seed here sown,
There to be with him who never
Ceases to preserve his own,
And with gladness
Give the praise to him alone.

HYMN DLXIII.

"*But none of these things move me.*"—ACTS xx. 24.

1 YES, I see thou art resolv'd,
'Tis thy purpose to depart,
Though the sacrifice involv'd
Presses heavy on thine heart;
Nothing that may come appals thee,
Since thine honour'd Master calls thee.

2 From thine home and native land
Thou art going far away;
Friends and kindred round thee stand,
Anxious all to make thee stay:
'Tis a trial, sent to prove thee,
Sore it is, but does not move thee.

3 Bent thou art to follow where
He who calls thee leads the way,
In the toil and strife to share,
Looking for the glorious day
When the Lord shall come from heaven,
And the crown of life be given.

4 Speed thee, then, thou man of God,
Speed thee to the distant shore;
Tell of pardon bought with blood
Where 'twas never told before.
Tell of him the Father gave us,
Him who came from heav'n to save us.

5 And may he, to whom is given
(Fruit of toil, and strife, and pain)
All the pow'r in earth and heav'n,
Guide thee, and thy soul sustain.
Keep thee still, and leave thee never,
Till thy conflicts end for ever.

HYMN DLXIV.

"*Their sound went into all the earth.*"—Rom. x. 18.

1 FROM the south to the north,
Let the message go forth;
From the west to the east let it run,
The message of grace
To man's fallen race:
'Tis for all who are under the sun.

2 O ye whom he loves,
Whom therefore he proves,
To know will they leave for his sake,
The home of their birth,
The scenes of their mirth,
With strangers their dwelling to make.

3 Should he bid you to go,
Where a mantle of snow
Envelopes both mountain and plain,
Though nature says nay,
Your Master obey;
Encounter and vanquish the pain.

4 Should he point to the place,
Where the sun in his race,
Darts his rays with a power intense,
Though sense bids thee stay,
Your Master obey;
Let faith conquer nature and sense.

5 To you is this word,
Whose spirit is stirr'd
To go on his errand of love;
Whose souls are on fire,
Who burn with desire
To move as impell'd from above.

6 Then take up the cross,
Whatever the loss;
The symbol of blessing it is.
The Lord as your guide,
The Lord on your side,
What more can you wish for than this?

HYMN DLXV.

"*Go ye into all the world.*"—MARK xvi. 15.

1 OVER sea and over land
See the missionary going;
Moving at his Lord's command,
Holy zeal within him glowing.
Zeal to make his Master known,
Known and lov'd in ev'ry quarter;
'Tis a spirit not his own,
Spirit of the ancient martyr.

2 'Tis the Lord inspires his heart,
He it is who makes him willing,
With his friends and home to part;
God's own purpose thus fulfilling.
Hence it is he quits his home,
Puts to sea and meets the danger;
Far away consents to roam,
Leaves his friends, and joins the stranger.

3 Ye who free from trouble are,
In your peaceful habitations;
Think of those, whose lot is where
Trials are and tribulations.
Think of them before the Lord,
Pray that he may still be nigh them;
Utt'rance give to speak his word,
And in time of need stand by them.

4 Sweet it is for them to know,
That the thousands here are praying;
That the Lord would with them go,
Pow'r and faithfulness displaying.
Think of this, and let your pray'r
Incense-like ascend to heaven;
So the Lord will hear it there,
And an answer will be given.

HYMN DLXVI.

"Whosoever will lose his life for my sake, the same shall find it."
LUKE ix. 24.

1 WHO is he that willing is,
At his Master's call to go
To a region far from this,
Leaving all he loves below?
Kindred, friends, and pleasant home,
All forsaking, not to meet,
Never till the general doom.
Who for things like this is fit?

2 Who but one that loves his Lord
Better than himself? and hence,
In obedience to his word,
Waives the things of time and sense;
Led by him, and mov'd by love,
Where his Master leads, he goes;
And empower'd from above,
What he bids him do, he does.

3 Such there are, who now far off
In the midst of strangers live,
Who while all around them scoff,
Bear it, pity, and forgive:
Men who look from things that are,
To the things that are to be;
Not cast down, though ill they fare,
Hoping soon their Lord to see.

4 'Tis the hope of this that cheers
Those who having all resign'd,
Quit their home midst many tears,
Leaving those they love behind,

What emotions must be theirs,
While they take a last farewell!
But when past, how sweet it is,
None but men thus prov'd can tell!

5 Men like these are what we need,
Full of faith, resolv'd in mind:
Men who love their Lord indeed,
And for him leave all behind,
All, nor count how dear it is,
Like the apple of the eye;
This they part with, even this,
For their Lord to live or die.

6 Who will give us men like these?
He whose dwelling is above;
Full of grace and pow'r he is,
And the name he bears is "Love."
Saviour, in thy mercy give
Men like these! to thee we cry:
Men who to thy glory live,
Nor refuse for thee to die.

HYMN DLXVII.

"*I was not disobedient unto the heavenly vision.*"—
ACTS xxvi. 19.

1 TO thy destination,
Man of God, away;
Why this hesitation?
Why this long delay?
Is it sad to think of,
All thou must give up?
Is it hard to drink of
Such a bitter cup?

2 Harder still, much harder,
Should the crown be lost.
O, for holy ardour!
Think not of the cost.
Leave thy home, though pleasant;
Man of God, be free;
Sacrifice the present,
Thine the future be.

3 What is it appals thee?
Dost thou fear the foe?
When thy Master calls thee,
Fear him not, but go.
Who or what shall harm thee,
When the Lord is near?
He for fight shall arm thee,
And remove thy fear.

4 Dost thou dread the ocean
With its mountain-wave,
And the wild commotion
That unmans the brave?
Dread it not, thy Master
Wave and tempest quells,
Hold his promise faster
As the billow swells.

5 Does the thought appal thee,
That, when far from home,
Trials will befal thee
In the time to come?
Trials full of danger,
In a foreign land;
No one but the stranger
Or the foe at hand?

6 Let not this dismay thee,
Fearful though it is;
Sad, if it should stay thee
In a time like this,
When the call so loud is,
And so much to do;
When the foe so proud is,
And so daring too.

7 To thy destination,
Man of God, repair;
Preach the great salvation
To the many there.
While thou art delaying,
Men are left to die:
To the idol praying,
And no teacher nigh.

8 Be not thou faint-hearted;
Brother, haste away.
Once the ties are parted
That have caused delay,
Then thy spirit will be
Happy, not before;
And thy comforts still be
Growing more and more.

9 Then it will be cheering
To thy soul to wait
For the Lord's appearing,
When, in royal state,
He will come from heaven:
Then the gladness is;
Then the crown is given:
Brother, think of this.

HYMN DLXVIII.

"*Every one that hath forsaken houses . . . for my name's sake, shall receive an hundred-fold.*"—MATT. xix. 29.

1 TO the far-off regions
Men of God, away;
Meet the hostile legions,
Face the proud array.
Hark! the distant shouting,
'Tis the battle-storm;
God his foes is routing,
And by whom?—a worm.*

2 Ye who are appointed
In this course to run,
Go ye forth, anointed
By the Holy One.
Go to toil and danger,
From your brother go;
Choose for him the stranger,
For your friend, the foe.

3 Think not of delaying
When your Master calls:
'Tis no time for staying
In the pleasant halls.
Home is sweet, but sweeter
Is it to obey;
This is wiser, better:
Men of God, away.

4 Be not griev'd to think of
All ye leave behind,
Though the cup ye drink of,
Bitter ye may find.

* Isaiah li. 14.

Good it is, though bitter,
  Full of joy and health,
And for blessing fitter
  Far than ease and wealth.

5 Soon the Lord appearing
  Will dry up your tears;
Wait, then, nothing fearing,
  Wait till he appears.
Gladness, without measure,
  Will be yours that day;
Holy joy and pleasure
  Not to pass away.

HYMN DLXIX.

"*Fear thou not, for I am with thee.*"—ISAIAH xli. 10.

1 BROTHER, art thou doubting whether
  Thou wilt leave thine home or no,
For, as yet, thou canst not gather
  That thy Master wills it so;
Right it is that thou should'st ponder,
  Ponder well ere thou dost move;
If thou doubtest, who can wonder?
  'Tis what wisdom must approve.

2 Pleasant home and friends to part with,
  Never to behold them more,
Till the very day thou art with
  Jesus, who is gone before;
'Tis the path of self-denial,
  Hard it is to break these ties;
Yet must thou abide the trial,
  Count the cost then; this is wise.

3 When the land is disappearing,
Where thy friends their dwelling have;
And thy ship, the channel clearing,
Floats on the Atlantic wave;
Then, perhaps, thy spirit sinking,
Thou wilt doubt thy Master's call,
And reproach thyself for thinking
Thou wast ever sent at all.

4 Past the perils of the ocean,
And the port is gain'd at last:
There's an end of the commotion,
And the ship is anchor'd fast;
Trials now await thee, many,
Needful all, but still severe;
Few will welcome thee, if any,
Foes, not friends, will meet thee there.

5 Such the cross that thou must take up,
But if Jesus bids thee go;
He for every loss will make up,
Be thou sure it shall be so;
Yea, the Lord himself has said it,
Thou shalt have "an hundred fold;"
Doubt thou not, but give him credit,
And in duty's path be bold.

6 Count the cost then, but forget not
Who has promis'd to be near;
If the Lord has called thee, let not
Doubt possess thy mind, or fear;
He sufficient is for all, who
Hear him and his call obey;
They are blessed, they who follow
Where the Saviour leads the way.

HYMN DLXX.

"*Who will go for us?*"—ISAIAH vi. 8.

1 WHO is prepared to go
Far off, to meet the foe,
Foe to mankind?
Who will the mountain-wave,
In the frail vessel brave,
Though it may prove his grave;
Whom shall we find?

2 Who can his home forsake,
Leave of his kindred take,
Far off to go;
Sail from his native land,
Bound for a foreign strand,
Dangers on every hand,
This who can do?

3 He who his Master loves,
He whom the Spirit moves,
He can do this;
He can the call obey,
He can, without delay,
Rise, and go far away,
Hard as it is.

4 He can behold the wave,
Though it should prove his grave,
Swelling apace;
And when the storm is high,
He can its rage defy,
Knowing the Lord is nigh,
Strong in his grace.

5 When in a distant land,
Troubles on ev'ry hand,
Yet is he glad;
Though he sees ev'rywhere,
Causes of grief and care,
Knowing who sent him there,
Should he be sad?

6 Though he may wait for it,
No fruit appearing yet,
Wait for it long;
Why should he faint or fear,
Since the Lord will appear,
Bringing the blessing near,
Can *he* do wrong?

7 Now he may sow in tears,
Yet after many years,
Then shall he reap;
Now it is grief and pain,
Then 'twill be joy and gain,
Blessings for those remain,
Those who now weep.

8 Seeing that this is so,
Blessed are they that go
Far, far away;
Far over land and flood,
Bearing the word of God,
Spreading the truth abroad,
Blessed are they.

HYMN DLXXI.

"*How shall they preach except they be sent?*"—Rom. x. 15.

1 THE missionary's work is sweet,
But nature from the work recoils;
The man of God alone is fit
To face its perils and its toils.

2 Let no man *hasten* hence away
To labour in a foreign land;
But let him think, and watch, and pray,
And wait for a divine command.

3 Unless the Saviour bids thee go,
Be sure, O man, thy work is vain:
Without him thou canst nothing do,
Nor pleasure wilt thou have, nor gain.

4 Thy zeal, if not a holy fire,
Derived and nourish'd from above,
Will soon grow slack, and then expire:
O man, be not in haste to move.

5 But if thy call to go be clear,
Then speed thee to the distant land;
Nor tarry thou, nor linger here,
But haste thee at thy Lord's command.

6 If thoughts about thy native land,
And pleasant home, and kindred dear,
Detain thee, think of his command,
Of his whom thou art bound to hear.

7 But think yet more of love; his love
Who drank for thee a bitter cup;
A motive this the rest above,
When others fail, 'twill hold thee up.

8 Be sure 'twill make thee full amends
For all that now forsaken is:
For native land, for home, for friends,
'Twill do all this, and more than this.

MISSIONARY PROSPECTS.

HYMN DLXXII.

"*And so all Israel shall be saved.*"—Rom. xi. 26.

1 YES, we hope the day is nigh,
When many nations, long enslavēd,
Shall break forth, and sing with joy,
"Hosanna to the Son of David"

2 Abrah'm's seed, cast off so long,
Shall then appear among the savēd,
Shall arise, and join the song,
"Hosanna to the Son of David."

3 Jews and Gentiles shall unite,
By Satan's power no more enslavēd,
And shall sing with great delight,
"Hosanna to the Son of David."

4 But a brighter day is nigh,
When Jesus shall collect his savēd,
Men and angels then shall cry,
"Hosanna to the Son of David."

HYMN DLXXIII.

"*Every man heard them speak in his own language.*"—
Acts ii. 6.

1 HOW many things combine to shew
The joyful day is near at hand,
When truth shall spread, and sinners know
The Saviour's name in ev'ry land!

2 When did the friends of truth unite
With so much zeal as now they do,
To spread abroad its glorious light,
And bring its excellence to view.

3 Mark how in this auspicious time,
A time by prophets not unsung,
The people hear, of ev'ry clime,
The Gospel in their native tongue.

4 It runs, it flies through ev'ry land,
We mark its progress with delight,
And bless his name at whose command
A day has risen, so fair, so bright.

5 Nor should his people give him rest,
Or cease their earnest cry to raise,
Until Jerusalem be blest,
And through the earth become "a praise."

HYMN DLXXIV.

"*The Lord shall reign for ever, even thy God, O Zion.*"—
PSALM cxlvi. 10.

1 ZION'S King shall reign victorious,
All the earth shall own his sway,
He will make his kingdom glorious,
He will reign through endless day:
What though none on earth assist him?
God requires not help from man;
What though all the world resist him?
God will realize his plan.

2 Nations now from God estrangēd,
Then shall see a glorious light,
Night to day shall then be changēd,
Heav'n shall triumph in the sight:
See the ancient idols falling!
Worshipp'd once, but *now* abhorr'd;
Men on Zion's King are calling,
Zion's King by all ador'd.

3 Then shall Isra'l, long dispersēd,
Mourning seek the Lord their God,
Look on him whom once they piercēd,
Own and kiss the chast'ning rod:
Then all Isra'l shall be savēd,
War and tumult then shall cease,
While the greater Son of David
Rules a conquer'd world in peace.

4 Mighty King, thine arm revealing,
Now thy glorious cause maintain,
Bring the nations help and healing,
Make them subject to thy reign:
Angels, in their lofty station,
Praise thy name, thou only wise;
O let earth, with emulation,
Join the triumph of the skies.

HYMN DLXXV.

"*I will bring thy seed from the east, and gather thee from the west: I will say to the north, Give up, and to the south, Keep not back.*"—Isaiah xliii. 5, 6.

1 MY soul, with sacred joy survey
The glories of the latter day;
Its dawn already seems begun,
Sure earnest of the rising sun.

2 The friends of truth assembled stand,
(A chosen, consecrated band,)
The standard of the cross display,
And cry aloud, "Behold the way!"

3 "Behold the way to Zion's hill,
Where Isra'l's God delights to dwell;
He fixes there his lofty throne,
And calls the sacred place his own."

4 "Behold the way!" ye heralds, cry,
Spare not, but lift your voices high;
Convey the sound from shore to shore,
And bid the captive sigh no more.

5 Swift on the wings of heav'nly zeal
They fly, nor seem their toils to feel;
But faithful to their Master's will,
Their sacred ministry fulfil.

6 The north "gives up," the south no more
"Keeps back" her consecrated store;
From east to west the message runs,
And either India yields her sons.

7 Auspicious dawn! thy rising ray
With joy I view, and hail the day;
Thou sun, arise, supremely bright,
And shed abroad thy holy light.

HYMN DLXXVI.

"*I have raised him up in righteousness.*"—ISAIAH xlv. 13.

1 THUS saith God of his anointed,
He shall let my people go,
'Tis the work for him appointed,
'Tis the work that he shall do;
And my city
He shall found, and build it too.

2 He whom man with scorn refuses,
Whom the favour'd nation hates,
He it is Jehovah chooses,
Him the highest place awaits:
Kings and princes
Shall do homage at his gates.

3 He shall humble all the scorners,
He shall fill his foes with shame;
He shall raise and comfort mourners,
By the sweetness of his name;
To the captives
He shall liberty proclaim.

4 He shall gather those that wander'd;
When they hear the trumpet's sound,
They shall join his sacred standard,
They shall come and flock around;
He shall save them,
They shall be with glory crown'd.

HYMN DLXXVII.

"*The Lord God omnipotent reigneth.*"—Rev. xix. 6.

1 HARK! the loud triumphant strains,
God, the King of Glory, reigns;
All the kingdoms own his sway,
Hail the happy, happy day;
Hail the day by God appointed,
Jesus reigns, the Lord's anointed.

2 Hark! the sound of sacred mirth,
Jesus reigns throughout the earth;
War, and strife, and tumult cease,
'Tis the time of love and peace;
See his people rest enjoying,
In his mountain none destroying.

3 Zion's King makes known his name,
He asserts his lawful claim;
His the kingdom, his the pow'r,
Hail, ye saints, the happy hour;
Worldly maxims cease to govern,
Jesus reigns, supreme and sov'reign.

HYMN DLXXVIII.

"*Prepare ye the way of the Lord.*"—Isaiah xl. 3.

1 LO! he comes! let all adore him,
'Tis the God of grace and truth!
Go, prepare the way before him,
Make the rugged places smooth;
Lo! he comes, the mighty Lord,
Great his work, and his reward.

2 Let the valleys all be raisēd,
Go, and make the crooked straight;
Let the mountains be abasēd,
Let all nature change its state!
Through the desert mark a road,
Make a highway for our God.

3 Through the desert God is going,
Through the desert waste and wild;
Where no goodly plant is growing,
Where no verdure ever smiled;
But the desert shall be glad,
And with verdure soon be clad.

4 Where the thorn and brier flourish'd,
Trees shall there be seen to grow,
Planted by the Lord, and nourish'd,
Stately, fair, and fruitful too;
They shall rise on ev'ry side,
They shall spread their branches wide.

5 From the hills, and lofty mountains,
Rivers shall be seen to flow;
There the Lord will open fountains,
Thence supply the plains below:
As he passes, ev'ry land
Shall confess his pow'rful hand.

HYMN DLXXIX.

"*The Lord hath made bare his holy arm in the eyes of all the nations.*"—Isaiah lii. 10.

1 YES, we trust the day is breaking,
Joyful times are near at hand,
God, the mighty God, is speaking
By his word, in ev'ry land;
Mark his progress,
Darkness flies at his command.

2 Let us hail the joyful season,
Let us hail the rising ray;
When the Lord appears, there's reason
To expect a glorious day;
At his presence,
Gloom and darkness fly away.

3 While the foe becomes more daring,
While he "enters like a flood,"
God, the Saviour, is preparing
Means to spread his truth abroad;
Ev'ry language
Soon shall tell the love of God.

4 O! 'tis pleasant, 'tis reviving
To our hearts, to hear each day;
Joyful news, from far arriving;
How the Gospel wins its way;
Those enlight'ning
Who in death and darkness lay.

5 Babylon's proud walls are falling,
All her wise men are perplex'd;
'Tis in vain we hear them calling,
On their gods; her cup is mix'd;
She must drink it,
God himself her doom has fix'd.

6 'Tis a time of expectation,
Awful signs are seen around;
Nation rising against nation,
Kingdoms falling to the ground;
Ancient kingdoms
Perish, and no more are found.

7 God of Jacob, high and glorious,
Let thy people see thy hand;
Let the gospel be victorious,
Through the world, in ev'ry land;
Let the idols
Perish, Lord, at thy command.

HYMN DLXXX.

"*Awake, awake, put on strength, O arm of the Lord.*"—
ISAIAH li. 9.

1 NOW let us crowd around the throne
Of him who hears and answers prayer;
The cause is his, and not our own,
The object of our Saviour's care.

2 Our land in darkness long has been,
A darkness like the gloom of night;
But streaks of radiant light are seen
Upon her sky. A cheering sight.

3 A token sure of coming day,
The sun itself will soon arise:
For this we look, for this we pray;
For this we raise our earnest cries.

4 Be gracious to our native land,
Our hope fulfil, thy people pray;
The morning dawns at thy command,
And thine it is to bring the day.

5 Except thou give thy blessing, Lord,
Our counsels and our plans are vain;
But if thy Spirit bless the word,
The mountain shall become a plain.

5 If thou wilt own the work in hand,
We need not fear, though foes combine;
For who is able to withstand
Thine arm, or frustrate thy design?

7 To thee, O Lord, to thee we cry,
Nor would we cease our voice to raise,
Till Zion is a name of joy,
And thy Jerusalem "a praise."

HYMN DLXXXI.

"*Let God arise.*"—PSALM lxviii. 1.

1 LET God arise, and let his foes
Be scatter'd wheresoe'er he goes;
As wax dissolves before the sun,
Let all his foes his presence own.

2 Let all the pow'rs of darkness fly
Before the God who reigns on high;
And when his ark appears, let all
The idols of the nations fall.

3 Let men from opposition cease,
Lay down their arms, and sue for peace;
From refuges of lies be driv'n,
Confess their sin, and be forgiv'n.

4 Let God arise, and win the day;
The mighty God his sceptre sway,
The golden sceptre of his grace,
Through ev'ry land, in ev'ry place.

5 And let his name, who shed his blood,
To bring the guilty nigh to God,
Be great in all the earth, and sung
In ev'ry land, by ev'ry tongue.

PERSEVERANCE.

HYMN DLXXXII.

"*Be not afraid of them, for the Lord thy God is with thee.*"—
DEUT. xx. 1.

1 NO; there must be no retreating:
Better death than have it so:
Ill were such a step befitting
Those who to the Saviour owe
Pardon, peace, and free salvation,
And on whom the Lord bestows
"Everlasting consolation:"
Talk not of retreat to those.

2 'Tis the Lord, he means to prove us,
Whether we will hear his call,
Whether his command will move us,
Whether we will give up all.
Give up all that may be needful
In a season such as this;
Of our Master's honour heedful,
Seeking not our own, but his.

3 Teach us, Lord, the self-denial
That becomes thy people here;
Help us in the hour of trial,
In thy grace and pow'r draw near.
Let us act as it behoves us
In a season such as this;
'Tis the trying hour that proves us,
Proves our faith what kind it is.

4 We have cause to mourn before thee,
That we have so little been
What we ought; and we adore thee
For the grace that we have seen.
On our part is provocation,
But forbearance, Lord, on thine.
Cause of love and admiration,
Wondrous all, and all divine:

5 Evil are we, Lord, and badly
Have we served thee hitherto;
Pardon this, and henceforth gladly
Let us all thy pleasure do.
Fain we would to thee now tender
All we are, and all we have;
And to thee the whole surrender,
Only bless us, only save.

HYMN DLXXXIII.

"*Because that for his name's sake they went forth.*"—
3 John 7.

1 NO, we must not quit the field,
Though the foe should come in pow'r;
We must neither fly nor yield.
In the very darkest hour;
Whom the Lord commands to go,
They shall vanquish ev'ry foe.

2 Such as we may fear, and shrink
From the peril and the toil,
Of our ease may too much think,
And to others leave the spoil;
But there are who nobly brave
Perils of the land and wave.

3 We should honour men like these,
Who, to make the Saviour known,
Part with friends and home and ease,
Counting not their lives their own.
By the love of Christ constrain'd,
By the pow'r of Christ sustain'd.

4 In the midst of foes they are,
Bearing much, and waiting long;
Theirs a life of toil and care,
While exposed to scorn and wrong.
Inly do they sigh and mourn,
But for evil good return.

5 Pray we, then, for men like these,
Pray we to our common Lord;
Theirs is labour, ours is ease:
Pray that he may help afford
To his servants, while they toil,
And from Satan take the spoil.

6 *Give* we too, 'tis meet we should,
As the Lord has giv'n to us.
In his eyes to give is good;
He is served and honoured thus.
And the workman worthy is
Of his hire. 'Tis justly his.

HYMN DLXXXIV.

"*For I will show him how great things he must suffer for my name's sake.*"—ACTS ix. 16.

1 BROTHER, hast thou much to suffer
Where thou art, and is the sea
On the which thou sailest, rougher
Than thou thoughtest it would be?

Art thou sometimes even tempted
To return and seek thine ease,
And to spend a life exempted
Henceforth from such ills as these?

2 Think not hardly of thy Master
That thou art thus sorely tried;
Only hold the promise faster,
Cleave more closely to his side.
'Tis not possible that *he* should
Fail the man who trusts in him.
Brother, 'tis not meet that *we* should
Blame him if our eyes are dim.

3 If we see not, as we should do,
That which may be plainly seen,
And as those whose sight is good do,
Then the fault with us has been.
Hagar had the fountain by her
At the time her hope had fled;
Could the Saviour have been nigher?
Yet was she as one half dead.

4 So it was, and so it still is,
What we want is eyes to see;
For we know our Master's will is
That his friends should happy be.
Brother, trust in him, and fear not,
"Should he slay thee," trust him still.
Though he seems as those who hear not;
Hear he does, and come he will.

5 Courage, brother, droop no longer,
Think not of a present home;
Stronger be thou, and still stronger,
Looking to the one to come.

Satan does, and will endeavour
To molest (he can't destroy);
Soon the strife will cease for ever,
Follow'd by immortal joy.

QUESTIONS FOR CONSCIENCE.

HYMN DLXXXV.

" *Ye are not your own.*"—1 Cor. vi. 19.

1 ARE we doing as we should do?
We, who have our pleasant homes?
Are we doing what we could do?
Will he say so when he comes?
He whose eyes are flame, whose voice is
Thunder, and whose will is fate;
Happy he who then rejoices!
We may think of this too late.

2 Are we giving, freely giving,
To maintain our Master's cause,
Due proportion of our living;
Looking not for man's applause?
Do we oft in spirit visit
Those who, far from friends and home,
"Labour in the word;" and is it
Sweet, in spirit thus to roam?

3 Does it make us more alive to
That which Jesus calls his own?
Do we with more ardour strive to
Spread his word, and make him known?
Are we feeling as we should do,
For our brethren far away?
Are we doing all we could do,
Waiting for the final day?

4 Are there men of God now ready
To embark, and face the deep?
Men of God, resolv'd and steady,
Wanting only what we keep?
Keep it not, when God requires it:
'Tis his own, then bid him take.
Shall we not, if he desires it,
Part with all things for his sake?

SOUTH SEA ISLANDS, WHEN INVADED BY THE FRENCH.

HYMN DLXXXVI.

"*Awake, why sleepest thou, O Lord?*"—PSALM xliv. 23.

1 AWAKE, awake, O Lord, awake!
Put on thy strength, and show thy pow'r;
O hear us, for thy mercy's sake,
And help us in this trying hour.

2 For those, O Lord, for those we pray,
Who in the distant islands dwell,
Who lately own'd the idol's sway,
But now of sov'reign grace can tell.

3 In this far distant quarter thou,
A mighty work, O Lord, hast wrought;
We tremble for the issue now,
But thou hast bid us tremble not.

4 The thought of thee alone, O Lord,
Of thee, the spring of pow'r and grace,
At such a time, can hope afford;
The case were else a hopeless case.

5 The fence that thou didst make has been
Thrown down, by those who fear not thee.
The foe has rudely enter'd in,
And is where he ought not to be.

6 To look for help to man is vain.
To thee we look, O Lord, to thee;
Relieve thy saints, thy truth maintain,
And let thy cause triumphant be.

7 Thy scattered sheep, O Lord, behold;
Till now so safe—no longer so:
The lion is within the fold:
Expel him, Lord, expel the foe.

8 Awake, awake, again we cry;
Awake, as in the ancient days.
To thee, and not to man we fly;
The work be thine, and thine the praise.

HYMN DLXXXVII.

"*Give us help from trouble, for vain is the help of man.*"—
PSALM cviii. 12.

1 NOW let us raise an earnest cry
To him who dwells, who reigns on high,
For our beloved islands plead,
To them the time is one "of need."

2 His arm not shorten'd is, we know,
Nor is his ear to hear us slow;
As truth unchangeable he is,
And pow'r, and grace, and love, are his.

3 Unite we all in earnest pray'r,
To him whose people are his care;
Nor think we that he will not hear,
Away with doubt, away with fear.

4 The foe is strong, and sure he is
To take the whole, and make it his;
No island does he mean to spare:
So means he, but the Lord is there.

5 The hungry man, when dreaming, thinks
(Though all is false) he eats and drinks,
But quick it passes all away:
'Tis thus the foe will miss his prey.

6 The Lord is with his saints, their friend,
Their cause and them he will defend;
And when they cry in time of need,
Will prove himself their friend indeed.

7 We know not why this darkness is,
But "God is love," we're sure of this;
The Lord his promise will fulfil,
He may delay, but come he will.

8 Take heed we make not flesh our arm,
There's nothing else can do us harm;
The Lord alone has pow'r to save,
And strength in him alone we have.

9 To save his own he will appear,
Their foes shall then be fill'd with fear;
'Tis ours to pray, to save is his,
How blessēd to be sure of this.

10 Then let us pray, and let us wait,
His time nor is nor can be late;
The darkness soon will pass away,
And then how bright will be the day.

HYMN DLXXXVIII.

"*The isles shall wait upon me, and on mine arm shall they trust.*"—Isaiah li. 5.

1 PRAY we for our lov'd Tahiti,
Pray we for her kindred isles;
Lord, behold thy saints with pity,
Guard them from the tempter's wiles.
From the arm of pow'r defend them,
From the rude invader's arm;
In the time of need befriend them,
And no foe can do them harm.

2 Little did we look for danger;
By surprise the evil came;
Not prepar'd, we think it stranger,
But the work is still the same.
His it is, who, lately driven
From his throne, returns again,
And defies the God of heaven,
Thinking to resume his reign.

3 But he will not, cannot do it,
Cannot, for the Lord is there:
He is strong, and they will rue it,
They who to assail him dare.
Lord, we know the cause thine own is,
For thy saints are one with thee;
But the glory thine alone is,
Thine it is, and ought to be.

4 Lord, behold thy foes are breaking
Through the fence, intending ill;
Through the fence of thine own making,
For they hate thy people still.

Fruitful trees of thine own planting,
'Tis their purpose to destroy;
Nothing but thy leave is wanting:
That obtain'd, there would be joy.

5 But thine arm is rais'd against them,
And thy people are secure;
With thy favour thou hast fenc'd them,
And hast made "their dwelling sure."
'Tis thy purpose, Lord, to try them,
Hence the darkness of this hour;
But thou art and wilt be nigh them,
Prove they shall thy grace and pow'r.

6 Soon the darkness will be over,
And the light will come again;
When it comes, it will discover
That which now is dimly seen.
What we thought an evil, will be
Not one, but a blessing prove;
And thy dealings, Saviour, still be
Found, as ever, fruits of love.

CHINA.

HYMN DLXXXIX.

"*Hear, ye that are far off, what I have done.*"—
ISAIAH xxxiii. 13.

1 WHO goes to China's distant shore,
The messenger of truth to those
Who never heard the truth before?
A blessing on the man who goes.

2 The man who goes with pure intent,
No selfish scheme or motive his;
Upon his Master's service bent;
This man the missionary is.

3 A blessing on the man who thus
Renounces friends and native land;
To aid his work belongs to us,
With loving heart and lib'ral hand.

4 Upon the ocean deep and wide,
He toils to reach the distant shore;
The Lord his hope, his stay, his guide,
The home he leaves he sees no more.

5 A better home is his by far,
The one where sinners, sav'd by grace,
Assemble, and with Jesus are.
A blessed and a glorious place.

6 How glorious, who is he can tell?
To know it baffles human thought;
The place where saints and angels dwell,
The place where evil enters not.

7 Where all is pure and all is bright,
No death, no pain, no grief, no fear;
The Lamb himself, the Lamb its light,
A sun that never sets is there.

HYMN DXC.

"*For a great door and effectual is opened unto me.*"—
1 Cor. xvi. 9.

1 FOR China's distant shore,
Embark without delay;
Behold an open door,
'Tis God that leads the way;
His call is clear and loud.
The missionary band
Should gather like a cloud,
And leave their native land.

2 From friend and brother go,
By sense of duty led;
The stranger and the foe
To cherish in their stead;
'Tis hard to break such ties,
But grace sufficient is,
And grace the strength supplies
For such a day as this.

3 Away, then, brother, go;
When Jesus says, Depart!
Let nothing here below
With him divide thine heart;
'Tis bitterness to leave
What so much valued is,
But soon thou shalt receive
"An hundred fold" for this.

4 Away, then, brother, go,
Whose spirit God has stirr'd;
To stranger and to foe
Convey the blessed word;
From friends and home away,
To China's distant shore,
The sacred call obey,
And hesitate no more.

5 The perils of the sea,
The perils of the land,
Should not dishearten thee,
Thy Lord is nigh at hand.
But should thy courage fail,
When tried and sorely press'd;
His promise shall avail,
And set thy soul at rest.

6 Nor wilt thou grieve for home,
The home that's left behind.
The thought of one to come
Will wholly fill thy mind:
And thou wilt bless the day,
When thou didst part with all,
And hasten far away,
At thy lov'd Master's call.

HYMN DXCI.

"*Behold, these shall come from far.*"—ISAIAH xlix. 12.

1 MEN we need, and means to send them,
Hence to China's distant shore;
Home has ties, but God can rend them,
He has rent them oft before.
He will rend them now again;
Means he will provide, and men.

2 Loud and urgent now the call is,
'Tis the Lord—we cannot doubt.
Levell'd to its base the wall is,
That which kept the stranger out.
Freely may we enter in,
And we must, or bear our sin.

3 Ye whom God has call'd to do him
Service in this distant field;
Stay not, but surrender to him
All he asks—'tis good to yield.
Go ye where he bids you go,
Do ye what he bids you do.

4 Think not that his service will be
Void of pleasure. Think it not;
What he has been, he still will be,
Banish ev'ry fearful thought.
One he is—the same in grace,
One, in ev'ry time and place.

5 Go ye, then, whom God is moving;
Go ye to the distant shore;
"Joy and gladness," sure of proving,
More than home can yield, much more.
Only do your Master's will,
And of blessing have your fill.

6 Ev'ry day will bring you nearer
To your rest, then rest indeed;
Bear the cross, 'twill make him dearer;
Him who suffer'd in your stead.
Only make his cause your own,
Blessings yours till then unknown.

Jubilee.

HYMN DXCII.

"Then shalt thou cause the trumpet of the jubilee to sound."—LEV. XXV. 9.

1 HARK! the solemn trumpet sounding,
Loud proclaims the jubilee;
'Tis the voice of grace abounding,
Grace to sinners rich and free;
Ye who know the joyful sound,
Publish it to all around.

2 Is the name of Jesus precious?
Does his love our spirits cheer?
Does his promise still refresh us,
By abating doubt and fear?
Is he good to us, and true?
Such he'll be to others too.

3 Were you once at awful distance,
Wand'ring from the fold of God?
Could no arm afford assistance,
Nothing save but Jesu's blood?
Think how many still are found
Strangers to the joyful sound.

4 Brethren, join in supplication,
Join to plead before the Lord;
'Tis his arm that brings salvation,
He alone can give the word;
Father, let thy kingdom come,
Bring thy wand'ring outcasts home.

5 Brethren, let us freely offer,
All we have is from above;
Let us *give*, and *act*, and *suffer*;
What is this to Jesu's love?
Did he die our souls to save?
Then we're his, and all we have.

6 Hark! the saints' triumphant chorus,
"Worthy is the Lamb," they cry;
They have gain'd the prize before us,
Soon we hope to share their joy;
But while here, remember still,
They who love him, do his will.

7 Till we reach the wish'd-for vision,
Till we see him as he is,
Let us bear the world's derision,
Let us prove that we are his;
Let us sound through all the earth
Christ's inestimable worth.

HYMN DXCIII.

"*Sing unto the Lord, all the earth.*"—Psalm xcvi. 1.

1 HALF an age, not more than this,
Half an age has pass'd away,
Yet the change, how great it is!
Sing we then, for well we may.

2 How the little cloud has grown,
Since it first appear'd in view!
'Tis the Saviour's work alone,
And to him the praise is due.

3 Raise we then our thankful songs,
Good it is to laud him thus;
Praise to him alone belongs,
Joy and thankfulness to us.

4 Sing the idols' fall and shame,
Sing the triumphs of the Lord;
His the work, the crown, the fame,
Ours his doings to record.

5 Tell we, then, of trophies won,
Trophies of his pow'r and love;
"From the rising of the sun,
To the going down thereof."

6 Lord, as thou art still the same,
Be thy spirit with the word;
Till the knowledge of thy name
Fills the earth. So be it, Lord!

7 Then shall many voices cry
Hallelujah, God is king;
Shouts of joy shall rend the sky;
Hope is ours, in hope we sing.
Hallelujah! Amen!

The Cross.

HYMN DXCIV.

"*But God forbid that I should glory, save in the cross.*"—
GAL. vi. 14.

1 THE Cross! how blessed is the sight,
To those who feel their guilt like me!
It shines with heaven's peculiar light;
No object half so bright I see:
And yet, how little do I know
Of what the Cross is meant to shew!

2 The spring of life I know is there;
The stream of blood that issues thence,
Has power, I know, and virtue rare;
It can the foulest conscience cleanse.
The sense of guilt it can remove,
And fill the soul with holy love.

3 That justice there, and mercy can,
And do together meet, I know:
I wonder at the gracious plan;
I gaze, and love to have it so.
Less terror, 'twould not awful be;
Less grace, it would not do for me.

4 Whatever I can want, it yields;
A sense of pardon thence I have:
My soul from Satan's pow'r it shields;
'Tis God's appointed way to save:
To save in ev'ry trying hour;
To save from ev'ry hostile pow'r.

5 Then teach me, Lord, to comprehend
The meaning of that wondrous sight:
Its source, its object, and its end.
O shed upon thy work a light,
A light from heav'n, that I may know
Whatever may be known below.

6 To some, I know, this grace is giv'n,
To search the mystery of love:
That love that higher is than heav'n,
And deeper than th' abyss below:
Like them, O Lord, I fain would be;
Like them would search, like them would see.

7 Then do thou clear my inward sight,
From clouds and mists that darkness cause:
And fill my soul with holy light,
That I may know the love that was,
That is, and cannot cease to be:
The love that reached and vanquished me.

HYMN DXCV.

"*But God forbid that I should glory, save in the cross.*"—
GAL. vi. 14.

1 WE sing the praise of him who died,
Of him who died upon the Cross;
The sinner's hope let men deride,
For this we count the world but loss.

2 Inscrib'd upon the Cross we see,
In shining letters, "GOD IS LOVE."
He bears our sins upon the tree,
He brings us mercy from above.

3 The Cross! it takes our guilt away,
It holds the fainting spirit up;
It cheers with hope the gloomy day,
And sweetens ev'ry bitter cup.

4 It makes the coward spirit brave,
And nerves the feeble arm for fight;
It takes its terror from the grave,
And gilds the bed of death with light;

5 The balm of life, the cure of woe,
The measure and the pledge of love;
The sinner's refuge here below,
The angel's theme in heav'n above.

HYMN DXCVI.

"*A covert from the tempest.*"—Isaiah xxxii. 2.

1 OUR rest be here, the Cross beneath,
The fittest place for such as we;
'Tis here the faint begin to breathe,
Th' insolvent here alone are free.

2 Pursued, and without pow'r to flee,
In debt, and having nought to pay,
The Cross our place of refuge be,
Our safety by the Cross to stay.

3 Beneath the shelter of the place
We'll stay until the storm is past;
For who would dare the storm to face?
Or who sustain its fatal blast?

4 But here we listen to the sound,
And safe within this hallow'd spot,
While desolation reigns around,
The angry tempest harms us not.

5 We owe him much, whose love provides
   A shelter from the furious blast,
The Lord, who thus his people hides,
   Until the storm is overpast.

6 Our refuge and our rest be here,
   The danger soon will pass away,
A cloudless sky will then appear,
   A blessed, bright, eternal day.

HYMN DXCVII.

"*The cross . . . whereby the world is crucified unto me, and I unto the world.*"—GAL. vi. 14.

1 THE Cross! my hope, my boast, my theme,
   There's music in the very word;
Compar'd to it, how worthless seem
   All earthly things, and how absurd
The thoughts and aims of men appear,
To those to whom the Cross is dear.

2 The Cross! the Cross! mysterious tree,
   On which the Saviour breath'd his last;
Thou wondrous Cross, I look to thee!
   The bitterness of death is past;
The sense of guilt, so keen before,
So terrible, is felt no more.

3 The carcase of the lion, thus
   Of old, did "meat" and "sweetness" yield;
A riddle then, not so to us:
   Its import is no more conceal'd;
What then lay hid, the Cross explains,
The type is past, the truth remains.

4 The Cross! the Cross! how safe he is
Who trusts in it, and it alone;
The promise and the blessing his:
'Tis better than a royal throne;
A throne, what is it but a toy,
Compar'd to what the saints enjoy?

5 The Cross! the Cross! 'tis shame, I know,
It may be death, I love it still!
The Cross be mine, come weal, come woe;
From it can come no real ill:
'Tis fraught with blessings rich and free,
And he who has them, blest is he.

HYMN DXCVIII.

"*But God forbid that I should glory, save in the cross.*"—
GAL. vi. 14.

1 GROUND of my hope, the Cross appears!
I see the "man of sorrows" bleed;
I bid adieu to guilty fears,
And in his death my pardon read.

2 And couldst thou, O my Saviour, die
To rescue me from endless woe?
Enough! there's none more blest than I,
Since thou couldst love a sinner so.

3 I leave the world its boasted store
Of pleasures that must quickly end,
I prize its vanities no more,
Since I have found the sinner's friend.

4 I care not if the world revile,
The world that hates my Master's cause;
The world, I know, would quickly smile,
Were I again what once I was.

5 Then farewell, world, and farewell all
That emulates a Saviour's claims;
I'll hear him, and obey his call,
Regardless who approves or blames.

6 I'll praise him while he gives me breath,
Nor then will cease to sing his love;
For, when my voice is lost in death,
I hope to join the choirs above.

HYMN DXCIX.

"*And they all condemned him to be guilty of death.*"—
MARK xiv. 64.

1 ON other points they may divide,
On this are all agreed;
By acclamation they decide
That Jesus ought to bleed.

2 And why? what evil hath he done?
Not one of them can tell;
His foes themselves are forc'd to own
"He doeth all things well."

3 Yet, he must die; his blood alone
Can satisfy his foes;
For well they know, till he is gone,
They never can repose.

4 They cannot bear the glorious light,
It dazzles and confounds;
In Jesus it appears so bright,
Their hatred knows no bounds.

5 "Away with him, away with him,"
With frantic zeal they cry;
Before our face he dares blaspheme,
'Tis fit that he should die.

6 'Tis thus the Scriptures are fulfill'd,
And mercy's work is done;
The Lord by wicked hands is kill'd,
And, dying, saves his own.

HYMN DC.

"*And they shall be unto you cities for refuge.*"—NUMB. xxxv. 12.

1 AND have I reach'd the sacred spot,
Where those who fly, a refuge find?
May I indulge my joy or not?
Speak, Lord, and ease my anxious mind.

2 A dreadful sound was in my ears;
The stern avenger follow'd hard;
My trembling soul was fill'd with fears,
For ev'ry door, I thought, was barr'd.

3 But here I seem to breathe at last;
I hear th' avenger's voice no more;
The danger seems as though 'twere past,
I feel a calm unknown before.

4 Is this delusion, Lord, or no?
What is not, though it seems to be;
O! tell thy servant, is it so?
Who fears to err, and looks to thee.

5 Or is it what it seems to be?
A blessed and a safe retreat,
Where sinners, who, pursued like me,
A refuge and a welcome meet.

6 I deem it such, and here abide
The issue of the final day;
When what we trust to, shall be tried,
And all but truth be swept away.

HYMN DCI.

"But God forbid that I should glory, save in the cross."—
GAL. vi. 14.

1 THE Cross! a theme of joy to some,
To others of contempt indeed,
To me the pledge of joys to come,
The only one I ask or need.

2 Take this away, and all is night,
A midnight gloom without a ray;
'Tis worse than fancy can indite;
'Tis night without the hope of day.

3 But sweet beyond expression is
The hope imparted by the Cross;
The world appears but loss to this,
A thousand worlds appear but loss.

4 And yet, how little do I know
The sweet attraction of his love,
Who came from heav'n, and stoop'd so low,
To raise me to the joys above!

5 The Cross, though life and health to me,
To him was agony and death;
A conflict none could bear but he,
With all on earth, and all beneath.

6 What pass'd in that mysterious hour,
The victim only can unfold;
To sound its depth exceeds our pow'r,
But all we need to know, is told.

7 He bore our sin, he paid our debt;
And, suff'ring, magnified the law:
'Twas here that "truth and mercy" met;
'Twas this that angels wond'ring saw.

8 My soul, forget not what is due
To him whose suff'ring pardon brings;
Nor cease to keep the Cross in view:
The Cross will teach thee wondrous things.

Israel in Exile.

HYMN DCII.

"*Turn again our captivity, O Lord.*"—PSALM cxxvi. 4.

1 WE turn to Zion, there is peace,
Nor can the treasures of the earth
Detain us here, or make us cease
To love the place that gave us birth.

2 The subjects of a foreign lord,
But here condemn'd awhile to mourn:
We hope, according to his word,
One day with singing to return.

3 Our Lord, whom now we know and love,
But cannot see, will then appear.
Appear in glory, far above
Whatever thought can fancy here.

4 His fame has reach'd us from afar,
And much we hear of his renown;
Yet such his wealth and glory are,
Not half of what is true is known.

5 But when in yonder place we see
The King himself, without a veil,
Shall angels be so bless'd as we,
Or equal joy and wonder feel?

HYMN DCIII.

"How doth the city sit solitary that was full of people!"—
LAM. i. 1.

1 O MOURNFUL sight! a city waste!
Her former glory may be trac'd
From what we see remaining;
'Tis Zion mourns her children gone,
She lies forsaken and alone,
And thus is heard complaining:

2 "My sons! ah, whither are they gone?
Of all I once possess'd, not one
Now soothes a mother's anguish:
My children, once my joy and pride,
Are torn with rigour from my side,
And I am left to languish."

3 Zion! the enemy is chief,
No friend is nigh to bring relief,
Because thou hast offended;
For *this* thy children are remov'd,
And thou art punish'd, though belov'd,
Thy profit is intended.

4 When thou wast lately full of mirth,
The joy and glory of the earth,
Then hadst thou many lovers;
For *this* thy God, who spar'd thee long,
Now takes away thy joy and song,
And all thy shame discovers.

5 O! hadst thou known thy happy lot,
Nor basely sold thyself for nought,
Thy gracious Lord forsaking,
Then had thy peace been as a stream,
But lo! 'tis vanish'd like a dream,
The loss of thine own making.

6 But though thy God thus makes thee know
What ills from disobedience flow,
He means not to forsake thee;
When he has made thee feel thy loss,
And purely purg'd away thy dross,
He means again to take thee.

7 Then shall thy children all return,
No more for ever shalt thou mourn,
Restor'd again to favour;
Zion shall gain a glorious name,
Her foes shall all be put to shame,
For God himself will save her.

HYMN DCIV.

"*How shall we sing the Lord's song in a strange land?*"—
PSALM CXXXVII. 4.

1 ON the boughs our harps suspended,
Exiles we and far from home,
When will days of grief be ended?
When the day of promise come,
Which, in prospect,
Sheds a ray that cheers our gloom?

2 Can we sing midst foes and strangers?
Can we sing when all revile?
When expos'd to snares and dangers,
Can we sing, or can we smile?
But not distant
Is the end of grief and toil.

3 Silent now, not without reason,
Many are our foes and strong;
But we hope to see a season
When we shall resume our song;
Songs of triumph
Shall be ours, we trust, ere long.

4 Sweet the prospect! how it cheers us!
Cheers us in the midst of foes;
And ev'n now our Saviour hears us,
Hears our cry, and soothes our woes:
Hope sustains us,
Hope of freedom and repose.

HYMN DCV.

"*The Lord hath done that which he had devised.*"—Lam. ii. 17.

1 AND is it here the temple stood,
The temple of the living God,
A structure once so splendid?
Its stately frame is seen no more,
Its vessels gone, with all its store,
And all its glory ended.

2 Should any ask, why this is so,
Why Isra'l's glory lies so low,
And Isra'l's foes are stronger?
'Tis Isra'l's God that gives them strength,
For Isra'l's sin was such at length,
That he could spare no longer.

3 For this, the temple fam'd so long,
The poet's and the prophet's song,
Nor honour has nor pity;
The city, too, in ruin lies,
That lately was so full of joys,
God's own beloved city.

4 But let not Isra'l's foes be glad,
To see the people fall'n and sad;
They shall not mourn for ever:
The Lord will cancel Isra'l's guilt,
The temple shall again be built,
The Lord will yet deliver.

5 That house the former shall exceed,
Its fame throughout the world shall spread,
The theme of future story;
The covenant's great Messenger,
Within it shall himself appear,
And fill it with his glory.

HYMN DCVI.

"*For we are saved by hope.*"—Rom. viii. 24.

1 VOICES mute, and harps suspended!
'Tis not meet that this should be!
Days of grief will soon be ended,
And the captive then be free:
God has promis'd.
Joyful days we soon shall see.

2 To the land of promise going,
Where our troubles are no more,
Shall we yield to sadness, knowing
We shall reach the peaceful shore,
And be free from
All that caused us grief before.

3 Hope of this may well awaken
Joy, though in the captive's breast;
When cast down, he's not forsaken,
Still sustain'd when most oppress'd;
Good awaits him:
His an everlasting rest.

4 Let us then dismiss our sadness;
Let us sing, for well we may;
Captives still, but hope brings gladness:
Hope of that forthcoming day,
When our sorrow
Shall for ever pass away.

Israel Victorious.

HYMN DCVII.

"*But fear not thou.*"—Jer. xlvi. 27.

1 "ISRA'L, *be not thou affrighted,*"
Though thy foes so num'rous be;
All thy foes shall be requited
For the hatred borne to thee;
Thou shalt see them
All before thy banners flee.

2 "*Isra'l, be not thou affrighted,*"
When thy foes in arms appear;
They are many, and united,
Yet hast thou no cause for fear;
He who saves thee
Stronger is, and he is near.

3 "*Isra'l, be not thou affrighted,*"
Though thy numbers are so small;
He, whose name on earth is slighted,
Knows thy wants, and hears thy call;
He is mighty,
And thine enemies shall fall.

4 "*Isra'l, be not thou affrighted,*"
Gloomy though the way appears;
Thou shalt never be benighted,
Banish therefore groundless fears;
He who saves thee,
Hears thy sighs, and counts thy tears.

5 Not a man shall stand before thee,
For the Lord shall make them flee;
This shall be from love he bore thee,
Ere the world began to be;
His the glory,
Guilt and shame belong to thee.

6 Where thou seest yon pillar hover,
Follow thou, nor thence decline;
Soon thy conflicts shall be over,
And a blessed rest be thine;
Light and glory
Shall for ever round thee shine.

HYMN DCVIII.

"*Faint, yet pursuing.*"—JUDGES viii. 4.

1 FAINT we are, though still pursuing,
See our foes before us fly;
'Tis our gain, but not our doing,
They might all our pow'r defy;
He whose arm is cloth'd with might,
Jesus, puts our foes to flight.

2 See our King before us going,
Follow him, nor fearful be;
Follow him with boldness, knowing
Strength is his, and victory:
Though we feel our pow'r but small,
Yet we trust our foes shall fall.

3 See them all before him flying;
All before our conqu'ring Lord;
Strong they seem'd, our force defying,
And we trembled at their word;
But he fill'd them with his dread,
And when he appear'd, they fled.

4 Since our foes then flee before him,
(For his arm almighty is,)
Let his people all adore him,
Let the glory all be his:
Let his people ever sing,
Glory, glory, to their King.

HYMN DCIX.

"But fear not thou, O my servant Jacob, and be not dismayed, O Israel, for behold I will save thee from afar."—JER. xlvi. 27.

1 ISRA'L shall obtain a pardon,
(Thus the Lord proclaims his love),
He shall be a water'd garden,
Isra'l shall no more remove;
He shall come from distant lands,
Thus my sov'reign purpose stands.

2 O my servant Jacob, fear not,
I have call'd thee, thou art mine;
Though thy glory yet appear not,
It will come, thy light shall shine;
Object of my love and care,
I will save thee from afar.

3 Though I make an end of others,
Fear thou not, but trust to me;
Greater than the love of mothers,
Is the love I bear to thee:
Though all other nations fall,
Jacob shall survive them all.

4 Yet thou shalt not be unpunish'd,
Thou shalt know that I am God;
Though belov'd, yet, still admonish'd,
Thou shalt feel the chastening rod;
But thy night shall soon be past,
And the day shall dawn at last.

5 When thy foes are all brought under,
When I gather all thy seed,
Then shalt thou be fill'd with wonder,
Then shalt thou rejoice indeed;
All thy warfare then shall cease,
And thy children shall have peace.

HYMN DCX.

"*Sing, O barren.*"—ISAIAH liv. 1.

1 "SING, O barren," cry aloud,
Thou who wast in youth rejected;
Lo! thy children crowd around,
Thou shalt be no more neglected;
Hear this word, this gracious word,
Lo! thy husband is the Lord.

2 Give thy tent a larger place,
Go, and let its chords be lengthen'd;
Spare thou not, provide it space,
And let all its stakes be strengthen'd,
All thy troubles now shall cease,
No one shall molest thy peace.

3 Lo! thy days of shame are past,
Fear thou not, nor be confounded;
In thy God a friend thou hast,
One whose kindness is unbounded;
Hills and mountains may remove,
But no change affects his love.

4 For a while thy God withdrew,
'Twas the time of his displeasure;
Short his anger is, and slow,
But his love, 'tis without measure:
Here let all thy mourning end,
God himself appears thy friend.

5 God will break with his own hand
Ev'ry weapon form'd to wound thee;
Thou shalt see at his command,
All thy foes to fall around thee;
Blest, and justified in him,
Thou shalt ev'ry tongue condemn.

HYMN DCXI.

"*Fear thou not, O Jacob my servant.*"—JER. xlvi. 28.

1 'TIS the time of Isra'l's trouble,
Lo! the enemy is chief;
Yet shall Isra'l have the double,
Double joy for all his grief:
Isra'l's Saviour
Will appear and bring relief.

2 Isra'l's foes rejoice to see him
Forc'd to bow to their command;
Who, they say, shall ever free him?
Who shall save him from our hand?
Can Jehovah
Now restore them to their land?

3 Yes, though Isra'l were removēd
To the world's remotest end;
Know ye, Isra'l is belovēd,
Isra'l has a faithful friend;
He will save him,
And with pow'r his cause defend.

4 Yes, Jehovah will restore him,
Isra'l yet shall have his day;
Darkness shall be light before him,
Ev'ry obstacle give way;
And Jehovah
Will his enemies repay.

5 Isra'l then shall fear no dangers,
Sav'd from ev'ry hostile hand;
Dwelling far from foes and strangers,
And increasing as the sand;
Joys abounding
Through his peaceful happy land.

HYMN DCXII.

"*Sing, O barren.*"—ISAIAH liv. 1.

1 "SING, O barren;" sing aloud,
Thou who wast rejected;
Lo! thy children, like a cloud,
Soon shall be collected;
Lo! they come, thy children come,
Spread thy tent, and give them room.

2 None shall slight thee after this,
None again upbraid thee;
For the Lord thy husband is,
He himself who made thee:
Thou shalt henceforth bear his name;
He will take away thy shame.

3 Thou hast been afflicted long,
Long been unbefriended;
Thou hast borne reproach and wrong,
But those days are ended;
Thou shalt no more taste of woe,
Thou shalt no more fear the foe.

4 Ev'ry danger, ev'ry harm,
Shall be now averted;
Thou shalt see a mighty arm
In thy cause exerted:
God himself thy friend appears,
God, thy Lord, will dry thy tears.

HYMN DCXIII.

"And the ransomed of the Lord shall return and come to Zion with songs."—ISAIAH xxxv. 10.

1 SEE the ransom'd now returning
From their long captivity;
They have bid adieu to mourning,
Since their King has set them free:
They are going
Where they long desired to be.

2 Long their harps were seen suspended
On the willows, and unstrung;
Till the days of mourning ended,
Zion's children never sung;
Grief restrain'd them,
And their harps had idle hung.

3 They who lately pined in sadness,
They who would not, could not sing,
Now are fill'd with joy and gladness,
Now awake the silent string;
Zion's children
Sing the praises of their King.

4 He who pleads their cause is stronger
Than the foe that held them fast;
They are captives now no longer,
Lo! their day is come at last:
Zion's children
Know the time of grief is past.

5 He who rules the savage lion,
He whom all the beasts obey,
Guards the road that leads to Zion,
Guards it from the beasts of prey;
Thus his people
Pass securely by the way.

6 Lo! they come, to Zion hasting,
Zion, object of their love;
Joy and glory everlasting
Is their portion from above:
Zion's children
Never shall again remove.

HYMN DCXIV.

"*When thou passest through the waters, I will be with thee.*"—
ISAIAH xliii. 2.

1 THUS saith the Lord to Jacob's seed,
In me, the mighty God, rejoice;
No hostile weapon shall succeed
Against the people of my choice.

2 When through the waters thou shalt go,
And through the fire thy way shall be,
The waters shall not overflow,
Nor shall the flame do harm to thee.

3 When many foes assemble round,
In hopes to make my people fall,
Their counsels I will then confound,
And bring destruction on them all.

4 Who dares to touch the chosen seed,
Toucheth the apple of mine eye;
'Tis mine my people's cause to plead,
And I, their advocate, am nigh.

5 Then fear not, Isra'l, thou art mine,
Rejoice and triumph in my name;
My strength and righteousness are thine,
Thou never shalt be put to shame.

Israel Forgetful.

HYMN DCXV.

"*Then sang Moses and the children of Israel.*"—Exod. xv. 1.

1 ISRA'L sung with joy and wonder,
When the Lord display'd his pow'r;
When he cleav'd the waves asunder,
Isra'l sung in that glad hour;
Then the sound of praise was heard,
Then Jehovah's name was fear'd.

2 But their joy was quickly over,
And complaints were heard around;
Thus did Isra'l soon discover
All that in his heart was found;
And the wonders lately seen,
Seem'd as though they had not been.

3 Thus do we forget too often
All the wonders God has shewn;
Countless mercies fail to soften,
And subdue our hearts of stone;
What though now we raise our song,
Yet we may repine ere long.

4 Where is folly such as this is?
Where is guilt that equals ours?
Where is patience such as his is?
Patience that so long endures?
Were he aught but what he is,
We had been consum'd ere this.

5 Teach us, Lord, to walk before thee,
As becomes thy people here:
Soon, we hope, we shall adore thee,
Free from sin, and free from fear;
Then shall all thy people sing,
Glory, glory to their King.

Israel Encouraged.

HYMN DCXVI.

"*Who is there among you of all his people? His God be with him, and let him go up to Jerusalem.*"—EZRA i. 3.

1 SONS of Zion, haste away,
'Tis the acceptable day,
'Tis the day expected long,
Burden of prophetic song;
Thus the mighty God has spoken,
Haste away, your chains are broken.

2 From the willows, where they've hung
Long neglected and unstrung,
Take your harps again, and sing,
Sound the praise of Zion's King;
Sing, for Zion's sons have reason,
'Tis a joyful, glorious season.

3 Come to Zion, haste away,
Here you need no longer stay;
Days of liberty are come,
God invites his exiles home;
Joyful times the Lord is bringing,
Come to Zion, come with singing.

4 Leave your sorrows all behind,
Give them, give them to the wind;
Sacred pleasures now invite,
'Tis the season of delight;
Bid adieu to grief for ever,
Yours are pleasures ending never.

HYMN DCXVII.

"They shall ask the way to Zion, with their faces thitherward."—JER. l. 5.

1 WHENCE come ye, weeping pilgrims, whence?
And whither do ye journey hence?

2 We travel from a distant land,
The scene of our disgrace,
We leave it by our King's command,
And haste to see his face;
We're bound for Zion's blest abode,
His people's joy to share;
O tell us, if thou know'st the road
That will conduct us there.

3 Ye happy pilgrims, come with me
To yonder eminence, and see
The city of your glorious King;
Then let your hearts rejoice and sing.

4 'Tis it, how glorious to behold!
We shall be there ere long;
O let the timid now be bold,
And let the faint be strong!
Sing, sing, ye pilgrims, on your way,
Let joy fill ev'ry breast!
Our King will all our toils repay,
We soon shall gain our rest.

HYMN DCXVIII.

"*So that we may boldly say, the Lord is my helper.*"—
HEB. xiii. 6.

1 OFT as I look upon the road,
That leads to yonder blest abode,
I feel distress'd and fearful;
So many foes the passage throng,
I am so weak, and they so strong,
How can my soul be cheerful?

2 But when I think of him, whose pow'r
Can save me in a trying hour,
And place on him reliance,
My soul is then asham'd of fear,
And though ten thousand foes appear,
I bid them all defiance.

3 The dang'rous road I then pursue,
And keep the glorious prize in view,
With joyful hope elated;
Strong in the Lord, in him alone,
Where he conducts I follow on,
With ardour unabated.

4 O Lord, each day renew my strength,
And let me see thy face at length,
With all thy people yonder;
With them in heav'n thy love declare,
And sing thy praise for ever there,
With gratitude and wonder.

Heaven.

HYMN DCXIX.

"*For we shall see him as he is.*"—1 John iii. 2.

1 TO see the Saviour as he is,
What can we look for more than this?
Of heav'n 'tis all his people know,
No more is needful here below.

2 A paradise let others feign,
Where all their fav'rite good obtain,
Where, free from all restraint and fear,
They feast on joys but tasted here.

3 We ask no other heav'n than this,
To see the Saviour "as he is;"
To take our place around his throne,
And know as we ourselves are known.

4 Where Jesus is, 'tis heav'n to be,
'Tis heav'n the Saviour's face to see;
We know, though all the world revile,
Celestial joy is in his smile.

5 The little that on earth is known,
Makes him the object of our love;
And us impatient to be gone,
To see him as he is, above.

HYMN DCXX.

"*Thine eyes shall see the King in his beauty.*"—
Isaiah xxxiii. 17.

1 WITH heav'n in view, we tread the path
That saints of former ages trod;
Like them, the children once of wrath,
But now, like them, the sons of God.

2 No room for any boast have we,
Upon another's wealth we live;
The pardon we enjoy is free,
The praise to God alone we give.

3 We seek a city far from this,
A distant city out of sight;
The Lord himself its builder is,
The Lord, its everlasting light.

4 In beauty there the King appears;
The King we love, and hope to see:
While here, his people sow in tears,
Their harvest shall hereafter be.

5 This King, the King of glory is,
His presence is the joy of heav'n;
How blest our lot, if we are his!
Opposers once, but now forgiv'n.

6 Our aim be this, to live below
As he would have his subjects live:
To those who own and serve him so,
The Lord eternal life will give.

HYMN DCXXI.

"*For he looked for a city which hath foundations.*"—
HEB. xi. 10.

1 BEYOND the world a city stands,
A city this, not made with hands,
Where God the Saviour reigns;
'Tis built for sinners bought with blood,
Redeem'd and sanctified to God,
And cleans'd from all their stains.

2 The cities of the world must fall,
However solid, they must all
The common ruin share;
But yonder city still appears
Unchangeable through endless years,
For God himself is there.

3 Happy the people who abide
Within those walls, and there reside
For ever with their King!
Our lot, we hope, will be to share
Their joys, and join the thousands there,
The Saviour's praise to sing.

4 With such a prospect, should we grieve,
When call'd our earthly house to leave,
And part with all below?
A nobler house is ours above,
From which we never shall remove;
Our God ordains it so.

HYMN DCXXII.

"*And the Lord said unto him, This is the land which I sware unto Abraham.*"—DEUT. xxxiv. 4.

1 WHEN we stand on Pisgah's summit,
We behold yon glorious scene,
Canaan's hills, we see them from it,
Canaan's hills, adorn'd with green;
O how fair the prospect seems!
Richer far than fancy's dreams.

2 While we view the land of promise,
'Tis our destin'd home we see,
Standing at a distance from us,
But where soon we hope to be;
Yes, we trust the day is near,
When we shall be happy there.

3 There the King of saints appearing,
Consecrates the glorious place,
Many crowns for ever wearing,
There he shews his smiling face;
Yes, he smiles on all around,
And he makes their joys abound.

4 Free from fears, and free from dangers,
There on ev'ry side enclos'd,
Far from foes, and far from strangers,
Unmolested, unoppos'd.
All his people live secure,
God has made their dwelling sure.

5 Oft we'll go to Pisgah's summit,
While we still continue here,
View the glorious prospect from it,
And rejoice with holy fear;
Waiting, wishing for the day
When we shall be call'd away.

Brotherly Love.

HYMN DCXXIII.

"*Endeavouring to keep the unity of the Spirit in the bond of peace.*"—EPH. iv. 3.

1 BRETHREN, let us walk together
In the bonds of love and peace;
Can it be a question, whether
Brethren should from conflict cease?
'Tis in union
Hope and joy and love increase.

3 Th
Lo
Th
W
4 M
B
A
O

"*I will*
west
not

1

2

3

2 Let the world dispute and cavil,
Brethren should abide in peace;
While to Zion's hill they travel,
They should learn from strife to cease;
Pilgrims in the heav'nly road,
They should seek each other's good.

3 Christ has said it, "Love each other,
Thus the world my people know;
He that loveth not his brother
Is a child of wrath and woe;"
Brethren, let us think on this,
Let us prove that we are his.

4 Love is more than mere appearance,
Let us learn to love indeed;
Mutual patience and forbearance
Well become our state of need:
When we stand around the throne,
We shall know as we are known.

Miscellaneous.

HYMN DCXXV.

"*Is not this a brand plucked out of the fire?*"—ZECH. iii. 2.

1 IS not this a brand,
Rescued from the fire,
By a mighty hand?
Look ye, and admire.
'Tis a sight for you,
Merit who have none.
See what grace can do;
See what grace has done.

2 Such a brand am I:
  Rescued from the flame;
And to death how nigh,
  When the Saviour came!
When he came to save:
  Came from heav'n above;
All my sin forgave,
  And reveal'd his love.

3 Great the debt I owe,
  More than tongue can tell;
Sav'd from wrath and woe;
  Sav'd from lowest hell.
Lord, it is to thee
  All this debt is due.
Let me thankful be;
  Full of love, and true.

4 Keep me by thy pow'r,
  Lest I fall away;
Keep me ev'ry hour,
  Lest my footsteps stray.
Keep me to the end,
  Till the strife is past:
Let me then ascend,
  And rejoice at last.

HYMN DCXXVI.

" *Who is he that condemneth?*"—Rom. viii. 34.

1 FRUIT we have of God's election,
  Pardon, peace, and holy joy;
Guidance here, and sure protection,
  Pleasures, too, that never cloy:
Earnest of the joy to come,
When our Father takes us home.

2 While the world had yet no being,
  Nor had time its course begun;
All-ordaining, all foreseeing,
  God, in purpose, gave his Son:
Gave him to the death for men,
Love its work was doing then.

3 'Tis indeed a wondrous story,
  One that time can never tell;
How himself, the Lord of glory,
  By the hand of justice fell:
But his purpose was to save,
By the cross, and through the grave.

4 God's elect may bid defiance
  To the foe, to ev'ry foe.
On the Lord their whole reliance,
  Just, because he counts them so.
Who on those in judgment sits,
Those whom God himself acquits.

5 Who, then, shall his people sever
  From the love of Christ, their Lord?
Jesus is the same for ever,
  Good and faithful is his word.
Hence no evil can affect,
Nothing injure God's elect.

HYMN DCXXVII.

"*I have loved thee.*"—JER. xxxi. 3.

1 THE God himself, who reigns on high,
  Has set his love on us,
And we, his people, wonder why
  He should have acted thus.

2 Why we should live, and others not,
We are not giv'n to know;
'Tis far too high for human thought,
For human thought below.

3 Perhaps in yonder glorious place,
We may be giv'n to know
Why we are objects here of grace,
And why distinguish'd so.

4 But should this knowledge be too high
For all but God alone,
Enough for us, if we enjoy
His love, the cause unknown.

5 Content with this, our aim should be
To live at all times thus;
That all the world around may see
The fruit of grace in us.

HYMN DCXXVIII.

"*And in sin did my mother conceive me.*"—Psalm li. 5.

1 BORN in sin, and doom'd to die,
Such are you, and such am I:
Nothing we can say or do,
Will or can make this untrue.
Bitter is the cup we drink of;
Sad it is—'tis sad to think of.

2 But how sad the case would be;
Sad for you, and sad for me,
Were it not for news from heav'n;
News of grace, of sin forgiv'n!
This can take away our sadness;
This can fill our hearts with gladness.

3 Grace it is—'tis grace indeed,
  When "a child of wrath" like me,
Is from guilt and ruin freed,
  And at length is brought to see,
Him whose voice is in the thunder;
Him whom angels view with wonder.

4 Grace, "the grace of God" it is;
His in act, in purpose his.
Wonder, O ye heavens, with me,
And thou earth, astonish'd be.
Grace is what for sinners meet is;
Grace is what to sinners sweet is.

HYMN DCXXIX.

"*Freely ye have received, freely give.*"—Matt. x. 8.

1 GO forth, and plant the sacred tree!
  The tree of life, 'tis God's command;
For health and healing it shall be,
  A blessing meant for ev'ry land.

2 In ev'ry soil and clime it grows,
  Beneath the sun its fruit is found:
It thrives amidst the winter snows,
  When all is waste and dead around.

3 Speed then your way to ev'ry land,
  Convey to all the gift of heav'n:
We thus obey our Lord's command,
  We freely give what's freely giv'n.

4 And, O may he, whose gift it is,
  A blessing on the word bestow;
And all the praise be his alone,
  Who saves the lost and ruin'd so.

HYMN DCXXX.

"*Behold, I come quickly: hold that fast which thou hast, that no man take thy crown.*"—Rev. iii. 11.

1 WHAT thou hast,
Hold it fast:
"Let no man take thy crown."
Watch and pray:
Thus the day,
The day will be thine own.

2 But beware;
Do not dare
To trust thy wicked heart.
False it is;
Look to this,
Or else expect to smart.

3 Christ alone
Keeps his own;
He keeps them safe from harm.
In his care,
Safe they are:
For mighty is his arm.

4 His is love,
Far above
What human tongue can teach;
When we try,
'Tis too high
For human thought to reach.

5 Happy day,
When we may
Behold the Saviour near;
Then to be
Safe, and free
From sin, from pain, from fear.

HYMN DCXXXI.

"*They that sow in tears shall reap in joy.*"—PSALM cxxvi. 5.

1 WHAT does the Lord for those to whom
He makes his mercy known?
He saves them from the fearful doom
Of those he does not own.

2 What privilege can equal theirs
Whom Jesus call his own;
While here, 'tis true, they sow in tears,
But this will cease, and soon.

3 The time to reap in joy is sure;
The Lord his word will keep.
How blessed is the joy, and pure,
Reserv'd for those that weep.

4 Whose tears from godly sorrow flow,
A golden harvest theirs;
They suffer with their Lord below;
Like him they sow in tears.

5 But when their Lord again appears,
What joy awaits them then!
'Tis only now they sow in tears;
They'll never weep again.

6 Then welcome be the glorious day,
When Christ our Lord appears,
When all we see shall pass away,
And with it sighs and tears.

7 When all his saints shall gather'd be,
Around their Lord above,
And sing, in blessed harmony,
His everlasting love.

HYMN DCXXXII.

"*For his great love wherewith he loved us.*"—Eph. ii. 4.

1 IF belovēd, why belovēd?
  Solve this question he who can.
Was I not from God removed
  Far as any other man?
Why, then, in his favour now?
Tell me if thou knowest how.

2 'Tis too hard for man—I know it;
  'Tis what angels cannot reach.
God, "the only wise," can show it:
  'Tis what he alone can teach.
He who spans the vaulted sky,
He can tell the reason why.

3 If the Lord has hid the reason,
  And reveal'd the fact alone,
Let me humbly wait the season,
  When the secret may be known.
To be lov'd may satisfy,
Though conceal'd the reason why.

4 Lord, if thou indeed dost love me,
  This sufficient is alone;
Things conceal'd, or things above me,
  May with safety be unknown.
'Tis enough, enough for me,
If I am belov'd of thee.

5 Yet there may arrive a season,
  When the secret will be told;
When the Lord will show the reason,
  And the mystery unfold.
Be it ours to wait till then,
Though we know not where or when.

6 But the message of salvation
Is to all—to all mankind.
In the gracious invitation
None excepted are, we find.
He who on the Son believes,
Everlasting life receives.

HYMN DCXXXIII.

"*I showed before him my trouble.*"—PSALM cxlii. 2.

1 IN trouble, Lord, I sought thy face;
In trouble, Lord, I found thy grace.
When trouble shall again arise,
To thee I hope to lift my eyes.

2 And what is there but trouble here?
It will be so till thou appear.
Till then thy people cannot be
From trouble and from trial free.

3 We do not, Lord, complain of this;
'Tis needful all, we know it is.
It makes us long to see the day,
When heav'n and earth shall pass away.

4 When Jesus shall "with clouds" descend,
'Tis then his people's troubles end;
But not till then—and we must wait,
The Saviour's time is never late.

5 For this we seek, for this we plead;
Be with us, Lord, in time of need;
Nor let us faint beneath the rod,
But let us know "that thou art God."

6 No trouble, be it what it may,
Can do us harm, if we can say,
"It is the Lord." The rod his own;
Our Father's will, not ours be done.

HYMN DCXXXIV.

"*Strangers and pilgrims.*"—1 Pet. ii. 11.

1 GOING home, and going quickly;
This may gladden ev'ry heart.
Should we suffer, be it meekly.
Soon the world and we must part;
Never more to meet again;
There's an end of suff'ring then;
There's an end of all that grieves us.
How the thought of this relieves us.

2 Going home—the thought is cheering;
Going to the place we love;
There in royal state appearing,
Midst the shining hosts above,
There our Father dwells and reigns;
Greater he than fancy feigns.
There his people live for ever;
Theirs enjoyment ending never.

3 Going home—there's nothing dearer,
To the pilgrim's heart than home;
Drawing nearer still, and nearer
To the place where pilgrims come.
Much he thinks of what will be;
Much of what he hopes to see;
Much of kindred, friends, and brothers,
But of Christ above all others.

4 'Tis the blessed hope of seeing
Him he loves in glory there,
'lessed hope of ever being
'Vith the Lord, his joy to share:

'Tis this hope that lightens toil,
And in sorrow makes him smile;
Cheers him in the midst of strangers;
Keeps him, when beset with dangers.

5 Going home—then it behoves us,
Now to live as pilgrims do.
When the trial comes, it proves us;
Proves if we have faith or no.
Let us make our calling sure;
Let us to the end endure.
In the Saviour's love abiding;
In the Saviour's strength confiding.

HYMN DCXXXV.

"*I said in my haste, I am cut off from before thine eyes.*"—
PSALM xxxi. 22.

1 'TWAS a foolish thing to say,
In my haste I said it;
Now I put the thought away,
It was sin that bred it.
Ought I to suppose that he,
Who his Son had given,
Ever could forgetful be
Of the heirs of heaven?

2 Those whom he had loved so well,
And to Jesus given;
Could they be consigned to hell?
Could they fail of heaven?
Yet I said ('twas in my haste),
And with words unguarded,
That my hope could fail at last,
I should be discarded.

3 So I feared, and this the cause,
I was full of evil;
When I look'd, I saw I was
On the lowest level.
On the scale, who lower is
Than myself, or could be?
Where's the wonder, knowing this,
Fearful if I should be?

4 Still I should not thus have said,
"I am lost for ever;"
Since the blood that Jesus shed,
Faileth never, never.
Still the same I gladly see,
As in the beginning;
Suited thus to one like me,
One that's always sinning.

5 Henceforth let me think of this
In the hour of sadness;
This, and this alone it is,
Fills the heart with gladness.
Why, my soul, shouldst thou be sad?
Why thus plung'd in sorrow?
Trust in God, and be thou glad,
Thou shalt sing to-morrow.

HYMN DCXXXVI.

"*Freely ye have received, freely give.*"—MATT. x. 8.

1 BEAR the Saviour's message, bear it,
Let the distant nations hear it;
Bear his word to every land.
Ye who know his love, declare it;
Ye who have the treasure, share it;
'Tis your Master's own command.

2 Idols soon shall fall before him,
And the nations shall adore him;
All the people then shall sing.
When the Saviour reigns victorious,
When he makes his kingdom glorious,
Hills and valleys then shall ring.

3 Ye who love the Lord's appearing,
Bid him welcome, nothing fearing;
Joyful is the day for you:
Then the Saviour will receive you,
And from ev'ry ill relieve you;
Gracious are his words, and true.

4 Faithful is the Saviour's promise,
Earth and hell would wrest it from us;
Earth and hell will strive in vain;
On the Lord is our reliance;
Thus we bid our foes defiance;
His the glory, ours the gain.

HYMN DCXXXVII.

"*To them that have no might he increaseth strength.*"—
ISAIAH xl. 29.

1 NO strength have I, no strength at all;
I know it, and I feel it, too.
To meet a trial, great or small,
Is what I would not, dare not do.

2 The proof that I am weak is this,
When left without support I fall.
The strength in which I stand is his,
Who to his saints is "All in all."

3 I do not grieve that thus it is,
Nor wish it otherwise to be.
The glory of the work is his;
The benefit belongs to me.

4 I walk "by faith, and not by sight:"
By faith in him my living head.
His word it is that gives us light:
It shines upon the path I tread.

5 That I do tread (if tread I do),
The holy path, from him it is.
I know it, and I feel it too,
The grace is his, the pow'r is his.

6 Supported by his arm of strength,
Though often tried and sorely pressed,
I hope, though weak and vile, at length
To gain an everlasting rest.

HYMN DCXXXVIII.

"For I am a stranger with thee."—Psalm xxxix. 12.

1 I'M going home, detain me not;
I must not loiter by the way,
Lest night come on; for who knows what
Might happen then—I must not stay.

2 'Twould ill become the man who says,
He's passing through, to be like those
Whose home is here. His words and ways
Should with his pilgrim state agree.

3 I must not love the things that are;
They only lead the pilgrim wrong;
They draw him from his purpose far:
They take away his joy and song.

4 I must not stop, no matter what
May notice claim—I'm going home.
Be mine the weary pilgrim's lot.
'Tis labour now, but rest will come.

5 And rest to those that weary are,
Is sweet, but sweet to such alone;
The hope of rest is better far
Than if the world were all our own.

6 The pilgrims soon will gather'd be,
Within their father's house above:
A holy, happy family,
By him made perfect then in love.

HYMN DCXXXIX.

"*I am alive for evermore.*"—Rev. i. 18.

1 SWEET is the savour of his name
Who suffer'd in his people's stead;
His portion here reproach and shame,
He liveth now, he once was dead.

2 *He once was dead*, the very same
Who sits on yonder throne above;
Who bears in heav'n the greatest name,
Whom angels serve, whom angels love.

3 *He once was dead*, the very same
Who made the worlds, a work of pow'r;
Who now upholds the mighty frame,
And keeps it till the final hour.

4 *He once was dead*, the very same
Who soon will come with glory crown'd;
His breath shall kindle then a flame
That shall consume the world around.

5 *He once was dead*, the very same
At whose command the dead shall rise,
To sorrow some, and endless shame,
And some to everlasting joys.

6 *He once was dead*, but now he lives,
His glory fills all heav'n above;
Its blessedness to heav'n he gives,
The fountain he of joy and love.

7 His people shall his triumph share,
With him shall live, with him shall reign;
In heaven their joy is full, for there
They see THE LAMB for sinners slain.

HYMN DCXL.

"*So Esther drew near and touched the top of the sceptre.*"—
ESTHER v. 2.

1 I TOUCH the golden sceptre, Lord,
The golden sceptre of thy grace,
And feel my sinking life restor'd;
He lives, who sees thy smiling face.

2 'Twas death I fear'd, for I was vile,
Nor knew how much thou couldst forgive:
How blessēd then to see that smile,
That seem'd to bid the rebel live!

3 And is it true, indeed, that he,
Who sits on yonder throne of light,
Will deign to smile on one like me,
Nor spurn the rebel from his feet?

4 Then may the vilest wretch draw near,
The sceptre of his grace to touch,
And nothing have the vile to fear,
His sceptre is held out to such.

5 The name the Saviour bears is LOVE,
His throne a throne of mercy is;
' they who touch his sceptre prove
'at mercy and what truth are his.

6 From him the poor are never driv'n,
He lifts the prostrate from the dust;
By him the rebel is forgiv'n,
And in his name is taught to trust.

7 Thus life is found when death was fear'd,
And to the objects of his grace
The Saviour's name is thus endear'd,
Their heav'n is to behold his face.

HYMN DCXLI.

"*He shall see of the travail of his soul.*"—Isaiah liii. 11.

1 THE highest place in heav'n above
Is his who bore the cross below;
In heav'n confess'd the God of love,
He wears a crown of glory now.

2 The waters troubled were and deep,
Through which he pass'd to yonder throne;
The Saviour oft was seen to weep,
The Saviour oft was heard to groan.

3 The Saviour's groans—how deep they were
That night, when prostrate on the ground,
In anguish he alone could bear,
Himself the Lord of life was found!

4 A deeper groan was heard that day,
When on the cross the Saviour died;
'Twas then he took our sins away,
And justice then was satisfied.

5 The name of Jesus precious is,
A rock, a sure defence, a tow'r;
No name a virtue has like his,
'Tis life and health, 'tis grace and pow'r.

6 To him who died that they might live,
Let praise by all his saints be giv'n;
For nothing have his saints to give,
But praise on earth, and praise in heav'n.

HYMN DCXLII.

"The Lion of the tribe of Judah . . . hath prevailed."—Rev. v. 5.

1 HARK! the voice of Judah's Lion,
Fearful to his foes it is,
But to all the friends of Zion
Mild as is the summer's breeze;
He to them no harm intends,
Happy then are Zion's friends.

2 When amidst angelic legions
None the volume could unfold,
None through all the blessed regions
Could the sacred book behold;
When the strength of others fail'd,
Judah's Lion then prevail'd.

3 He the seven seals has broken,
And the volume open lies,
Wondrous things the Lord has spoken,
Wondrous in his people's eyes;
Things to come while time shall last,
Till the trumpet's final blast.

4 Now, with all the host of heaven,
Let us make his glory known,
Praise by all to him be given,
He is worthy, he alone;
His the glory, and the pow'r
Is the kingdom evermore.

HYMN DCXLIII.

"*The God of glory thundereth.*"—Psalm xxix. 3.

1 HARK! the God of glory thunders,
Swift his vivid lightnings fly;
Who is this that works these wonders?
Who is this that shakes the sky?
O! what mighty hand is this?
Moving all, unseen it is.

2 Not unseen by those who credit
What the word of God makes known;
He who cannot lie has said it,
Jesus reigns, and reigns alone;
At his word the thunder rolls,
He it is that shakes the poles.

3 When the thunder-clouds are clashing
O'er our heads, in midnight peals,
And the lightnings round us flashing,
Then the stoutest spirit fails;
Yet is this the Saviour's voice,
And his people may rejoice.

4 Yea, and in that awful season,
When the world shall pass away,
Then, ev'n then, the saints have reason
To rejoice, and bless the day;
Then is their redemption come,
Then they reach their wish'd-for home.

5 Saviour, grant us hope with patience,
Looking to that awful day;
Then fulfil our expectations,
Joyful let us hear thee say,
"Come, ye blessed, and receive
All a Father's love can give."

HYMN DCXLIV.

"*The land that is very far off.*"—ISAIAH xxxiii. 17.

1 A LAND I know there is,
Though far away from this,
Where toil and trouble are no more;
This land I sometimes see,
And then I fain would be
In safety on the happy shore.

2 'Tis trouble here and grief,
But hope affords relief;
The hope of an eternal rest,
The hope of reaching home,
The hope of joys to come,
The hope of being ever blest.

3 'Tis labour here, and strife
That only ends with life,
For here we dwell amidst our foes;
On yonder happy shore
Our foes are seen no more,
And there we shall enjoy repose.

4 This mind be always mine,
A fervent wish to join
With those who from their labours rest:
And yet a will to stay,
Till God sees fit to say,
"Come up, and be for ever blest."

HYMN DCXLV.

"*Of faith, that it might be by grace.*"—ROM. iv. 16.

1 GRACE is the sweetest sound
That ever reach'd our ears;
When conscience charg'd, and justice frown'd,
'Twas grace remov'd our fears.

2 Grace is a theme indeed,
A hope-inspiring theme,
'Tis all we can desire or need,
'Tis more than fancy's dream.

3 'Tis freedom to the slave,
'Tis light and liberty;
It takes its terror from the grave,
'Tis joy and victory.

4 Grace is a mine of wealth,
Laid open to the poor;
Grace is the sov'reign spring of health,
'Tis life for evermore.

5 Of grace then let us sing,
A joyful, wondrous theme;
The God of grace is Isra'l's King,
And grace proceeds from him.

6 We hope to see his face,
With all the saints above,
And sing for ever of his grace,
For ever of his love.

HYMN DCXLVI.

"*Or, canst thou thunder with a voice like him?*"—JOB xl. 9.

1 SAY, canst thou thunder with a voice
Like his whose hand the thunder made?
Then may'st thou in thyself rejoice,
Of nothing need'st thou be afraid.

2 Then has thine own right arm the pow'r
To make thee safe when others flee;
Nor need'st thou fear the evil hour,
For evil hour there's none to thee.

3 But if thy strength be small, then why
Against the God of glory fight?
And when he brings his mercy nigh,
O! why that mercy boldly slight?

4 'Tis mercy such as suits thy case,
It reaches guilt of deepest dye,
The richest and the freest grace,
The ground of hope, the spring of joy.

HYMN DCXLVII.

" *Heaven is my throne.*"—Isaiah lxvi. 1.

1 HEAV'N is the throne of Isra'l's God,
And earth his footstool is;
His is the sceptre and the rod,
To save and punish his.

2 Great is the terror of the Lord,
His arm is cloth'd with might;
And when he whets his glitt'ring sword,
No eye can bear the sight.

3 This God is ours, he reigns above,
And bless'd his people are,
The objects of paternal love,
And of paternal care.

4 Wisdom is his, and pow'r and grace,
And truth that cannot fail;
And bless'd are they who see his face,
Who see without a veil.

5 This grace, we trust, will yet be ours,
And with a hope like this,
Let all the time, and all the pow'rs,
That God has giv'n, be his.

HYMN DCXLVIII.

"*I will sing of mercy.*"—PSALM ci. 1.

1 SWEET were the sounds that reach'd our ears,
When mercy rais'd her heav'nly voice;
'Twas mercy that dispell'd our fears,
And bade our souls in hope rejoice.

2 All other sounds discordant seem,
Compar'd with mercy's heav'nly song;
So sweet and joyful is the theme,
It bears our willing souls along.

3 O may we never cease to hear
The voice that gives our conscience rest,
That dissipates our guilty fear,
And tells us we are truly blest.

4 May mercy still remove our fear,
And bind our souls with cords of love;
Mercy that soothes our sorrows here,
And gives us hope of joys above.

HYMN DCXLIX.

"*Let every one that nameth the name of Christ depart from iniquity.*"—2 TIM. ii. 19.

1 LET all who name his blessed name,
Who once for sinners shed his blood,
Depart from sin, and count it shame
To live like those who know not God.

2 "What kind of persons should they be,"
Whose names appear enroll'd above,
The people whom the Lord makes free,
To whom he manifests his love?

3 "What kind of persons should they be?"
How blameless should their life appear,
Who hope the Lord in heav'n to see,
And dwell with him for ever there!

4 With hopes so blessed and so bright,
Of heav'n they well may think and talk.
And being children of the light,
As children of the light should walk.

5 The sons of God, they well may scorn
The highest honours here on earth,
To heav'n's eternal honours born,
To stoop would ill become their birth.

6 And when a few short years are past,
What's promis'd now will then be giv'n;
A goodly portion theirs at last,
The glories and the joys of heav'n.

HYMN DCL.

"*Besides me there is no Saviour.*"—ISAIAH xliii. 11.

1 SALVATION *is of God alone,*
The glorious plan is all his own;
In love he form'd the great design,
And here his grace and wisdom shine.

2 *Salvation is of God alone,*
One only victim could atone
For human guilt; that victim he
Who claims with God equality.

3 *Salvation is of God alone,*
'Tis he who breaks the heart of stone,
Who makes self-righteous boast to cease,
nd gives the troubled conscience peace.

4 *Salvation is of God alone,*
'Tis he who leads his people on,
'Tis he who makes their burdens light,
And shields them in the day of fight.

5 *Salvation is of God alone,*
He sets his people on his throne;
'Tis rapture all, and triumph then,
They never taste of grief again.

6 *Salvation is of God alone,*
This truth let all his people own,
And to his name the praise be giv'n,
By saints on earth, and saints in heav'n.

HYMN DCLI.

"*God is love.*"—1 John iv. 16.

1 "GOD is love," his word has said it,
This is news of heav'nly birth;
Fly abroad and quickly spread it,
Make it known through all the earth
That "*God is love.*"

2 Not in yonder blessēd regions,
Where the Lord, with glory crown'd,
Reigns amidst angelic legions,
Will the brightest proof be found
That "*God is love.*"

3 'Tis on earth the Lord discloses
All his love, how vast it is;
Earth's the favour'd spot he chooses
To convince the world of this,
That "*God is love.*"

3 Then shall Isra'l, long dispersēd,
Mourning seek the Lord their God,
Look on him whom once they piercēd,
Own and kiss the chast'ning rod:
Then all Isra'l shall be savēd,
War and tumult then shall cease,
While the greater Son of David
Rules a conquer'd world in peace.

4 Mighty King, thine arm revealing,
Now thy glorious cause maintain,
Bring the nations help and healing,
Make them subject to thy reign:
Angels, in their lofty station,
Praise thy name, thou only wise;
O let earth, with emulation,
Join the triumph of the skies.

HYMN DLXXV.

"*I will bring thy seed from the east, and gather thee from the west; I will say to the north, Give up, and to the south, Keep not back.*"—Isaiah xliii. 5, 6.

1 MY soul, with sacred joy survey
The glories of the latter day;
Its dawn already seems begun,
Sure earnest of the rising sun.

2 The friends of truth assembled stand,
(A chosen, consecrated band,)
The standard of the cross display,
And cry aloud, "Behold the way!"

3 "Behold the way to Zion's hill,
Where Isra'l's God delights to dwell;
He fixes there his lofty throne,
And calls the sacred place his own."

ain and strife,
is life;
repose,
a close.

se,
all his foes;
their pow'r,
that hour.

day is won,
ork is done;
ruit of toil,
spoil.

come,
n a home;
appear,
gers here.

ll pass away,
great day;
be blest,

the morrow."—
JAMES iv. 14.

row,
to-day,
morrow;
say,
r call,
it all."

2 Happy they, who, all committing
  To their Father's care and love,
Let him choose what most is fitting,
  And of all he does approve;
They are free from anxious care,
Blest in this his people are.

3 Teach us, O our God and Father,
  Teach us to obey thee thus;
Be thy choice our portion, rather
  Than what might seem good to us;
'Tis not meet we should refuse
Aught that thou, our God, shalt choose.

4 Future things with thee are present,
  All to come thine eye can see;
Safe it is for us, and pleasant,
  Future things to trust to thee;
Then thy people happy are,
When on thee they cast their care.

HYMN DCLIV.

"*For when I am weak, then am I strong.*"—2 COR. xii. 10.

1 NO strength at all belongs to us,
  Our strength in Jesus is;
Nor should we grieve to have it thus,
  Since all the praise is his.

2 Some cause to boast, however small,
  Some store we fain would have;
But Jesus strips his saints of all,
  That his own arm may save.

3 We nothing lose. We nothing had.
  'Twas all a fancied store.
Though weak we're strong, rejoice though sad.
  And we are rich though poor.

4 With strength sufficient for the day,
The Lord his saints supplies;
This thought should keep them from dismay,
Though many foes arise.

5 Though hosts should press them in the rear,
And lofty mountains flank their sides;
Though in their front a sea appear,
The cloud is there, the cloud that guides.

6 The Lord will open for his saints
A passage through the sea;
His arm will break through all restraints,
And what he wills shall be.

7 O happy people of his choice!
Redeem'd and sav'd by grace,
'Tis yours for ever to rejoice,
In yonder glorious place.

HYMN DCLV.

"*Rejoice in the Lord.*"—PHILIP. iii. 1.

1 IN him, whose presence gladdens heav'n,
We do and will rejoice;
And blest are they to whom 'tis giv'n
To hear and know his voice!

2 Against the Lord we once bore arms,
His mercy we oppos'd;
The charmer's voice had then no charms,
For then our ears were clos'd.

3 He might have left us to endure
The wrath we seem'd to brave;
Our case would then admit no cure,
For who but he could save?

4 But though resisted long, he strove,
His purpose was to save;
He show'd the greatness of his love,
And, though provok'd, forgave.

5 Then let us sing of grace alone,
And magnify the name
Of him who sits upon the throne,
And join to praise THE LAMB.

HYMN DCLVI.

"*I will trust, and not be afraid.*"—ISAIAH xii. 2.

1 WHEN we cannot see our way,
Let us trust, and still obey;
He, who bids us forward go,
Cannot fail the way to show.

2 Though the sea be deep and wide,
Though a passage seems denied,
Fearless let us still proceed,
Since the Lord vouchsafes to guide.

3 Though it seems the gloom of night,
Though we see no ray of light,
Since the Lord himself is there,
'Tis not meet that we should fear.

4 Night with him is never night,
Where *he* is, there all is light;
When he calls us, why delay?
They are happy who obey.

5 Be it ours, then, while we're here,
Him to follow without fear;
Where he calls us, there to go,
What he bids us, that to do.

HYMN DCLVII.

"*In whom we have redemption.*"—COL. i. 14.

1 IN our Lord we have redemption,
   Full remission in his blood;
From the curse entire exemption,
   From the curse pronounc'd by God:
What a Saviour Jesus is!
O what love, what love is his!

2 See the Lord, our nature wearing,
   This is wondrous in our eyes;
See him all our sorrows bearing,
   Hark! 'tis he, 'tis he who cries,
While he bears the curse for us,
"Why am I forsaken thus?"

3 Awful cry! it shows his suff'ring
   Far above the reach of thought;
When he gave himself an off'ring,
   And with blood his people bought:
When their sins on him were laid,
And their ransom fully paid.

4 Praise be his, all praise transcending,
   Praise on earth, and praise in heav'n;
Praise through ages never ending,
   To the Lamb of God be giv'n:
He alone the Saviour is,
Everlasting praise be his.

HYMN DCLVIII.

"*Truly the light is sweet.*"—ECCLES. xi. 7.

1 THE light is sweet, and pleasant is
   The sun to mortal sight;
But fairer light we know than this,
   We know a sun more bright;

2 A sun that sheds a purer ray,
That gives to heav'n its light;
A sun that yields perpetual day,
That goes not down by night;

3 A sun that shines upon the way
That leads to joys above;
That cheers the pilgrim with its ray,
And warms his heart with love.

4 This sun is ours; it gilds with light
Th' eternal vault of heav'n;
'Tis faintly view'd by mortal sight,
As yet no more is giv'n.

5 But soon, we hope, a day will be,
When clouds shall be no more;
This glorious sun we then shall see
In beauty, not before.

6 Till then it yields sufficient light
To shew the heav'nly way;
And now and then it seems more bright,
And darts a warmer ray.

7 Fair is the lot that 's cast for them,
On whom this sun has ris'n;
This sun illumines with its beam
The darkness of a pris'n.

HYMN DCLIX.

"Yea, he did fly upon the wings of the wind."—
PSALM xviii. 10.

1 THE Lord, his way is in the storms,
The lightnings fly at his command;
He gave to nature all its forms,
And nature owns his guiding hand.

2 The mountains tremble at his look,
The everlasting hills remove;
The sea is dried at his rebuke,
At his rebuke who reigns above.

3 And is it true, indeed, that he
Whom heav'n itself cannot contain,
Will dwell on earth? and will he be
Our God, and bless his feeble train?

4 What grace is this! what grace to us!
O Lord, we wonder and adore,
That such as we are favour'd thus,
Who fought against thy grace before.

5 O may that grace our fear remove,
And render captive ev'ry thought
To him who came from heav'n above,
And with his blood his people bought.

HYMN DCLX.

"*By grace ye are saved.*"—Eph. ii. 5.

1 NOTHING but the purest grace
Could have sav'd and set us free;
Saviour, when we see thy face,
O what thanks we'll give to thee!
How we'll tell to all around us,
What we were when mercy found us!

2 We were then the heirs of woe,
Guilty, and condemn'd to die;
Yet, not knowing it was so,
We were in a dream of joy:
Such we were when mercy found us,
So we'll tell to all around us.

4 Stand thou still this day, and see
Wonders wrought, and wrought for thee;
Safe thyself on yonder shore,
Thou shalt see thy foes no more:
Thine to see the Saviour's glory,
Thine to tell the wondrous story.

5 Yea, thy God shall yet be known,
Far and wide, as God alone;
At his word shall idols fall,
For thy God is Lord of all:
Strength is his, and his salvation;
He shall reign in ev'ry nation.

HYMN DCLXII.

"*Having a desire to depart and to be with Christ.*"—
PHIL. I. 23.

1 IF I had wings, then would I go
With speed to yonder realms of light;
I'd bid farewell to all below,
And take my everlasting flight.

2 I'd ask admittance there, as one
Without pretension aught but this—
A sinner sav'd by grace alone,
That grace that for the vilest is.

3 I'd join in praise with those above,
Who owe, like me, their place in heav'n
To royal mercy; much they love,
Because that much has been forgiv'n.

4 I thought (vain hope!) that I might clain
A place in heav'n to merit due;
'Twas then I gloried in my shame,
And deem'd him wise who nothing kne\

2 The wisdom of the world must fail,
'Tis found deficient in the scale;
When guilt and pain and death assail,
Ah! what will *such* a friend avail?

3 It may with pride the heart inflame,
It may exalt a man to fame,
It may procure a splendid name,
But cannot save from endless shame.

4 There is a wisdom from on high,
No food for pride will it supply,
But guilt and pain it may defy,
And cheers us when we come to die.

5 Who shall *this* wisdom's worth declare?
Or what shall we to her compare?
To her, bright gems, however rare,
But faintly shine, and worthless are.

6 Who wisdom find, are truly blest,
The "tree of life" is then possess'd;
Of all that's valued this is best,
'Tis present and eternal rest.

HYMN DCLXV.

"*O Nebuchadnezzar, we are not careful to answer thee in this matter.*"—DANIEL iii. 16.

1 WHEN all were enjoin'd by decree,
Before the great image to fall,
The tyrant expected to see
His mandate complied with by all.
Whatever their master ordain'd
Was done by the flexible crowd;
By fear of his anger constrain'd,
Before the great image they bow'd.

2 But some there were found who refus'd
To prostrate themselves at his word;
They would not obey him, unus'd
To adore any god but THE LORD.
In vain did the tyrant proclaim
His purpose to make them comply,
In vain did he point out the flame,
And bid them obey him, or die.

3 The champions with confidence said,
"Let others, O king, dread thine arm;
In vain are thy terrors display'd,
For to us they convey no alarm.
Our God, whom we worship, is nigh,
To save us, O king, from thine hand;
But know, we choose rather to die,
Than yield to thy impious command."

4 'Tis thus that the saints must obey,
Their work must be thoroughly done;
Though death should appear in the way,
Their duty is still to go on.
The Lord will approve at the last
Those only who thus persevere;
And such, when the conflict is past,
Before him with joy shall appear.

HYMN DCLXVI.

"*For there is none other name .... given among men whereby we must be saved.*"—ACTS iv. 12.

1 THERE'S not a name beneath the skies,
Nor is there one in heav'n above,
But that of JESUS, can suffice
The sinner's burden to remove.

2 Sweet name! when once its virtue's known,
How weak all other helps appear,
The sinner trusts to it *alone*,
And finds the grand specific there.

3 'Twas long before I knew this truth,
And learn'd to trust the Saviour's name;
In vanity I spent my youth,
The thought now fills my heart with shame.

4 But since I've known the life and pow'r
With which his name is richly stor'd,
The world can keep my heart no more,
Nor can its joys content afford.

5 The things I once esteem'd the most,
I now account as worthless dross;
Thy name, dear Saviour, is my boast,
For which the world appears but loss.

6 Lord, grant me boldness to proclaim
(Unmov'd by any fear but thine)
The saving virtues of thy name,
And prove its influence divine.

7 Nor let its savour be confin'd,
Through ev'ry region let it spread;
Impart its blessings to mankind,
And by its pow'r revive the dead.

HYMN DCLXVII.

"*Behold, he shall come, saith the Lord of hosts.*"—Mal. iii 1.

1 HE comes! the Saviour full of grace,
By ancient prophets sung;
The smile of mercy in his face,
And truth upon his tongue.

2 In him the world no beauty sees,
"No form nor comeliness,"
Rejected and despised he is,
And plung'd in deep distress.

3 But there's a people taught by grace
To know his matchless worth;
They own him, though accounted base,
And shew his praises forth.

4 They own him as the Lord of all,
Their Saviour and *their* God;
Before his feet they prostrate fall,
The purchase of his blood!

5 'Tis thus the Saviour is receiv'd,
The world accounts him vile;
While sinners, by his grace reliev'd,
Can live but by his smile.

6 To him, who bore the sinner's shame,
Be endless glory giv'n,
Immortal honours crown his name,
The Lord of earth and heav'n.

HYMN DCLXVIII.

"*Reward her even as she rewarded you, and double unto her double.*"—REV. xviii. 6.

1 NOW reward her, give her double,
Babylon is doom'd to fall;
'Tis her day, her day of trouble,
Vain her broad and tow'ring wall;
Not a friend will now remain,
None her honour to maintain.

2 Long she hurl'd a proud defiance
At the God that reigns above;
On her strength plac'd vain reliance,
Thought she never would remove;
But her triumph now is past,
Vengeance, ling'ring, comes at last.

3 Blood she shed in vast profusion,
Blood that flow'd in martyrs' veins;
'Tis the day of retribution,
God to shew his justice means;
All the blood her servants shed,
God will visit on her head.

4 O, ye people, now forsake her,
Ye whom God his people calls,
Lest her judgments overtake her,
While ye stay within her walls;
Sharers in her sin, prepare
In her judgments too to share.

5 Those who once conspir'd to raise her,
Join to bring her glory down;
Ev'ry friend she has betrays her,
All unite to take her crown;
Vain her broad and tow'ring walls,
Lo! "the queen of kingdoms" falls.

6 She who, by her pomp and splendour,
Dazzled all the world around,
Calls in vain—there's no defender,
None to plead her cause is found;
All her pomp and glory dies,
See! she sinks, no more to rise.

HYMN DCLXIX.

"*Come and hear, all ye that fear God, and I will declare what he hath done for my soul.*"—Psalm lxvi. 16.

1 O YE that fear the Lord, attend,
While I relate a wondrous case,
Of one whom Christ, the sinner's friend,
Redeem'd and rescued by his grace.

2 I knew this man, I know him still,
In devious paths he long had stray'd;
Blind ignorance and proud self-will
Conceal'd the path that wisdom made.

3 He was no infidel, 'tis true,
(As men now understand the name,)
No; he condemn'd the *naughty crew*,
Himself *essentially* the same.

4 From gross abominations free,
The pharisaic robe he wore,
He seem'd a man of piety,
And such the character he bore.

5 Caress'd by friends, and often told
Of goodness which he never had,
He thought that all his dross was gold,
Nor ever dreamt his state was bad.

6 Whatever men may think of such,
Their enmity to truth is great;
They think that they possess so much,
That nothing can improve their state.

7 Deluded thus by golden dreams,
They oft sleep on without alarm;
The whole a solid treasure seems,
Till *death* dissolves the fatal charm.

8 Thus did *he* sleep whose case I tell,
And gaz'd upon his fancied store;
He thought, vain fool! that all was well,
Nor did he know that he was poor.

9 But while he slept, a gracious voice
Struck on his ear, and seem'd to say,
"Sleeper, awake to real joys!
Lo! Jesus is the living way."

10 This voice prevail'd, and now he knows
That he indeed was in a dream;
From Jesus *now* his comfort flows,
His life, his peace, his hope, from him.

11 The world can keep his heart no more,
Since Jesus has reveal'd his love;
And when life's pilgrimage is o'er,
He hopes to see his Lord above.

HYMN DCLXX.

"*Woe be unto the pastors that destroy and scatter the sheep of my pasture, saith the Lord.*"—Jer. xxiii. 1.

1 WOE to the pastors, saith the Lord,
Who scatter and destroy my sheep!
Though you should now despise my word,
Your end will be to mourn and weep.

2 The flock you should have kept with care,
Is left to stray without a guide;
Behold, the lion and the bear
An unresisting prey divide.

3 As when some unexpected shock
Awakens terror by surprise,
'Tis thus I will require my flock,
Nor shall you then escape by lies.

4 Hear this, ye idol shepherds, hear,
Who think of nothing but your gain;
When the chief shepherd shall appear,
Ye then will gnaw your tongues for pain.

5 O hear his voice while yet he speaks,
To warn you of your awful state!
The man who *here* forgiveness seeks,
Will find he never seeks too late.

6 When you have learn'd his voice to know,
You then may show his flock the way;
And when he comes, he will bestow
A crown that never will decay.

HYMN DCLXXI.

"*Who will shew us any good?*"—PSALM iv. 6.

1 "WHO will shew us any good?"
Thus the hopeless worldling cries;
Pleasure, though with zeal pursued,
Still from his embraces flies.

2 Is there nothing here below
Can supply the soul with food?
Hear the general answer—no!
"Who will shew us any good?"

3 Solomon the trial made,
Brought all nature to the test,
Tried the palace, tried the shade,
Yet he sought in vain for rest.

4 What can others now expect?
What will all their projects gain?
Are they likely to effect
What the king has tried in vain?

5 Must we then all hope resign?
Is there nought can yield repose?
Saviour, make thy face to shine,
This is what will heal our woes.

6 Ye who seek for peace of mind,
Ye who would be truly blest,
If you seek it here, you'll find
Jesus gives his people rest.

HYMN DCLXXII.

"*And Jesus said unto him . . . To-day shalt thou be with me in paradise.*"—LUKE xxiii. 43.

1 JESUS sav'd the dying thief,
Welcome news for one like me;
Now I know there is relief,
When the world no hope can see:
Sav'd by grace, by sov'reign grace,
By the cross I'll take my place.

2 Saviour of the dying thief,
Lo! a wretch as vile as he,
Fill'd with shame, remorse, and grief,
Draws his hope, O Lord, from thee;
In the view of so much grace,
Can despair at all have place?

3 Nothing but the richest grace
Could relieve a wretch like me,
This alone could reach my case,
And I see this grace in thee;
Saviour of the dying thief,
In thy grace I find relief.

HYMN DCLXXIII.

"*If the Son therefore shall make you free, ye shall be free indeed.*"—John viii. 36.

1 JESUS gives his people freedom,
Freedom to the world unknown,
Liberty from heav'n decreed 'em,
Such as they possess alone;
They are free whom Jesus saves,
All the rest, we know, are slaves.

2 Slaves of sin—a yoke how grievous!
Thanks to him who made us free;
O that men would but believe us,
Happy, happy would they be;
They who by the truth are freed,
Jesus says, are free indeed.

3 But though sin no more enslaves us,
This may well our wonder move,
That to him who freely saves us,
So unfaithful we should prove;
O how base, how vile are we!
And how "full of grace" is he.

4 Grace supports us, grace unbounded,
Hope would perish but for this;
All our hope on grace is founded,
O that sound, how sweet it is!
Sweet to those, who hope have none,
Save what grace supplies alone.

5 Let us sing the Saviour's praises,
He alone could set us free;
And we hope he soon will raise us,
With himself in heav'n to be;
Let us think with joy of him,
Let his grace be all our theme.

HYMN DCLXXIV.

"Therefore I take pleasure in infirmities, in reproaches."—
2 Cor. xii. 10.

1 WHAT! take pleasure in distresses,
Glory in reproach alone!
He who can do this possesses
Something to the world unknown,
Something that can furnish joys,
When the world its smile denies.

2 Love to him, who once was offer'd
On the cross, and bore its shame,
Who on earth a victim suffer'd,
And a curse for men became,
Love to him can furnish joys,
Nobler far than earth supplies.

3 This can make reproach a blessing,
Pain a pleasure, loss a gain;
Joyful hope in Christ possessing,
What is loss, and what is pain?
What is shame, and what is death,
What to him who lives by faith?

4 Far from earth he has his treasure,
'Tis laid up with God above;
What though earth afford no pleasure?
Happy in his Father's love,
He can smile, though all around
Stript of ev'ry joy be found.

5 He is blest, and they who blame him
Know not whence true joys arise;
When his Master comes to claim him,
Then his foes will own him wise;
When the world exists no more,
Heav'n will yield him boundless store.

HYMN DCLXXV.

"*Let us break their bands asunder.*"—PSALM ii. 3.

1 "LET us break their bands asunder,
Let us cast their cords away;"
Hear these words, my soul, and wonder,
What is this the people say?
Will they join against the Lord,
Join to fight against his word?

2 O ye people, why this madness?
Why contend against the strong?
Soon your joy must end in sadness,
All your hopes expire ere long;
Think, O think with whom you fight,
Him whose arm is cloth'd with might.

3 See, he sits, your efforts viewing
With a smile of conscious strength;
Why your frantic schemes pursuing,
As though God would fail at length?
Look at heav'n, and then despair—
Can he fail, whose throne is there?

4 Thus saith God of his anointed,
"He shall reign on Zion's hill;"
So Jehovah has appointed,
He who works his sov'reign will;
This his further pleasure is,
That the heathen should be his.

5 Vain is human opposition,
God is stronger than his foes;
Treats resistance with derision,
And his pow'r by vict'ry shews;
When he stretches out his hand,
Who his purpose can withstand?

HYMN DCLXXVI.

"*And they all condemned him to be guilty of death.*"—
MARK xiv. 64.

1 O REVOKE the fatal sentence!
What has Jesus done amiss?
Soon you'll mourn in deep repentance,
Mourn a deed so black as this.
Think, O think on what you're doing,
Drawing down vindictive fire,
In his blood your hands imbruing,
Blood that God will soon require.

2 O unwise, ungrateful nation!
Will ye crucify your King?
When you write his accusation,
What's the charge you have to bring?
True, he says he comes from heaven,
True, he boasts the highest name;
But the proofs that he has given
Fully vindicate his claim.

3 Stop! O stop! and closely view him;
View the man whom ye reject;
Foolish people! not to know him,
Not to know the Lord's elect;
Search the prophets, ask of Moses,
Let their evidence be heard;
Each in turn the deed opposes,
All bear witness to his word.

4 'Tis in vain ye still deny him,
Rage has lock'd up reason's pow'rs;
Still ye cry out "Crucify him,
Be his blood on us and ours."

Why on truth this bold reliance?
  Truth knows nothing of the deed;
God accepts the proud defiance,
  It shall be as you have said.

5 Lo! from you the kingdom wrested,
  Shall on others be bestow'd;
You, of all your rights divested,
  Long shall feel the arm of God:
Far from the belovēd city,
  Isra'l's tribes their days shall waste:
None shall spare, and none shall pity,
  Till they own their King at last.

HYMN DCLXXVII.

"*Turn not away the face of thine anointed.*"—
PSALM CXXXII. 10.

1 JESUS is the Lord's anointed,
  Come, eternal life to bring;
Lamb of God, to death appointed,
  Isra'l's prophet, priest, and king;
Object of his people's trust,—
God, and yet allied to dust.

2 Ere created thing existed,
  Blessed in himself alone,
Jesus was; and, unassisted,
  Made the world, by pow'r his own;
'Tis the building of his hands,
And, by him upheld, it stands.

3 This is he, whom man despises,
  He with whom the world contends,
Till the light of heav'n arises,
  Then its opposition ends;
What the sinner scorn'd before,
Render'd wise, he scorns no more.

4 This is he, whom heav'n confesses,
"King of kings, and Lord of lords;"
They are blessēd, whom he blesses,
Sweet the joy his smile affords;
Jesus is the God of grace,
And 'tis heav'n to see his face.

HYMN DCLXXVIII.

"*But also to die at Jerusalem for the name of the Lord Jesus.*"—ACTS xxi. 13.

1 O FOR a martyr's glowing zeal!
He fears no danger, shuns no pain;
He stands oppos'd to earth and hell,
And tells them all their threats are vain.

2 See where the faithful champion stands!
Undaunted by his num'rous foes;
He listens to his Lord's commands,
And life itself for him foregoes.

3 The kindling flames around him blaze,
His courage stands the awful test;
The dying saint no fear betrays,
Nor does he ask his foes for rest.

4 His treasure they cannot destroy,
And while they think to cast him down,
They do but hasten on his joy,
And brighten his celestial crown.

5 "Farewell," he cries, "to all below,
I mount to yonder blest abode,
To join the saints in heav'n I go;
To dwell for ever with my God."

6 How blest are they whose work is done,
Who now enjoy the glorious prize!
Be this our care, the race to run,
That we may know and share their joys.

HYMN DCLXXIX.

"For it is not possible that the blood of bulls and of goats should take away sins."—HEB. X. 4.

1 THOUGH all the beasts that live and feed
Upon a thousand hills should bleed,
Though all their blood should flow,
The sacrifice would be in vain,
The stain of sin would still remain,
Sin is not cancell'd so.

2 A "better sacrifice" than these
Must bleed, in order to appease
The anger of the Lord;
No blood has virtue to atone
For man's offence, but his alone,
Whose title is THE WORD.

3 His, who could say, though styl'd a son,
"My Father and myself are one;"
His only could atone:
His, who Jehovah's "fellow" stood,
Who claim'd equality with God,
And made the world alone.

4 He came, in love to sinners came;
Eternal honour to his name!
He bow'd his head and died:
A full atonement now is made,
The ransom by his death is paid,
And justice satisfied.

5 What news is this! how sweet to hear!
Though sinners, we may now draw near
To God, the righteous God:
The obstacles that stood before
To bar the way, are now no more,
Since Jesus shed his blood.

6 Eternal honour be to him
Who plann'd the great, the gracious scheme,
And found the ransom too:
Let all his saints their voices raise,
And sing the great Redeemer's praise,
While endless ages flow.

HYMN DCLXXX.

"*Having made peace, through the blood of his cross.*"—
COL. i. 20.

1 OURS is a pardon bought with blood,
Amazing truth! the blood of one,
Who, without usurpation, could
Lay claim to heav'n's eternal throne.

2 No victim of inferior worth
Could ward the stroke that justice aim'd.
For none but he, in heav'n or earth,
Could offer that which justice claim'd.

3 But he, the Lord of glory, came,
On yonder cross he bow'd his head;
He suffer'd pain, he suffer'd shame,
And lay a pris'ner with the dead.

4 But, lo! he rises from the grave,
And bears the greatest, sweetest name;
The Lord, almighty now to save,
From sin, from death, from endless shame.

5 Sweet is the pardon thus procur'd,
And, oh! how dear the Saviour is
To him for whom he thus endur'd
The punishment that else were his!

HYMN DCLXXXI.

"*Awake, psaltery and harp.*"—PSALM cviii. 2.

1 JESSE'S son awakes the lyre,
Listen while the psalmist sings;
His the Spirit's sacred fire,
All his theme, the King of kings.

2 Others sing of worldly things,
Themes like these to men belong;
But when Isra'l's prophet sings,
Sacred themes inspire his song.

3 Listen, listen while he sings,
Jesus is his glorious theme;
Jesus is the King of kings,
'Tis his joy to sing of him.

4 How should we delight to hear
Strains that hope and love impart!
Strains of joy for mortal ear,
Strains that purify the heart.

5 Son of Jesse, sound the lyre,
Bear our willing souls along;
Thine the prophet's holy fire,
Thine his theme, and thine his song.

HYMN DCLXXXII.

"*Enter ye in at the strait gate.*"—MATT. vii. 13.

1 THERE is a way that leads to death,
A way that many go,
In spite of all that wisdom saith,
In spite of future woe.

2 This way is smooth, 'tis fair and broad,
'Tis pleasant to the sight;
But woe to those who take this road!
It leads to endless night.

3 Another way there likewise is,
That leads to joys above;
But few, alas! will travel this,
'Tis not the way they love.

4 This road is rough and narrow too,
Nor does it please the eye;
But though 'tis difficult to go,
Its end is certain joy.

5 How blest are they whose feet are found
In wisdom's sacred way!
They soon shall reach the happy ground,
And there for ever stay;

6 Where sorrow ends in purest joys,
Where no complaint remains;
Where hope before its object dies,
And love triumphant reigns.

HYMN DCLXXXIII.

"*He humbled himself.*"—Phil. ii. 8.

1 THE God of glory dwells on high,
He rules the armies of the sky;
Ten thousand thousand round him stand,
Obedient to their King's command.

2 The God of glory, mov'd by love,
Descends in mercy from above;
And he, before whom angels bow,
Is found a man of grief below.

3 This love is great, too great for thought,
Its length and breadth in vain are sought;
No tongue can tell its depth and height,
The love of God is infinite.

4 But though his love no measure knows,
The Saviour to his people shews
Enough to give them joy, when known;
Enough to make their hearts his own.

5 Constrain'd by this, they walk with him,
His love, their most delightful theme;
To glorify him here, their aim;
Their hope, in heav'n to praise his name.

HYMN DCLXXXIV.

"*He said, It is finished.*"—JOHN xix. 30.

1 "IT IS FINISH'D!" sinners, hear it,
'Tis the dying victor's cry;
"IT IS FINISH'D!" angels, bear it,
Bear the joyful truth on high:
"IT IS FINISH'D!"
Tell it through the earth and sky!

2 Justice, from her awful station,
Bars the sinner's peace no more;
Justice views with approbation
What the Saviour did and bore;
Grace and mercy
Now display their boundless store.

3 Hear the Lord himself declaring
All perform'd he came to do;
Sinners, in yourselves despairing,
This is joyful news to you;
Jesus speaks it,
His are faithful words and true.

4 "IT IS FINISH'D!" all is over,
Yes, the cup of wrath is drain'd;
Such the truth these words discover,
Thus the vict'ry was obtain'd:
'Tis a vict'ry
None but Jesus could have gain'd.

5 Crown the mighty conqu'ror, crown him,
Who his people's foes o'ercame!
In the highest heav'n enthrone him!
Men and angels, sound his fame!
Great his glory!
Jesus bears a matchless name.

HYMN DCLXXXV.

"*And he led them on safely.*"—PSALM lxxviii. 53.

1 SAVIOUR, through the desert lead us,
Without thee we cannot go;
Thou from cruel chains hast freed us,
Thou hast laid the tyrant low:
Let thy presence
Cheer us all our journey through.

2 With a price thy love has bought us;
(Saviour, what a love is thine!)
Hitherto thy pow'r has brought us;
(Pow'r and love in thee combine;)
Lord of glory,
Ever on thine Isra'l shine.

3 Through a desert waste and cheerless,
Though our destin'd journey lie,
Render'd by thy presence fearless,
We may ev'ry foe defy;
Nought shall move us,
While we see our Saviour nigh.

4 When we halt (no track discov'ring),
Fearful lest we go astray,
O'er our path thy pillar hov'ring,
Fire by night, and cloud by day,
Shall direct us;
Thus we shall not miss our way.

5 When we hunger, thou wilt feed us,
Manna shall our camp surround;
Faint and thirsty, thou wilt heed us;
Streams shall from the rock abound:
Happy Isra'l!
What a Saviour thou hast found!

6 When our foes in arms assemble,
Ready to obstruct our way,
Suddenly their hearts shall tremble,
Thou wilt strike them with dismay;
And thy people,
Led by thee, shall win the day.

7 Then lead on, almighty victor,
Scatter ev'ry hostile band;
Be our guide, and our protector,
Till on Canaan's shores we stand:
Shouts of vict'ry
Then shall fill the promis'd land.

HYMN DCLXXXVI.

"*Behold the man!*"—JOHN xix. 5.

1 BEHOLD *the man!* how glorious he!
Before his foes he stands unaw'd,
And without wrong or blasphemy,
He claims equality with God.

2 *Behold the man!* by all condemn'd,
Assaulted by a host of foes;
His person and his claim contemn'd,
A man of suff'rings and of woes.

3 *Behold the man!* he stands alone,
His foes are ready to devour;
Not one of all his friends will own
Their Master in this trying hour.

4 *Behold the man!* though scorn'd below,
He bears the greatest name above;
The angels at his footstool bow,
And all his royal claims approve.

5 *Behold the man!* a pris'ner now,
And with transgressors doom'd to die;
A crown shall soon adorn his brow,
A crown of glory and of joy.

6 *Behold the man!* the world is his,
Yet who on earth so poor as he?
For others he submits to this,
For them he stoops to poverty.

7 *Behold the man!* he knew no sin,
Yet justice smites him with her sword;
He bears the stroke that else had been
The sinner's portion from the Lord.

8 *Behold the man!* so weak he seems,
His awful word inspires no fear;
But soon must he, who now blasphemes,
Before his judgment-seat appear.

9 *Behold the man!* a King he is,
His throne is built in heav'n above;
And there, the people who are his,
Shall see his face, and sing his love.

HYMN DCLXXXVII.

"Thus saith the Lord, I remember thee, the kindness of thy youth, the love of thine espousals."—JER. ii. 2.

1 O WHERE is now that glowing love
That mark'd our union with the Lord?
Our hearts were fix'd on things above,
Nor could the world a joy afford.

2 So strange did love like his appear,
That love that made him bear the cross,
No other subject pleas'd our ear,
The world for this appear'd but loss.

3 Where is the zeal that led us then
To make our Saviour's glory known;
That freed us from the fear of men,
And kept our eye on him alone?

4 Where are the happy seasons spent
In fellowship with him we lov'd?
The sacred joy, the sweet content,
The blessedness that then we prov'd?

5 To thee, our God, we own our sin,
Of thee we have forgetful prov'd;
As one who leaves her lord we've been,
As one unfaithful, though belov'd.

6 Behold, again we turn to thee;
O cast us not away, though vile!
No peace we have, no joy we see,
O Lord our God, but in thy smile.

7 And, oh! renew our former love;
Yea, let it never cease to grow,
Till, brighten'd and refin'd above,
A pure celestial flame it glow.

HYMN DCLXXXVIII.

"*Ho, every one that thirsteth!*"—ISAIAH lv. 1.

1 HO, ye thirsty! here's a spring,
Open'd by the King of heav'n;
Ye who nothing have to bring,
Here are waters freely giv'n:
Whither would you go? oh, whither?
Here's the spring of life; come hither.

2 Come, ye thirsty, here's the spring,
Whence the living waters flow;
Hear the message of a King,
Whither, whither would you go?
'Tis in Zion's sacred mountain
Men will find the living fountain.

3 Hearken, O ye sons of men!
Stop in time, O stop and think!
You will thirst, and thirst again,
While at other springs ye drink:
This alone is satisfying,
Everlasting life supplying.

HYMN DCLXXXIX.

"*Behold what manner of love the Father hath bestowed upon us.*"—1 JOHN iii. 1.

1 WHAT love is this the Father shows,
To us who once appear'd his foes;
That, spar'd so long, and now forgiv'n,
We should become the heirs of heav'n?

2 Our Father is not known on earth,
And any who derive their birth
From him, are like himself unknown:
The world will know and love its own.

3 We ask not for the world's applause,
The world that hates our Master's cause;
As *he* was, so we wish to be,
Not more esteem'd and lov'd than he.

4 The sons of God, our title here;
It does not, cannot yet appear
What God our Father will bestow
On those whom he adopts below.

5 But this we know, nor more is giv'n,
That when the Saviour comes from heav'n,
They shall be like him, who are his,
For they shall see him as he is.

6 They who from God derive their birth,
Cannot like others cleave to earth;
Their hope an influence imparts,
That warms and purifies their hearts.

HYMN DCXC.

"*Ask ye of the Lord rain.*"—ZECH. x. 1.

1 THE former and the latter rain
Was Isra'l's portion from the Lord;
Did he his gracious hand restrain,
No produce would the field afford.

2 'Twas thus the Lord his people shew'd
That all they had was from above;
That from himself their comforts flow'd,
And all depended on his love.

3 If he should have withheld his hand,
And first or last refused to give,
Their fields unfruitful would remain,
Their stores no harvest would receive.

4 'Tis still the same, his people now
Depend upon his care and love;
'Tis only then they live and grow,
When he supplies them from above.

5 Their fruitfulness on him depends;
The seed and culture are in vain,
Unless the rain of heav'n descends,
The former and the latter rain.

HYMN DCXCI.

"Who shall lay any thing to the charge of God's elect?"—
Rom. viii. 33.

1 WHO shall condemn the Lord's elect?
Or what their safety shall affect?
No matter who in judgment sits
On those whom God himself acquits.

2 His saints find favour in his eyes,
'Tis God himself that justifies;
He cancels ev'ry charge with blood,
His people they, himself their God.

3 Who shall condemn? 'tis Christ that died,
'Tis Christ our Lord was crucified;
Yea, rather, who is ris'n again,
His work, his off'ring not in vain:

4 Who even sits at God's right hand,
While wond'ring angels round him stand;
Who maketh intercession there,
For all his ransom'd people here.

5 What then shall part us from his love?
Shall aught below, or aught above?
Nay, since the Saviour died and rose,
His saints shall vanquish all their foes.

HYMN DCXCII.

"*The Lord is good.*"—NAHUM i. 7.

1 YES! "the Lord is good," I know it,
  I have prov'd it from my youth;
All his gracious dealings shew it,
  Shew the soul-reviving truth:
Though all others silent stood,
I must say "the Lord is good."

2 Long ere yet I had a being,
  He, to whom all things are known,
Knew what I should be, and seeing
  I should perish, left alone,
Then my soul with mercy view'd;
This declares "the Lord is good."

3 While I lived in mad defiance
  Of his pow'r who gave me breath,
Though my soul had made alliance,
  And was leagued with hell and death,
Yet his gracious purpose stood;
This declares "the Lord is good."

4 Since, thro' grace, I've learn'd to know him,
  What forbearance has he shewn!
I have been unfaithful to him,
  Yet his mercy is not gone;
What he bore, no other would;
'Tis a truth, "the Lord is good."

5 Of this truth I'm oft forgetful,
  And repine against his will;
Yes, my heart is most deceitful,
  Yet he spares and pardons still;
And in yonder blest abode,
I shall sing "the Lord is good."

HYMN DCXCIII.

"*For he knoweth our frame.*"—PSALM ciii. 14.

1 MY Father knows my feeble frame,
He knows how poor a worm I am,
Untold, he knows it all.
The least temptation serves to draw
My footsteps from my Father's law,
And make me slide and fall.

2 Of this I give him daily proof,
And yet he does not cast me off,
But owns me still as his;
He spares, he pities, he forgives
The most rebellious child that lives,
So great his patience is.

3 And shall I thence a pretext draw,
Again to violate his law?
My soul revolts at this:
I'll love, and wonder, and adore,
And beg that I may sin no more
Against such love as his.

4 O love divine! eternal source
Of good to man, I mark thy course,
I mark it with delight;
To Bethlehem I follow thee,
And there the wondrous babe I see,
A cheering, glorious sight.

5 I trace thee thence to Calvary,
And there the "man of sorrows" see,
His body bath'd in blood;
The stream I follow'd from its source
Now pours with a resistless force,
A rapid swelling flood.

6 Its waters health and healing bring,
They make the waste rejoice and sing,
Their progress thus we trace;
They pour their virtues through the earth,
They fill the world with sacred mirth,
And gladden ev'ry place.

HYMN DCXCIV.

"*Who hath believed our report?*"—ISAIAH liii. 1.

1 SAY, who they are who have believ'd
Th' offensive truth that God approves?
His testimony have receiv'd,
And own'd the character he loves.

2 In him mankind no beauty sees,
Whom God the Father sends and seals;
He has no charms the world to please,
In whom the Spirit fully dwells.

3 Messiah's claims are set at nought,
He lives rejected and contemn'd;
And when he dies, he then is thought
By justice and by truth condemn'd.

4 As *he* was once, *his Truth* is now,
Rejected and despis'd of men;
Loving or hating *that*, we shew
How we'd have view'd the Saviour then.

5 Who then are they who now believe
The truth that men revile and hate?
Who thence their peace and hope receive,
And for the Saviour's coming wait?

6 His people are, as he was here,
An object of contempt to men;
And when he shall again appear,
They shall be like their Master then.

HYMN DCXCV.

" *Casting all your care upon him.*"—1 Pet. v. 7.

1 THE privilege I greatly prize,
Of casting all my care on him,
The mighty God, the only wise,
Who reigns in heav'n and earth supreme.

2 How sweet to be allow'd to call
The God whom heav'n adores, my friend;
To tell my thoughts, to tell them all,
And then to know my pray'rs ascend!

3 Yes, they ascend; the feeblest cry
Has wings that bear it to his throne;
The pray'r of faith ascends the sky,
And brings a gracious answer down.

4 Then let me banish anxious care,
Confiding in a Father's love;
To him make known my wants in pray'r,
Prepar'd his answer to approve.

5 My Father's wisdom cannot err,
His love no change nor failure knows;
Be mine his counsel to prefer,
And acquiesce in all he does.

HYMN DCXCVI.

" *Hereby perceive we the love of God, because he laid down his life for us.*"—1 John iii. 16.

1 ETERNAL honour be to him,
Who sav'd us by his blood!
His love shall be our joyful theme,
The boundless love of God.

2 But few would die to save a friend,
He died to save his foes;
His love nor measure has, nor end,
'Tis such as no man knows.

3 No words can tell its depth or height,
No love can equal his;
The love of God is infinite,
Like God himself it is.

4 No sacrifice appear'd too great,
The love of God to prove;
And thence we learn to estimate
The greatness of his love.

5 Yet all we know is, that his love
Exceeds all others far;
How far, not all the hosts above
Are able to declare.

6 But what we know makes wealth, and fame,
And pleasure seem but loss;
And renders dear the glorious name
Of him who bore the cross.

HYMN DCXCVII.

"*And base things of the world . . . hath God chosen.*"—
1 Cor. i. 28.

1 I NEED not blush to own that he,
On whom my hope of heav'n is built,
Was crucified on yonder tree,
Since 'tis his blood that cancels guilt.

2 Nor need I blush to call him Lord,
Whom heav'n adores with all its hosts;
Yes, Jesus is by heav'n ador'd,
In him the brightest seraph boasts.

3 What, though the world no glory sees
In him my soul admires and loves,
I wonder not—how should he please
The man who of himself approves?

4 I too could boast of merit once,
And Jesus had no charms for me,
But all such claims I now renounce,
No merit but in him I see.

5 He is my refuge and my boast,
The LORD, my righteousness and strength:
Through whom, though now by tempests tost,
I hope to enter heav'n at length;

6 There to behold that glory near,
Which at a distance now I see;
And undisturb'd by pain or fear,
Repose throughout eternity.

HYMN DCXCVIII.

"*A friend of publicans and sinners.*"—MATT. xi. 19.

1 WE need not be asham'd to own
That he, on whom our hopes depend,
Though now he fills the highest throne,
Was styl'd on earth "the sinner's friend."

2 The title came from those who sought
To bring dishonour on his name;
But Jesus then refus'd it not,
Nor sought to vindicate his fame.

3 And now, though yonder throne is his,
He bears the gracious title still;
Jesus, "the friend of sinners" is,
He owns the charge, and ever will.

4 The title that was meant in scorn,
He takes and binds upon his brow;
And thus the guilty and forlorn
Are taught his character to know.

5 And while his name is set at nought,
By those who on their worth depend,
The wretched and the vile are taught,
To bless him as "the sinner's friend."

HYMN DCXCIX.

"*The heavens declare the glory of God.*"—PSALM xix. 1.

1 THE heav'ns declare thy glory, Lord!
The thousand worlds that meet our eyes
Sufficient evidence afford,
That thou art great, that thou art wise.

2 Who but the only wise could form
A world contriv'd with so much skill;
Or who but he, whose mighty arm
Could execute his sov'reign will?

3 But though the things we see around,
Thy wisdom and thy pow'r declare,
No argument can there be found,
To save a sinner from despair.

4 Not from thy works, but from thy *word*,
The soul-reviving news is known;
That pardon may with truth accord,
And mercy can to man be shewn.

5 When a few seasons have revolv'd,
The world will pass away, and then
The works thereof shall be dissolv'd,
And not a wreck or trace be seen.

6 Not so thy word, it stands secure;
The blessed truths that it contains
Eternal are, and shall endure
When nothing of the world remains.

7 And they who from thy word derive
Their hope, and are of thee forgiv'n,
The wreck of nature shall survive,
And find eternal life in heav'n.

HYMN DCC.

CHILDREN'S HYMN.

"*If these should hold their peace, the stones would immediately cry out.*"—Luke xix. 40.

1 CHILDREN once were heard to sing,
When so many silent were;
Glad they welcom'd Isra'l's King,
And hosannas fill'd the air.

2 David's Son, and David's Lord,
Heard their praises, and approv'd:
Be our Saviour's grace ador'd;
Be our Saviour's name belov'd.

3 Count us not, O Lord, too bold,
If we try our song to raise;
Children we, like those of old,
Taught, like them, to lisp thy praise.

4 Jesus, hail! we sing of thee;
Welcome to thine house of pray'r:
Let our hearts thy temple be;
Lord, set up thy kingdom there.

5 Make us wise, thy name to know;
Let us feel thy pow'r and love:
Ours to serve thee, Lord, below;
And to dwell with thee above:

6 There to sing hosannas loud;
There a Saviour's praise to sing;
Mix with yonder joyful crowd,
And for ever praise our King.

HYMN DCCI.

ANOTHER CHILDREN'S HYMN.

"*Hosanna to the Son of David.*"—MATT. xxi. 9.

1 WHEN Jesus to the temple came,
The voice of praise was heard;
The very children own'd his claim,
And in his train appear'd.

2 Hosannas made the temple ring,
For many tongues agreed;
Hosanna to the heav'nly King,
To David's holy seed.

3 When some would have rebuk'd their zeal,
Thou, Lord, the thought didst check:
If they were harden'd, stones would feel;
If silent, stones would speak.

4 Lord, let the days be now renew'd,
When children lisp thy praise;
Thou art as powerful and good,
As in the former days.

5 Work, Lord, on all our children's hearts,
And this will loose their tongues;
The love that heav'nly truth imparts
Will animate their songs.

HYMN DCCII.

"And they cried out all at once, saying, Away with this man."—LUKE xxiii. 18.

1 "AWAY with him," the people cry,
Ten thousand voices raised on high,
His instant death demand;
In vain a heathen would restrain
Their impious rage; his voice is vain,
And their decree must stand.

2 Are these the people, who but now
Appeared as forward to allow
The Saviour's royal claim?
Who fill'd the city with their cry,
And rais'd triumphant songs of joy,
In honour of his name?

3 How much, and O how quickly chang'd!
How suddenly from him estrang'd,
Whom lately they extoll'd!
Before, they rais'd him to the sky;
They now require that he should die,
With fury uncontroll'd.

4 And yet not chang'd, but still the same;
A splendid work had rais'd his fame,
And led them to suppose
That he would now erect his throne,
And make a conquer'd world his own,
Thence came their joy arose.

5 But when they see their hope is vain,
They join the Saviour's foes again,
(Their minds unalter'd stood:)
They scorn'd his blessed name before,
But, disappointed, scorn it more,
And clamour for his blood.

HYMN DCCIII.

"*Without shedding of blood is no remission.*"—HEB. ix. 22.

1 LIFE for life, or no remission,
  Thus the Lord proclaims from heav'n;
Blood must flow—on this condition,
  This alone, is sin forgiv'n:
Yes, a victim must be slain,
Else, all hope of life is vain.

2 But the victim, who shall find it,
  Such a one as sinners need?
To the altar, who shall bind it?
  Who shall make the victim bleed?
Questions these, of anxious thought,
And with difficulty fraught.

3 Though the beasts around us feeding
  On a thousand hills, were slain,
What would this avail? their bleeding
  What avert, or what obtain?
Such a victim as must die,
All the world could not supply.

4 God himself provides the victim,
  Jesus is the Lamb of God;
Heav'n, and earth, and hell afflict him,
  While he bears the sinner's load:
'Tis his blood, his blood alone,
Can for human guilt atone.

5 Joyful truth, he bore transgression,
  In his body on the cross;
Through his blood, there's full remission
  For the vilest, ev'n for us:
Jesus for the sinner bleeds,
Nothing more the sinner needs.

HYMN DCCIV.

"*The wages of sin is death.*"—ROM. vi. 23.

1 DEATH is sin's tremendous wages,
This we never should forget;
'Tis the Lord himself engages
To discharge the awful debt:
Sin and death together go,
Truth requires it should be so.

2 Awful tidings! who can shew us
How a sinner yet may live?
How can God be gracious to us?
How can God our sin forgive,
Yet invariably declare
Sin and death united are?

3 Come, behold a great expedient,
God reveal'd in flesh appears,
God himself becomes obedient,
And the curse for sinners bears;
'Tis a great, a gracious plan,
Wounding sin, yet sparing man.

4 O the wisdom of contrivance,
O the grace that shines therein!
God forgives without connivance,
He forgives, yet spares not sin;
Justice sees the victim bleed,
Nothing more can justice need.

5 Whither should we go, oh! whither,
Whither from the glorious sight?
Truth and mercy meet together!
Righteousness and peace unite:
'Tis the cross that gives us rest,
Makes us safe, and makes us blest.

HYMN DCCV.

"For ye know the grace of our Lord Jesus Christ."—
2 Cor. viii. 9.

1 YES, we know the grace of Jesus,
All his people know his grace;
'Tis a theme that always pleases
Those in whom the truth has place:
Never can his friends admit
Aught that would detract from it.

2 Jesus saw the sinner's danger,
Saw from heav'n, and stoop'd to save;
In the world appear'd a stranger,
And his life for sinners gave:
Come, ye saints, behold and see,
Who so rich, so poor as he.

3 Grace like this delights, amazes,
Grace unbounded, grace divine;
Lord, accept our feeble praises,
For we know this grace is thine:
Thou wast poor, that we might be
Rich in glory, Lord, with thee.

4 Yes, our Lord was rich in glory,
Yet he stoop'd, and bore the cross;
Tell, ye saints, the joyful story,
Tell how poor the Saviour was;
If ye can, declare how low
Jesus stoop'd to rescue you.

5 Jesus, without controversy,
Is the God that reigns above;
Source alone of sov'reign mercy,
God of everlasting love;
This is he who came from heav'n,
He whose life for men was giv'n.

HYMN DCCVI.

"*Therefore the world knoweth us not.*"—1 John iii. 1.

1 UNKNOWN by men, the Christian lives;
Enough, if he is known above,
By him who all his sin forgives,
And loves him with a father's love.

2 To know him, and be known again,
Is all he seeks; he asks no more;
And should he feel the scorn of men,
'Tis what his Master felt before.

3 The mark of universal scorn
His Master stood, nor hid his face;
Like one deserted and forlorn
He seem'd: by all accounted base.

4 The liker to their Master here,
The more abundant joy they prove:
A joy, though not unmix'd with fear,
Yet full of sweetness, full of love.

5 Then make us like thyself, O Lord;
As thou wert, let thy people be:
We look above for our reward;
We look to reign in heav'n with thee.

HYMN DCCVII.

"*I wot that he whom thou blessest is blessed.*"—Numb. xxii. 6.

1 THE stream that from the fountain flows,
The fountain of eternal love,
Imparts its virtue as it goes;
A gift all other gifts above.
'Tis life and peace divinely giv'n,
'Tis mercy coming down from heav'n.

2 How blessed to enjoy the gift,
  To taste of mercy here below;
In humble thankfulness to lift
  Our hearts to him who saves us so!
To know his love, how great it is,
To own and feel that we are his.

3 How blessed is the hope of good,
  The good that without measure is,
Of seeing him who shed his blood
  To save us, and to make us his!
Redeem'd by blood, and sav'd by grace,
We look to see the Saviour's face.

4 We look to see him as he is;
  This honour to his saints is giv'n.
To see the glory that was his,
  Before the world began, in heav'n;
To see his face, to share his throne,
And give the praise to him alone.

HYMN DCCVIII.

"*Out of the depths have I cried unto thee, O Lord.*"—
PSALM CXXX. 1.

1 TO whom should those in trouble flee?
  To whom, O Lord, but unto thee?
For thou alone canst soothe our grief,
And thou alone canst give relief.

2 When in the lowest depths we are,
When all is grief, and all is care,
We cry to thee, and not in vain;
A word of thine relieves our pain.

3 'Tis sweet to be assur'd of this,
To taste the comfort sweeter is;
But sweeter far, to reach the shore,
Where grief and trouble are no more.

4 To see the object of our love
Enthron'd in majesty above;
To see the angels own his claim;
To hear the angels sound his name.

5 We look, not without hope, for this;
For all is ours, if we are his:
The Lord will "grace and glory" give;
His people shall for ever live.

6 Yes, the delight of heav'n is theirs;
From sorrow free, aud free from cares;
No conflicts there, no toil, no strife,
A blessed and immortal life.

HYMN DCCIX.

"*Unto thee, O Lord, will I sing.*"—Psalm ci. 1.

1 SEE our foes before us driv'n;
Sing we to the God of heav'n;
Sing of grace, of sin forgiv'n;
Sing a Saviour's love.

2 'Tis a theme of boundless range;
Love it is that knows no change;
Love surpassing thought, and strange;
Others far above.

3 Spread abroad the "joyful sound,"
Make it known to all around;
'n the truth a joy is found,
One they know not of.

HYMN DCCX.

"*That ye sorrow not, even as others.*"—1 Thess. iv. 13.

1 WHY weep for the dead?
He rests on his bed,
Till the day when the trumpet shall sound.
That voice he shall hear,
And shall then re-appear,
Wherever his grave may be found.

2 The voice of the Lord;
His powerful word,
Shall awaken the dead in that day,
And they who have wept,
Who in Jesus have slept,
No more shall complain of delay.

3 Now time has expir'd;
The day they desir'd,
Is come to rejoice them at last.
The veil is remov'd,
And the Lord, whom they lov'd,
Now makes them amends for the past.

4 Why weep for the dead?
In Jesus his head,
His life is for ever secure.
The promise is giv'n,
The pillars of heav'n
Are not than the promise more sure.

5 Why weep for the dead?
His spirit has fled;
But his true life in Jesus is found.
His race he has run;
The prize he has won;
Rejoice that a brother is crown'd.

6 Let us who survive,
Who still have to strive
With the foe, and the fight to maintain,
Invoking the Lord,
And strong in his word,
Press forward the blessing to gain.

HYMN DCCXI.

"*The city of the great King.*"—PSALM xlviii. 2.

1 "BEAUTIFUL for situation,"
And the joy of all the earth,
Zion is; the favour'd nation
Worships there—and there no dearth
Ever is of what is good;
Zion is the saints' abode.

2 Foes of Zion, walk around her,
See what strong defence is hers;
God her builder is and founder,
'Tis the spot that he prefers.
'Tis the spot in all the world,
Where his banner is unfurl'd.

3 Glorious things are spoken of thee,
Zion, dwelling-place of God:
They shall prosper, they that love thee,
But thy foes shall feel the rod.
Feel his rod who dwells in thee,
And their fall shall fearful be.

4 But thy time shall be for ever,
Stable thy foundations are;
Never shalt thou fail, no, never,
Zion is Jehovah's care;
All around is doom'd to fall,
Zion shall survive it all.

HYMN DCCXII.

"*Mighty to save.*"—Isaiah lxiii. 1.

1 MIGHTY is the arm that saves us,
Who is he can tell its pow'r?
Why then fear the foe that braves us,
As if "ready to devour?"
Should we faint, or be dishearten'd?
Shall we to the foe give way?
When the Saviour's arm is shorten'd,
Then, and not till then, we may.

2 Mighty is his arm, we know it;
Yes, his arm is cloth'd with might;
Many are the proofs that shew it,
His the day, and his the night.
His the earth and heav'ns; the wonders
That we see around are his.
His the lightning and the thunders:
This, and more than this, is his.

3 Mighty is his arm, we prove it,
When our burthen heavy is;
Who is able to remove it?
Is there any pow'r but his?
When our foes in arms assemble,
Thinking to prevail in fight:
Who is he that makes them tremble?
Who puts all our foes to flight?

4 Blessed be his name for ever,
Might and majesty are his;
Nothing from his love can sever
Those he claims and owns as his.
'Tis our privilege to know him,
Ev'ry day our tribute bring:
Own how great a debt we owe him,
And his praise for ever sing.

HYMN DCCXIII.

"*Having obtained a good report through faith.*"—HEB. xi. 39.

1 THOUSANDS have, from age to age,
Put their trust in thee, O Lord;
Both the simple and the sage
Have rejoic'd to find thy word:
Sweeter is its taste than honey,
And its price is more than money.

2 Much they suffer'd, Lord, for thee,
From the world that knew thee not;
For the world could nothing see,
Nothing blessed in their lot.
Hence the world their claim derided,
And with Satan ever sided.

3 Much they suffer'd for thy sake,
But they bore it, nor complain'd;
In the prison, at the stake,
True and valiant they remain'd:
Ev'ry loss for thee enduring,
Losing all, yet all securing.

4 O may I and others still,
Who profess to know thy name,
Prove obedient to thy will,
Whether men approve or blame:
In thy strength alone confiding,
Faithful unto death abiding.

HYMN DCCXIV.

"*The name of the Lord is a strong tower.*"—PROV. xviii. 10.

1 'TIS sweet to know the sacred name
Of him who bore the cross for us;
Who suffer'd pain, and grief, and shame,
In love to man he suffer'd thus.

2 'Tis sweet to know the sacred name,
Of him whom truth declares to be,
To-day as yesterday, "the same,"
"The same" throughout eternity.

3 How wonderful is he! how great!
Who neither change nor weakness knows;
His people have a sure retreat,
He keeps them safe from all their foes.

4 They hide themselves behind his pow'r,
And thence look round upon their foes;
They fail not in the trying hour,
For God is with them to the close.

5 And when the final day is come,
When heav'n and earth have pass'd away,
The Lord will take his people home,
And oh! what joy is theirs that day

HYMN DCCXV.

"*Declare plainly that they seek a country.*"—HEB. xi. 14.

1 THUS far upon our way we're come,
The farther on, the nearer home;
Sweet home! the home so dear to all
Whom God has call'd, or yet shall call.

2 The children of one Father they,
One Lord they own, one faith, one way;
Redeem'd with blood, and sav'd by grace,
In heav'n they see the Saviour's face.

3 Where all the heav'n-born children meet,
My home is there; and O how sweet
To join them where the Saviour is,
And live in heaven with him and his!

4 But often (to my shame I speak)
In worldly good my rest I seek:
I then lose sight of things to come,
No longer then I love my home.

5 Forgive my sin, O Lord, forgive,
And suffer even me to live;
Then make me what I ought to be,
Devoted wholly, Lord, to thee.

6 Let thoughts of home be always sweet,
That home where all thy children meet:
The goodly company above,
Of saints made perfect there in love.

HYMN DCCXVI.

"*He kept him as the apple of his eye.*"—DEUT. xxxii. 10.

1 AS the apple of his eye,
So the Lord his people keeps;
Ever gracious, ever nigh,
Never slumbers he, nor sleeps.
O how blest his people are!
Objects of his love and care.

2 Ye who serve another god,
Tell us, is your "rock" like ours?
In the fire, and in the flood,
Saves he, and from hostile pow'rs?
Can he cheer the heart, when sad?
Can he make his people glad?

3 Happy they whose God he is,
He who reigns in earth and heav'n:
Happy whom he owns as his,
They to whom this grace is giv'n:
They alone on earth are blest,
But in heav'n they find their rest.

HYMN DCCXVII.

"*By the grace of God I am what I am.*"—1 Cor. xv. 10.

1 MINE was a hopeless case,
'Twas hopeless, but for grace;
I thought myself accurst,
But when I fear'd the worst,
'Twas then the Saviour shew'd his face,
'Twas then I saw the worth of grace.

2 I live by grace alone,
Take that, and all is gone:
'Twas this reliev'd my pain,
'Twas this that broke my chain:
'Twas grace that made me whole, if whole,
And out of pris'n brought my soul.

3 No wonder grace should be
Thus dear to one like me;
No wonder I should dwell
On what I love so well:
For who can say how much I owe,
To what I'm taught to value so?

4 Nor less do I esteem,
Nor *now* less needful deem,
This grace, than in the hour,
When first I felt its pow'r:
'Twas precious then, 'tis precious still,
Its worth I more than ever feel.

5 And when the end is near,
'Twill take away my fear:
The Saviour's grace, that day,
Will be my hope and stay;
No wonder, then, if grace I deem,
Of themes that are, the sweetest theme.

HYMN DCCXVIII.

"*Broken cisterns.*" – JER. ii. 13.

1 YE who have the fount forsaken,
Whence the living waters flow:
Be not, oh, be not mistaken,
Nothing good from this can grow.
Broken cisterns
Empty are, and must be so.

2 Here's a fountain full of blessing,
God himself the fountain is;
In his love all good possessing,
They are blessēd who are his:
Here's a fountain:
All who will may drink of this.

3 Sinner! what infatuation
Binds thee, that thou canst not move?
Mercy woos thee to salvation,
But entreaties fruitless prove.
Art thou proof, then,
Proof against a Saviour's love?

4 In the day of visitation,
Can thine heart, O man, endure?
In the coming desolation,
Canst thou make thy dwelling sure?
And, though threaten'd,
Dost thou think thyself secure?

5 Let a fellow-man remind thee
Of the coming judgment day;
Should the judge of all then find thee
Walking still in error's way:
O bethink thee!
Who will then thy ransom pay?

HYMN DCCXIX.

"*As Christ also loved the church.*"—EPH. v. 25.

1 JESUS leaves his throne of glory,
Leaves it, and comes down to earth;
Sinners, hear the wondrous story,
Joyful news—the Saviour's birth.
What but love could bring him *here*?
His the name to sinners dear.

2 His is love, all thought too high for,
Angels cannot reach its height;
Saints, 'twas you he came to die for,
You he clothes in robes of white,
You he washes with his blood,
Makes you "kings and priests to God."

3 "Life for life"—'tis justice claims it,
Life for life is freely giv'n:
Awful stroke! 'tis justice aims it,
And he falls, "the Lord from heav'n;"
Dies a victim, on the tree;
Dies, O sinner, dies for thee.

4 *Here* discordant things agreeing,
Meet in blessed harmony;
Sinners to this refuge fleeing,
Are from guilt and terror free:
Justice here and grace unite,
'Tis a joyful, wondrous sight.

5 Here we should abide for ever,
Loving and admiring too;
Keep thy servants, Lord, and never
Let us say, or let us do
Ought displeasing in thy sight,
Ought that will not bear the light.

HYMN DCCXX.

"*Be strong in the Lord.*"—Eph. vi. 10.

1 THE Lord is my strength,
This lesson at length
I have learn'd, though so slow to receive it.
Though taught in the word,
I deem'd it absurd,
But now do I know and believe it.

2 How foolish are we!
How little we see,
That the strength we require from above is:
In conflict with sin,
Without or within,
The sinner unable to move is.

3 But good is the word,
That comes from the Lord,
That bids us lay hold of his power;
'Tis blessed to know,
Since strong is the foe,
The Lord is our strength and our tower.

4 This, then, is his word,
"Be strong in the Lord,"
His truth and his promise secure us:
Whoever assails,
His word never fails,
And this is enough to assure us.

5 With this as our stay,
We go on our way,
Rejoicing in full expectation:
That when he appears,
He'll dry up our tears,
And give us "eternal salvation."

HYMN DCCXXI.

"*Suffered for sins, the just for the unjust.*"—1 Pet. iii. 18.

1 I HAVE sinn'd, but thou hast suffer'd,
Thou hast suffer'd, Lord, for sin:
Thou art, Lord, the victim offer'd,
And by thee we enter in:
Enter into favour here,
And at length in heav'n appear.

2 This affords me consolation,
All that I, a sinner, have;
'Tis thy love, thy free salvation,
'Tis thy grace, and pow'r to save.
These are themes that make me glad,
Silent otherwise, and sad.

3 Thee, O Lord, I love to think of,
Good it is to think of thee.
When I stood upon the brink of
Ruin, thou didst think of me.
When all other doors were clos'd,
Then thy mercy interpos'd.

4 Now I look, through grace, to see thee,
As thou art, in heav'n above;
Time there was, when I would flee thee,
When I valued not thy love.
But for grace, 'twould be so still,
Grace alone could change my will.

5 Thou hast done it; praise I give thee,
But what shame belongs to me!
Saviour, let me cease to grieve thee,
Let me not unthankful be.
Take this evil heart of mine,
Take it, Lord, and make it thine.

HYMN DCCXXII.

"Who died for us."—1 Thess. v. 10.

1 JESUS died, he died to save us,
Wonder, O ye heav'ns, at this;
Wonder at the proof he gave us,
Proof of love, such love as his.
Fous its object,
Wondrous in our eyes it is

2 Well it may be, 'tis the wonder
Of the thousands round his throne;
He whose voice is heard in thunder,
He who reigns in heav'n alone:
Leaves his glory,
Comes to earth, and is not known.

3 Comes to die, the Lord of glory,
Comes to die, O think of this!
Ye who know it, tell the story,
Keep not back this love of his.
Spread the tidings:
This his people's business is.

4 Tell it to the world around you,
Tell the love of God to man:
Tell them of the love that found you,
Mention make of mercy's plan.
'Tis what sinners
May enjoy, but cannot scan.

5 Strange it is, and full of wonder,
Love's unfathom'd mystery;
That which sin had rent asunder,
Reunited here we see;
Praise the Saviour,
Who has caus'd it thus to be.

HYMN DCCXXIII.

"*Passeth knowledge.*"—Eph. iii. 19.

1 'TIS strange, 'tis passing strange, the love
That brought the Saviour from above,
And made him die for man.
No other subject equals this,
Too deep, too high, too large it is,
For human thought to scan.

2 But though to know this love aright,
Its breadth, its length, its depth, its height,
Is far beyond our pow'r,
Enough is told to make us blest,
To give us peace, to give us rest,
Until the final hour.

3 The Lord will then descend from heav'n,
And to his people will be giv'n,
A joy all joys above.
With eyes immortal they shall see,
With him for ever they shall be,
Whom now, unseen, they love.

4 The prospect bright and cheering is,
And they are blest he owns as his.
Then keep, O keep us, Lord!
Uphold our steps, nor let them slide;
And let us in the truth abide,
According to thy word.

5 His people, in their place above,
Will better know the Saviour's love,
And on his glory gaze.
But 'tis eternity alone
Will make his love be fully known:
His love no measure has.

HYMN DCCXXIV.

"*Endured the cross, despising the shame.*"—HEB. xii. 2.

1 MUCH I love the honour'd name
Of "the man" who bore the cross;
Bore its weight, and bore its shame,
Treasure this, the rest is dross.

2 Here I find the thing I want,
Pardon, peace, and hope of heav'n;
This I have by royal grant,
And the rest will soon be giv'n.

3 Hope will shortly cease to be,
When the promis'd joy is giv'n;
When the Lord himself I see,
Seated on the throne of heav'n.

4 Yet the question will intrude,
Shall I see the Saviour's face?
Will he not from heav'n exclude
One so barren and so base?

5 Lord, I turn my eyes to thee,
Source and channel, too, of grace;
And I look, thy face to see,
Though so barren and so base.

6 Limits thou hast added none,
To the grace thy word reveals:
Here I rest my hope alone,
And my spirit comfort feels.

7 When upon myself I think,
Then, like Peter on the sea,
I begin to fear and sink,
Till I turn my eyes to thee.

8 'Tis thine arm alone can save;
And the man who trusts in thee,
On the land, or on the wave,
Safe and blest is sure to be.

HYMN DCCXXV.

"*Woman, why weepest thou?*"—JOHN XX. 15.

1 WEEP no more, ye saints, why should ye?
If ye do, for others weep:
Would ye ask for more, or could ye?
Will not God his promise keep?
Life eternal Jesus gives,
Ye shall live, because he lives.

2 Weep no more, ye saints, bethink ye
That the Saviour is at hand;
Of his spirit deeply drink ye,
'Tis his will, and his command:
This it is will calm your fears,
This it is will dry your tears.

3 Weep no more, ye saints; the morning
Dawns, and day comes on apace;
What is hatred? what is scorning?
What to be accounted base?
Saints should never shun the cross,
Though it brings them shame and loss.

4 Weep no more, ye saints, but gladly
Look to the approaching day:
Saints should not complain, or sadly
Think of ills that pass away:
Hark! the final trumpet sounds,
Grief has vanish'd, joy abounds.

HYMN DCXXXVI.

"Say unto my soul, I am thy salvation."—Psalm xxxv. 3.

1 "SINNER, I am thy salvation,"
[illegible]
Sweet, and full of consolation,
Are these words of thine, O Lord.

2 Hearing words like these, I wonder:
Words so far our thoughts above:
When we might expect the thunder,
'Tis the "still small voice" of love.

3 He to whom these words are spoken,
All things has. I'm sure of this.
Other promises are broken,
But this promise faithful is.

4 Saviour, speak these words with power,
To my soul, and make me glad:
If thou art my shield and tower,
Who or what can make me sad?

5 'Tis to those alone who fear thee,
That "thy secret," Lord, is known:
They who live in spirit near thee,
Know thy voice, and they alone.

HYMN DCXXXVII.

CHILDREN'S HYMN.

"Out of the mouth of babes and sucklings thou hast perfected praise."—Matt. xxi. 16.

1 WHEN the teachers of the law
In the Saviour nothing saw,
Nothing that they wanted,
Children saw what they did not:
Children, by the Spirit taught,
Loud hosannas chanted.

2 Thus the saying was fulfill'd,
Thus was "the avenger still'd,"
When, with hearts undaunted,
Children round the Saviour flock'd,
And while "elders" rudely mock'd,
Loud hosannas chaunted.

3 Thus did they, who wise were thought,
Fail to find ("their own the fault")
What to babes was granted.
And the Lord made known his pow'r,
When the children, in that hour,
Loud hosannas chaunted.

HYMN DCCXXVIII.

"*Cast thy burden upon the Lord.*"—PSALM lv. 22.

1 ON the Lord thy burden cast,
Whatsoever grief thou hast:
Make it to the Saviour known,
Trust in him, and him alone.

2 Be thy troubles great or small,
Few or many, bring them all;
Bring the whole to him who bears
All his people's griefs and cares.

3 In the time of deep distress,
When thy troubles sorely press:
Thou art tempted then to think
That the Lord will let thee sink.

4 Think it not—this cannot be,
Stand thou still, O man, and see
God's salvation, come it will,
Trust in him, and be thou still

5 Painful it may be to wait,
But it cannot come too late;
God's appointed time is best,
They who wait for him are blest.

6 "Hope deferr'd," is grief and pain,
But the end is solid gain;
When it comes, O man, to thee,
"As a tree of life" 'twill be.

HYMN DCCXXIX.

"He divided the sea, and caused them to pass through."—
PSALM lxxviii. 13.

1 ISRAEL dryshod pass'd the flood,
While the waves on either side,
Like a rampart, upright stood,
Keeping off the pressing tide.
Nature bow'd to Israel's God,
When his servant wav'd his rod.

2 Then when Israel, safe from harm,
Stood upon the further shore,
Did the prophet raise his arm,
And he wav'd his rod once more.
Suddenly the chasm is fill'd,
And the hostile shout is still'd.

3 Where he lately pass'd on foot,
There he saw the mighty foe
Check'd and stay'd in his pursuit:
Little thought he 'twould be so.
There he saw him swallow'd up,
Draining thus the bitter cup.

4 Israel well might think of this,
But he did not: strange to say.
Israel, prone to do amiss,
From Jehovah went astray.
To the idol Israel bow'd,
Israel, foolish, weak and proud.

5 Yet have we no right to blame
Israel for his wicked thought;
'Tis with us, alas! the same,
To the idol we have sought.
We have had our golden calf,
And, like him, have fed on chaff.

6 Saviour, all our sin forgive;
Take the idol-love away.
To thy glory let us live;
Let us do so from this day.
Let us cease to "walk as men:"
Happy then, and only then.

HYMN DCCXXX.

"*Having made peace through the blood of his cross.*"—
COL. i. 20.

1 WHAT should keep me from the cross?
Emblem it of peace procured:
Peace with God: all else is loss;
Let me be of this assur'd.
Peace with God includes the rest,
Be it mine, and I am blest.

2 This includes atonement made,
Full atonement made for sin.
Yes, the debt, the debt is paid,
Sinners now may enter in.
That which barr'd their way before,
Bars it, joyful news! no more.

2 The Lord is my help and my shield;
The truth and the blessing is here;
Who have it, ought never to yield
To sloth, or to doubt, or to fear.
Enough there is in it to give,
In time of the greatest alarms,
A peace that no mind can conceive,
Save his whom it cheers and it arms.

3 The Lord is my help and my shield,
Then why this misgiving within,
As though I should finally yield,
And own the dominion of sin,
Forsaking the Lord, whom I love,
And serving another, abhorr'd?
O thou who art ruler above,
Forbid it, forbid it, O Lord!

4 His only, his only I am,
Who laid down his life for my sake;
Allegiance is due to the same,
Allegiance that nothing can shake:
No, nothing, with boldness I say.
If God be "my help and my shield,"
'Tis this that gives strength for the day,
'Tis this that forbids us to yield.

5 Yet still I am not without fear,
Lest all that I prize should be lost,
For trials await us while here,
As many have found to their cost.
To thee, Lord, my case I commit,
Thy strength and thy blessing impart.
Do with me as thou seest fit;
But give me a place where thou art.

HYMN DCCXXXIII.

"*When the enemy shall come in like a flood.*"—Isaiah lix. 19.

1 YES, a call there is,
One that must be heard;
For the call is his,
His who should be fear'd.
'Tis a call for fruit,
Fruit of faith and love,
And, beyond dispute,
Coming from above.

2 'Tis a call to be
Valiant for the truth;
'Tis to you, to me,
'Tis to age, to youth.
He that hath an ear,
Let him hear, and do.
Nothing need we fear,
For the Lord is true.

3 When the foe comes in,
Flood-like, and defies:
When the man of sin
Fills the world with lies;
When he claims it all,
And asserts his claim,
Is there not a call
To defeat his aim?

4 How resist his claim?
Think we well of this.
How defeat his aim?
This the question is.
'Tis by faith and pray'r,
By the Spirit's sword;
These the weapons are,
Furnish'd by the Lord.

5 These it was, we know,
Some three ages past,
Smote our mortal foe,
And he stood aghast;
Caus'd his heart to quail,
And his knees to shake.
These will never fail,
Why then others take?

HYMN DCCXXXIV.

"*Thy way, O Lord, is in the sea.*"—PSALM lxxvii. 19.

1 "THY way, O Lord, is in the sea,"
"Thy footsteps are not known."
How foolish and how weak are we!
And thou art great alone.

2 All things that are, or great or small,
Their being have from thee;
Thy work they are—thou mad'st them all,
Or else they could not be.

3 How happy, Lord, thy people are,
Possessing all in thee!
A portion theirs, surpassing far
The things we hear and see.

4 The future only will disclose
Thy people's blessedness,
The perfect blessedness of those
Who here thy name confess.

5 For them thou hast reserv'd a place,
Not distant from thy throne:
For them, the heirs of sov'reign grace,
Of sov'reign grace alone.

6 Then welcome be the promis'd day,
  When Jesus comes again;
For this we look, and well we may:
  His people triumph then.

HYMN DCCXXXV.

"*And having spoiled principalities and powers, he made a show of them openly.*"—COL. ii. 15.

1 THE final struggle has begun,
  The war 'twixt light and darkness is;
All other strife beneath the sun
  Is nothing worth, compar'd to this.
Shall Satan hold or yield his pow'r?
All rests upon this fearful hour.

2 'Tis passing strange, yet so it is,
  That one of those whom God has made,
Should be at war with him and his,
  At open war, nor be afraid
To bide the issue of the day:
This moves our wonder—well it may.

3 That he who made this world, has been
  Supplanted by the evil one,
No proof requires but what is seen,
  And what is heard, and what is done.
Go where we may, or here or there,
We find the idol everywhere.

4 The few who serve the God of heav'n,
  That made the world, and all therein,
Were once to idol-worship giv'n,
  And they were then the slaves of sin.
The evil one their master was,
But now they keep the Saviour's laws.

5 The time is coming, when our King
Will trample on the rebel bands.
The hills and valleys then shall ring,
And all the trees shall clap their hands,
For joy that God the Saviour reigns,
And all his pow'r on earth regains.

6 The Lord may in that day explain
What now to us mysterious is:
Why Satan was allow'd to reign,
To seize this world, and make it his?
And why he should refuse to yield,
And dare his Maker to the field?

7 The Lord will conquer. Must he not?
Who can resist Omnipotence?
This truth the foe will soon be taught:
Against the Lord there's no defence.
His house will soon a ruin be;
One comes, that stronger is than he.

8 'Tis not the pow'r of force, but love;
'Tis truth victorious over sin.
Her weapons temper'd are above;
The mortal warfare is within.
'Tis thus that Satan vanquish'd is,
And yields the throne that now is his.

9 How great is he, surpassing great,
Who, by the power of his word,
Drives the usurper from his seat!
'Tis David's Son, and David's Lord.
'Tis he who casts the tyrant down,
Who wins, and who deserves the crown.

10 For this it was that evil came,
And was allow'd to enter in,
That God might glorify his name;
That he might "make an end of sin;"
That "grace thro' righteousness might reign,"
And saints eternal life might gain.

11 A glorious day not distant is,
When that which here mysterious seem'd,
Will be explained; when he and his,
Redeemer he, and they redeem'd,
Shall stand before a wond'ring world,
And foes be into darkness hurl'd.

HYMN DCCXXXVI.

"*Thou knowest not what a day may bring forth.*"—
PROV. xxvii. 1.

1 IN this world of sorrow,
Who can tell to-day,
What will be to-morrow?
Here we lose our way.
When we try to know it,
All is dark as night;
He alone can shew it,
Who himself is light.

2 Of the future he can
Tell the whole before;
Of the present we can
Speak, but nothing more.
Yet of what to come is,
Much the Lord has told;
And his word of promise
Cheer'd his saints of old.

3 Looking to a season
Distant yet, they smil'd;
Cheer'd, not without reason:
For a wondrous child
Promis'd was, who should be
To the world its light;
What more blessēd could be?
Day 'twas, after night.

4 Still the Lord discloses
Much of things to come,
And in mercy shews us
Of our future home;
But for this we should be
"Cleaving to the dust."
So with us it would be,
So it would, and must.

5 'Tis the hope of what will
Be, when time is past,
Keeps us now, and *that* will
Keep us to the last.
That it is that charms us,
From a world of sense,
That for conflict arms us,
Else without defence.

6 'Tis the hope of being
With the Lord above;
'Tis the hope of seeing
Him we trust and love:
This it is that gives us
Courage for the fight,
And, when faint, relieves us,
Else we "have no might."

7 What, then, though we know not
  What to-morrow brings?
Better that we do not,
  These are "secret things."
Is it not enough for
  Those who know the Lord?
Should they have to suffer,
  He will strength afford.

8 He will give to-morrow,
  What to-morrow needs;
Then away with sorrow,
  Wise are all his deeds.
Has he ever fail'd us,
  In the time of need?
When the foe assail'd us,
  Then our "sun and shield."

HYMN DCCXXXVII.

"And when they had platted a crown of thorns, they put it upon his head."—MATT. xxvii. 29.

1 'TWAS a crown of thorns he wore,
  A befitting diadem.
Gold and gems are dust—no more;
  What had he to do with them?
While the crown of gold he scorns,
He accepts the crown of thorns.

2 Thus, with taunts and ridicule,
  Were the Saviour's claims disown'd;
But his day will come to rule.
  All shall see him then enthron'd;
But the scorner, where is he?
Will he then a scorner be?

3 When the "Son of Man" appears
In the clouds, and fills his throne,
What will cries avail, or tears?
Justice then presides alone.
He that then unpardon'd is,
Pardon never can be his.

4 O ye scornful men, beware!
There's a time of wrath at hand.
Terror then, and wild despair
Will invade the scornful band.
Fool he is, who trusts in lies:
Now or never, be ye wise.

HYMN DCCXXXVIII.

"*The seven heads are seven mountains, on which the woman sitteth.*"—Rev. xvii. 9.

1 CITY of the seven hills!
Thou art doom'd, and fall thou wilt.
Thus it is, for so he wills,
He who knows, and weighs thy guilt.
He, the Holy One and just,
He will lay thee in the dust.

2 Thou hast fought against the Lord,
Thou hast shed his people's blood.
Ruin comes—thy just reward,
Rushing like a mighty flood;
All-destroying in its course,
Nothing can withstand its force.

3 City of the seven hills!
Know thou that thy day is nigh.
He that takes the sword, and kills,
By the sword himself will die.
Righteous retribution this,
And the hand of God it is.

4 Blood thou lovest, and art drunk
With the blood of slaughter'd saints.
Deeds from which all others shrunk,
Thou hast done; by no restraints
Or of pity, or of shame,
Ever mov'd, but still the same.

5 City of the seven hills!
Thine has been an iron rule;
Cause to man of many ills,
Man, thy simple, ready tool.
But a change has come at last,
Thou art not what once thou wast.

6 City of the seven hills!
Who is there to mourn thy fate?
Ev'ry heart with pleasure thrills,
Save of those who goodness hate.
All rejoice who love the light,
Gladden'd by the joyful sight.

7 Sing, thou heav'n, and sing, O earth;
"Prophets and apostles," sing;
'Tis a time of sacred mirth.
Praise our Saviour and our King,
"True and just" in all his ways,
He has done it; his the praise.

HYMN DCCXXXIX.

"*The Lord is on my side.*"—PSALM cxviii. 6.

1 MUCH there is to try us here,
Much without, and much within;
Much there is to make us fear;
Much to draw us into sin.
Snares are scatter'd all around,
Pitfalls everywhere abound.

2 Much there is to cheer us too;
   Much to give us strength, when tried.
What can those against us do,
   When the Lord is on our side?
Have we not a sure defence,
In the Lord's omnipotence?

3 Hence the saints, tho' weak, are strong,
   Strong in him who makes them so.
Heav'n and earth to him belong,
   All above, and all below;
And the objects of his care
Trust in him, and happy are.

4 Trust in him, for ever trust,
   Strong he is, and faithful too;
They who do not, will and must,
   Perish all, his word is true.
Trust in him who dwells above,
Fountain he of grace and love.

HYMN DCCXL.

"*For there is none to help.*"—PSALM xxii. 11.

1 NONE to help us, no, not one,
   No one but the Lord alone;
But his arm is strong to save,
   Other arms we need not have:
His alone sufficient is,
Trust we then alone in this.

2 Saviour, when we would do so,
   Then comes in a chilling thought.
Then it is we fain would know
   Are we thine, or are we not;
All, we know, depends on this,
'Tis for thine the promise is.

3 When we think of what we are,
And of what we ought to be,
Then our minds are full of care;
Can we, Lord, belong to thee?
Talk we as thy people talk?
Walk we as thy people walk?

4 All the past, O Lord, forgive,
Let it not remember'd be.
Let us now begin to live,
As we should do, Lord, to thee.
Let us love thy precious name,
Let thy glory be our aim.

5 Let thy promise sweeter be
Far than honey to our taste.
Better to belong to thee,
Living in a howling waste,
Than have all that men desire,
And at last eternal fire.

6 Save us from the sinner's doom;
Save us, Lord; and when we lie
Buried in the silent tomb,
Let us wait the midnight cry,
Then arise, our Lord to see,
And with him in heav'n to be.

HYMN DCCXLI.

"*The things which are not seen are eternal.*"—2 Cor. iv. 18.

1 A CLEARER view of things unseen,
'Tis this we need: the want of this
Allows the world to come between
The Lord and us—how sad this is!

2 How sad it is, that things which have
So little worth, should valued be:
Should steal our hearts, and half enslave
The freeman whom the Lord makes free.

3 But we are weak. Then help us, Lord;
Thy strength alone can help the weak,
Who, self-condemn'd and self-abhorr'd,
Thy mercy crave, thy blessing seek.

4 No strength have we, nor can we have,
Except it comes from thee alone.
Thine arm, O Lord, is strong to save:
This truth we feel, this truth we own.

5 Nor do we ask or wish to be
Dependant less upon thy pow'r;
'Tis sweet to have our strength in thee.
This keeps us in the trying hour.

6 And this will keep, in time to come,
Till conflict ends, and toil, and strife.
This past, thy people gain their home;
Their portion, everlasting life.

HYMN DCCXLII.

" *Ye are not your own.*"—1 Cor. vi. 19.

1 THE demon, Lord, expel,
Who from the lowest deep,
The very depth of hell,
Possession tries to keep,
Of that which should be thine.
(I thought it once my own.)
My title I resign,
O be it thine alone!

2 I would surrender all,
Without reserve, to thee.
I would obey thy call,
And quite devoted be.
I would keep nothing back,
But freely all resign:
That thou may'st nothing lack,
Of all that should be thine.

3 Thy Spirit, Lord, impart;
Let him possession take
Of this my evil heart.
'Twill all resistance make.
But power is his, and he
The evil can expel.
'Tis his, the slave to free,
The slave of sin and hell.

4 For freedom, Lord, I plead:
A slave I would not be.
And they are free indeed,
Who live, O Lord, to thee.
To thee, then, let me live!
Thy service freedom is.
Thy Holy Spirit give,
For power and grace are his.

5 No strength at all have I:
The pow'r is all thine own.
Then hear my feeble cry,
And leave me not alone.
Let all within me feel
The working of thy pow'r;
Both soul and body seal,
Against the final hour.

6 And when the day appears,
That brings the Lord from heav'n,
To wipe away all tears
From those he has forgiv'n,
Then let my portion be,
Thy people's lot to share;
In heav'n thy face to see,
And be for ever there.

HYMN DCCXLIII.

"*Who am I, O Lord God?*"—2 SAM. vii. 18.

1 AND am I, Saviour, one of those
Who destin'd are, by sov'reign grace,
When this mysterious scene shall close,
To dwell in yonder holy place.

2 The place wherein thine honour dwells,
All other places far above,
Where ev'ry saint his story tells.
'Tis one of love, redeeming love.

3 His story full of wonder is;
It touches him who fills a throne;
The one in heaven, the kingdom his,
The glory and the power his own.

4 It touches him, who, full of grace,
Appear'd on earth, and shed his blood,
In favour of the guilty race:
The Son of man, the Son of God.

5 He saw the cross; knew all it meant,
Its pain, its shame, were full in view,
But forward still, unaw'd, he went,
Resolv'd his Father's work to do.

6 The mortal struggle came at length,
'Twas fearful, but 'twas final too,
For darkness put forth all its strength;
When Jesus fell, he crush'd the foe.

7 The vanquish'd foe will rise no more,
The victor fell to rise again,
To bear a name all names before:
The angels' boast, the scorn of men.

8 But those on earth who know his name,
As precious ointment, say it is;
And for his sake encounter shame,
Content to know that they are his.

HYMN DCCXLIV.

"Let us have grace, whereby we may serve God acceptably."—
HEB. xii. 28.

1 SAVIOUR, this is what I ask,
Cause me, Lord, to serve thee better,
Not as slaves fulfil their task,
This is nothing but the "letter."
Set me from all idols free,
Then thy yoke will easy be.

2 Sweet the service (else not so),
When the servant loves his master.
'Tis to thee, O Lord, I owe
Rescue from the great disaster,
That which fell upon our race:
Mine was once a fearful case.

3 Under guilt, and under curse,
And the very slave of sin,
What was there to make it worse?
All was dark and dead within,
Still without, all goodly seem'd,
Man approv'd, while God condemn'd

4 From this state, if not deceiv'd,
I may say that thou hast sav'd me.
Bought with blood, by grace reliev'd
From the power that once enslav'd me;
Pleasant should thy service be:
Pleasant, Lord, to one like me.

5 Saviour, what I ask is this,
Make it so, and so it will be,
Else it will be as it is;
What I have been, I shall still be.
Lord, increase my love to thee,
Make me what I ought to be.

HYMN DCCXLV.

"*The spirit indeed is willing, but the flesh is weak.*"—
MATT. xxvi. 41.

1 I KNOW I should be wholly his,
Who bought me with his precious blood:
I love the thing that better is;
I know the evil and the good.

2 But am I what I ought to be?
And do I what I ought to do?
It is not so; alas for me!
I mourn because it is not so.

3 I wish to be, without, within,
What God, the Lord, would have me be.
I would not be the slave of sin;
Appear, O Lord, and set me free.

4 Thyself alone, in whom I live,
Can break the chains that bind me still.
'Tis thine, O Lord, 'tis thine to give
The power to do, the power to will.

5 Let no reserve within me dwell,
No wish to hide a thought from thee.
The evil from my heart expel.
A living temple let me be.

6 Within me, Lord, set up thy throne,
And reign without a rival there.
My heart be thine, be thine alone,
For ever thine. O hear my pray'r!

HYMN DCCXLVI.

"*Why art thou cast down, O my soul?*"—PSALM xliii. 5.

1 SAY, why art thou cast down, my soul?
And why is this disquiet, why?
Is grace a fiction? and the whole
Of what thou hast believ'd, a lie?

2 If so, then give it up, and be
What once thou wast; then eat and drink,
And merry be; for better they
Who think not, than are those who think.

3 But O, my soul, thou knowest well,
That grace no fiction is; for thou
Hast prov'd its virtue, and canst tell
Its worth; then wherefore doubt it now?

4 Thou knowest it no limit has:
'Tis far beyond the reach of thought.
For sinners meet it is, it was,
And ever will be: fear thou not.

5 But though it may no fiction be,
And though no limit it may have,
Perhaps it was not meant for thee:
'Twas others it was meant to save.

6 The secret things to God belong;
  They lie far off, beyond our ken.
To donbt because of these, is wrong;
  The things reveal'd belong to men.

7 Then wish not, O my soul, nor try,
  Above what's written to be wise.
Enough, the word of faith is nigh,
  And ev'ry needful thing supplies.

8 Then be not, O my soul, cast down,
  But trust in him whose name is LOVE.
All blessings shall be thus thine own,
  On earth below, in heav'n above.

HYMN DCCXLVII.

"*In many things we offend all.*"—JAMES iii. 2.

1 "IN many things we all offend;"
  This should not be, why is it then?
It is not thus we treat a friend,
  It is not thus we deal with men.
The people of the Lord should be
From evil, as from error free.

2 A father and a friend they have;
  He dwells above, he fills the throne.
On earth he was, he came to save:
  On earth the mighty work was done,
That fills all heav'n with wonder now:
My soul, attend, and wonder thou.

3 O think of this: that he who hung
  On yonder cross, was "Lord of all."
Himself a man, and men among,
  His was the "wormwood and the gall,"
The bitterness of death was his.
Awake, my soul, and think of this!

4 Be often, then, before the cross;
'Tis there the mystery of love
Unfolded is. All else is loss
To it: itself all price above.
Wisdom is there, and pow'r, and grace,
Then dwell we in this holy place,

HYMN DCCXLVIII.

"*Ye are the light of the world.*"—Matt. v. 14.

1 A CHRISTIAN, in his proper sphere,
Should be a light to all around;
His business is to labour there,
And happy he if faithful found.
His field of labour may be small,
If God appoints it, this is all.

2 But let him often think of those
Who have a sterner work to do:
Who none but strangers see, and foes.
And let him oft in spirit go
To where *they* are, and count their tears,
Their labours witness, and their fears.

3 And when he does so, let him then
Reflect on all the sweets of home:
And let him love and honour men,
Who leave all this; content to roam
Where all is strange, and hostile much.
'Tis right to love and honour such.

4 In doing so, we only own
Our common Master's power and grace.
Then let us, when before his throne,
Entreat him that in ev'ry place
The missionary may be found
Imparting light to all around.

HYMN DCCXLIX.

"So David prevailed over the Philistine with a sling and with a stone."—1 SAM. xvii. 50.

1 "WITH a sling, and with a stone,"
David met his giant foe;
Arm'd with these, and these alone,
David struck the mortal blow.
Quelling thus the giant's boasts,
Spreading joy through Isra'l's hosts.

2 Who that saw the stripling go,
"With a sling, and with a stone,"
To encounter such a foe,
And to fight with these alone,
Could suppose he car'd for life,
Else would he have shunn'd the strife.

3 But the stripling wiser was
Than the rest, though later born.
"Is there not," he said, "a cause?"
Shall the foe thus shew his scorn?
Is there no one on our side,
No one to rebuke his pride?

4 David 'twas that slung the stone,
But the Lord ordain'd its course.
David look'd to him alone,
To direct, and give it force.
Thus directed and impell'd,
Isra'l's vaunting foe it fell'd.

5 When the king was fain to save,
From a strife he deem'd so sore,
One so young, and yet so brave,
David said he fought before:
And the Lord was with him then,
He would trust the Lord again.

6 David's Son, and David's Lord,
Had another foe to fell.
Words of truth the deed record,
But the whole, what words can tell?
Time, that nothing leaves untold,
Time will all the truth unfold.

7 When the Lord appears again,
What is now but half-discern'd,
Will be seen distinctly then;
From the book no longer learn'd,
Precious book! it has its day,
But with faith will pass away.

8 Be it so; then come, O Lord:
Thus we say, or ought to say;
Come, according to thy word;
Come, and bring the promis'd day,
'Tis the day thy people love,
Day of days, all days above.

HYMN DCCL.

"*As thy days, so shall thy strength be.*"—Deut. xxxiii. 25.

1 SAVIOUR, send us help from heav'n,
Strength proportion'd to our day;
Let this grace to us be giv'n;
While we journey, speed our way,
Till we reach our happy home,
Whence thy people never roam.

2 Nothing is there, there to harm:
All is peace, and all is love;
Nothing there to cause alarm:
Joy is there, all joy above.
'Tis a safe, a blessed place,
Destin'd for the heirs of grace.

3 And we should be glad to think
That the day not distant is,
When we shall begin to drink
At the source, O think of this!
At the very fountain-head:
Thither by the Saviour led.

4 Is there anything like this?
Anything like this below?
Rest on earth, a fiction is,
This we've learn'd, and this we know.
'Tis above that rest is found,
Not on this unholy ground.

5 Rest in heav'n, and elsewhere not;
Rest from care, from toil, from strife;
Rest from sin, in deed and thought.
God's own gift, "eternal life:"
This is, Lord, thy people's rest,
This is, to be fully blest.

6 Be it ours, O Lord, to fear;
Ours to trust, to watch, to pray:
That we may at length appear,
'Mong thy saints, in that bright day
When the ransom'd enter heav'n,
And the promis'd rest is giv'n.

HYMN DCCLI.

"*They that sow in tears, shall reap in joy.*"—Psalm cxxvi. 5.

1 NOW we sow in tears;
When the Lord appears,
We shall reap the fruit of joy.
Shall we then complain?
Life is what we gain:
What we lose is but a toy.

2 Jesus, when on earth,
Even from his birth,
Knew and felt what sorrow was.
Many tears he shed;
On the cross he bled:
Love the motive, sin the cause.

3 See the Saviour now,
Crowns adorn his brow:
Fruit of tears profusely shed.
What had here its root,
Has in heav'n its fruit:
Pain and grief to glory led.

4 So it is with those
Whom the Lord may choose
To rejoice when he appears.
They who will have joy,
Free from all alloy,
Must consent to "sow in tears."

5 Precious seed it is,
But how precious his,
His, who liv'd all worlds before!
Such no age had seen,
Such had never been:
Tears like his will flow no more.

6 Godly sorrow still
Does its work, and will:
Precious is the seed that's sown.
Here it has its root,
But in heav'n its fruit:
There we reap, and there alone.

HYMN DCCLII.

"*Having nothing, and yet possessing all things.*"—
2 Cor. vi. 10.

1 HAVING nothing, yet possessing all things;
This is strange, yet so it is.
In this world it is the day of small things,
We must wait, if we are his:
His, who look'd himself beyond the present,
Waiting for a glorious day.
We must wait in hope, but hope is pleasant;
Wait we then, nor chide delay.

2 He who made the world (tho' strange to tell it)
Had not where to lay his head.
When the storm arose, his word could quell it,
And his voice could raise the dead.
He was poor, because that poor he would be;
Thus the Father's will was done.
Thus it was, and thus alone it could be,
If he would enrich his own.

3 His is love no line we have can measure;
Why repine because of this?
Rather wait his time, and his good pleasure:
All is ours, if we are his.
All in him, our living head, possessing:
All in him, in him alone.
Ours the present hope of future blessing,
Ours a place around his throne.

4 Sad it seems, to see a man bereft of
All he had, and now alone;
Nothing left, no, nothing left of
All he once could call his own.
Yet, if he be Christ's, how is he poorer?
Ye who know it, tell me this.
Is there aught that's plainer, aught that's surer:
All is ours, if we are his.

HYMN DCCLIII.

"*They have seen thy goings.*"—PSALM lxviii. 24.

1 SAVIOUR, we have seen thy goings:
Seen them in the holy place.
We have witness'd, too, thy doings,
Full of love, and full of grace.
Who can do the things thou doest?
Who on earth, or who in heav'n?
Who can know the things thou knowest?
Praise to thee alone be giv'n.

2 When thou workest, who can stay thee?
Who resist thy sov'reign will?
Who can stop, or who delay thee?
Thine to save, and thine to kill.
Thine "the spirit without measure;"
Thine it is to cancel guilt:
Thine to work thy sov'reign pleasure,
When and in what way thou wilt.

3 Who will ask thee what thou doest?
Lord of earth, and Lord of heav'n.
Wisdom thine, who all things knowest,
And all pow'r to thee is giv'n.
Hope be ours; though strong our foes are,
He who saves us, stronger is.
Safe, we know, and happy those are,
Whom the Saviour owns as his.

4 Little know we, Saviour, of thee,
Though we ought to know so much.
Happy they who trust and love thee;
Make us, Lord, O make us such!
Henceforth let us leave thee never;
To thyself our hearts incline.
Thine the kingdom, thine for ever;
Thine the power, the glory thine.

HYMN DCCLIV.

"*Dying, and behold we live.*"—2 Cor. vi. 9.

1 MANY perils, many crosses,
Many trials, many losses,
Here await the Lord's elect.
Here it is, where none are for them,
But, as his, where all abhor them,
What but grief can they expect?

2 But the Lord makes all their trials
Bring them good, nor are his vials
Pour'd upon them from above.
When they ask him, he advises;
When they need it, he chastises:
All is love, a Father's love.

3 In the midst of foes and strangers,
And beset with many dangers,
Dying, and, behold they live.
'Tis his work, who lives for ever,
Wise and good, and changing never;
And to him the praise we give.

4 Much there may be yet to prove us,
Ere the Lord from earth remove us,
We may yet be sorely tried.
Think not that the foe will leave us,
To the end he will deceive us:
But the Lord is on our side.

5 If it is so, then we should be
Strong in faith, and so we would be.
Saviour, on thy people shine;
Welcome trials then, and crosses;
Welcome pain, and welcome losses:
All is ours, if we are thine.

HYMN DCCLV.

"*None of these things move me.*"—Acts xx. 24.

1 WHEREVER our Master may call us,
Our duty is, thither to go;
No matter what there may befall us,
No matter how mighty the foe,
Our part is to follow our Master,
The Lord, our infallible guide.
When fearful, to hold him the faster;
'Tis his to defend and provide.

2 Whatever he says, he will do it;
The will and the power are his.
He lives, and his people shall know it,
In him their security is.
He lay in the grave for a season,
But now he is high above all;
His people can trust him with reason,
And gladly respond to his call.

3 Our Master himself will provide us
With all we can want or desire.
Then what if the world should deride us,
Its favour we do not require.
Enough if our Master will own us;
Though strange it appears, and it is;
His purpose is then to enthrone us
Beside him: such kindness is his.

4 This joy set before us, then be it
Our care and our aim to obey,
That when the day comes, and we see it,
The great and the "terrible day,"
To us it may be full of gladness,
Of gladness but tasted before;
The end of all sighing and sadness,
Enjoyment, with life evermore.

HYMN DCCLVI.

"*When thou passest through the waters, I will be with thee.*"—
ISAIAH xliii. 2.

1 THRO' the fire, and thro' the water,
'Tis the way to yonder place.
Think we of "the day of slaughter,"
"When the towers fall." 'Tis grace,
Grace alone can bring us through it,
Through the flame, and through the flood.
'Tis the Lord himself will do it;
He is "faithful," "he is good."

2 "Forward," then; from trial shrink not,
When the Lord points out the way;
Of the things forsaken think not,
'Tis the Lord we must obey.
"Forward," then, and cease we never,
Till we gain the promis'd rest.
There we shall be safe for ever,
Blessing, and for ever blest.

3 Ye whose timid hearts misgive you,
Why this fear? This should not be:
For the Lord will never leave you,
Nor forsake you—faithful he.
Sweet it is, when evil presses,
To rely upon his arm;
They are blessèd whom he blesses;
Who or what shall do them harm?

4 Forward, then, and be not fearful;
Forward, 'tis the Lord's command.
In the view of danger cheerful,
Led by an almighty hand.
Kept by pow'r, that not your own is:
His it is, who governs all.
Trust to this, for this alone is
Able to prevent your fall.

5 Trust in this; it will not fail you,
Passing through the flood and flame.
Trust in this when foes assail you,
Still at hand, and still the same;
Trust in this till life is over,
Fear ye not, but trust in this.
At the last ye shall discover
What a mighty pow'r it is.

HYMN DCCLVII.

"*Thou didst cleave the fountain and the flood.*"—
PSALM lxxiv. 15.

1 "FLOOD and fountain thou didst cleave,"
And thy people, struck with awe,
Seem'd as if they would believe,
And would keep thy holy law.
'Twas but nature, nature still:
Stubborn and unchang'd the will.

2 While they heard, and while they saw,
Then they felt a present pow'r,
And their minds were fill'd with awe.
'Twas but for the passing hour:
Unbelief return'd again,
And they felt like other men.

3 Strange, that things so lately seen,
Should so soon forgotten be,
And as though they had not been,
Or been like what others see;
Should so little move the mind,
And should leave no trace behind.

4 Strange, indeed, except to those
Who are taught themselves to scan;
They could things as strange disclose,
Evils of the inner man:
Things less gross, but not less bad:
Things that make the spirit sad.

5 They can tell of wonders wrought,
By the arm of God made bare;
Favours granted—some unsought,
Others giv'n to their pray'r.
Wonder'd at indeed, when seen,
Then, as though they had not been.

6 "Flood and fountain thou didst cleave,"
Yet are we unthankful still.
Lord, we do but half believe:
Give the pow'r, and give the will.
Without thee we nothing have,
Without thee there's none to save.

HYMN DCCLVIII.

"*He took not on him the nature of angels.*"—Heb. ii. 16.

1 WHAT is man, O Lord, that he
Should be favour'd thus by thee?
Angels fell, and they were left,
In their fall, of hope bereft.
Not so, fallen man, for he
Safe and blessed still may be.

2 Tell the reason, ye who can,
Why this grace to fallen man?
Why does God his sin forgive?
Why is he allow'd to live?
Tell us, ye who know it, why
Man is not condemn'd to die?

3 Why should God his Son have giv'n?
  Why should he have come from heav'n,
And be "made a curse" for man?
  Tell us this, whoever can.
'Tis the Lord, a sov'reign he;
What he wills, 'tis that must be.

4 Secret things belong to him,
  Not to us: our sight is dim.
What he shews us, that alone
  Know we; all the rest unknown.
Let us be content, nor try
Into "secret things" to pry.

HYMN DCCLIX.

"*What is man, that thou shouldst magnify him?*"—
JOB vii. 17.

1 WHO are we, or what are we,
  That we should be favour'd thus,
Destin'd with the Lord to be?
  Why this grace? and why to us?
Who can tell us? He alone,
He to whom all things are known.

2 Why have we, who sought it not,
  Gotten that we look'd not for?
Why is theirs a blessed lot,
  Whom the Lord might well abhor?
Who can answer give to this?
Deep, too deep for us it is.

3 Deep as the abyss below,
  And from human eye conceal'd,
Who is he can think to know
  That which God has not reveal'd?
'Twill be known, if ever, when
He reveals it—not till then.

4 Yet the love that makes us glad,
Is the love that has no end,
That which no beginning had,
And the simple "comprehend;"
This they know, and this can tell,
"All is well," for ever well.

HYMN DCCLX.

"*What is man?*"—Psalm viii. 4.

1 "WHAT is man," O Lord, what is he,
That for him thou should'st take thought?
Toiling ever, ever busy
About that which profits not.
Why not let him gather fruit,
Bitter as its parent root?

2 Why to him have thoughts of kindness?
Or why think of him at all?
Why not leave him to his blindness,
Let him stumble, let him fall?
Why not let it be as when
Angels fell?—they perish'd then.

3 Lord, we know not; 'tis a matter
Far too high for us to reach;
Thine it is alone to scatter
Clouds and darkness; thine to teach;
Thine to tell what may be told,
And what may not, to withhold.

4 This we know, and this enough is,
'Tis enough for us to know.
That no more is told, a proof is
That we need it not below.
Angels fell, and all was lost:
Man is sav'd, but, O the cost!

HYMN DCCLXI.

"*Beloved, let us love one another.*"—1 JOHN iv. 7.

1 O HOW good and pleasant
'Tis where love is found;
There the Lord is present,
Blessings there abound.
'Tis the foretaste giv'n
Of the joy to come,
When the saints in heav'n
Gain their happy home.

2 With the peaceful, God is,
These he counts as his;
But our Father's rod is
Where contention is.
"God of peace" his name is,
His who dwells in light.
Love a holy flame is,
Burning pure and bright.

3 Be it ours to follow
Where the Lord may lead;
Gladly owning all who
Own our common head:
Those who know what grace is,
And its blessings share;
Those in whom the traces
Of his image are.

4 Kindred these, and brothers:
And a union this,
Stronger than all others:
From above it is.
Who or what can sever
That which God makes one?
This endures for ever,
This, and this alone.

5 Do we love each other?
This the question is;
He who loves his brother,
Shews that he is his.
His whose precept this is,
"Thou thy brother love,"
He who does so, his is:
His who reigns above.

6 Be we then united
By the bonds of love,
Though by others slighted.
Welcome, holy dove.
'Tis where thou art present,
Peace and love are found.
Good it is, and pleasant,
When these fruits abound.

7 Plead we then for union,
'Mong the Lord's elect,
Blessēd their communion,
Blessēd its effect.
Be it ours to love it,
'Tis the Master's will,
But to taste and prove it,
This is better still.

HYMN DCCLXII.

"*He preserveth the way of his saints.*"—Prov. ii. 8.

1 MUCH there is to turn us
From the "narrow way;"
Some there are would burn us,
If they had their way.
But they cannot do it;
Well for us they can't;
O! how we should rue it,
Had they what they want.

2 Some there are who scorn us,
And our foolish way;
Others frown, and warn us:
We must change, they say.
They can bear no longer,
What they hear and see;
He who proves the stronger,
Master let him be.

3 Others give a reason
Why they think us wrong.
All things have their season:
Pray'rs may be too long.
If we're always praying,
Life is at a stand;
This is not obeying
The divine command.

4 One there is we see not,
Who can do us harm,
Hinder'd if he be not
By a mighty arm.
He will try to make us
Leave the "narrow way;"
Should the Lord forsake us,
He would win the day.

5 But the Lord will save us
From the wily foe;
He himself will have us:
Onward let us go.
If the Lord be for us,
What can do us harm?
In the midst of sorrows,
Trust we in his arm.

6 Through a world of dangers,
Though our passage be;
Foes around, and strangers,
Hostile all we see;
Trust his word, 'tis stable,
And his word we have;
Trust his arm, 'tis able,
Able 'tis to save.

HYMN DCCLXIII.

"*The fear of man bringeth a snare.*"—PROV. xxix. 25.

1 SHALL I, Lord, evade the cross!
Shame, O shame, if I should do it;
Shame it would be, shame and loss,
Yet I'm often tempted to it.
When with those who know thee not,
Then I feel my courage failing;
Fearing man, how sad the thought!
And before my fellow quailing.

2 Lord, I know this should not be;
This is what I am lamenting,
And I turn my eyes to thee,
Sorrowing and repenting.
How I mourn because of this!
How I hate it, and condemn it!
Like a winter's flood it is,
Far too strong for me to stem it.

3 Shall I fear the face of man?
Who is he, or what his power?
He whose life is but a span,
Like a fading, falling flower,

Yet I quail before his frown.
Arm me, Lord, with courage arm me,
Let me learn thy name to own,
Careless who or what may harm me.

4 Yet I know how weak I am,
And how oft I have offended.
Still, O Lord, thou art the same,
And I live by thee befriended.
Power belongs to thee alone,
Weakness without limit mine is;
Mine to plead before the throne;
Thine to hear, to answer thine is.

5 Should the bigot reign again,
And the faggot blaze to try us;
O be with thy people then,
In the time of need stand by us.
Lord, should such a day arrive,
Cause us to abide the trial.
Let our faith the shock survive,
Be it death, but not denial.

HYMN DCCLXIV.

" *We were like them that dream.*"—Psalm cxxvi. 1.

1 DO we dream, or is it real?
Is it freedom—such indeed?
Something solid, not ideal?
Are we from our bondage freed?
Whence this doubt, and why the question?
'Tis that all things wondrous seem.
Hence the thought, the mind's suggestion,
'Tis, perhaps, some pleasant dream.

2 No, 'tis truth; the chain is broken,
That which crush'd us to the ground.
God has done it: 'tis the token
Of his love. Let songs abound;
Let our "mouths be fill'd with laughter;"
Holy mirth becomes us now.
We shall have to fight hereafter,
And the Lord will teach us how.

3 Sing we then with joy and gladness;
He who late our master was,
He who fill'd our souls with sadness,
He no more the power has.
Galling was the chain that bound us,
Yet we dreamt that we were free,
Till the Saviour sought and found us:
Lord, we give the praise to thee.

4 'Tis thy mighty arm that broke it,
Broke our chain: 'twas done by thee.
'Twas thine awful voice that spoke it,
Spoke the word that made us free.
Now we know that serving thee is
Freedom: nothing else but this.
In the world, no being free is,
Save thy servant: freedom his.

5 Sing we, then, of him who frees us
From our bondage: sing of him.
Sing of love, the love of Jesus;
'Tis a sweet, a blessed theme;
'Tis a theme exhausted never,
New it is through countless days.
Sing the Saviour's love for ever;
His be never-ending praise.

HYMN DCCLXV.

"Are ye able to drink of the cup that I shall drink of?"—
MATT. XX. 22.

1 Of the cup that I shall drink of,
Canst thou drink? I cannot, Lord;
'Tis a thing I dare not think of;
But if thou wilt strength afford,
Bitter though it be, I need not
Fear to take it from thine hand.
Be it what it may, I heed not,
If I drink at thy command.

2 What I do for thee, I do it
In thy strength, and not my own,
If I dream of adding to it,
In a moment all is gone.
In my weakness, Lord, thy strength is
"Perfect made." 'Tis even so.
Precious truth, that now at length is
Mine, wherewith to meet the foe.

3 Ask me now, Lord, can I do it?
And I humbly answer, yes!
Thine the strength, and trusting to it,
Can I say, or ought I, less?
Were I on myself relying,
Sin and folly this would be.
In thy strength all ills defying,
Doing this, I honour thee.

4 Still I fear, much fear, I should not
Stand the test, if sorely tried.
Why should I, if others could not,
And at last the faith denied?
Yet in thee no failure could be;
Gracious art thou, Lord, and true;
All thou doest is what should be,
Not to thee their fall is due.

5 Yet I own it checks my gladness,
When I think on such a case,
And a feeling like to sadness
Enters in, and takes its place.
Pity, Lord, and do not chide me;
Save, O save me, first and last.
In thy secret chamber hide me,
Till the storm is overpast.

6 Then a sun will rise, that never,
Never will go down again.
Blest the people are for ever,
Chosen from the sons of men,
Vessels chosen to salvation,
Objects of eternal love;
Seal'd before the world's foundation.
Praise to him who reigns above.

7 Praise the Lord, and never doubt him;
What he wills, must surely be.
Clouds and darkness are about him:
What he hides, we cannot see.
Let us do what he would have us,
Trust him, and dismiss our fears.
From all evil he will save us,
In the day when he appears.

THE END.

PRINTED BY ROE AND BRIERLEY,
42, Mabbot-street, Dublin.

PUBLISHED BY MARCUS MOSES, DUBLIN.

FIFTY PSALMS, arranged for One, Two, or Three Voices, and Organ or Piano-Forte, by D. WEYMAN. 1 vol. 12mo. Price 4s.

"We have experienced much gratification from inspecting a splendid stereotype edition of WEYMAN'S MELODIA SACRA, edited by Dr. SMITH, which has just been brought out at a great expense. This unequalled collection of Sacred Music we hope soon to see in general use, as, from the low price at which it is now published, it well may be. To have the members of the Established Church duly qualified to join in singing the praises of their Creator in the great congregation, would be one of the most desirable objects that could be accomplished; and nothing is so well calculated to achieve such a *desideratum* as their becoming possessed of a work like WEYMAN'S MELODIA SACRA, which, we are convinced, far outrivals anything of the kind ever before acquired by the Christian world. For the purpose of private devotion, and as a most useful auxiliary to social and family worship, the MELODIA SACRA cannot be equalled. If this invaluable compilation of Sacred Melody, which the late Mr. DAVID WEYMAN left in so admirable a state of perfection, were diffused through society as universally as it ought to be, and habitually practised in the social circle, the service of the Established Church, which is of such surpassing dignity and purity, would soon be enlivened by that fervour and exalted animation, which the tuneful voices of the numbers who now crowd our places of national worship would be capable of communicating to it. We hail, as a national boon, the stability which the publisher has given to a collection of music so decidedly associated with the National Church of these realms, and which is now rendered accessible to every family of moderate means."—*Warder*.

"The selected Melodies have been chosen with care and judgment, and New Music has been composed for many of the Psalms, by the first composers in the sister island; and no expense spared to render the publication elegant, useful, and gratifying. Many beautiful traits of sweetly solemn Air and ably fabricated Harmony fill and adorn the pages; and the aggregate collection constitutes a valuable body of Sacred Music."—DR. BUSBY *on* "*The Melodia Sacra.*" *Vide London Monthly Magazine.*

"The MELODIA SACRA, published by the late Mr. WEYMAN, approaches so nearly to perfection, and contains so many approved Airs, that it appears unnecessary, in forming a new selection of Psalm tunes, to introduce any other melodies than those contained in it. . . . The MELODIA SACRA alone has afforded an abundant variety, and fully satisfactory employment for the Society's meetings."—*Church Music Society, Trinity College, Dublin.*

"The MELODIA SACRA is a work which never can be superseded; we would recommend it to every one who has a taste for Psalmody."—*Record.*

A NEW SELECTION of SIXTY PSALMS, from WEYMAN'S MELODIA SACRA, for the use of the Church Music Society, Trinity College. 1 vol. royal quarto, 7s. 6d.

FIFTY-NINE CHANTS, for Four Voices, or for Organ or Piano-Forte, arranged by R. W. BEATY, 2s.

CHANTS and RESPONSES, arranged by Dr. J. SMITH, 2s.

CHANTS for the Use of the Church Music Society, Trinity College, arranged by J. RAMBAUT, 1s.

SEQUEL to WEYMAN'S MELODIA SACRA, Two Hundred HYMNS and ANTHEMS, by approved Authors, arranged for One, Two, Three, or Four Voices, and Organ or Piano-Forte, by D. WEYMAN, Dr. JOHN SMITH, R. W. BEATY, and others: in Nos. at 1s. each; or complete in Two Vols., each 10s.

PSALM BOOK for the Use of Churches. The One Hundred and Fifty Psalms, Authorized Version, as set to Music in WEYMAN'S MELODIA SACRA, the first line of Music at the head of each Psalm ; neatly bound, 1s., or 10s. per dozen.

HYMN BOOK for the Use of Churches, containing Two Hundred HYMNS, as set to Music in the Two Volumes of SEQUEL to MELODIA SACRA, with Seventy additional Hymns. The first line of the Music proper for each, given with every Hymn. New Edition, with a Second Appendix of Forty Hymns, 18mo, fine paper, neatly bound, 1s., or 10s. per dozen.

PSALM and HYMN BOOK, the 150 Psalms and the 310 Hymns, as above, with first line of Music, &c., in One Vol., neatly bound, 1s. 6d., or 15s. per dozen.

ONE HUNDRED and FIFTY HYMNS of the above Collection, with first line of Music to each, 6d., or 5s. per dozen.

MINIATURE EDITION of the above Hymn Book, containing 310 Hymns, neatly bound in cloth, gilt edges, 32mo, 1s., or 10s. per dozen.

PSALM and HYMN BOOK, 150 Psalms and 310 Hymns, Miniature Edition, gilt edges, 32mo, 1s. 6d., or 15s. per doz.

MINIATURE HYMN BOOK, containing a Selection of 150 Hymns from the above. Cloth, 32mo, gilt edges, 6d., or 5s. per dozen.

ONE HUNDRED HYMNS for Public Worship, selected from the SEQUEL to WEYMAN'S MELODIA SACRA, by the Rev. Maurice F. Day, cloth, 6d.

Lightning Source UK Ltd.
Milton Keynes UK
175847UK00002B/61/P